The Making of
Modern British Politics
1867–1939

To the memory of my grandparents

The Making of
Modern British Politics
1867–1939

MARTIN PUGH

BLACKWELL
Publishers

Copyright © Martin Pugh, 1982, 1993

The right of Martin Pugh to be identified as author of this work has been
asserted in accordance with the Copyright, Designs and Patents Act 1988.

First published 1982
Second edition published 1993
Reprinted 1993, 1995, 1996, 1998

Blackwell Publishers Ltd
108 Cowley Road, Oxford OX4 1JF, UK

Blackwell Publishers Inc
350 Main Street, Malden, Massachusetts 02148, USA

British Library Cataloguing in Publication Data
A CIP catalogue record for this book is available from the British Library

Library of Congress Cataloging in Publication Data
Pugh, Martin
The making of modern British politics 1867–1939 / Martin Pugh—2nd ed.
p.   cm.
Includes bibliographical references and index.
ISBN   0–631–17928–3 (pbk)
1. Great Britain—Politics and government—1837–1901.
2. Great Britain—Politics and government—1901–1936.
3. Great Britain—Politics and government—1936–1945.
4. Political parties—Great Britain—History. I. Title.
DA560.P79   1993   92–18662
941.08—dc20   CIP

Typeset in 10 on 12pt Plantin
by Graphicraft Typesetters Limited, Hong Kong
Printed and bound in Great Britain by
Athenæum Press Ltd, Gateshead, Tyne & Wear

This book is printed on acid-free paper

Contents

List of Illustrations   viii

Preface   ix

Part One 1867–1900   1

1   Party and Participation   3
    1867–1900

    Voting and Non-voting   5
    Electoral Practice and Malpractice   10
    The Rise of the Party Activist   15
    Party, Parliament and the 'Independent Member'   18

2   The Evolution of the Gladstonian Liberal Party   23
    1867–1895

    Liberalism, Reform and Religion   25
    The Building Blocks of Liberalism   26
    The Programme versus the Single Issue   31
    1886: the Radicalization of the Party   36

3   The Conservative Revival   44
    1874–1900

    The Impact of Middle-class Conservatism   46
    Organizing the Democracy   50
    Tradition and Change   53
    Salisbury and Liberal Unionism   57
    The State and Social Reform   62

4   The Social Roots of Political Change in Late Victorian Britain   68

    Trends and Issues   68
    Rural Radicalism   73
    Working-class Politics and Socialists   76
    Women, Politics and Labour   82
    Working-class Conservatism, Empire and Patriotism   83
    The Lower Middle Class   90

                    Part Two 1895–1914   95

5   The Edwardian Crises   97
    1895–1914

    The Waning of Radicalism   97
    Liberal Imperialism   103
    'National Efficiency' and Tariff Reform   106
    The Crisis of Conservatism   109

6   Edwardian Progressivism   113

    Origins of the New Liberalism   113
    The Politics of the Pact 1903–1914   121
    Edwardian Labourism   130
    The Workers and State Welfare   136

7   The Electoral Struggle   137
    1906–1914

    The Containment of Labour   138
    The Franchise Factor   142
    The Local, Municipal and Regional Dimension   145
    When the Lights went out   153

                   Part Three 1914–1920s   159

8   The Impact of the Great War on British Politics   161

    Disintegration of the Progressive Alliance 1914–1916   161
    Lloyd George and the Conservatives 1916–1918   169
    Labour's Change of Course   176

9   A Mass Electorate at War   182

    Impact on Civilians   182
    Impact on the Troops   188
    The Coupon Election 1918   193

10 Party, Ideology and the State in the Great War 200

 The Myth of *Laissez-faire* and Interventionism 200
 Conservatism, Capitalism and the State 1914–1922 204
 Labour's Socialist Commitment and the Liberal
  Inheritance 1914–1929 210

Part Four 1918–1939 217

11 The Elevation of Labour and the Restoration of Party Politics 219
 1918–1924

 Fragmentation of the Coalition 219
 The New Strategy 1922 222
 Baldwin and Normality 1923 225
 The MacDonald–Baldwin Axis 1924 228

12 Origins of the Conservative Electoral Hegemony 236
 1918–1931

 The Impact of the Electoral System 236
 The Conservatives and the Constituencies 240
 Labour's Grass Roots 1918–1929 244
 Women in Inter-war Politics 249
 The General Strike and the Realignment of the
  Working Class 252
 The Election of 1931 259

13 The Eclipse of the Extremes 261
 1931–1939

 Labour, Socialism and Keynesianism 261
 The National Government and Liberal Toryism 269
 The Threat from the British Union of Fascists 275
 The Left, Rearmament and Public Opinion 278
 The General Election of 1935 and its Aftermath 284

Epilogue 289

Notes 293

Guide to Further Reading 303

Index 322

Illustrations

Mr Gladstone Attacking the Front Bench from Harry Furniss, *Pen and Pencil in Parliament*, 1897   4

The Irish "Vampire" from *Punch*, 24 October 1885   37

'Joey' from Harry Furniss, *Pen and Pencil in Parliament* 1897   60

"The Liberals' Pal" from Conservative pamphlet 'Topical Tips for Typical Tykes', 1906   87

The Patient Ass from *Punch*, 18 April 1896   116

The Triangular Test from *Punch*, 10 July 1912   146

The Triumph of "Culture" from *Punch*, 23 August 1914   163

Ramsay the Unruddy from *Punch*, 20 February 1924   232

? from *Punch*, 15 November 1922   251

Preface

This book is designed to meet a need among students and teachers in the field of modern British history. Few areas of historical study can have generated as much scholarly work over the last twenty years, and the result has been a barrage of books and articles directed at the academic territory between the 1860s and the Second World War. Not surprisingly undergraduate and A level students, who are often asked to cope with quite sophisticated questions of interpretation these days, frequently wear a slightly shell-shocked expression beneath the torrent of material. While the quantity of original, specialist work is difficult to handle, the traditional textbooks seldom take the student beyond a basic chronological account of the rise and fall of ministries. It is depressing to find how rarely even recently published general works reflect the central contributions made in books like Peter Clarke's *Lancashire and the New Liberalism* (1971) or John Vincent's *The Formation of the British Liberal Party 1857–68*, published as long ago as 1966, which have indisputably changed our view of the period. I hope that this volume will, if nothing else, help students to get to terms with some of the important and interesting questions raised by the study of British political history between 1867 and 1939, though I am conscious that it is a rash undertaking on my part. Readers should be warned that while I provide a guide to alternative views, especially in the bibliographies, I have made no attempt to act as a neutral referee on matters of controversy. Students who believe that an academic approach means refusing to commit oneself to anything definite ('safety first') might remember Lloyd George on Sir John Simon: 'The Rt. Hon. Gentleman has spent so long sitting on the fence that the iron has entered his soul.'

Although the treatment in this volume has been influenced strongly by the published and unpublished work of other historians, I have also tried to indicate areas where our knowledge is still relatively thin. My own research for the book has been deliberately directed upon areas in which it seemed likely to do most good. For example, while the archives of the Labour Party are, in general, rather thoroughly worked, certain parts, like the material relating to municipal elections, appear to be less used, although most relevant to the interpretation of Edwardian politics; I have also made considerable use of the Ramsay MacDonald papers which were unavailable for a considerable period. The popular basis of Conservative support remains a relatively untrodden field, despite some stimulating contributions in recent years, and here I have given more than usual prominence to the evidence of Primrose League activity.

Naturally in preparing a volume of this kind I have been unusually grateful for the earlier efforts of other scholars – some indication of which is given in the bibliographies and notes. But I have a particular debt to those who read and commented on the book at various stages. Henry Pelling very kindly brought his critical gaze to bear on the whole manuscript with, I hope he would agree, beneficial results. I have also been greatly helped by David French who scrutinized chapters 8, 9 and 10; by Bill Purdue on chapters 5, 6 and 7; and by Maureen Calcott on chapters 11, 12 and 13. All of them would rightly dissent from much of what has been written here, and in thanking them I do not shirk my responsibility for the flaws of judgement and errors of fact which may persist.

Several academics have generously given me permission to make use of material published in tabular form in their own work: Hugh Berrington in 'Partisanship and Dissidence in the Nineteenth Century House of Commons', *Parliamentary Affairs*, 21(1967–8); J. P. Cornford in his essay 'Parliamentary Foundations of the Hotel Cecil', Robert Robson (ed.), *Ideas and Institutions of Victorian Britain* (Bell, 1967); Michael Kinnear in *The British Voter: an Atlas and Survey since 1885* (Batsford, 1968); and Alan J. Lee in *The Origins of the Popular Press 1855–1914* (Croom Helm, 1976). I am also very grateful to Peter Liddle for allowing me access to his 1914–18 Personal Experience Archives presently held at the University of Leeds; and to Mr Leslie Gould of Leeds and the Librarian of the Leeds Library who made material available to me. I have been assisted in various other ways . The Research Fund of Newcastle University made a grant towards the costs of the research. In the early stages Robert Baldock gave valuable support and encouragement; and in the later stages Janice Cummin typed a number of the chapters expertly and rapidly. I would like to express my thanks to all those friends and relations who provided me with accommodation, without which it would be difficult to cover the archival resources of the country from Newcastle; and finally to my wife who was consistently supportive and tolerant of the moodiness of a pregnant author.

Part One
1867–1900

1
Party and Participation
1867–1900

> We have only to imagine, if we can, a Pitt or a Castle-
> reagh stumping the provinces, and taking into his
> confidence, not merely a handful of electors, but any
> crowd he could collect in any part of this island.
>
> *The Times*, 26 December 1879,
> on the first Midlothian campaign

Between the 1860s and the turn of the century, British politics, in the constituency, party and parliamentary spheres, took on recognizably modern characteristics. Although the transition necessarily proved a lengthy and patchy process, the 1880s stand out as the key decade of change. Indeed the general election of 1880 may, with some justification, be regarded as the first modern election. It was a *general* election in that five-sixths of the constituencies were actually contested, and in that it produced a national campaign as distinct from the sporadic, localized contests typical of mid-Victorian elections. Voters were offered an un-usually clear-cut choice largely, through the initiative of the *de facto* leader of the opposition W. E. Gladstone who promised to reverse the imperial and foreign policy of Disraeli if he was returned with a majority. In contemporary eyes the novelty of the Midlothian campaign, that 'ten days' waterspout dealing with all human affairs' as *The Times* put it, consisted in a prospective Prime Minister taking voters so ser-iously as to deliver to them lengthy speeches on weighty subjects more properly addressed to the Houses of Parliament. The year 1880 brought to a climax that polarization of loyalties between the two party leaders which, since Gladstone's championing of franchise reform in 1866, had begun to transcend the local and personal patterns of allegiance; and which imprinted upon British politics for decades thereafter two stereotyped party positions in both foreign and domestic affairs.

MR. GLADSTONE ATTACKING THE FRONT BENCH.

Harry Furniss, Pen and Pencil in Parliament *(1897).*

Moreover, the 1880 election physically resembled a modern one. Hitherto the leaders had usually avoided speaking in other men's constituencies after nominations lest they be seen to interfere in a community's private affair; now they found ever more excuses to permit the electorate the novelty of oratory from outside. Gladstone pioneered the nearest approach to a whistle-stop tour as he journeyed up to Edinburgh descending from his train at Grantham, York and Newcastle to deliver short harangues, somewhat to the annoyance of the ordinary passengers, thence proceeding to an intensive programme of two daily speeches for a fortnight on his second campaign in Midlothian. Though many of the thousands who attended his progress around the constituency could not hear his speeches, Gladstone's every word at West Calder or Dalkeith was caught up by eager journalists to be reprinted in the dense black columns of the provincial and national press, to be bandied about by the more obscure participants up and down the country. 'This duty of making political speeches', Lord Salisbury complained to Queen Victoria in 1887, 'is an aggravation of the labours of your Majesty's servants which we owe entirely to Mr Gladstone.' One should not allow Salisbury's weary cynicism to obscure his own successful adaptation to a variety of political practices, including regular speech-making, of which he disapproved. It would be rash to conclude that the mass of voters felt moved to return Gladstone to power in 1880 because they shared the same concern with the affairs of Afghanistan and the Balkans. The impact of the controversy that had begun in 1876 over the Bulgarian atrocities and culminated in the Midlothian campaigns fell more forcefully upon the partisan activists and local backers of Liberalism, that vital intermediate group whose voluntary efforts and high morale were increasingly indispensable in harnessing the voters at large; but these party workers comprised a characteristic and central element in the political transition of late Victorian Britain.

Voting and Non-voting

Victorians did not claim that their system was democratic, a term that smacked of continental abstraction and implied an excess of equality characteristic of American society; rather, it produced effective government, it guaranteed 'liberty', and it was representative. What it represented directly was those considered fit by reason of their independence, their material stake in society, their education and political knowledge to exercise the parliamentary franchise with beneficial effects upon political life. Men wholly absorbed in the daily struggle for existence were unlikely to develop the capacity for political judgement, still less the opportunity to exercise it freely. Conscious of the defects of even the existing electorate, radicals of the 1860s accepted that drastic and ill-considered extensions of the franchise would only open further opportunities for corruption; the business of a reformer was to find a form of words in law which in practice would define those who were beyond corrupting pressures. Moreover, the late Victorian conception of corruption extended beyond the traditional individual type to the more formal, institutional forms practised in the United States in which politicians offered groups of voters specific pledges of material gain in return for support. Political integrity required that a man who depended upon the state for his maintenance should be ineligible to vote for the government; hence in Britain men in receipt of relief from the poor law guardians remained disqualified until 1918.

In fact an election was not primarily about the individual's rights, but about the representation of his community, from which it followed that the interests of non-electors could be represented quite adequately by the leaders of their community. Thus a landowner spoke for his labourers politically as an extension of his other duties towards them; similarly the interests of the largest single group of non-voters, women, were upheld by their fathers and husbands. In a family, as in any other community, there was no special merit in every individual member voting in person, for 'mere numbers' provided no guarantee of efficiency or morality. Women were generally perceived by male politicians to be deficient in the intellectual and temperamental qualities appropriate for politics, to lack the independence, inclination and even the energy which was devoted instead to the vital task of childbirth.[1] 'Woman' in short was equated with married woman despite the fact that nearly a quarter of adult females were actually spinsters or widows in the 1860s, many of whom paid local rates and managed property; even wives were permitted, under the Married Women's Property Acts 1870, 1874 and 1882, to retain their property instead of surrendering it to their husbands on marriage. Faced with the fact that some women were 'fit', even on men's terms, for the franchise, politicians allowed female participation, in discreet numbers, in municipal elections, on school boards and on boards of guardians. However, despite the growing similarity between local and national government in the late nineteenth century, most politicians stuck to the view that the great parliamentary issues of Empire, war and national security ought not to be exposed to the vacillating and emotional judgements of women. Moreover, once a majority of men had obtained enfranchisement after 1884, the impetus behind Victorian reform waned noticeably; the remaining male non-voters stood pat upon their superior status as *men*, and eschewed making common cause with women.

The male non-voter himself was by no means uninvolved in the political process. Particularly in smaller boroughs elections were characterized by popular participation if only in the form of processions, rioting and intimidation. This attendant disorder obliged the authorities to extend the poll over two to three weeks (as in modern India) in order to allow the police to transfer scarce resources from one group of constituencies to another; not until 1918 did they feel confident enough to risk one-day polling. However, popular involvement also took on a political tone. Since the days of the Chartists non-electors had made a practice in some towns of gathering at the hustings when nominations were due, proceeding thence to elect, on a show of hands, an 'MP' as an alternative to the formal poll. Also, disfranchised radical working men in such towns as Rochdale, Stockport, Warrington, Stoke and Morpeth took to boycotting the shops and pubs of their political opponents, thereby playing a more independent role than some enfranchised workers

TABLE 1.1   *Parliamentary electors in the United Kingdom*

1866	1,364,000
1869	2,445,000
1883	3,152,000
1885	5,708,000
1911	7,904,000

who were more subject to employers' pressure at elections.[2] In addition the disfranchised invariably shared with the electors themselves a vicarious sense of participation in elections by aligning themselves with one candidate or party; millions of people wore ribbons and rosettes in party colours, or sported primroses on Disraeli's birthday. For a generation not yet in thrall to the personalities of football, films or popular music, political leaders and their contests provided a great entertainment or spectacle, a cause to belong to, and a link with the lives of the great.

Although the debate over franchise was conducted on the high ground of principle, the translation of 'fitness' into law proved to be severely limited by sheer ignorance of the numbers involved, by the exigencies of parliamentary management, and by assumptions about the help or hindrance newly enfranchised groups would lend to the legislating party. Disraeli's inability to patch together a temporary majority in the Commons in 1867 except by offering concessions to radical Liberal backbenchers produced a dramatic increase in the borough electorate, extending the suffrage to householders and to occupiers and lodgers paying an annual rent of £10, while leaving the county electorate but slightly modified. This lopsided, typically English pattern proved indefensible, and led to the rationalization of 1884 when the new borough franchises were extended by Gladstone to counties. The numerical effect of these changes provided the underlying dynamic to late Victorian political evolution (see table 1.1).

Under this system the proportion of adult males entitled to vote fluctuated usually between 63 and 66 per cent; the more imminent a general election the greater incentive for the parties to ensure that their supporters were on the register. However, the figures overstate the true proportion since half a million men were registered more than once; therefore, no more than six out of every ten men, at most, were parliamentary voters before 1914. Industrial towns, where enfranchisement had traditionally been much lower than that in medieval boroughs and counties, experienced particularly dramatic rises: in Blackburn 1,800 voters became 9,700 in 1868; Newcastle's 6,600 voters had increased to

TABLE 1.2 *Parliamentary franchises 1885–1918*

		Proportion of the 1911 electorate (%)
Household	franchise for inhabitant occupiers, whether owners or tenants, of a separate dwelling house	84.3
Occupation	franchise for those who occupied as owners or tenants, any land or tenement of £10 annual value	
Lodger	franchise for those who rented rooms valued unfurnished at £10 p.a.	4.6
Property	franchise for 40s freeholders and other freeholders, copyholders and leaseholders (almost wholly confined to counties)	8.4
Service	franchise for inhabitant occupiers of a separate dwelling house through their employment or office, not as owner or tenant	1.8
University	franchise for graduates	0.6
Freemen's	franchise for freemen by birth or apprenticeship in boroughs where the qualification had existed before 1832	0.3

Source: Parl. Papers 1911, LXII, pp. 679–700.

21,400 by 1872. However, considerable unevenness persisted until 1914 in that residential towns (Oxford 75 per cent) and counties (Cornwall 80 per cent) enjoyed substantially higher enfranchisement than industrial boroughs (Oldham 63 per cent), the extremes being characteristic of large conurbations (Glasgow 52 per cent, Bethnal Green 42 per cent). This pattern was in fact a built-in consequence of the system adopted in 1884. For although the third Reform Act rationalized the existing pattern it nonetheless bequeathed a complex structure of seven distinct types of qualification (see table 1.2).

Those who were expressly excluded by the electoral law fell into three groups; first, women who had been eliminated since the 1832 Act which adopted 'male persons' for the first time; secondly, such categories of men as lunatics, aliens, criminals, peers, receivers of poor relief, those guilty of corrupt practices in elections, and some officials involved in elections; thirdly, men such as sons living in their parents' home and servants residing with their employers who were effectively excluded as they could not claim to be householders. In this way some 1.5 million men (by 1914) found themselves excluded. However, this still left a much greater number – 3.75 million by 1914[3] – who failed to make good their claim (usually as householders or lodgers) simply because of the complicated process of registration. To introduce his name onto the register a potential householder or lodger had to demonstrate continuous residence for 12 months at a given address from July of one year to June of the next. On this basis his name could be entered on the preliminary list in April or May, and if it survived the scrutiny in September–October, would appear on the new parliamentary register in December, which became operative in January of the next year – an 18-month cycle. If the voter moved outside his borough or county constituency, or if his move involved a change of qualification, say from householder to lodger, he had not maintained continuity of residence for 12 months and forfeited his place. Since in working-class boroughs in the large conurbations up to 30 per cent of the population commonly moved each year, massive disfranchisement was inevitable.

The system was also less than democratic in allowing the opportunity to vote many times. Joseph Chamberlain apparently possessed six qualifications, though this was by no means a record; given the leisurely spread of polling some men claimed to cast as many as ten votes. Overall the plural voters amounted to over half a million or 7 per cent of the total,[4] concentrated in commercial seats, in London and in county seats adjacent to or surrounding parliamentary boroughs. Supporters of plural voting argued that it properly reflected the stake a man had in each particular community. However, if every piece of property a man possessed fell within a single parliamentary borough or in a single division of a county he could vote but once; plural voting was possible only if his property was spread over different constituencies. Moreover, under the anachronistic convention that a borough was part of a county, freeholders in parliamentary boroughs exercised this vote in a neighbouring county seat with which they often had no interest or connection.

The final dimension of inequality lay in the marked variation in constituency size despite the effect the 1885 redistribution had in correcting the historic over-representation of the south and south-west. By adopting a basic population unit of 50,000 to justify new seats it proved possible to grant 39 additional metropolitan representatives, 15 to

Lancashire and 13 to Yorkshire. Some 36 constituencies whose population was above 15,000 but below 50,000 lost one of their two members, while 72 boroughs under 15,000 were simply merged into surrounding counties. However, this still left many small boroughs returning their own members, for example Windsor, Durham, St Andrews and Salisbury, all with around 3,000 actual electors. At the other extreme the largest electorate by 1910 was the Romford division of Essex (61,000). An imbalance, moreover, remained marked between certain areas of the British Isles, notably Ireland whose 103 members represented an average electorate of 6,700 by contrast with the English average of 13,000. Ireland's exaggerated representation at Westminster had profound effects upon British politics before the First World War. In abandoning the traditional two-member constituencies for the more geographically restricted single-member seats in 1885 the legislators hoped to preserve the community basis of politics. However, the effect in the mature industrial society of late Victorian Britain was a system of constituencies frequently characterized by one dominant class; this was the reality behind what seemed to MPs rather artificial entities – North-East Norfolk, North-West Manchester – that were deficient in the prestige previously attaching to the representation of a county or major borough. This was symptomatic of the changing orientation of politics from the local to the national level, and from community to class.

Electoral Practice and Malpractice

Victorian elections were expected as a matter of course to be punctuated by excessive drinking, mob action ranging from exuberance to intimidation, an exchange of cash and a judicious application of the 'screw'. However, 'influence' covered a multitude of practices and forms, many of which were regarded as perfectly natural and proper. By tradition county politics was the preserve of landed gentlemen who both provided candidates and effectively determined the outcome through the loyalty they commanded among farmers and smallholders. The exercise of such influence could be effortless and inconspicuous, not necessarily coercive or unwelcome to the lower levels of rural society. So long as party politics remained a remote and intangible concept the typical county elector would act within the ambit of his local community; it was the county or community that his MP represented rather than either individuals or a party. Moreover, as the person who remitted rent in bad years, provided work in inclement weather, and contributed financially and socially to the life of the village or estate, the squire could legitimately expect political support; the relationship between squire and local electorate rested upon a mutual sense of duty and responsibility. In so far as voters anticipated a flow of benefits from an election it was these regular, tangible ones rather than legislative programmes at Westminster. Studies of politics in counties such as Lincolnshire from the 1830s to the 1880s suggest that 'politics' comprised certain agricultural matters, notably the malt tax and the tariff, which tended to unite farmers and landowners thus offering few openings for genuine party alternatives.[5]

However, this is to describe an ideal situation of rural stability characteristic of the capital-intensive and profitable agriculture of the mid nineteeth century; it could not survive unscathed the contractions and changes in ownership brought on by falling agricultural profitability after 1875.[6] As unprofitable estates were disposed of and the gentry rented out a number of country houses to families without local, traditional connections, influence inevitably waned or, at least, required to be more deliberately exercised than before. While a landowner who was resident or played a full part in the life of the community might legitimately command loyalty, one who attempted to exercise it as an absentee or negligent owner encountered opposition and resentment.[7] This had always been the case; influence had never been easy to extend to a second candidate connected merely by party not by ties of family or county.[8]

Nor was a coercive element entirely absent, though it had always been more prevalent in Wales and Ireland than in the English counties, at least in the obvious form of eviction of tenants after elections. As late as 1894, however, Northamptonshire farmers took reprisals against agricultural labourers who had shown the temerity to stand successfully for election in the new parish councils.[9] On the whole influence was most effective when no active steps were necessary to exercise it; in the 1860s it was still regarded as bad form, as well as being futile, to canvass a landowner's tenants without first seeking his permission. Significantly the formal canvass seems to have become more normal from 1885, and was widely associated with undue pressure; Joseph Arch (founder of the Agricultural Labourers Union and Liberal MP for N.W. Norfolk) carried his inbred fear of the canvass to the extent of refusing to adopt it when himself a candidate, describing it as a 'mean subterfuge. Its object is to get at a man's vote in an indirect way.'[10]

It is often asserted that the apparently slight impact of the secret ballot, introduced by Gladstone in 1872, is an indication of the general absence of undue pressure. This is by no means consistent with the actions of many politicians themselves. In order to arrest their declining control in rural areas Conservative landlords often stationed an estate manager or agent outside the polling station to take down the names of those who voted;[11] and since ballot boxes were separately counted one observed how many votes each village had cast for the other side.[12] It was thus not difficult to undermine the rural elector's confidence that the ballot really was secret as the radicals claimed. Naturally voters who were habitually deferential towards their social superiors did not suddenly change their practice in the absence of strong political pressures to do so. Ireland provided a dramatic explosion following the introduction of the secret ballot in the form of 57 Home Rulers elected in 1874. In Wales 1874 brought gains for the Liberals, despite a national tide against them, but this was no more than a continuation of a well-established trend. In both these countries the basis of political revolt lay in the fact that landlord and rural voter were frequently not of the same community; a well-developed alternative community of a cultural–religious type generated an early break with political practice. In Scotland large landowners were often Liberal, albeit Whiggish, in allegiance and therefore pulled in the same direction as their tenants wished to go. In England the ballot made little impact under the restricted franchise before 1884; but it was a different matter under the reformed electorate and the subsequent widespread politicization of the counties. It is unlikely that Liberal gains in hitherto Conservative counties in 1885 would have been so extensive had the poll remained open, or that the rebellious Crofter candidates would have prised Highland seats from Whig control.

Influence in the boroughs had for long been more obviously corrupt and coercive. Small boroughs often saw an election as the best means of attracting money to the town. Indeed, an immediate objection to the Ballot Act was that it facilitated the taking of bribes from *both* sides by electors. Contemporary alarm over excessive levels of expenditure during the elections of 1868, 1874 and 1880 stimulated the Gladstone government to enact a Corrupt and Illegal Practices Prevention Act in 1883 which set maximum expenditure limits according to size of electorate, imposed upon a single designated agent the responsibility for making a complete return of his candidate's expenses, and made it the duty of the Director of Public Prosecutions to initiate cases where corruption had occurred. Although this appears to have been relatively effective in setting limits to spending during campaigns, it would be optimistic to think that it radically altered attitudes. Neither a politician guilty of corrupt practices nor a voter who took bribes were ostracized for what were regarded as minor peccadilloes. In ancient parliamentary boroughs bribery amounted to a tradition rather than a venal sin; as late as 1911, for example, when Worcester was investigated by a Royal Commission, no less than 500 electors emerged guilty; by this period bribery had settled at an unspectacular level of 2s 6d or 5s[13] plus a few drinks per vote, and the Worcesters had ceased to be typical. Such practices dwindled essentially because they ceased to be efficacious; in substantial boroughs with 10,000–20,000 voters large-scale bribery was hardly worth the cost and was too blatantly obvious.

However, politicians circumvented the Act of 1883 to a considerable extent by spending money outside the election campaign period and by allowing others to spend it on their behalf, or in their interest. For the public still regarded it as a proper function of the MP to assist the borough, notably as an employer, and as a regular investor in community projects, charities and sporting clubs. MPs frequently distributed coal and blankets in winter, showered sweets upon the children, and saw that tea parties and 'knife and fork' suppers were thrown on suitable occasions. In addition the member's postbag would be full of begging letters from individual constituents seeking money or jobs. On top of this came the costs of being in Parliament. After 1885 expenditure of £800 to £1,000 was typical for a campaign; the candidates paid the, often exaggerated, costs of the returning officer; and the member commonly provided a salary of £100 to £300 per annum for his agent, plus additional sums for registration work each year. Thus the fact that by the First World War petitions alleging electoral malpractice had shrunk to a handful cannot obscure a certain continuity of practice and of attitude in the relation between a politician and his constituents.

Victorian reformers who hoped that judicious expansion of the electorate would foster a mature and informed debate on political issues in place of corruption and influence invariably lived to be disillusioned. Historians have rightly grown sceptical about any quick emergence of a 'politics of opinion' based upon the thinking individual voter after 1867. Indeed good evidence has emerged to suggest that the pattern in new industrial boroughs often repeated in certain respects that of county or medieval borough seats. Some employers, for example, appear to have mobilized the votes of their workers as effectively as any rural squire, and many a self-made manufacturer was known to give his men breakfast on polling day before marching them off to cast their votes for himself or his candidate. A number of medium-sized towns made it a practice to return the largest employer of labour – J. J. Colman the mustard manufacturer at Norwich, Joseph Pease the Quaker ironmaster at Darlington, or Charles Mark Palmer whose shipyards supported the economy of Jarrow; similarly industrialized county seats such as Northwich (Cheshire) returned the local chemical magnate Sir John Brunner, and the Mansfield division of Nottinghamshire elected the coal-owner Arthur Markham. Detailed study of Blackburn and Bury has demonstrated a distinct pattern in which working-class voters who resided near and worked in a factory owned by an active Liberal or Conservative reflected overwhelmingly his allegiance.[14] In such circumstances the result of an election could be as predictable from the relative strength of Liberal and Conservative employers as in a county from the number of the landlords' retainers. This is explicable especially in 1868 if one envisages the 1867 Act as enfranchising urban villages in which the factory served as the rural estate; here the pressures for unity around one's place of work against rival, external forces could be stronger than the individual's political opinion. Though dismissal of the politically rebellious introduced an occasional coercive element it was apparently the exception; coercion was more likely to be applied by a voter's own workmates than by his employer.[15]

Lest this should be seen as the universal pattern of urban politics in the late nineteenth century certain qualifications may be entered. Employer influence was characteristic of medium-sized towns where the range of employment was limited to one or two trades, and where the owners still resided near their workers in the 1880s. Where there existed a more varied economy and no dominant employers, a more rapid emergence of political opinion was a natural consequence.[16] Also the greater likelihood of residential separation of owner from worker in the larger conurbations, and even in the smaller Lancashire and Yorkshire towns by the 1890s, undermined the paternal relationships of the 1860s. Nor was the voter–employer relationship merely a passive, non-political one on the worker's part. In the constant shifting of house and job a workman of, say, Liberal views could deliberately seek a connection with a radical mill-owner. Just as a rural magnate who changed his politics did not expect the tenantry to switch allegiance automatically, so the employer had to recognize the existence of loyalties that were political or party as distinct from personal. Finally, the exercise of influence was naturally marked in the election following immediately upon the 1867 Reform Act when large numbers or working men voted for the first time but under the old conditions of open voting. By the 1880s even entrenched MPs were vulnerable to political issues; Brunner lost his seat in 1886; Palmer found himself almost unseated by a socialist in 1900. Moreover, any owner had to be known as a good employer or face a battery of criticism and innuendo during a campaign. As a result of personal and political considerations, by the turn of the century entrepreneurs with political ambitions were migrating away from the seats of their business: Richard Holt of Liverpool found a constituency at Hexham in Northumberland; Walter Runciman of Tyneside sat for Dewsbury; Alfred Mond of Cheshire represented Swansea. Such movements reflected the fact that it was no longer enough to be a local employer; allegiance to a political party furnished the safest guide to a constituency's representation.

TABLE 1.3   *Uncontested seats at general elections*

1857	333	1880	109	1900	243
1859	383	1885	43	1906	114
1865	302	1886	225	1910 (Jan.)	75
1868	212	1892	63	1910 (Dec.)	163
1874	188	1895	189		

The Rise of the Party Activist

One of the most striking features of mid-Victorian elections is that barely half the constituencies actually experienced a contest; and where seats were contested a third or more of voters normally split their two votes across party lines – an indication that Whig and Tory were not sharp political divisions but amorphous and overlapping groupings. Since two members had to be returned, Whigs and Tories frequently agreed to nominate a single candidate each with a view to avoiding the trouble and expense of a contest. Thus an election was often the result of a split *within* one side, between radicals and Whigs or on personal grounds, rather than between parties. Such cosy arrangements were, of course, anathema to the dedicated party activists of the late Victorian era whose objective in manning the constituency organization on a permanent basis was to ensure a fight at every election. After 1885 single-member constituencies[17] eliminated traditional Whig–Tory collusion, and the advance of formal party organization, stimulated by franchise extensions, may be measured from the decline in unopposed returns (see table 1.3). As the table shows 1885 marked the nearest approach to the mid-twentieth-century practice in which virtually every constituency is contested; around 30 of the unopposed returns occurred in staunchly Nationalist areas of Ireland which the Unionists found it futile to fight. Even so, the large totals for 1886, 1895 and 1900, when the Liberal organizations were either split or starved of resources, indicate how incomplete the evolution remained.

Hitherto parliamentary election campaigns had rested in the hands of small groups of landowners, professional men or employers who used solicitors to organize the poll and the registration. However, an alternative approach based upon the assumption of a regular party conflict evolved particularly in those towns whose government had been reformed under the 1835 Municipal Corporations Act;[18] the municipally inspired prototype did not generally displace the improvisations at parliamentary level until politicians had to face the challenges and problems raised by the new franchises, the redistribution, and the restrictions upon expenditure in the 1880s, which generated a permanent, institutional framework eventually covering the whole country.

Three major manifestations of organized party activity may be identified. First the professional party agent began to displace the solicitor for whom electoral work was just a sideline. This was no more than a natural consequence of the complexity of the franchise and registration process after 1885. The agent's responsibility was to ensure that his party's supporters appeared on the preliminary list of voters in May, to put in further claims and defend them before the revising barristers in the autumn, and particularly to lodge objections against the names of known opponents. Such work could make all the difference to the lodgers' vote since they had to make a fresh application every year; if they or householders shifted house the party agents pursued them in an annual charade. Some found that lodging objections paid higher dividends than making claims. In Newcastle the Conservatives objected to 9,500 names between 1888 and 1891 and in nearby Gateshead where the population rose by 16 per cent between 1885 and 1891 the electorate dropped by 301![19] In 1908 the Leeds Liberals secured a net advantage from registration of 257 (98 claims, 159 objections) over their opponents; in Keighley the Conservative agent claimed net gains ranging from 69 in 1892 to 238 in 1897.[20] In dozens of seats a turnover of these proportions was enough to determine the result of an election, and the party that neglected registration work for a year or two suffered badly. Where both agents were alert and thorough they habitually met privately before the revising courts got to work for a mutual withdrawal of objections; there is thus no little substance in the view that the parties, as much as the law, determined the franchise before 1918. Agents had also to keep abreast of legal cases which modified the interpretation of the Act; for example the 'latchkey' decision of 1907 by which 'lodgers' who held a front door key to the building could qualify as 'householders' produced a sudden influx of new voters. Sensible of their role in winning elections the party agents asserted their status by establishing professional associations, the Liberals in 1882 and the Conservatives in 1891; they adopted examinations for full membership, endeavoured to impose minimum salary levels upon the parties, set up benevolent funds, and published semi-secret journals to brief members on the latest tricks of the trade.

A second characteristic of the post-1867 system was the local party-sponsored club. Especially in Lancashire and Yorkshire working men's clubs were a long-standing feature, but politicians felt so apprehensive of losing touch with the urban electors of 1867 that they threw considerable resources into extending the network. A typical neighbourhood club was a modest affair of two or three rooms, one for lectures, one for reading, drinking, billiards or smoking; even a strongly radical town like Keighley boasted 13 such Conservative clubs in 1907. A popular extension of club activity during the summer involved mass picnics and excursions by train to the country home of the MP, candidate or other party dignitary; in September 1900, we learn, 600 North Salford Liberals picnicked at Matlock Bath in Derbyshire by day and enjoyed a Venetian fete on the river by night.[21] On a more regular basis urban party associations developed their own brass bands and football clubs which the MP was expected to subsidize. In such ways the parties helped to fill the role nowadays occupied by a vast and varied entertainments industry. Their motives in moving deliberately beyond strictly political activity were to inculcate the values of the parliamentary system among the new voters, to impart political education at least to the activist elite, and to foster an habitual loyalty on the part of those who were uninterested in or ignorant of politics. In addition the parties frequently sponsored benefit societies, friendly societies, sick and burial societies, and even building societies; according to one Liverpool Tory in 1879: 'working men in the north country always wanted to see some return for their money, and would therefore more willingly join a benefit club than an association for a purely abstract object.'[22] The success of the clubs and the Primrose League shows how misleading, in the British context, is the assumption that traditional parliamentary parties were simply parties of 'individual representation' that failed to involve their supporters except intermittently at election times; the evidence suggests that the Conservatives, rather than any of the extra-parliamentary socialist or labour bodies, approximated to a party of 'social integration' in that they permeated the daily lives of their members.

Finally, party growth manifested itself in the emergence of formal constituency associations based upon individual membership running into hundreds or thousands, divided between branches for each ward or polling district. This provided the centre for volunteer activists whose time and efforts now provided free much of the canvassing, transport and propaganda work previously paid for on an *ad hoc* basis. Representative constituency bodies were pioneered by radical Liberals – it was dubbed the 'caucus' system – who gave it central institutional form in the National Liberal Federation (NLF) of 1877. Rank and file Conservatives encountered greater opposition from landed and parliamentary patrons who sensed a threat to their own control, and eschewed the Liberals' pretensions to policy-making and selection of candidates; nonetheless, after a slow start in 1867 the National Union of Conservative and Constitutional Associations (NUCCA) attained official approval and spawned affiliated associations across the country during the mid-1880s. By this stage few candidates stood without the benefit of an agent, a permanent association, or the backing of a network of social organizations which gave them links with the mass of voters no longer attainable simply through the personal connections of leading families. By building up habitual party loyalty the politicians themselves helped to replace older forms of community and group influence with institutional, political ones.

Party, Parliament and the 'Independent Member'

By 1900 observers of British politics had begun to draw certain conclusions, often pessimistic ones, from the experience of the reformed system since 1867. Graham Wallas in his *Human Nature in Politics* (1908) highlighted the irrationality of a mass electorate in contrast to the liberal ideal. Also in 1908 the American academic A. L. Lowell in *The Government of England* dwelt upon the centralization of power in the Cabinet and the corresponding decline in the authority and independence of the House of Commons. The roots of this change had already been identified in M. Ostrogorski's *Democracy and the Organisation of Political Parties* (1902), which drew attention to what he saw as the debilitating effects of caucus politics upon Parliament. Seen in perspective Ostrogorski's pessimism seems exaggerated, even misplaced, since, despite the pretensions of Victorian party organizations in the 1870s, by 1900 both Liberal and Conservative parliamentary leaders had harnessed their extra-parliamentary forces to serve their ends; they appealed directly to the voters over the heads of their critics for the 'mandate' as the fashionable term had it; their command of patronage and policy was rarely challenged successfully even in the Labour Party whose roots and strength lay, as yet, outside the House of Commons. Very few politicians used the party organization as their highroad to power; even Joseph Chamberlain and Lord Randolph Churchill merely toyed with it before reverting to playing the game by the existing rules.

However, this should not obscure the very real changes that took place in the career and functions of the backbench politician in the late nineteenth century. Until this time membership of the House of Commons was still widely regarded less as a career than as a part-time activity undertaken along with other unpaid duties towards the community. This was held to be no small advantage in deterring carpet-baggers and in attracting to public service representatives of independent means. 'Once pay a member for his votes collectively,' declared Sir William Harcourt, 'and he will very soon make a market for his individual votes.'[23] Yet both tighter party discipline and the growing demands made by governments upon MPs undermined the conventional conception of the MP in our period. By tradition membership of the Commons impinged lightly upon the MP's time. Government business occupied only a fraction of the time of the House; attendance was frequently fitful and whipping slack, even unnecessary, for a ministry rested upon administrative rather than political support. Each August Parliament rose for the shooting season, members displaying a marked reluctance to return until the following February.

However, under Gladstone and his successors the parliamentary year grew longer. Governments appropriated sittings hitherto reserved for backbench legislation; and severe pressure upon government business caused by regular Irish Nationalist obstructionism prompted Gladstone in 1882 to pioneer the procedure for closure of debate by simple majority vote, a practice ritually condemned but nonetheless adopted by all governments anxious to squeeze legislation through. With the burgeoning scope of official activity came both lengthier and more complex legislation and financial proposals. Both the Public Accounts Committee of 1861 and the Estimates Committee of 1912 represented attempts to maintain the principle of Commons' scrutiny and control of finance without absorbing excessive amounts of time on the floor of the House. In practice Commons debates on Supply evolved into a largely ritual aspect of Parliament's work; in 1896 A. J. Balfour simply fixed the number of Supply days after which all remaining votes were taken by closure; they ceased to be opportunities for criticism of expenditure in detail and became instead occasions for general discussions initiated by the opposition. Thus governments grew to dominate the timetable and members to depend upon the party whip to keep them in touch with business from hour to hour. As attack by the opposition became normal practice so the whips displayed increasing intolerance of non-attendance or revolt. Life gradually ceased to be congenial for what Lord Salisbury described as 'the old judicial type of Member who sat rather loose to his party'.

Whereas the governments of the 1850s regularly suffered 10 to 15 defeats each year, by the 1900s their successors experienced only one per session on average. We may measure the growth of disciplined party behaviour by the number of Commons divisions in which 90 per cent of a party's representatives went into the same lobby (see table 1.4). Two features are particularly striking. First, the Conservatives in office and in opposition displayed tighter discipline or cohesion than the Liberals. This is quite at odds with contemporary criticism of the caucus for supposedly subjecting the politicians to its dictates; in practice the NLF invariably lent encouragement to MPs in rebellion against the

TABLE 1.4   *'Party votes' in the House of Commons 1850–1903*

	No. of divisions	Conservatives (%)	Liberals (%)
1850	321	45	37
1860	257	31	25
1871	256	61	55
1881	199	71	66
1883	253	65	52
1890	261	87	64
1894	237	92	84
1899	357	91	76
1903	260	83	88

Source: H. Berrington, 'Partisanship and Dissidence in the Nineteenth Century House of Commons', *Parliamentary Affairs*, 21 (1967–8), p. 342.

leadership. Secondly, the lax discipline prevailing up to the 1860s tightened up after 1868, but weakened somewhat during the early 1880s when the party leaders were inclined to seek co-operation from their opponents against their own rebellious supporters. However, the great divide on Home Rule in 1886 drove both sides towards greater cohesion than ever before, reaching a peak under the management of Salisbury and Balfour. A fundamental alteration had taken place since mid-century when government and opposition had been more fluid and relaxed, and neither side represented rigid parties. After 1886 governments ceased to be able to rely upon support from oppositions which now criticized everything but without prospect of defeating anything. All now turned upon maintaining the allegiance of one's own party majority; the older traditions of cross-bench voting by a large proportion of members gradually died out. Thus when Edwardians looked back nostalgically to a golden age of the 'Independent Member' they had in mind what we would think of as a House of 'moderates' whose fluctuating votes reflected the blurred and ambiguous lines of party demarcation.

Such developments seemed to many contemporaries to undermine the status of the MP while encroaching upon his time and freedom. Life in the Commons began to lose its attractions for young gentlemen. This is not to say that landed families did not continue to play a prominent role in both parties; simply that they had to make more deliberate efforts than before and acquiesce in the restrictions of parliamentary life. But the social composition of the Commons underwent a steady modification during the late Victorian era. It has been found that between 1868 and 1910 landowners fell from 46 to 26 per cent as a proportion of Conservative members and from 26 to 7 per cent among Liberals;[24] in the same period those whose livelihood lay in industry and trade rose from 31 to 53 per cent of Conservatives and from 50 to 66 per cent of Liberals; while those from legal and professional occupations grew from 9 to 12 per cent among Conservatives and from 17 to 23 per cent among Liberals. The dominance of lawyers in particular at cabinet level was a noticeable feature of the Liberal governments of 1906–14 which included very few industrialists. This march of the middle classes, which some Edwardians professed to abhor as an invasion by 'wirepullers', professional politicians and men on the make, reminds us how very protracted was the process of penetration initiated by the famous 'middle class' victories of 1832 and 1846.

In fact by 1900 many a rising bourgeois had discovered a short cut if not to power at least to prestige by obtaining a knighthood, baronetcy or peerage, often after (though not necessarily because of) generous contributions to party funds, aid to ailing party newspapers and services at elections. The rate of creation of peerages during the 1880s and 1890s was twice that of the 1830–60 period. Moreover the proportion of industrial and professional middle-class men among the newly ennobled reached 43 per cent during 1897–1911 by comparison with 14 per cent during 1867–81.[25] Certain types of recruit, notably brewers and newspaper proprietors, attracted criticism for their prominence; Guinesses were elevated in 1880 and 1891, and a Bass and an Allsopp both in 1886; Lord Glenesk arose from the *Morning Post* in 1899, Lord Burnham from the *Daily Telegraph* in 1903, and Lord Northcliffe from the *Daily Mail* in 1905. Yet the solid centre of British industry was well represented by Lords Armstrong (armaments) in 1887, Inverclyde (shipping) in 1897, Joicey and Allendale (mining) in 1906, and Mount Stephen (railways) in 1891, to take only a few examples. Though both parties, especially the Liberals, were under more pressure to raise central funds from wealthy men by the 1880s, financial contributions were not the sole factor. After 1886 Gladstone had to fortify the depleted Liberal ranks in the Lords. Conversely Salisbury, whose 1885–6 ministry was a turning-point in rapid creations, felt obliged to dispense honours as an alternative to posts now thinly spread between Conservatives and Liberal Unionists.

In the quest for office the new men competed under the old rules in that until 1911, when MPs were awarded a £400 salary, the backbencher had to live off a fortune amassed before his entry into politics; by 1900 of course many a second-generation industrialist could use his father's business to launch him into politics in his youth. But party loyalty now demanded that aspiring members should first tackle one or two hopeless or marginal constituencies before being nominated for a safe seat for life. For the politician's essential lifeline lay through his party rather than in his roots in his locality. As Augustine Birrell remarked to Asquith and Haldane one day as they gazed out across the Firth of Forth to the country beyond: 'What a grateful thought that there is not an acre in this vast and varied landscape that is not represented at Westminster by a London barrister!'[26]

2

The Evolution of the Gladstonian Liberal Party

1867–1895

A Liberal reform is never simply a social means to a social end, but a struggle of good against evil.

Sidney Webb, *Nineteenth Century*, September 1901

'Like the Kingdom of Heaven,' Sir William Harcourt could say as late as 1891, 'the Liberal Party is a house of many mansions.' Indeed before the 1870s the 'Liberal Party' was so amorphous and diverse both politically and organizationally as to be quite unlike a twentieth-century party. Mid-Victorian parties were primarily loose parliamentary parties, and such cohesion as the Liberals possessed derived initially from their role as the normal governing party of the period, and subsequently from Gladstone's dominating effect from 1866 until his retirement in 1894. Yet although diversity and dispute attended the party during these years, historians simplify too much if they overlook the steady and emphatic evolution of Liberalism towards a cohesive modern party framework and approach. The 1850s had seen the emergence of the parliamentary party under Palmerston; the 1860s brought new links between Liberals in the country and politicians like Bright and even Gladstone. In the 1870s formal party organization began to characterize the constituencies; and during the 1880s came the climax of political radicalization and a purging of the ranks which left popular Liberalism closer to parliamentary Liberalism than ever before. Gladstone's last government, 1892–4, saw the nearest approach to a programmatic party government and a drastic departure from the Palmerstonian era.

The origins of the parliamentary party may be traced back to 1850 when the death of Sir Robert Peel released his free trade followers to find permanent homes. Aberdeen's Coalition of 1852–5 provided a vital step in the transition by permitting the absorption of the Peelites into the Whig–Liberal governing group. Although this ministry came to grief in the Crimean War it provided the formula that was repeated with greater success by Palmerston in 1855–8 and 1859–65. On this latter ministry, which is usually thought of as the first Liberal one, Palmerston stamped his leadership effectively enough to ensure that the Whig–Liberal–Peelite combination would be more than a mere stopgap. Its breadth of support and its range of leading administrators made it the natural ruling party of the time.

However, Palmerston's party was essentially a parliamentary one quite unrepresentative of many of the people who regarded themselves as Liberals in the country. Half of its members were landowners or gentlemen with private incomes; indeed, despite the famous victories over reform in 1832 and the Corn Laws in 1846, government remained largely in the hands of the traditional landed men. Yet if the middle classes had not acquired power they showed an increasing interest in penetrating the world of politics; and what made the Liberals more of a national party than their rivals was that they embraced much more of commercial and industrial Britain. They also incorporated many of the most active politicians who devoted themselves to causes, to public speaking in the country, and to building links with the press and pressure groups. In contrast, politics for most politicians remained a part-time affair rather than a profession, and a local rather than a national or party matter. The other 'professionals' were the frontbenchers, often Whig peers like Granville, Kimberley, Spencer and Ripon, who, immersed in the great departments of state, addressed their energies more to administration than to a party audience outside Parliament; they resembled civil servants as much as modern politicians. In 1880 Gladstone still packed five earls, a duke and a marquess into his Cabinet of only 12 members. Later in the century many Whig peers abandoned politics, or at least Liberal politics; but those like Ripon and Spencer who chose to adapt continued to play a major role even on the Liberal side. However, their hold on cabinets was relaxed in favour of men who were typically party politicians such as Joseph Chamberlain, Sir Charles Dilke and John Morley. As the 1880 Cabinet shows, Gladstone had no prior intention to advance these men, convinced as he was of the virtues of government by disinterested gentlemen. Yet the talents of Chamberlain, Dilke, Morley, W. W. Forster, Sir William Harcourt, John Bright, Henry Fawcett and H. H. Asquith won them posts under Gladstone notwithstanding their radical views; in fact after 1886 a Liberal cabinet could hardly be formed without such men.

Liberalism, Reform and Religion

One of the consequences of the detailed study made by historians of policy-making and internal party debates has been to create an exaggerated impression of division and disunity in Victorian Liberalism. To some extent the quantity of high politics source material makes this unavoidable. But it sometimes leads to the assumption that nothing held Liberals together except power and opportunism; asked to explain what it meant to be a Liberal in late Victorian times, the student is often perplexed for an answer.

Nonetheless, the common basis of Liberalism is tolerably clear. Above all the party was dedicated to the cause of free trade which many Liberals saw not merely as the key to economic prosperity but as a great moral good. In addition Liberals advocated a range of constitutional, legal and religious reforms which reflected their desire to restrict excessive privilege, to open up opportunities and to improve civil liberties for the individual. One expression of this was parliamentary reform which, after the row over the 1866 Reform Bill had subsided, became a characteristic Liberal theme. This, however, was qualified by the developing split over women's suffrage. Similarly on the religious front some Liberals wished to travel further down the road than others; while the disestablishment of the Church in Ireland commanded general assent in 1868, most stopped short of disestablishing the Church of England. Again, Liberals usually disliked autocratic and clerical regimes abroad, hence their support for self-determination among Greeks, Italians and Germans; but few were as yet ready to extend this principle to Irishmen and Indians. On this basis, however, it is clear that by the 1860s Liberalism represented something coherent and distinct from Conservatism. Indeed, it was largely because of his stand on these questions that Gladstone himself eventually became a Liberal after his early career as a Tory politician.

Recently historians have begun to go rather further than this in emphasizing the significance of ideology in Victorian politics. This has taken the form of reasserting the centrality of religious and moral issues for Whigs, Liberals, radicals and Conservatives alike. It is certainly striking to note how much time and energy late Victorian governments devoted to questions with troublesome religious complications. After 1868 Gladstone was embroiled in arguments with Nonconformists over elementary schools and disestablishment, and his government suffered defeat over the Irish Universities Bill. The 1880s brought the Church Burials Act, repeated attempts by the atheist Charles Bradlaugh to take his seat in Parliament, the Deceased Wife's Sister's Bill and the Welsh Sunday Closing Act. The 1890s saw debates over clergy discipline in the

Church of England, Church tithes, Welsh disestablishment, rate aid for Church schools and the Marriages Act of 1898. The Conservatives were equally troubled – notably by the controversy about ritualism in the Church – and the downfall of Balfour's government was partly the result of the religious implications of the 1902 Education Act.

A number of circumstances help to account for the preoccupation with religion in this period. Since the religious census of 1851 Victorians were afraid that large sections of society had escaped the influence of the Church. Thus Anglicans had been investing heavily in the construction of new urban churches, in Sunday Schools and, after the 1870 Education Act, in new elementary schools. Competition within the Christian world was growing fiercer both because of the challenge posed by Nonconformists and because of the general advance of Roman Catholicism. Gladstone spoke for many when he expressed concern about the resurgence of papal authority in Europe – on the assumption that the citizen could not be loyal both to the Pope and to his Queen and government. Yet there were many prominent conversions to Catholicism, including Lord Ripon (Liberal) and Henry Matthews (Conservative). Moreover, the steady growth of High Church practices provoked a running controversy over 'ritualism' from the 1870s to the end of the century. And the continuing influx of Catholics from Ireland fuelled Protestant extremism in several parts of the country.

There was a close connection between the role of religion and the peculiar centrality of Gladstone during this period. For he both benefited from and contributed to the prevailing mood. Though suspect to many as a High Churchman and a zealot, he undoubtedly articulated religious and moral questions in a way that neither Disraeli nor, significantly, Joseph Chamberlain could do. He had to pay a price for his position, for example, in steadily accepting the grievances of Nonconformists as political objectives. But equally Gladstone's followers surrendered themselves to his unique status as spokesman for the 'Nonconformist Conscience'; no one could rival his capacity to articulate a sense of morality in politics and lift men's sights above vulgar materialism. The classic example of Gladstone's approach in action was provided by his famous campaign over the Bulgarian atrocities in the late 1870s. While many Whigs and Tories regarded his efforts with suspicion, his crusade aroused notable enthusiasm among both Nonconformists and High Churchmen.

The Building Blocks of Liberalism

Important as Gladstone was, the Liberal Party had a life of its own, and was evolving steadily by the third quarter of the nineteenth century.

Until the 1870s few MPs had to deal with organized parties in their constituencies. But whatever the Liberal forces lacked, as yet, in formal organization they made up for in vociferousness. Most had been drawn into political activity for a specific objective or cause often through a pressure group such as the United Kingdom Alliance (temperance), the National Education League (free, undenominational, state education), or the Liberation Society[1] (Church disestablishment); the outstanding common element here was Victorian Nonconformity engaged in a prolonged campaign to eliminate other grievances such as the payment of Church rates, denial of burial rights in churchyards and exclusion from the ancient universities. Other causes, represented by the Ballot Society, the Reform Union and the Peace Society, were fragments of the anti-Corn Law movement of the 1840s. Still others catered more specifically to radical working men organized in radical clubs, the 'new Model' unions and in the Reform League which harked back to Chartism. In addition there were the campaigns for moral improvement including not only temperance but the abolition of the Contagious Diseases Acts (which permitted the army to license prostitutes in certain garrison towns), the trade in child prostitution and capital punishment. The foot soldiers in this phalanx of pressure groups ranged from self-made manufacturers and merchants through the lower middle class of shopkeepers, teachers and journalists to craftsmen and miners. Whereas the parliamentarians were typically landed, Anglican and Whig, provincial Liberals were more commonly urban–industrial, Nonconformist and radical.

Disparate as these elements appear, they did in fact provide the fabric of local Liberalism; and although much of their energy was devoted to fighting Whigs rather than Tories, during the 1860s and 1870s they were harnessed to parliamentary Liberalism so effectively that by the 1890s it had come to reflect their views fairly well. Articulate in its incoherence, pressure-group Liberalism was much more cohesive than it appears at first sight. For its forces were concentrated socially and geographically in the towns of midland and northern England, Scotland and Wales. Membership of the groups overlapped so much that there was a natural attraction in the idea of an institutional umbrella such as the Liberal Party. This was especially true for middle-class Nonconformists whose desire to become integrated into national political life and throw off the stigma attaching to them led them to the parliamentary Liberal Party, which, for all its imperfections, provided the best quick route to power. It is no exaggeration to say that Nonconformity was the factor that turned many Victorians into active politicians, for those who neglected to exercise their political influence were, in the words of the Congregationalist minister R. W. Dale, 'guilty of treachery both to God and man'. Only 64 Nonconformists were elected to the Parliament of 1868, but their numbers rose steadily to 95 by 1886, 177 by 1892 and 210 in 1906.

Unity also arose from a common perception of the means and purpose of radical politics. While some objectives could be realized at municipal level or by pressure applied through bodies like the Trades Union Congress, all were hindered by the essential unresponsiveness of Parliament. By the 1860s it seemed plain that the key to further advance lay, as Cobden and Bright had perceived years before, through extensive reform of the franchise and the ballot. Political reconstruction invested Liberal politics with an elevating and unifying theme; its business was the removal of privilege and artificial restriction and the opening up of political opportunity to the talents of every man. Herein lay the basis for common action through the identification of common enemies by middle- and working-class radicals which had been pioneered in such places as Birmingham and Rochdale. Radicals discerned a model and a moral reinforcement in the politics of the United States.[2] Working people were encouraged by reports from emigrants who dilated upon the greater opportunities there, the social equality and the absence of a dominant landed elite. Similarly for middle-class radicals a system that was democratic in being open to energy and talent at the grass roots represented their ideal. America played an important role in drawing together not just popular radicals of Bright's stamp, but also many of the intellectuals and academics of the 1860s. James Bryce, Henry Fawcett and John Stuart Mill were all drawn towards Liberal politics at this time partly through their sympathy for the North in the American Civil War,[3] this gave them not only contact with urban radicals, but also a sympathetic appreciation for working men who appeared to take a moral view of politics by their advocacy of the Northern cause. Indeed, along with Oliver Cromwell and the Italian nationalists Mazzini and Garibaldi, Abraham Lincoln remained for years a hero to British radicals; and 'John Brown' and other American tunes served as rallying songs for reformers right through to Edwardian times.

This need for leadership and unity was also appeased to some extent by the provincial press, which in its Victorian heyday was highly political and disproportionately Liberal in sentiment. Papers like the *Leeds Mercury, Manchester Guardian* or *Newcastle Chronicle* provided a focus for radical activity, and by extensive reproduction of major speeches built a vicarious bridge between the people and leading politicians. The keystone of this arch was undoubtedly Gladstone. For until his emergence as a popular figure in the 1860s Liberalism continued to run on two parallel lines; the movement in the constituencies looked to parliamentarians like Bright, who was only a backbencher, remote from the seats of power. Thus when Gladstone began to speak on franchise reform and to visit industrial centres like Tyneside (which led to his abandonment of his university seat in favour of a popular constituency in 1865), he found a huge reservoir of 'virtuous passion' waiting to be tapped. As Chancellor of the Exchequer and destined Liberal leader Gladstone was the first major figure to take the trouble to come to the people; the experience proved immensely flattering for both sides.

It is a distinctive feature of British politics that by the 1860s most politically active working men seem to have been content to operate under the umbrella of Liberalism. They found their champions in such men as Gladstone, Abraham Lincoln and Charles Bradlaugh, the radical member for Northampton; and many of their ideas were derived from intellectuals such as Henry Fawcett or John Stuart Mill, or Henry George the American land reformer whose book *Progress and Poverty* had sold 400,000 copies by the time of his triumphant tour of Britain in 1882. Though Chartism had dwindled after 1848 there was a good deal of continuity of ideas and individuals who rallied to John Bright and were eventually led into the pale of the constitution by Gladstone when he championed the cheap press and parliamentary reform in the 1850s and 1860s. The culmination came in 1874 when the first working men – Thomas Burt (Morpeth) and Alexander McDonald (Stafford) – were elected MPs. Known as 'Lib–Labs', these members took the Liberal whip and fervently espoused Gladstonian causes. Lib–Lab candidates were usually miners' union officials who stood in constituencies where their members were so concentrated as to enable them to bargain with the local Liberal Associations for the nomination. Burt and McDonald were joined by other miners, notably William Abraham (Rhondda), Charles Fenwick (Northumberland Wansbeck), John Wilson (Mid-Durham) and Ben Pickard (Yorkshire Normanton). But the other Liberal working men should not be overlooked, for example, Joseph Arch, the agricultural labourers' leader (N.W. Norfolk), and in London George Howell a former bricklayer (N.E. Bethnall Green), Randall Cremer, a carpenter (Shoreditch) and James Rowlands, a watch-case maker (East Finsbury). Clearly the Liberalism of this era enjoyed a powerful democratic reputation; it represented 'the people' at least in the sense of the artisans and small shopkeepers who derived a gratifying sense of self-respect from their participation in Gladstonian politics. The link was consolidated by the popular radical press, particularly the *Daily News*, and by the mass circulation working-class Sunday papers, *Lloyds Weekly News*, *Reynolds Newspaper* and the *News of the World*.

Yet historians have sometimes found it surprising that a traditional party could mobilize working-class support on a frugal diet of constitutional reform, retrenchment and moral causes. However, the relationship evidently also had a material rationale. The obvious element was free trade which provided cheap food; working men looked for the further lifting of duties levied on essential items of consumption. Social reform as yet generated no significant demand. This was partly because existing social policies represented an unwelcome interference in working-class life, and because the benefits were not seen to be justified by the costs in terms of local rates and national taxation. Approximately 70 per cent of government expenditure was devoted to the army, navy and the national debt; then there was the police, civil service, and civil list to be paid for. Since much of the revenue required derived from taxes on consumption paid by relatively poor people it followed that the Gladstonian cry of retrenchment commanded much popularity. This also helps to explain the loyalty of working-class leaders to Gladstone over foreign and imperial questions. His preference as Prime Minister after 1868 for settling disputes with other powers by negotiation rather than by war, his efforts to withdraw troops from colonies such as New Zealand, and his reluctance to be dragged into fresh imperial expansion all made eminent sense. In fact in 1869 and 1870 Gladstone's government met expectations by reducing expenditure and lowering taxation. The only flaw was that it proved difficult to sustain this strategy. Moreover, the rise in money wages in the early 1870s carried growing numbers of working men over the annual income threshold of £100 which made them liable for income tax. In this context Gladstone's promise in 1874 to abolish the income tax was wholly consistent with the popular appeal of Victorian Liberalism.

However, Gladstone retained his control of the popular and parliamentary strands of Liberalism more by inspiration than by skilful management, and showed an alarming penchant as leader for withdrawing altogether in times of difficulty. Eschewing the vulgar arts of party management he tried to hold to the higher ground of national interest. No doubt this reluctance to become involved was a useful tactic for keeping him above the sectional interests, and indeed reflected his own distaste for pressure-group politics, which he thought would lead to mediocrity among politicians and the corruption of class legislation. This was a characteristic view for a man of his generation; yet Gladstone also levelled criticisms of self-interest at the 'upper ten thousand', and cultivated the lower classes because he discerned in them a capacity for moral and responsible behaviour that would improve political life. He therefore engaged in a dual enterprise of trying to govern through the best representatives of the traditional ruling class, while involving the lower classes in morally improving issues rather than pandering to their material welfare. The collapse of Whiggery and the aggrandizement of the caucus had defeated these aims well before his retirement, but his struggles decisively influenced the development of Liberal politics. Although Gladstone's reputation for radicalism was exaggerated, he made the Liberal party a vehicle for a certain kind of reform during 1866–74 and gave the radicals their best means of determining government policy; yet his evident alienation from many specific items in the radical programme commended him to the Whigs as a bulwark against drastic change until the 1880s. So long as both sides accepted his leadership and manoeuvred for his support Gladstone could play a pivotal and unifying role in the evolution of the party.

The Programme versus the Single Issue

Although Gladstone's followers were often captivated by the novelty of participation in national politics they also expected their support to be translated into precise reforms; yet their expectations were bound to be dashed because neither Gladstone nor the MPs as a whole approved of demands for Church disestablishment or temperance reform. Instead of allowing his priorities to be influenced by the rank and file Gladstone intended rather to use their 'virtuous passion' to strengthen his case in Parliament for the changes he did believe necessary. This strategy hinged upon his ability to create a single transcending issue which both Parliament and the constituency activists would accept as the priority. In this process the Reform Bill promoted by him and Lord John Russell in 1866 formed a vital step. For when the Bill perished as a result of Whig opposition Gladstone declined to carry on in office as, on past precedent, he might have been expected to do. His resignation meant that although the Whigs had won a limited victory over that particular Bill, they were going to lose the wider battle for control of future Liberal policy; the incoming minority Conservative administration would sooner or later be driven to an election that Gladstone intended to fight on the franchise question, thereby purging the rebels and producing a majority pledged to reform.

Since in the event Disraeli managed to pass a bill of his own by making concessions to radical backbenchers, Gladstone promptly found another overriding cause – disestablishment of the Church in Ireland and Irish land reform. On this basis he won a majority in 1868 which enabled him to impose both Irish reforms and several other measures during 1868–73. In this period of reform the authority of the gentry was curtailed by Forster's elected school boards and by the secret ballot; upper-class privilege was limited by reforms in the civil service and the army; and the status of the Church and the rights of property were encroached upon in Ireland. This was all of a piece with franchise reform itself as far as the radicals were concerned in that it attacked the sources of privilege and inefficiency which many had been criticizing since the Crimean War and even earlier. By 1874 the Palmerstonian mould had been decisively broken.

However, while the attack upon privilege furnished a fine theme, the omissions and shortcomings in detail strained the loyalty of Gladstone's supporters sufficiently to produce his defeat over the Irish Universities Bill in 1873. Many radicals believed that Irish disestablishment should lead rapidly to Welsh and Scottish; temperance men were highly irritated by the Licensing Act which regulated public houses and thus made drinking more acceptable not less; trade unions gained legal standing but their right to picket was left in doubt; and Nonconformists felt outraged at the use of ratepayers' money for subsidizing Anglican schools through the new school board system. The 1870 Education Bill best demonstrates the divisive tendencies in the party, for 132 Liberal members voted against it, while 133 abstained; it passed only with Conservative support. These examples show Gladstone's difficulties in trying to govern in the general interest on the strength of sectional interests, many of whom he believed to be propagating unpopular 'fads'; these he pronounced 'unripe' and urged their proponents to convert a majority in the country before expecting the government to risk adopting them. Unfortunately for Gladstone he could not easily command the country without the active assistance of the pressure-group radicals. Temperance fanatics and militant Nonconformists were the quintessential volunteer workers whose withdrawal could cripple the party locally; and the Liberal defeat in 1874 was widely ascribed to the recalcitrance of disappointed groups like the National Education League. No doubt the NEL deliberately fostered the impression that without them victory was impossible, and they overlooked the loss of support from those who considered that Gladstone had been far too sweeping. Eventually the 1874 defeat sobered many of the 'faddists'; they applied themselves to filling the gap left by conservative defections because the Liberal Party was still their best route to power.

However, the erosion of upper- and middle-class support was a more permanent phenomenon because they did have a political alternative. In 1874 many urban seats returned Conservatives, while in the counties – another portent – Whigs often withheld money and influence from Liberal candidates. The fact is that although in retrospect Victorian Liberalism may seem basically the party of free trade, individualism and self-help, by the 1880s contemporaries were more aware of the growing emphasis on state intervention and compulsion at the expense of individual rights. Temperance and education were two major spheres in which radicals had rapidly concluded that the inadequacy of individual effort could be remedied only by state compulsion. And during Gladstone's second ministry the 1880 Employers Liability Act and the 1881 Irish Land Act, which introduced tribunals empowered to revise rents, were seen as an even graver threat to private property than his earlier measures. Consequently the 1880s saw the resignation of men like the Duke of Argyll from the Cabinet and the creation of the Liberty and Property Defence League. By 1885, with Joseph Chamberlain in full flood against those 'who toil not, neither do they spin', many a traditional Liberal was inclined to take seriously the warning of the jurist A. V. Dicey that if one gave up individual freedom 'you can find no resting place until you reach the abyss of Socialism.'

In fact Gladstone's tactics in 1874 had been to offer abolition of the income tax. But after his defeat he retired for two years before re-emerging in September 1876, 'pamphlet in hand', to assume the leadership of the provincial crusade against Disraeli's pro-Turkish policy in the Balkans. This campaign was a classic illustration of his capacity for drawing the radicals from their narrow concerns by an appeal to moral righteousness. He began by condemning the Prime Minister for condoning the massacres of Bulgarian Christians merely because he thought it in Britain's interest to back up the Ottoman Empire; and by the time of the two Midlothian campaigns of 1879 and 1880 he had widened the attack to one on 'Beaconsfieldism', that is, the use of military power for imperial aggrandizement as in South Africa and Afghanistan. In fact the policy of their governments was much closer than the rhetoric suggested. Disraeli had been drawn unwillingly into the conflicts with the Boers and the Afghans by British representatives on the ground, Sir Bartle Frere (high commissioner) and Lord Lytton (viceroy) respectively. Gladstone was to encounter the same problems, especially in Egypt and the Sudan.

Nevertheless, as an expedient for polarizing politics and recapturing the leadership of radicalism the campaign against 'Beaconsfieldism' proved a triumph; but it was no solution to the problem that led to 1874. Others had begun to consider how to overcome the incoherence endemic in Liberalism. In particular Joseph Chamberlain, Mayor of Birmingham 1873–6, diagnosed the problem in terms of the dispersion of radicalism over innumerable causes. To be successful radicals had to concentrate on a single question as Cobden and Bright had done over the Corn Laws; the trouble was that their success had led to the disintegration of the forces that had brought it about, and ever since 1846 Bright had vainly sought a similar rallying point. Initially Chamberlain himself believed that either disestablishment or education would serve to concentrate radicalism and tighten its grip on the party, but 1874 had shown him the inadequacy of such causes when it came to rousing the electorate. Making a virtue of necessity, therefore, he abandoned the single-issue strategy in favour of programme politics. His main vehicle for this, the National Liberal Federation, was established in 1877 from the ruins of the National Education League with the object of radicalizing both the policy and the organization of the Liberal Party. It would represent the active, democratic constituency Liberals in the country who would select candidates who reflected their views. The annual assembly of the NLF would become a kind of Liberal Parliament in the country, especially when the party was out of office; and being representative of the party's supporters it could legitimately prepare a programme of measures and indicate the priorities to the leaders. In this way it was hoped to harness radicalism's scattered forces to the governmental machine.

The basis of the NLF's claims to represent Liberalism lay in local parties whose membership was open to all supporters. The Birmingham Liberal Association, two-thirds of whose membership was reckoned to be working class, provided a model for others to emulate. Although middle- and working-class co-operation had long been a feature of Birmingham politics, similar systems had been pioneered in Oldham and Rochdale which inspired popular organization in places like Newcastle in the 1870s.[4] Every Liberal in the city was entitled to attend his local ward meetings which elected representatives to a 'Liberal 600', and this in turn chose an executive committee. At its inauguration in 1877 the NLF drew representatives from 95 such organizations.

Initially Gladstone's dislike of the pretensions of the caucus and programme politics was obscured; for when the NLF timed its inaugural meeting in May 1877 to catch the wave of excitement over the Bulgarian issue the Liberal leader graced the occasion with a speech at the Bingley Hall, Birmingham. Each believed they had caught the other. By hitching Gladstone's prestige to the NLF Chamberlain calculated that he was bound to strengthen radicalism at the expense of the Whigs who were undoubtedly embarrassed by the Bulgarian campaign. Ultimately this proved a shrewd assessment. But in the short run the NLF found itself swept along in Gladstone's crusade in which its own objectives were obscured. By maintaining his grip on radical affections, especially in imperial and foreign affairs, Gladstone succeeded for some years in checking the programmatic form of politics desired by Chamberlain. The year 1877 thus began the process of driving the two men apart.

As a result the Liberals swept home in the 1880 general election on a wave of moral righteousness with a negative mandate to undo Disraeli's policy, but little else. The victory seemed unrelated to the issues of radical politics, and as the new administration staggered on without achievement the whole Midlothian strategy began to appear as a ruse designed to sidetrack radicalism. In fact Gladstone's difficulties during 1800-85 were partly due to the engrossing problems of South Africa, Afghanistan and Egypt; to the coercive measures for Ireland and the consequent obstructionism of the Nationalist MPs; and to time-consuming controversy over the entry into the Commons of the atheist MP, Charles Bradlaugh, who had refused to take the oath. However, the Prime Minister had no priorities for legislation, and important reforms of land and local government were frustrated. Consequently the faddists grew voluble again, and their clamour was stilled only by the introduction of a major measure, the 1884 Franchise Bill, which was passed before the government broke up over its defeat on the budget in June 1885.

In fact the two leading radical ministers, Dilke and Chamberlain, had already resigned in May, the latter to concentrate on a ferocious campaign against the landed upper class which was designed to win the newly enfranchised county voters for radicalism at the 1885 elections. In interpreting Chamberlain's proposals (dubbed the 'Unauthorised Programme'), one has to disentangle the ideological element from the tactical objective. His list included free elementary education, elective county government, land reforms, graduated taxation, death duties, disestablishment, devolution-all-round, manhood suffrage and payment of MPs. In part this grew out of Chamberlain's municipal experience in Birmingham where the council had shown its middle-class ratepayers the virtues of public enterprise in the provision of such services as gas, water, sewerage and lighting. This willingness to extend the collective element in economic and social matters marked Chamberlain out as what was often called a 'constructive radical'; conversely, eminent 'radicals' like John Morley shrank from 'construction' on both economic and political grounds, the more so as it was increasingly coupled with the demand for graduated taxation.

In other respects, however, Chamberlain's approach was less radical. The idea of local government reform or devolution was really to allow divisive matters such as temperance or education to be settled outside Parliament. Nor did he wish to offend the middle-class belief in private enterprise, witness his cautious approach to housing.[5] For him the chief issue was land because it served to concentrate the attack upon the upper classes and to pre-empt any separate working-class onslaught on property in general. In the long run, he believed, middle-class radicals had to mobilize the new mass electorate before someone else did.

The tactical significance of the Unauthorised Programme is less obvious. On the face of it Chamberlain's object was to gain such a preponderance of radical MPs in the new Parliament that it would be impossible for Gladstone to repeat the experience of 1880-5. Historians have therefore tried to calculate the number of his supporters. One study suggests a growth from 80 in 1874 to 120 in 1880 and 160 after the 1885 election when 333 Liberals were returned altogether.[6] Another writer suggests 180, using as the criterion for radicalism an MP's support for even one point in the programme;[7] but this contrasts sharply with the chief whip's estimate of only 101 'Chamberlainites'. Retrospective assessments exaggerate Chamberlain's strength because they define radicalism in domestic terms and forget that the foreign–imperial dimension was equally important. Most radicals had inherited their creed from Cobden and Bright: trade not rule was the virtue of Empire: Britain should abstain from entanglements abroad and avoid expenditure and armaments. The irony is that on these matters the two leading radicals, Dilke and Chamberlain, were out of step with most radical opinion; they resented the failure of Gladstone, as they saw it, to stand up for British interests as much as the Whigs. Another weakness in Chamberlain's appeal was that, though a Unitarian himself, he remained essentially a secular radical, not much motivated by religious or spiritual concerns; the 'Nonconformist Conscience' always remained elusive. Consequently Chamberlain could never prise radicalism away from Gladstone. During the early 1880s he began to recognize this: for many radicals now looked to Morley – a staunch 'Little Englander' – as a more suitable leader than Chamberlain; and the first working-men MPs such as Thomas Burt also followed the Gladstonian line on foreign affairs. Thus 'Chamberlainites' should not be equated with 'radicals'. There was little prospect of a takeover of the party by him in 1885; and herein lies the explanation for his otherwise extraordinary abandonment of the Liberal Party in the company of Lord Hartington and the Whigs in 1886.

1886: the Radicalization of the Party

The fall of Gladstone's government over the 1885 budget was followed by a minority Conservative administration and a general election in which the Liberal lead of 86 over the Tories was matched by the election of 86 Irish Nationalists. The deadlock was resolved by the launching of the 'Hawarden Kite' in December 1885 when Gladstone's son, Herbert, released the news of his father's conversion to Irish Home Rule. Thereupon Liberals and Nationalists combined to eject Salisbury from office; Gladstone introduced a Home Rule Bill which failed owing to the opposition of 93 Liberal MPs who withdrew under Hartington and Chamberlain to stand as Liberal Unionists at the ensuing general election of 1886.

THE IRISH "VAMPIRE."

From Punch, *24 October 1885*.

This crisis reflected much more than a simple division of opinion over the principle of Home Rule. It was easy for men like Sir William Harcourt, who disliked the Bill intensely, to remain loyal to Gladstone. In so doing he had opted for one strategy; Chamberlain in withdrawing had opted for another. Having absorbed the lesson of 1880 he had no intention of allowing the Grand Old Man to lead the party off on another crusade, and thus forget the real business of radical polit- ics. Since the 1885 election had confirmed that he could not dominate the party Chamberlain had sought a short cut by co-operating with Hartington and the Whig elements to topple Gladstone. The basis for a Hartington–Chamberlain government consisted in their common dislike of Gladstone's supine and unpatriotic foreign policy; within such a government Chamberlain believed that Hartington, lacking Gladstone's influence with the radicals, would be obliged to allow him to determine the pace of domestic reform. This prospect of an alternative Liberal ministry posed a dilemma for Gladstone from which he escaped successfully by seizing the initiative over Home Rule. The joint withdrawal of Hartington and Chamberlain was a logical consequence in that it reflected their common failure to ditch Gladstone, and Chamberlain's inability to win control of the radical forces.

The ultimate significance of this turning-point in politics is as much misunderstood as its origins. Superficially the Home Rule crisis appears merely a divisive, weakening factor that deprived the party of its radical strength. The reality was different. It clarified Liberal politics by introducing a simple test of orthodoxy, and completed the process initiated unwittingly by Gladstone in 1866 when he refused to abandon franchise reform. The purging of the Whig elements had been proceeding apace during 1880–5 when the Dukes of Argyll and Bedford and the Marquess of Lansdowne, to name only the most illustrious, had left the party. Of the 73 Liberal Unionist MPs who survived the 1886 election only 20 were radical supporters of Chamberlain; by 1892 only 11 of the latter remained and several had rejoined the Gladstonians. In short, 1886 virtually completed the radicalization of Liberalism. Although only 191 Gladstonians were returned in 1886 they comprised a much more cohesive party than ever before. For the first time Gladstone appointed radicals such as Tom Ellis and Arnold Morley as party whips, and when next he came to form a government in 1892 he had no option but to draw upon radicals to fill the cabinet posts.

The fact that the majority of radical politicians chose to stay with Gladstone reflected the loyalties of Liberals in the country. Evidence of the attitudes of the three layers of Liberalism suggests that Home Rule sentiment was at its weakest among parliamentarians, stronger among the electors, and as its strongest among the activists. It is easy to exaggerate the electoral unpopularity of Home Rule. Rebellious Liberal Unionists secured election in 73 seats because the Conservatives stood down in their favour, thus presenting them with around two-thirds of the former Conservative vote to add to a quarter to a third of the old Liberal vote. They managed this most easily in areas where the development of party organization had lagged, and where it proved difficult to obtain and finance a new Gladstonian candidate at short notice. In such cases the prestige of the sitting member served to carry sufficient support, particularly in parts of the south-west and western Scotland where the strategic implications of Home Rule seemed to lend force to the Liberal Unionists' case. On the other hand, in a straight contest between a Gladstonian and a Conservative the loss of Liberal votes was much slighter; in fact many Liberals improved their poll over 1885 and actually regained seats in such places as Huddersfield, Leeds East, Liverpool Exchange, Manchester South-West, Wednesbury and Wolverhampton West.

These victories in the towns constitute further evidence of the strength of Home Rule sentiment where Liberalism was well organized. Indeed one study suggests that only 5–10 per cent of party activists felt sufficiently opposed to Gladstone's policy to leave the party.[8] To them Home Rule appeared an eminently radical issue on which they could sympathize with the Irish for fighting a common enemy. The swiftness with which the caucus fell into line behind Gladstone undoubtedly surprised Chamberlain. Following the introduction of the Home Rule Bill on 10 April 1886 the local organizations selected delegates for an NLF council meeting on 5 May: the 'Newcastle 600', the 'Nottingham 800', the 'Leicester 500' and many others declared emphatically for Gladstone; even at Birmingham the 'Two Thousand' dissented only on details. At the NLF meeting a motion mildly critical of the Bill was thrown out by 575 votes to 25, which led to the resignation of Chamberlain and his Birmingham loyalists Jesse Collings and Powell Williams. Moreover, sitting members who were prevaricating at Burnley, Nottingham West, Buckingham and Hastings found their local caucuses insisting that they endorse official policy; those who remained obdurate like G. O. Trevelyan and George Goschen were denied renomination; other prominent figures were ejected by a vote of the local party, notably Hartington at Rossendale and Sir Henry James at Bury. In general the wealthier Liberal supporters were more prone to withdrawal, so that the local parties became noticeably poorer if more cohesive politically. The year 1886 actually helped to reunite Liberal associations formerly in disarray at Bradford, Dewsbury and Newcastle. As many as 50 associations affiliated to the NLF for the first time, thus making its hold more complete than ever. In September 1886 it shifted its headquarters to London next door to the Liberal Central Association so that the two bodies could enjoy a common secretary, Francis Schnadhorst, and put an end to the rivalry between them.

The crystallization of the radical forces as a result of Home Rule is particularly noticeable in Scotland, which, though strongly Liberal, had been sharply divided between a Glasgow-based organization of radicals and an Edinburgh-based association of Whigs and moderates. The former vigorously propagated the two central issues of Scottish politics –

land reform and disestablishment – and were conciliated by a new Secretaryship of State for Scotland in 1885 and the Crofters Bill of 1886. The radicals had long felt that a reformed county franchise would expose the inability of the Whigs to mobilize public opinion; they therefore established an NLF for Scotland on the English pattern and put up candidates against Whiggish Liberals in 28 of the 72 Scottish constituencies in 1885. Home Rule finally alienated the Scottish Whigs who had been trying to hold on to Gladstone during the 1880s, though the immediate price was the loss of 23 Liberal MPs opposed to Home Rule, 17 of whom secured election in 1886. On the other hand the disestablishment radicals and land reformers who had grown impatient with Gladstone saw the futility of leaving and rallied to the Irish cause; Gladstone was now thrown into their arms.

Similarly the English pressure groups appreciated the tactical advantages of sticking to the Grand Old Man. The loss of so many local patrons plainly left the party more dependent than ever on the network of Nonconformity in the provinces. Even before 1886 the faddists had steadily reconciled themselves to long-term work within the party. The National Education League had actually disbanded after 1874 to channel its energies through the NLF and into school board elections, thereby becoming an integral part of Liberal electoral machinery. Similarly the Liberation Society dropped its coercive tactics after 1874 in the hope that loyalty would bring its reward, which it did in the shape of a Welsh Disestablishment Bill in 1894. The more closely these groups associated themselves with the Liberals the more their opponents backed the Conservatives; then the faddists could plausibly argue that Liberal candidates could not poll the full potential radical vote unless they aroused the enthusiasm of their own adherents. On balance, the changing relationship between the party and the pressure groups between the 1860s and 1890s was to the advantage of the former. After the franchise extensions and introduction of the secret ballot it was much more difficult for the proponents of any cause to claim credibly that the abstention of their supporters had brought about the defeat of a candidate. By the 1890s, therefore, 'faddism' was for the most part neatly marshalled in the annual programmes of the National Liberal Federation.

One major element of weakness hampered the post-1886 Liberal party: the absence of an effective radical leader in the front rank of parliamentarians who could succeed Gladstone whose age and intellectual rigidity increasingly limited his usefulness. It was indeed an irony that Chamberlain should have left the party at the very moment when it became the embodiment of programmatic radicalism. Initially he expected his severance from the party to be temporary, which is why the Liberal Unionists tried to avoid voting with the Conservatives in the Commons; this was intended to facilitate their return to Liberalism when Gladstone retired. In fact he stayed on, and the overtures for reunion in 1887 were easily rebuffed by those like Morley who disliked Chamberlain's brand of politics. While the Grand Old Man remained leader until 1894 Chamberlain gradually learnt to work with Salisbury whose government he joined in 1895. Gladstone and Morley were content to await the gradual return of the lesser figures embarrassed by association with Salisbury. The drift would have been faster but for Chamberlain's ability to secure certain reforms during 1887–92, particularly those for land and education.

Some writers still regard Home Rule simply as the 'most potent divisive force' in Liberalism after 1886;[9] this is a natural conclusion to be drawn from the correspondence of a few leading politicians who disagreed on the details of Home Rule as on the details of every policy. However, this is scarcely applicable to the party as a whole which, as we have seen, rallied round the principle of Home Rule. By 1888 the Conservative coercion policy in Ireland had given Gladstone a useful angle on the Irish Question because it allowed him to avoid discussing details and concentrate his fire on a simple moral issue. Resistance to government oppression dramatized the Irish Question for English audiences; 'Justice to Ireland does not arouse enthusiasm', observed the cynical Labouchere, 'unless it be wrapped up in what they regard as justice to themselves.'[10] English working men were therefore urged to see the threat to their own rights of combination and organization inherent in the suppression of similar bodies in Ireland.

In time, however, Home Rule assumed a less prominent role in Liberal politics. The destruction of Parnell's career in 1891 as a result of a divorce scandal sapped the will of many British Home Rulers; and the inevitable rejection of the second Home Rule Bill by the peers in 1893, followed by Gladstone's retirement in 1894, turned the issue into a cul-de-sac for ambitious Liberals instead of the highway to office that it had been for Morley in the 1880s. Since the party had to have a post-Home Rule policy, programme politics enjoyed a heyday encouraged by Harcourt and the faddists. The culmination of this process occurred at the NLF's Newcastle conference in 1891 which endorsed the full range of reforms: taxation of land values, ground rents and royalties, death duties, free elementary education, Welsh and Scottish disestablishment, a 'direct popular veto' on the liquor traffic, parish councils, home-rule-all-round, the 'free breakfast table', and reform of the franchise and the House of Lords.

This had been the staple radical diet for some years. What made the 'Newcastle Programme' significant was its apparent endorsement by Gladstone only a year before his victory in an election fought on its provisions. In fact Gladstone paid only cursory attention to the items on the list at Newcastle, ignoring those he disliked and concentrating on Ireland. Regardless of his real attitude, the programme's importance became evident when his Home Rule Bill suffered rejection at the hands of the peers. Their action posed a dilemma for the Cabinet. If Home Rule was so vital then they must resign and ask the country to overrule the House of Lords. But Gladstone's colleagues declined to take this course. In 1892 they had compelled him to embody much of the party programme in the Queen's Speech, and it seemed to them that after six years out of office they must press ahead with the reforms on which they had recently won election. The ministers, in short, now thought along the same lines as the NLF. Hence 1894 brought Harcourt's famous 'Death Duties' budget and the establishment of parish and district councils, as well as unsuccessful attempts at legislation for employers' liability and Welsh disestablishment.

It would, therefore, be beside the point to say that the Cabinet never allowed the NLF to dictate its policy, for the two had moved so close together that as a rule aggressive tactics were not necessary. The 1892–5 Liberal government represented an important stage in the party's evolution in so far as it showed the absorption of programmatic radicalism both in principle and in detail. Where the rank and file chose to adopt aggressive tactics, as on Welsh disestablishment, it was not because of disagreements on the merits of the issue but because the leaders felt that the peers' hostility made it a futile cause; they nonetheless went ahead with a bill. Undoubtedly the party still had major unresolved problems, notably a solution to the House of Lords question, the emergence of independent working-class politics, and the resurgence of imperial sentiment. Yet it had substantially resolved the problems of the 1860s; and in the process it had abandoned the passive, parliamentary form of politics and shaken free from the upper-class control that had inhibited both its role as assailant of privilege and its evolution as a modern political party.

Gladstone's role in all this is ambiguous. As we have seen, his brand of Liberalism was a viable, not an anachronistic, one, especially in the 1860s and 1870s. However, it is also clear that by the 1890s many of the changes in the party had come about in spite of Gladstone not because of him. Moreover, the conditions of politics were now changing in several ways. First, Home Rule inevitably waned as it became clear that the electors would not give the Liberals a mandate on this question alone. Second, by the mid-1880s religious issues had reached their peak. Many of the Nonconformists' grievances had now been settled. Although the bulk of Liberal candidates were now committed to disestablishment, the force behind the issue was fading; this is clear from the loss of members and funds by the Liberation Society in the late 1880s and 1890s, especially in England. Third, it emerged that the Gladstonian formula based on retrenchment and low taxation was not viable in the long run. Far from being abolished, income tax rose under Liberal governments. In fact Chamberlain's emphasis on land taxation and a graduated income tax offered a more realistic way forward. But Gladstone proved reluctant to recognize this, as his resignation over higher government spending in 1894 underlines. Liberalism's new agenda was beginning to be born.

3

The Conservative Revival
1874–1900

> It is significant that ... the reformed constituency of
> Westminster should have preferred the unknown Con-
> servative who sold books [W. H. Smith] to the famous
> Liberal – JOHN STUART MILL – who wrote them.
>
> *The Times*, 7 October 1891

At the death of Disraeli in 1881 the Conservative Party stood in some
apprehension about its future. Since the repeal of the Corn Laws in 1846
it had not won a majority at a general election except for 1874, and,
in view of the drastic reforms made and anticipated, no one could
feel confident that the pattern had been decisively broken. Before 1846
the Conservatives had established themselves as a national party representing agriculture while also promoting the economic innovation
desired by urban, industrial England. But for the defection of the
Peelites in 1846 they might have gone on to perform the role subsequently filled by Victorian Liberalism. Instead they lingered for 30
years a sectional rump, suspect in the eyes of the electorate for their
inexperience of office, the prominence of the distrusted Disraeli, and
the protectionist tendencies of the country gentlemen. As late as 1874
Queen Victoria noted with evident relief that Disraeli's new ministers
included only one duke and were 'not at all retrograde'!

Yet the Conservative reputation for wildness and instability was
somewhat exaggerated. Their dilemma really lay in the absence of any
distinctive policy with which to win the electorate. There was little that
a mid-Victorian Conservative government might do with respect to
Empire, economy, property or monarchy that one under Lord Palmerston could not do better.[1] Not until the forces of popular radicalism
gained the ascendancy in the Liberal Party, and Palmerston's chau-
vinistic conservatism gave way to Gladstone's moralistic reformism,

did the Conservatives begin to appear a better vehicle for the aspirations of 'respectable' England once again. Disraeli was lucky, if rather late in life, in the events of the 1860s; but he knew how to exploit his opportunities. He saw how to divide and rule the House of Commons in 1866–7 by taking up franchise reform; and how to appropriate Palmerston's mantle by seizing upon the radical 'conspiracy' to dismember the Empire, and by pursuing the Crimean War policy in 1875–8.

Yet Disraeli's contribution to the Conservatives' restoration as a governing party and as a majority in the country has been much exaggerated. When Derby and Disraeli expanded the electorate by enfranchising many working-class householders and lodgers in 1867 they were not making a bold appeal for new Conservative voters. Had they wished to do that it would have been natural to extend the new franchises to the *counties* where the party was strongly entrenched; but this would almost certainly have provoked a Tory revolt and thus torpedoed the Bill. What Disraeli was really attempting in 1867 – largely by judicious manipulation of the constituency boundaries – was a limited experiment in making the existing Conservative support count for more. Nor is there much evidence that the newly enfranchised voters, outside Lancashire, gave the party additional support in 1868. Even the Conservatives' great victory in 1874 was won on the basis of a smaller share of the popular vote (1.09 million to 1.28 million) than the Liberals; clearly the maldistribution of seats gave Conservatives a major advantage. In the long run the most important aspect of the new electorate was its *indirect* effect in accelerating the radicalization occurring within Liberalism, thereby allowing the Conservatives under Lord Salisbury to inherit the naturally conservative forces in the country. In the long run the party grew less in a 'Disraelian' mould than a 'Peelite' one. Disraeli's own pilgrimage from impecunious notoriety to the peerage left intact his fondness for pre-industrial society united by the deference of the labourer and the duty of the landowner. He could not easily accommodate an urban middle class or an organized proletariat and like Gladstone he regretted the explosion of wealth in the hands of men who did not recognize it as a duty 'to endow the Church, to feed the poor, to guard the land, and to execute justice for nothing'. For him government was best conducted by disinterested gentlemen through local communities not central bureaucracies. This reluctance to come to terms with industrialization restricted the scope for an active policy for the working classes because this implied bureaucracy and taxation; instead Conservatism returned to an accommodation with middle-class industrial wealth. The return of the latter-day Peelites, though not at all what Disraeli envisaged, nevertheless gave the party its increasing strength and much of its organization and policy in the late nineteenth century.

The Impact of Middle-class Conservatism

In 1865 the Conservatives' strength lay in England where 221 of their 294 MPs held seats, particularly in counties and small boroughs. Their representation even in counties was threatened by urban expansion. Yet their perilously narrow electoral base was to be modified in three ways. First, the Liberal hold on Scotland strengthened slightly, and on Wales greatly, while in Ireland the Home Rulers mopped up 80 per cent of the seats after 1874. In this way the Conservative position as the English party was considerably accentuated. Second, the Liberals extended their base in the counties following the 1884 franchise reforms. Thus, whereas in 1868 Conservatives had won 115 out of 154 English county seats, in 1885 they held only 105 out of 239; counties had become a key element in an overall Liberal majority.

Conservatives were saved only by their growing support in large boroughs and suburban seats, which reached a climax in 1900 when they took 177 English boroughs as against 162 English counties. There were indications of this trend in Lancashire after 1852 and in London after 1859; and in 1868, despite its overall defeat, the party gained 34 seats in boroughs whose population exceeded 20,000. Loss of formerly radical constituencies like Middlesex and Westminster was a warning to the Liberals that urbanization had created middle-class residential communities whose aspirations were not those of radical artisans.

However, the large towns remained under-represented in the Commons, and, since they returned two members from undivided constituencies, the improved Conservative poll frequently left the party a larger minority but still unrepresented. If Conservatives were to realize their strength, tactics required a drastic redistribution based upon equal constituencies and a single-member system. This is why one finds such radical notions being urged by Salisbury and Sir Michael Hicks-Beach in 1884–5; they seized their opportunity when Gladstone, hoping to close a somewhat barren term of office with a radical triumph, introduced a bill to extend the household suffrage to the counties. This the peers could plausibly reject unless a redistribution scheme were attached. In the ensuing compact between the party leaders the Conservative desire for equal single-member seats coincided with the objectives of the Chamberlainites who hoped to eliminate Whigs in small boroughs. Thus, boroughs with a population under 15,000 lost their separate representation, while those with under 50,000 lost one of their two members. This drastically reduced the representation of the south-west to the advantage of London and Lancashire, both of which proved to be Conservative for 20 years. All counties and all but 23 boroughs were

TABLE 3.1   *Conservative MPs in London*

Pre-1867 (total 18)		Post-1867 (total 22)		Post-1885 (total 59)	
1859	0	1868	3	1885	35
1865	0	1874	10	1886	47
		1880	8	1892	36
				1895	51
				1900	51

divided into single-member seats along boundaries that were designed to reflect 'the pursuits of the people'. This scheme helped the Conservatives, first, by increasing the scope for plural voting in the divided constituencies at a time when the propertied classes were coming adrift from Liberalism. Second, the Conservatives believed that by keeping agricultural areas separate from mining or urban areas they could maintain the territorial influence of the landowners. Third, in conurbations the same principle involved creating separate working-class, commercial, and residential middle-class seats. This would at least save the Conservative minority from being swamped. Liberals like Leonard Courtney and Sir John Lubbock argued in vain that minority representation would best be secured by a proportional system. At the time few politicians perceived that in a mature industrial society characterized by residential separation the effect of trying to preserve homogeneous communities would be to facilitate class-based voting. The consequences were obvious in formerly radical cities like Leeds where Conservatives subsequently won two of the five seats, and Sheffield where they took three of five. London, however, provided quite the most striking example of Conservative gains (see table 3.1). Redistribution could not, of course, have had this effect without shifts of allegiance, but it facilitated the translation of urban votes into new members. Indeed his work in 1884–5 alone entitles Salisbury to be considered a major architect of his party's revival; in combination with the Home Rule crisis of 1886 the redistribution of 1885 made these years the decisive turning-point for Conservatism.

The broader base of Conservatism gradually modified the party's social composition in Parliament; an analysis of the MPs according to the date of their election to the Commons brings out the extent and timing of the change (see table 3.2). Only among MPs elected in 1885–6 who had previously sat in Parliament was the landed element the predominant one; in each new set of recruits after 1885 a substantial

TABLE 3.2   *Social origins of Conservative MPs*

| Parliamentary group | | Landed classes | % from | | Other |
			Industry and commerce	Professional and public service	
1885–6	Old	54.8	28.7	15.2	1.4
1885	New	34.1	34.2	26.5	5.1
1886	New	36.7	27.5	29.2	6.7
1892	New	41.9	32.0	19.6	6.0
1895	New	36.0	28.0	24.9	10.9
1900	New	28.7	42.5	18.1	10.6

Source: J. P. Cornford, 'Parliamentary Origins of the Hotel Cecil', in R. Robson (ed.),
    Ideas and Institutions of Victorian Britain (1967), p. 310.

TABLE 3.3   *Social origins of Conservative MPs 1885–1900 (%)*

	1885	1886	1892	1895	1900
Landed classes	45.8	43.3	46.2	41.2	38.5
Industry and commerce	31.1	29.5	28.1	28.3	32.0
Professional and public service	19.9	23.2	20.7	23.2	21.3
Others	2.9	4.0	4.7	7.3	8.6

Source: J. P. Cornford, 'Parliamentary Origins of the Hotel Cecil', in R. Robson (ed.),
    Ideas and Institutions of Victorian Britain (1967), p. 310.

majority were drawn from the industrial and professional middle classes, a reflection of the fact that suburban seats, which were likely to adopt bourgeois candidates, had become safer for Conservatives than many counties.

On the other hand an examination of the entire parliamentary party after each election brings out the continuity (see table 3.3). Clearly the composition of the party changed rather gradually. For whereas the sons of the upper classes normally entered the Commons before the age of 30, the businessman had first to establish his financial independence by building up his company, so that a seat in Parliament crowned his career in his fifties. Professional men, especially barristers, could enter earlier, but were apt to treat politics as an aid to their legal careers rather than as the prime objective. Both groups were more likely to take on marginal or hopeless constituencies, and to die or retire after short periods as MPs. The squires elected before 1885 enjoyed particularly long terms as MPs, but began to drop out in substantial numbers only after 1900.

Consequently the ultimate reward of cabinet office, being the due of men who had established their reputation in the House, fell disproportionately to the landed gentlemen. A businessman could be caught between the need to attend his business and to devote time to a minor role as parliamentary private secretary or junior whip, which was a necessary step on the ladder of office. It is not surprising that both Disraeli and Salisbury drew criticism for neglecting the claims of middle-class supporters, though the latter quickly learnt to make lavish use of honours to compensate for shortage of jobs. Despite the competition a number of bourgeois recruits obtained major office under Disraeli and Salisbury as a result of the dearth of administrative talent and debating skills to combat the Liberal heavy artillery. The 1874 ministry saw Richard Cross as Home Secretary, Gathorne-Hardy at the War Office, Sclater-Booth at the Local Government Board, and W. H. Smith whose elevation to the Admiralty in 1877 caused a flutter at the palace and W. S. Gilbert's satirical creation 'Sir Joseph Porter' in *HMS Pinafore*. Salisbury appointed C. T. Richie to three ministries, George Goschen to the Exchequer, and relied heavily on Smith as Leader of the Commons from 1886 until his death in 1891. Smith and Cross, derided by Lord Randolph Churchill as 'Marshall and Snelgrove', reached the top through personal ability rather than as representatives of urban middle-class Toryism, though business expertise was, perhaps, a factor in Goschen's appointment as Chancellor in 1887. Yet it took more than a few pioneers to kill Lord Randolph's snobbery or the ingrained condescension of the traditional leaders. Witness Arthur Balfour's advice to Salisbury on the choice of a new Postmaster-General in 1891 in which he commended W. L. Jackson (MP for Leeds North) who,

> has great tact and judgement – middle class tact and judgement I admit, but good of their kind . . . he is that *rara avis*, a successful manufacturer who is fit for something besides manufacturing. A cabinet of Jacksons would [be] rather a serious order, no doubt: but one or even two would be a considerable addition to any cabinet.[2]

What is clear is that middle-class ministers were chosen, apart from the special cases like Chamberlain, on the strength of administrative competence and forensic talent. The epitome of urban Conservatism and the National Union, Sir John Gorst, conspicuously failed to make the Cabinet; however, Gorst, who largely ruled himself out by rebelliousness over labour questions, was never dangerous enough to command a place at the top. Indeed the only politician who can in any sense be said to have used the National Union to advance himself to the Cabinet, Churchill, was an aristocrat without a real following.

Organizing the Democracy

As the Conservative leaders contemplated the growth of urban political organization on the Liberal side they realized that they would have to match it eventually; yet it was Salisbury rather than Disraeli, who actually came to terms with this distasteful necessity.

Since the 1830s the party had made do with a rudimentary organizational structure emanating from the Carlton Club whence amateur officials attempted to stimulate registration work in the constituencies. However, continued electoral failure and the establishment of the Liberal Registration Association in 1861 were so worrying that by 1867 Disraeli was ready to respond to John Gorst's passionate demand that the party should deliberately consolidate its traditional links with the people. One expression of these links already existed in working men's Conservative clubs, and the first modest gathering of these – the National Union of Conservative and Constitutional Associations (NUCCA) – in 1867 received Disraeli's blessing. Whether through dismay at the election defeat of 1868 or through being apprehensive of the popular body, he also created in 1870 a separate Conservative Central Office which was designed to stimulate new associations, maintain contact with them and compile lists of candidates. Since these functions duplicated those of the NUCCA the dual system inevitably produced friction. Initially, however, both bodies made progress in the declining years of Gladstone's administration; and by 1872 Central Office and the National Union were closely linked through a common headquarters and Gorst's position as both principal agent and honorary secretary of the National Union.

The objects of the National Union were modestly conceived. As Gorst had reminded the approving delegates in 1867, it was 'not a meeting for the discussion of Conservative principles on which we are all agreed, it is only a meeting to consider by what particular organization we may make these Conservative principles effective among the masses'.[3] Initially the task of extending Conservative associations through the country proved congenial; and by 1877 some 791 bodies had affiliated, though many of these were clubs and registration societies not constituency associations. The victory of 1874, when 65 of the 74 Conservative gains in England and Wales occurred under the auspices of active Conservative associations, encouraged the National Union to ignore the indifference and hostility exhibited by much of the party which preferred to rely upon traditional *ad hoc* committees of solicitors and gentlemen to organize elections. Particularly in the rural areas local dignitaries disliked anything that smacked of the caucus. They were also deeply suspicious of the voluminous body of literature eulogizing Disraelian reforms generated by the National Union in the 1870s; the Conservative case, they believed, should never be based upon programmes of exceptional legislation for the working class.

Gladstone's surprise victory in 1880 emboldened the National Union delegates to offer the party advice on the shortcomings of its attitude towards organization. They demanded more attention to speeches in the country by parliamentary leaders, and greater expenditure on new Conservative clubs which considerably facilitated registration work; and they condemned the habit of leaving organization in the hands of amateur 'gentlemen who practically knew nothing of election matters and undertook the management merely as a professional duty in their capacity of lawyers'.[4] In addition they pointed out that the 1883 Act on expenses and illegal practices would curtail the practice of paying for canvassing and conveyancing to the poll, and leave the party greatly handicapped against the radicals.[5] The expectation of an extended county franchise at this time was one of the considerations that impelled Lord Randolph Churchill to champion the party organization.

He was not the only one who was alive to the dangers posed by the rapidly changing rules of the electoral battle. Gorst, aware that the associations often existed only on paper and lapsed between elections, tried to encourage them to contest the municipal elections regularly and to find extra money for the building of clubs. But although the National Union took pains to dissociate itself from the National Liberal Federation and to abjure pronouncements on policy its conferences eventually became the scene of lively debates, and not simply on organization. After 1885 the rank and file showed enthusiasm for various issues that the parliamentary leaders studiously avoided – alien immigration, women's suffrage, state subsidies for house purchase, and an imperial tariff policy; indeed the successful battle for protectionism waged in annual conferences during the 1880s and 1890s prepared the way for the Chamberlainite takeover after 1903.

Despite these undercurrents the National Union never directly confronted the leadership except in the early 1880s and then not over policy but over organization and the role of urban middle-class

Conservatism. By 1880 Gorst, frustrated by Disraeli's neglect of the machine and by personal chagrin at not being offered a major post, sought a leader for his cause. Through his membership of the 'Fourth Party' (a self-appointed group of four MPs who tormented the Gladstone government), he found one in Churchill; it is significant that it took someone of Churchill's rank to spearhead the campaign. After securing election to the Council of the National Union in 1882 he proceeded to attack the practice of co-opting on to the Council 12 members nominated by Central Office which had little interest in improving organization in the country. He railed against the Central Committee, which Disraeli had established and was dependent on the leader for funds and personnel, for effectively reducing the National Union to an impotent, advisory role. Churchill demanded that control of organization and funds be removed from the irresponsible body to the elected Council. Culminating in a meeting with Salisbury in 1884, Churchill's campaign produced a face-saving compromise. The Central Committee was abolished, the Council freed of co-opted members and a little more money was granted to the national Union. None of these details, however, materially improved the power or status of the National Union.

Beneath the rhetoric Lord Randolph Churchill had never shared Gorst's objectives, and certainly not his hostility towards the traditional leaders of the party from whose ranks he came.[6] In 1882 he declined an invitation to contest Manchester, preferring to remain safely in the family borough of Woodstock until its abolition in 1885. He made a single foray on behalf of urban Conservatism by fighting a Birmingham seat against John Bright, but thereafter reverted to a safe seat at Paddington. Churchill had no intention of putting his career at risk for the cause of middle-class Conservatism, which is why, once he felt he had done enough to win a place in the next government, he dropped the National Union. It would be flattering both Churchill and the National Union to suppose that he endeavoured to use it as a power base from which to secure the party leadership – was too young, too inexperienced in office and too lacking in support in Parliament. Salisbury pandered to Churchill's pretensions because he appreciated that his campaign was not directed against himself but against Northcote, and because he recognized that Churchill's platform oratory was an asset to the party. There was consequently no objection to elevating him to cabinet rank in 1885 provided that nothing of substance had to be conceded to the National Union. Churchill was safe because he was no Chamberlain.

Thus, after 1884 the National Union settled down to its functions of branch-building, propaganda and speech-making; and from 1885 all Conservative associations were automatically affiliated to it. A signal

indication of the leadership's control over the organization was Salisbury's ability to ensure the withdrawal of Conservative candidates in
all but a handful of the 93 seats held by Liberal Unionist MPs in 1886.
Local constituency interest was simply overruled by parliamentary
strategy. The party in the country was tended by 'Captain' R. W. E.
Middleton, the principal agent from 1885 and honorary secretary of the
National Union from 1886, who co-ordinated his work smoothly with
Salisbury and the chief whip. Where Gorst had been prickly and
ambitious Middleton was loyal, tactful and ready to accept the subser-
vient role of the organization. This was congenial to Salisbury who
enjoyed consulting him both over election statistics, of which he became
a keen student, and over the awarding of honours in the party, which he
was determined not to neglect. Much of Middleton's work consisted in
creating a network of professional agents that covered half the constituencies by 1900 with an intermediate layer of officials in each region.
They provided headquarters with electoral intelligence, and the public's
reaction to legislation, particularly Liberal legislation that might be
safely rejected by the Lords if it was not really popular. In retrospect the
electoral successes of the Middleton era seemed to prove the advantages
of a professional corps of organizers over the larger but more troublesome structure of associations represented by the National Union.

Tradition and Change

In the past much of the writing about Conservative history has approached the subject by considering how liberal or progressive the party
was; hence the prominence traditionally accorded to men like Peel and
Disraeli who are seen as great reformers who helped to modernize the
Tory Party. Yet concentration on such exceptional figures may well
produce a distorted idea of Conservative history. The 'reactionary' Lord
Salisbury for example, enjoyed a more successful career than Disraeli,
and, as we have already seen, was rather more alive to the needs of a
modern electoral system. Salisbury serves to remind us that historically
the purpose of most Conservatives involved resisting change and
limiting it when it proved to be unavoidable. On the face of it, Disraeli's
impressive record of social reform after 1874 appears to contradict this
view. But its significance seems to be very limited. Not only did Disraeli
himself display little interest in the subject, he had opposed social
reforms in the past – 'those Gallic imitations' – through a dislike of
central bureaucracy. Most of his reforms emerged from civil service
attempts to extend or improve legislation passed by previous Liberal
governments.

A more consistent interest of Disraeli's, both in and out of office, was to cut national taxation, relieve the burden of local rates and generally to restrict government. For example, the Artisans Dwellings Act was simply permissive legislation allowing the demolition of slums but not requiring replacements; in practice those few local authorities that did wish to build homes for the working class found themselves prevented because Conservative governments refused to allow them to raise the necessary loans.

This negative approach to taxation and social policy was arguably more popular than the interventionist one; and it was certainly more typical of late Victorian Conservatism. From the 1870s onwards the party relied little on novel policies and instead resorted increasingly to *traditional* causes. Essentially this involved defending the Church establishment, religious education, private property, the Empire, the monarchy, and the union with Ireland against the depredations of radicalism. The surprise in all this was not that Conservatives adopted such a strategy but that it seemed to be successful even under a larger electorate. Thus, late Victorian Conservatism presents an interesting paradox. On the one hand there is a strong impression from the improved electoral fortunes that the party adapted more successfully than its opponents to the conditions of a mass electorate. On the other hand this seems inconsistent with the leaders' patent distaste for popular organization, and their determination to keep the National Union strictly within bounds; indeed, although constituency associations became the norm after 1885, the organizations were often a mere formality, as small and remote as ever. The need to match the radicals in practical political skills was only partly met by the Conservatives' superior finances and the creation of full-time constituency agents. For they could by no means dispense with the efforts of a large corps of volunteer workers. In this respect the deficiencies of the formal party structure in the National Union and the constituency bodies were more than compensated for by the Primrose League, a key political institution in this period which has been remarkably neglected by the historians of the Conservative Party.

Founded in November 1883, the 'Primrose Tory League', as it was originally known, claimed to promote 'Tory principles – viz the maintenance of religion, of the estates of the realm, and of the Imperial Ascendancy of Great Britain'; by adopting both the primrose – supposedly Disraeli's favourite flower – and such slogans as 'True Union of the Classes', its leaders sought to emphasize the Disraelian source of their inspiration. The League offered one class of membership at a guinea a year for 'Knights' and 'Dames', and another for associate members whose much lower dues went to their local branches; these branches were actually known as 'Habitations', the honorary president as the 'Grand Master', the ruling body as the 'Grand Council', the executive head as the 'Chancellor', official notices as 'Precepts', and subscriptions as 'Tribute'. All this delightfully anachronistic escapism made the Primrose League as appealing as a Masonic lodge or a collegiate university, and it reminds us that the members created a political role that was as enjoyable as it was useful. By 1886 membership had reached 237,000, by 1891 it exceeded 1 million, and by 1910, 2 million. These figures are exaggerated because the League invariably added new members to the total while making no deductions for losses. However, the pattern of its growth broadly reflected Conservative fortunes. Membership more than doubled in 1886–7 under the stimulus of the Home Rule crisis, slackened in the early 1890s as Salisbury's government ran out of steam, quickened dramatically before and during the Boer War, and stagnated thereafter until 1910. By that year some 2,645 Habitations existed in the British Isles. Far from being a purely rural phenomenon the League entrenched itself in industrial Britain too, and claimed that nine-tenths of the members were working class.

Why was the Primrose League such an asset to the Conservative Party? Fundamentally because it provided a practical application of class and rank as a unifying force in society. Part of the difficulty with a body like the National Union was that Conservatives had felt uncomfortable with an organization designed for working men or the urban middle class. 'I have never been myself at all favourable', Disraeli once said, 'to a system which would induce Conservatives who are working men to form societies confined merely to their class.'[7] Whereas the National Union suffered embarrassment at the lack of participation by working men, the League adopted a frankly hierarchical structure that not only mirrored the gradations of society but dramatized them; by accepting class as a virtue not as a matter for apology the League comfortably embraced the Conservative view of social unity.

In the same way the League enjoyed an advantage over the National Union in that though it was a popular body it never appeared a threat to the leadership. Its relationship with the party remained spiritually close but organizationally loose. By confining its politics to fairly general principles like the Empire which would endure beyond the passing excitements of legislation, the League avoided either taking sides on divisive issues or presenting programmes to the parliamentary leaders. This is why Salisbury and Balfour were quite content to accept roles as 'Grand Master' and to present annual addresses. This arrangement gave them a friendly alliance with a large body of like-minded people who, by remaining separate, could not make unreasonable demands upon them.

As an electoral machine the League served the party in several crucial ways. It deluged the constituencies with its own and Central Office propaganda. The Warden of a Habitation was frequently entrusted with responsibility for preparing annually lists of voters and canvassing those on the register; its dense network of local contacts especially in rural areas enabled the League to mobilize the Conservative vote efficiently at elections. However, it was the League's regular round of activities *between* rather than during elections that gave Conservatives the edge over their Liberal rivals, whose activity and vote was apt to fluctuate much more according to the ebb and flow of national political issues. By avoiding a formal 'Conservative' title the League also made it easier for non-Conservatives to participate in their events. Indeed they offered a great deal more than mere politics: Habitations readily accepted the warning that meetings should not be 'so distinctly elevating as to be pronounced dull'. They offered cheap dances, their own brass bands, and evening entertainments involving singing, conjurors, ventriloquists, jugglers, waxworks, marionettes and pierrots. Such programmes, available in each locality, formed an irresistible attraction especially in country areas where they might be the only form of regular social event. In this way the League often integrated itself into the fabric of a community more effectively than political parties could do. Frivolous League activities provoked much hilarity and contempt from Liberals and socialists, who were not convinced that politics was meant to be enjoyable. However, they saw that the teas, fetes and visits to country houses served a real function by providing a coveted opportunity for the lower ranks to mingle briefly with the great. Nor was the mixture purely social, for a fete or evening entertainment usually included its political address. A political message was delivered less directly though doubtless more effectively by techniques that were a novelty in themselves such as magic lanterns and *tableaux vivants* which displayed a series of images of imperial splendour such as the Queen enthroned as Empress of India, Gordon at Khartoum, Nelson on the *Victory*, Lords Roberts or Kitchener in Afghanistan or South Africa. This blend of patriotic history with recent controversial incidents was more shrewdly aimed than many more cerebral pieces of propaganda.

Another merit of the Primrose League lay in its capacity for involving women in the political process. From 1883 women had been admitted as members, and sometimes formed their own Habitations. Middle- and upper-class ladies threw themselves enthusiastically into arranging League functions, canvassing, contacting the outvoters, conveying electors to the polls in private carriages, raising funds and generally keeping the grass roots of Conservatism vigorous. By the 1890s the sight of the Primrose Dame speeding through villages on her 'safety' bicycle or descending *en masse*, as the 'Primrose Cycling Corps' at by-elections became a painfully familiar sight to radicals. Here again, it suited the men of the party that women should involve themselves so constructively but without pressing for power or for their enfranchisement. Nonetheless both Salisbury and Balfour followed Disraeli's example in indicating personal sympathy for votes for wealthy women. This early association between women activists and the Conservative Party doubtless laid the foundations for the party's organizational superiority in the twentieth century. More immediately the Primrose League generated the voluntary labour so necessary under the reformed electoral system of the 1880s and challenged the radicals' political skills effectively. By extending the Conservative influence beyond small groups of partisans the League succeeded where politicians invariably failed in keeping the cause healthy between elections, which goes some way to explaining the stability of the Conservative vote between the 1880s and 1914 by comparison with the more volatile Liberal performance.

Salisbury and Liberal Unionism

The third Marquis of Salisbury who led no less than four governments between 1885 and 1902 from the lonely eminence of Hatfield and the House of Lords, was a most unlikely leader in a democratic age of which he thoroughly disapproved. This period of dominance has long been neglected by historians; even by Conservatives his accomplishments have been ignored in favour of the more superficially attractive figure of Disraeli. This is not altogether surprising: Disraeli does have a contemporary appeal where Salisbury seems inflexibly old-fashioned; Disraeli's name is easily linked with a creed and with a watershed in history whereas Salisbury seems to have left no permanent tradition; most of all, Salisbury basically despised his party, accepting it merely as the best available vehicle for his objectives; with his austerely intellectual approach he detested any pandering to the sentimental nostrums of Conservatism.

His opportunity to become leader arose after Disraeli's death in 1881 which inaugurated an unhappy experience in dual leadership by Sir Stafford Northcote in the Commons and Salisbury in the Lords. The outcome of this period – Salisbury's premiership in 1885 – was not expected in 1881. For Salisbury's record suggested the dangerously ideological backwoodsman; Northcote was safer, and was for some time the Queen's first choice. This failed to materialize because as Leader of the Opposition Northcote, by his conciliatory and lacklustre performance, threw away his main advantage over Salisbury, that he could directly confront Gladstone in the Commons. This was repeatedly emphasized by the lively attacks made by the 'Fourth Party' comprising Churchill, Gorst, Arthur Balfour and Sir Henry Drummond Wolff. It is now clear that one object of Churchill's activity in the Fourth Party as in the National Union was to facilitate Salisbury's attainment of the leadership in place of Northcote.[8] For his part Salisbury appreciated that Churchill's popular oratory obscured his traditional Conservatism, and welcomed a compromise that weakened Northcote's supporters in the National Union. The effect of the protracted controversy was to focus attention upon Salisbury as the one who could handle the popular body, and to edge Northcote off stage as an irrelevancy.

However, if the rumpus served to elevate Salisbury, it also drew attention to his political rigidity. Unlike most politicians he thought seriously about the long-term development of society. A quintessential conservative, Salisbury believed that the defects in man's condition were to a large extent congenital and consequently not susceptible to new ways of ordering society. Since what could be achieved through politics was quite limited it was desirable to restrain the state from trenching too far upon the private sphere as most reforms threatened to do. In government one should concentrate on administration rather than mere 'politics'. Like several other late Victorians with experience of India (Secretary of State 1874-8), Salisbury absorbed a firm belief in the superiority of strong, just, arbitrary government by a highly qualified elite, as opposed to systems in which authority hinged upon representation and efficiency was hampered by political parties and assemblies.

Herein lay the menace of contemporary British society. In 1867 Salisbury had resigned from the Conservative government in disgust at franchise reform, and spent much of his nervous energy composing withering attacks upon Disraeli for his unprincipled opportunism and betrayal of Conservative principles – much as Disraeli had once berated Peel. The slide towards a democratic franchise seemed to him destructive of a stable and unified society. For once the Commons had, in the name of the people, aggrandized all power at the expense of the other elements in the mixed constitution (the monarchy and aristocracy), government would fall into the hands of men without property and lose its impartiality. Britain could easily slide into an American type of corruption in which politicians gained office by offering specific rewards to distinct groups or classes, thereby helping their society towards eventual disintegration.

Although these sentiments were never far from the surface they reflect the younger Salisbury, a man who had not yet acquired the mellow confidence that political success and a happy marriage gradually gave him. In practical terms, much as he preferred the 1832 system, he accepted that he could never hope to reverse the drift away from it.

Salisbury's apprehensions had materially abated by the time he became Prime Minister. He grew to appreciate Disraeli's desire to make Conservatism the British national party rather than the organ of a sectional interest. He realized, too, that the defence of 'liberty' could be accomplished within the framework of democracy; even the United States took on a more attractive appearance, for its federalism, its Senate and its judiciary imposed admirable curbs on the power of central government. The problem was how to extend the role of local against central government in Britain without simply handing over power to the radicals as had happened with the school boards. The best substitute for an American arrangement of checks and balances lay in reliance on the House of Lords and the Conservative Party.

Therefore Salisbury set himself to master some of the arts of party leadership, gratefully relying on his chief whip and principal agent. Yet he resented the obligation to immerse himself in the trivia of political life: 'Why should I spend my evenings being trampled upon by the Conservative Party?' He retreated to Hatfield as often as possible and kept social contact to a minimum. Fortunately his chief whip, Aretas Akers-Douglas, a congenial country gentleman from Kent, helped to save him from the consequences of his own aloofness, and managed efficiently an increasingly loyal parliamentary party. Though Salisbury could never attain popularity, his followers were in a sense grateful, for, as one historian has put it: 'A nobleman from a Tory family with illustrious forbears, Salisbury came from the class among which Conservatives wanted but rarely managed to find a leader.'[9]

His practical strategy was determined by the knowledge that his party had won a general election only in 1874 followed by what appeared to be traditional Liberal victories in 1880 and 1885. This, he believed, was simply because the party alignment still reflected the divisions of 1832 and 1846 – now irrelevant. Since the Liberal reforms had been absorbed into the system the Whigs ought logically to join the Conservatives in defending the *status quo*. Eventually Salisbury's major achievement was to facilitate the post-1886 realignment without forfeiting his own control. For him the detachment of the Whigs would ensure either a Conservative government, or, still better, a radical government with such a small majority that it lacked the authority to force through drastic changes; in such circumstances the House of Lords would step in as the guardian of the national will against sectional interests entrenched in the House of Commons.

The critical point in the unfolding of this strategy came after December 1885 when Gladstone's commitment to Irish Home Rule became public knowledge, and began to alienate a substantial section of Liberals under Lord Hartington's leadership. However, Salisbury had to

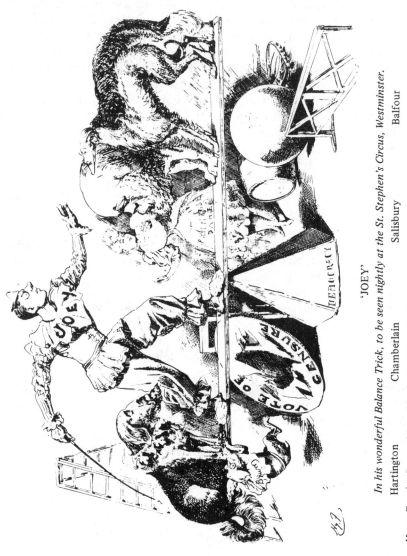

'JOEY'

In his wonderful Balance Trick, to be seen nightly at the St. Stephen's Circus, Westminster.

Hartington   Chamberlain   Salisbury   Balfour

Harry Furniss, Pen and Pencil in Parliament (1897).

move skilfully, for Hartington had ambitions of his own. He seemed acceptable to a sufficiently wide range of opinion in both Liberal and Conservative camps to form his own government, which would have been tantamount to a restoration of the Palmerstonian alliance in the centre. Since this made him a threat to both Salisbury and Gladstone they endeavoured to prevent any coalescence in the centre. Gladstone forced the issue by preparing a Home Rule Bill, speedily dissolving Parliament after its defeat and elevating Home Rule as the test of Liberalism. For his part Salisbury contributed a strident anti-Home Rule speech in May 1886 in which he derided the Irish as comparable with the Hottentots in their unfitness for self-rule, and advised them to emigrate to Manitoba to alleviate their hardship. This inflammatory speech was calculated to polarize the debate between himself and Gladstone so as to drive Hartington to one side or the other, thereby losing the centre ground.

What was to be the relationship between the 93 Liberal Unionists, of whom 78 survived the general election, and the Conservatives? It was no part of Salisbury's intention in 1886 to absorb them immediately. Cooperation in the constituencies had served its purpose by reducing the Gladstonians to 191 while leaving 316 Conservatives. In view of the dangerous concatenation of Joseph Chamberlain and Lord Randolph Churchill he refused to bring the Liberal Unionists into his government; their joint energies harnessed to programmes of reform would certainly disrupt the Cabinet or take it out of his own hands. When in 1886 Churchill rashly offered his resignation as Chancellor of the Exchequer in protest at the Cabinet's refusal to accept economies, the Prime Minister made a tentative offer to Hartington because he felt confident it would be declined; thereupon the vacancy was filled by recruiting another ex-Liberal, Goschen, leaving the party relationship unchanged. Similarly the Liberal Unionists declined to throw in their lot fully with the Conservatives. Susceptible to their Liberal critics in the country who had rebelled solely over Home Rule in many cases, they seized every chance to distance themselves from the new government by refusing to vote for it except over Ireland or when it stood in danger of actual defeat, which was rare.

However, the Gladstonian revival prior to 1892 convinced Salisbury that it was unwise to take Liberal Unionism for granted. He therefore determined to incorporate them into his next government by offering four cabinet posts. His belief that Chamberlain would accept the limitations of a Conservative cabinet was vindicated when the ex-radical asked only for a committee of investigation on old age pensions, and, for himself, the Colonial Office. In the long run this led to new problems, but for the time being it served to draw the two together and harness

Chamberlain to a cause that was dear to the Conservative Party. Technically Salisbury, with 341 members in 1895, could have dispensed with a coalition. Yet he found some advantage in diluting his embarrassingly large majority with Liberal Unionist elements. For one thing he had discovered that the Nonconformists brought in by Chamberlain were not necessarily subversive radicals; and even radicals contributed to the checks and balances within the coalition. In practice major measures like the 1896 Education Bill succumbed entirely to Conservative attack; and the 1897 Bill for Workmen's Compensation only reached the statute book emasculated by the peers. While this process created friction on particular matters, Salisbury could at least rejoice that it served the higher purpose of setting limits on central government.

The State and Social Reform

Though Salisbury's approach to domestic affairs sprang from a cynical distrust of government, it was softened by fear of adopting an entirely negative policy and by a modicum of compassion towards the poor. Fortunately elections could be won without stooping to 'class legislation' at the expense of the propertied section, for, as Churchill's meteoric rise had demonstrated, the working classes would respond to quite traditional Tory appeals in defence of Church, Empire and monarchy. However, this strategy succeeded best only when the opposition co-operated by concentrating on such questions as Home Rule. When in office after 1886, Conservatives felt obliged to adopt a constructive attitude on domestic matters, if only to disprove the Gladstonian argument that all progress was blocked by the refusal to concede Ireland's demands. This accounts for the quantity of minor legislation, designed to be economical and undisturbing, enacted under Salisbury's premierships.

This policy should not be interpreted, as it sometimes is, as a resurrection of a Conservative tradition for strong paternalist government, unhampered by liberal individualism, which developed into a pragmatic collectivist ideology.[10] The origins of such a view lie in the historic Tory preference for strong government which had been characteristic of the revolutionary and Napoleonic war period and which did reassert itself in exceptional circumstances such as the First World War; but this is not to be confused with or causally linked with collectivism. Conservatives of the 1880s inherited the prevailing Victorian preference for curtailing government in favour of local autonomy and economy where this was seen to be effective. The basis of Salisbury's *laissez-faire* convictions was more political than economic; they sprang from his veneration of private property and hostility to interfering government rather than from the business liberalism that inspired many of his colleagues. Though he did not shrink from a little judicious state assistance for the poor, he believed that little could be accomplished by this means without causing financial and social damage; on the whole, therefore, he prescribed self-help as a general rule, but without the optimism that an early Victorian Liberal might have displayed. Conservatives also accepted the inevitability of free trade, though their candidates in agricultural constituencies still pandered to protectionism;[11] but as free traders they lacked the intense moral conviction with which many Liberals invested the issue. Salisbury, like many Conservatives, seems to have been undogmatic about free trade, accepting in principle by the 1890s the idea of retaliation against other countries.

There was, of course, a tradition of Tory radicalism from the early Victorian period when some politicians had attempted to defend the workers against the effects of a rampant capitalism; typically this took the form of support for limiting the working day to ten hours and opposing the new poor law. However, by the 1880s these traditions had begun to wither from neglect. Conservatives were increasingly to be found among those who defended the principles of 1834, while the critics of the poor law were radicals and Fabians who looked to the county councils and central government to shoulder its responsibilities. Similarly the demand for an eight-hour day often met a stony response in the 1880s from the middle-class employers who were now joining the Conservatives. In fact by 1892 the official party view condemned the eight-hour day for raising prices and lowering efficiency, as well as for interfering with the worker's freedom to determine his own conditions of work;[12] in short the party was preaching the arguments of classical economics more readily than their opponents. Nor was Disraeli's recognition of the right to picket in 1871 followed up by his successors who were more impressed by unions and militancy; indeed the Salisbury–Balfour era culminated with the Conservatives putting themselves at odds with labour by refusing to reverse the Taff Vale judgement of 1901 (see p. 123). The working man now seemed too assertive and powerful to fit the Disraelian conception.

By the 1880s the remnants of Disraelian Tories, Lord John Manners and Lord Cranbrook, were old and uninfluential. The real reformers were C. T. Ritchie (at the Local Government Board, the Board of Trade and the Home Office successively); A. J. Balfour, at least on education and Ireland; and Chamberlain from outside. Yet Chamberlain's influence proved less formative than that of men like George Goschen who, in becoming Chancellor in 1886, intended to help 'purge them of the cant of Tory Democracy', and irritated even Salisbury in his defence of the rights of property and hostility to social reform. Goschen's career demonstrates the crystallization of the naturally conservative forces around Salisbury and the abandonment of Disraelianism; he epitomized the middle-class recruits who had not quit Liberalism in order to pay higher taxes or suffer more legal regulation under the Conservatives.

Yet there was much more consistency in the negative approach than is often recognized. Ever since 1846 Disraeli had been keen to compensate landowners for the loss of protectionism; the favoured method involved relieving their tax burdens by grants-in-aid from the Exchequer to local authorities. Thus after 1874 Disraeli doubled grants to local authorities, transferred the costs of prisons to the Exchequer, and raised the limit for income tax liability from £100 to £150. This proved to be the real legacy of Disraeli. Between 1887 and 1892 the Conservatives doubled central support for local authorities from £4 million to £8 million and lowered the income tax rate to $6\frac{1}{2}d$ in the pound. Later in the 1890s they found an extra £1.5 million to relieve rates on agricultural land, several times reduced rates for voluntary schools, and even attempted to relieve Anglican parsons of rates. Two aspects of this policy are significant. First, it enabled the Conservatives to claim the Gladstonian ground as the party of retrenchment, which Liberal governments could no longer do with credibility. Harcourt's achievements in 1892–5, for example, were to raise income tax to $7\frac{3}{4}d$ and add some £9 million to taxation. Second, by the 1890s Tory finance had become a blatant exercise in providing doles for the party's wealthy landed supporters, which urban Conservatives resented as much as Liberals. Any Disraelian claim to represent all classes began to look implausible.

Land reform epitomized the Conservatives' dilemma, for radical propaganda among agricultural labourers threatened electoral disaster, while legislation for Scottish Crofters and Ireland provided precedents. Hence the passage of an Allotments Act in 1887 (extended in 1890), which empowered local authorities to purchase land for letting at economic rents, and the 1892 Smallholdings Act. Salisbury resisted these measures on the grounds that compulsory purchase was tantamount to confiscation, and that infringement of the rights of property owners would be economically counter-productive; yet his colleagues forced him to give way.[13] Some anticipated that the legislation would be relatively ineffective in view of the reluctance of landowner-dominated county councils, especially in the south, to make use of their powers.

Indeed the establishment of county councils in 1889 and the peers' amendments of the Liberals' Parish Councils Bill in 1893 proved an effective check on social reform. Though loath to disturb the existing management of county affairs through the Courts of Quarter Sessions by

JPs appointed by the Lords Lieutenant, Salisbury knew that reform was a radical priority from which the 1880-5 government had narrowly been deflected;[14] further radical attempts had to be forestalled. Many Conservatives resisted direct elections for county councils because they would be expensive and, by introducing a political element, would exclude the best men – an argument typical of Salisbury. However, Ritchie, backed by Chamberlain who saw this as a test of his influence with the Conservatives, managed to scotch the idea of indirect election. Yet the county franchise was restricted to occupiers, and a quarter of the membership of the councils was reserved for co-opted aldermen; in addition special restrictions on expenditure were imposed, and the poor law administration was withheld from them for fear that the radicals might gain control.

Fear of popular involvement also inspired educational reform in this period. Salisbury himself largely lacked sympathy with the idea of education for the masses which would deprive employers of child labour; but he failed to stop the extension of free elementary education in 1891 by Balfour and his ally Chamberlain for whom it was a long-standing objective. The problem lay in the school boards, always seen as subversive bodies, which had taken to widening the range of subjects taught and had established secondary schools in many places. Apart from the cost to ratepayers it was thought to be destructive of social harmony to educate people beyond their station in life. The 1896 Education Bill, which proposed to remove control to county councils, proved abortive due to opposition within the Cabinet. Thereafter other ways were found of undermining the school boards. In 1899 the Board of Education instigated a case against the London School Board for spending money from the rates on science and art schools; the resulting 'Cockerton Judgement' made higher grade education illegal. Balfour's famous Act of 1902 finally ended the school boards by placing responsibility for education with committees of the county councils.

In contrast, housing did engage Salisbury's interest to the extent that he personally initiated the 1885 Royal Commission on Housing. Nonetheless his government refused to allow any infringement of the urban landlords' and landowners' rights over their property; they resisted any state involvement in house-building, though permitting the London County Council to act; and they adhered to permissive legislation in the bleak hope that market pressures would disperse population away from overcrowded urban centres.[15]

In Ireland dire necessity pushed the Conservatives well beyond what was thought safe for England. After 1881 when a shocked Salisbury found that the landowners did not want him to save them from Gladstone's Land Act, the rights of property were effectively thrown overboard. A combination of rents lowered by tribunals, agricultural depression and rural violence gradually destroyed the landowners' resolve to the extent that by 1900 they were ready to sell their land given attractive terms. During the 1880s the Conservatives had begun to appreciate the idea of creating peasant proprietors (at least in Ireland) in the conviction that to turn tenants into small owners was tantamount to converting agitators into supporters of stable government, and thereby undermining 'Home Rule'. Beginning with the £5 million allocated for land purchase in Ashbourne's Act of 1885 and continuing with similar measures in 1888 and 1891, this policy culminated in Wyndham's Land Act of 1903 under which a quarter of a million Irishmen bought farms before 1914. As Salisbury observed dolefully in 1887, 'It is the price we have to pay for the Union, and it is a heavy one.'[16] It is significant that those Conservatives most closely associated with this policy, Horace Plunkett, Lord Dunraven and George Wyndham, suffered a permanent check to their careers.

Ireland also afforded more scope for experiments in social interventionism than England. As Chief Secretary, Balfour applied state funds to pay wages for relief work in the most distressed counties and for the construction of light railways. His Congested Districts Bill of 1890 created boards in the west of Ireland (where the people were too poor to take advantage of land purchase schemes) with resources to acquire land, amalgamate uneconomic holdings, distribute seed potatoes and assist tenants to migrate from congested districts or to emigrate. The nearest approach to a similar policy in England came in 1905 in the form of Walter Long's Unemployed Workmen's Act, which involved using rate finance for relief work schemes in London. However, Balfour, now Prime Minister, retreated from the radical implications of the measure by limiting it to a three-year experiment only, and by appointing a Royal Commission on the Poor Law to avoid the necessity for further action.

This reluctance to deal boldly or constructively with social problems brought the Salisbury–Balfour era to an unimaginative end. Throughout these years Conservatives had been caught in the dilemma of financing social policies under a free enterprise system. Although this is sometimes seen as a Liberal problem it afflicted the Conservatives more, partly because they found themselves more frequently in office, but also because, in the absence of the political reform espoused by the Liberals, they felt an obligation to pass safe social legislation. Paradoxically Chamberlain's influence was probably greater during 1886–92 when he remained outside the government and felt anxious about justifying his co-operation by means of the measures for county councils, education and allotments. Later he sought influence through a vigorous imperial policy and a formidably long list of social reforms which he presented to Salisbury in a memorandum of 1894: compensation for industrial injuries, amendment of the Artisans Dwellings Act, loans to working men for house purchase, an eight-hour day for miners, reduction of alien immigration, old age pensions, labour exchanges, arbitration courts to settle industrial disputes, earlier closing for shops, and cheaper train travel for workmen. In fact his colleagues were amenable to action on several of these items, notably immigration and workmen's compensation. But by now Chamberlain had reconciled himself to playing a limited role. Although pensions did receive official sanction in the *Campaign Guide* for 1895, there was agreement only on a contributory scheme that would have omitted those most in need. The Cabinet drifted into the South African War and lost its opportunity to outflank the Liberals. Its whole approach to social questions was crippled by its addiction to retrenchment and inhibited by apprehension about the pressure of organized labour and the social investigations of the 1890s. Innovation was to be adopted only where it would forestall a more radical change. In this way Conservative thinking stagnated until the explosive reappraisal triggered by Chamberlain's disastrous tariff campaign of 1903.

4

The Social Roots of Political Change in Late Victorian Britain

When you stand in the voting booth with your card and your pencil in your hand, think of this: I am going to vote either for robbing God or against it.

Warwickshire clergyman, quoted in The Nonconformist,
3 December 1885

Up to 1841 British general elections remained essentially parochial in character: that is, the shifts of opinion from one constituency to another fluctuated over a wide range that reflected the multitude of local factors at work. Thereafter the range narrowed as more general influences common to the whole country made an impression. However, historians have characterized this as a regional rather than a national pattern which reached its height around 1868–85.[1] Using Dr Pelling's calculations[2] of the Conservative and Unionist share of the poll we may distinguish the broad party loyalties of the regions as they appeared in 1885 (see table 4.1). To a considerable extent these regional loyalties already reflected the uneven distribution of social classes in each area. But classes had by no means come to behave in a uniform fashion across the country. Working men in London and Lancashire were much less inclined to Liberalism than working men in north-east England or Wales; the middle classes of Scotland and Yorkshire were far more likely to vote Liberal than those of south-east England.

Trends and Issues

In terms of party fortunes the period from 1865 to 1900 falls into two phases with the watershed in 1885–6: the first saw a continuation of the mid-Victorian Liberal dominance interrupted only in 1874; and the

TABLE 4.1   *Conservative and Unionist % vote 1885*

Strongly Conservative		Intermediate		Anti-Conservative	
S.E. England	54.5	East Anglia	49.2	Northern	
Wessex	51.5	Bristol region	48.7	England	41.7
Lancastria	51.4	Yorks region	45.8	Peak-Don	41.5
London County		West Midlands	45.5	Wales	39.6
Council area	51.0	Central England	44.7	Scotland	36.3
		Devon and			
		Cornwall	44.3		
		East Midlands	43.7		

TABLE 4.2   *General election results 1865–1900 (seats won)*

	1865	1868	1874	1880	1885	1886	1892	1895	1900
Conservative	294	274	356	238	250	316	268	341	334
Liberal Unionist						78	47	70	68
Liberal	364	384	245	353	334	191	273	177	184
Irish Nationalist			51	61	86	85	81	82	82
Labour							(ILP)1		(LRC)2

second from 1886 saw it replaced by Conservative predominance with the partial exception of 1892 (see table 4.2).

Broadly two kinds of changes are at work here; there are certain underlying movements in the allegiance of social, religious and cultural groups, in the entry of new groups of voters, and modifications of the constituency boundaries; and there are also short-term factors to be considered – the impact of particular issues and controversies, the timing and tactics of each election, and switches by the leading personalities. We have already noted one important long-term trend, namely the shift of middle-class and propertied interests towards Conservatism from the 1860s culminating in the schism of 1886. However, long-term group loyalties never entirely account for fluctuating election results, for every group has its soft, wavering fringes that respond to the ebb and flow of events and personalities. It would be too much to claim that the great Victorian issues, however passionately debated by the politicians, actually influenced more than a fraction of the electorate directly; party loyalty tends to be an impervious thing. But a small turnover of votes always produced drastic effects; as Lord Salisbury observed, a mere 2,000 strategically placed votes made 1880 a Liberal victory instead of a Conservative one. In addition, although economic questions had not yet become the staple of election debates, it does seem that party fortunes were vulnerable to sudden economic fluctuations; the downfall of Disraeli in 1880 and of Rosebery in 1895 was sealed by a slump immediately preceding each election, while Salisbury was saved from heavy losses in 1900 in part by the sudden buoyancy in the economy.

In 1868 Gladstone rallied radical sentiment with his bold programme of Irish reform; but the election, despite the extended electorate, essentially confirmed the traditional Liberal majority, marred only by a distinct ebbing of middle-class Palmerstonians. Coming after a plethora of innovations, 1874 exacerbated this trend. Essentially a reaction by those whose interests seemed to have been threatened by Gladstone's reforms, this election saw both a suspension of Whig support for Liberalism in the counties, and a subsidence of radical–Nonconformist enthusiasm owing to dissatisfaction with recent legislation. In the long run the regular school board elections necessitated by Forster's Act probably consolidated the Nonconformist habit of voting Liberal, while also strengthening Conservatism among Anglicans and Catholics; for Conservative defence of independent religious schools was one means of neutralizing the Liberal appeal to the Irish. After 1875 the prevailing sense of economic depression, though exaggerated, shook Conservative loyalties especially among farmers suffering bad harvests and high grain imports; and social distress doubtless told more forcefully with the lower classes than the scarcely perceptible benefits of Disraelian social legislation. Although ostensibly the election turned upon the Midlothian onslaught on 'Beaconsfieldism', the outcome reflected this issue only indirectly in that the anti-imperial campaign restored radical morale and thereby helped the Liberals to poll their full strength again.

The election of 1885 appears more complicated. That it was less of a victory for the Liberals than 1880 was due primarily to Parnell's decision to withhold the Irish vote in England, to the unpopularity of Gladstone's imperial policies culminating in the death of General Gordon at Khartoum in 1885, and to renewed alarm among the urban middle classes at the radical tone of Chamberlain's 'Unauthorised Programme'. Yet Conservative urban consolidation was balanced by Liberal gains in the counties now under a new franchise. The question of Church disestablishment attained considerable prominence in England in 1885. For many years Nonconformists had been strenuously engaged, through the Liberal Party, in removing the obstacles to their participation in national life, so much so that religious assignation had become central to party loyalty; wherever the 'free churches' were thickly distributed (as in Wales, Scotland, the north-east, Yorkshire, Cornwall and the midland and East Anglian towns), Liberalism was very strong. But the party still commanded much Anglican support too; the MPs were still mostly Anglicans and led by a prominent Anglican. However, this proved to be a waning asset in this period. Gladstone steadily eliminated Nonconformist grievances such as church rates in 1868; he disestablished the Church in Ireland in 1870, passed the University Tests Act in 1871, and the Church Burials Act in 1880. The next obvious step was disestablishment for Wales and Scotland, and the Liberation Society hoped to exploit the new county franchise to generate sufficient pressure to oblige Gladstone to take action. Since Chamberlain gave prominence to disestablishment, the Conservatives raised the cry of 'the Church in danger' in 1885, hoping to win over middle-class Anglicans from Liberalism. Even Nonconformists, once their keenest grievances were rectified, showed some tendency to side with Conservatism as the embodiment of the status quo to which they now belonged. In fact the political behaviour of the free churches did increasingly reflect the social class of their members; furthest down the social scale – and highest in political radicalism – were the Primitive Methodists, followed by Baptists, Congregationalists and, finally, Wesleyan Methodists. The latter were longer in existence, more comfortably middle class, nearer to Anglicanism, less antagonistic to the established Church, and more receptive to a national political outlook. Hence Wesleyans displayed some reluctance to join radical campaigns by comparison with other Nonconformists; and by the 1890s many of them preferred Rosebery's brand of Liberal Imperialism to Gladstonianism, and provided recruits for the Conservatives.

The Home Rule crisis of 1886 proved to be a watershed because it crystallized the attitudes of many Liberal followers already wavering for other reasons, and enabled them to take a coherent position as Liberal Unionists. Yet the impact of Ireland varied greatly from region to region. Western Scotland was considerably stirred because of the proximity of both Ireland and the Irish, while eastern Scotland remained relatively unmoved; north-east England and Yorkshire stayed largely Gladstonian while Lancashire moved even further to Unionism; in East Anglia the question seemed remote, yet in the south-west Home Rule seemed strategically relevant, and the St Ives division of Cornwall manifested the most marked shift to Unionism. Today it seems remarkable that for years afterwards the Irish Question provided a staple item in constituency campaigns; both parties clearly thought it worth keeping the issue alive. When taking the high ground of principle the Gladstonians urged the virtues of self-determination, and the Conservatives the threat to imperial unity and security. However, on the low ground of self-interest it was articulated differently. Conservatives repeatedly urged English working men to remember that a Dublin Parliament would destroy business confidence and thereby cause an even greater influx of destitute immigrants into English cities. The Gladstonians countered by warning that the bloody suppression of Irishmen's rights implied a threat to those of English workers too, and by arguing that an independent Ireland would in fact retain the population presently compelled to seek its livelihood abroad. While the Liberals plainly forfeited working-class support notably in the northwest, they enjoyed the compensation of a solid and organized Irish vote which gave them the edge in many urban constituencies right up to 1914.

By 1892 the Gladstonians had managed to effect a limited recovery from the débâcle of 1886, but one based more upon county seats, a sign that they had revitalized the issues of 1885 but could not restore their full 1880 strength. Three years later, after expectations had been dashed by the inability of both Gladstone and Rosebery to deliver the innovations promised, the party went down to a heavy defeat. Essentially a negative reaction, the election saw Liberal abstentions and Conservative victory by default. The year 1895 also brought into general prominence the local veto on alcoholic sales (or 'Local Option') partly because it was taken up by Sir William Harcourt as he cast around rather desperately for fresh issues. Although temperance reform had acquired some political salience as long ago as 1871 as a result of Bruce's Licensing Bill, there had not been as sudden or complete an alienation of the drinking classes to the Conservatives as contemporaries often alleged. For years Gladstone fended off demands for the Local Veto in the belief that free trade and competition would eventually reduce the harmful effects of alcoholic consumption; also a number of brewers and publicans remained in the Liberal camp despite its connection with temperance; and in any case temperance became an election issue only where a candidate adopted a belligerent attitude on the subject. Although it was undoubtedly advantageous to the Conservatives in working-class seats to be able to defend a man's right to his beer, the party's association with the drink interest could not be too vociferously asserted. For one thing the improving working man was often a keen abstainer; for another, the party actually incorporated much middle-class temperance sentiment in the shape of organizations like the Church of England Temperance Society. Moreover, 1886 had brought many Liberal Unionists to their side who would merely be driven back to the Gladstonians if they were antagonized over licensing or education. Despite these qualifications, however, it is true that many a Liberal candidate risked alienating his staunchest backers if he remained lukewarm about temperance.

Between 1895 and 1899 the Liberals again appeared to claw back much of their support; but the by-election trend in their favour was suddenly interrupted shortly after the outbreak of the Boer War. There can be little doubt that the preservation of the 1895 Conservative majority was due to the shrewd timing of the 1900 general election fought in an atmosphere of embattled patriotism and an economy stimulated by the demand for war production. The government lost only ten English and four Welsh seats while gaining five in Scotland. In fact, in terms of votes there was a swing in their favour everywhere except in Wales where foreign adventures seemed less relevant, and traditional issues, which favoured the Liberals, reasserted themselves. To a lesser extent the same was true of the remoter parts of England; Conservatives benefited most in the big towns especially London which was always quick to grow excited over international crises.

Rural Radicalism

The introduction of the secret ballot in 1872 produced little immediate impact upon English county politics; 1885, when the electorate was trebled, proved to be the turning-point in that it led to an attempt to politicize areas hitherto somewhat insular and remote from national politics. Whether the traditional, conservative and Conservative pattern of rural politics could resist the new depended upon certain underlying social characteristics, notably the type of settlement pattern and the prevailing religious affiliation. For radical politics flourished only where it could establish roots in an alternative community to that epitomized by the joint authority of the squirearchy and the Church. The links between politics and religious figures – Anglican, Nonconformist and Catholic – were often active and blatant; one Lincolnshire vicar piously informed Lord Salisbury in 1885:

> I am canvassing the labourers here in Mr Stanhope's interest, and find that a Liberal canvasser has been endeavouring to gain votes with the false assertion that the Conservatives are the enemy of the agricultural labourers, and wish to give the country a dear loaf. . . .
> As it is part of my duty to protect my parishioners from false doctrines of all kinds and from the father of lies and his progeny, I shall be glad to receive your reply on Saturday so that I may be able to state the truth publicly on Sunday.[3]

Political management by parson and squire attained maximum effectiveness in the 'closed' villages typical of the southern and midland counties and great estates in which all who lived depended upon the landowner for their cottage and employment. However, over the years the surplus population drifted to the 'open' villages which, in consequence, often grew into small towns. Here housing and sanitation were sometimes inferior and more expensive, while employment was irregular. Yet the residents, freer from the influence of their social superiors, tended to deviate in social and religious behaviour, often becoming islands of radicalism.[4] Nonconformists had frequently worsted the Church of England in the struggle for the allegiance of such communities; and the prevalence of their chapels in the small towns and villages of Wales, East Anglia and the south-west underpinned radicalism there. Nonconformity thrived also in areas of more scattered settlement based upon small farms and holdings remote from villages; this was typical of much of the heath and fenlands in eastern counties such as Norfolk, Cambridgeshire and Lincolnshire, of Cornwall and parts of Devon, and in the vast upland chain of Pennine country stretching from Derbyshire north to Yorkshire, Durham and Northumberland.

The significance of settlement and religion is very evident in a highly agricultural and traditionally Conservative county such as Norfolk, where less than half the agricultural population resided in closed villages and where the chapels were vigorous. Enfranchised in 1884, the labourers promptly delivered four of Norfolk's six county seats to the Liberals in 1885. Realization that the county electorate was not so amenable as previously led the Conservative chief agent to advise Salisbury in both 1892 and 1895 that the election should ideally coincide with harvest time when the labourers would be distracted and less politically involved.[5]

From the 1870s rural radicalism was being integrated with national politics at several levels. It enjoyed national leadership from Gladstone, through whom Liberalism spoke for the small man again the Establishment, and from Chamberlain's three-acres-and-a-cow approach. Radical newspapers like the *Daily News* also took a keen interest, for example by assisting the new agricultural trade unions in the 1870s by writing up the story of their strikes and encouraging urban radicals to provide funds urgently needed to sustain their action. Urban workers such as dockers often thought it worthwhile subsidizing land reform propaganda on the grounds that this would eventually retain the population on the land and thus mitigate the overcrowding and wage-cutting caused by migration to the towns. Similarly during the 1880s all kinds of essentially external organizations propagandized the counties often through mobile vans bearing lecturers, leaflets and lantern shows; the Land

Restoration League's Red Van, the Land Nationalisation Society Van, the Sunrise Radical Van, the Beaconsfield Van, the Church Association Van, and the Home Rule Van were some of the entertainments from both parties at this time.

However, neither pressure groups nor national leaders could make lasting inroads against the underlying Conservatism without a network of sub-contractors able to link the party cause with the lives of the people. Without missionaries from small towns or chapels it was often difficult to find speakers and chairmen for village meetings, and a small shopkeeper or merchant, Nonconformist minister or even a travelling lecturer would fill this role. When parish councils were established in 1894, many labourers did come forward as candidates, though it was felt safer for an independent entrepreneur to take the risk of offending his superiors. One valuable source of stump orators was the agricultural labourers trade unions which sprang up especially in Warwickshire, Oxfordshire, Norfolk and Suffolk during the 1870s. Regular union activity proved very difficult to sustain, for even in the strongest counties only a third of the men became members; farmers could therefore draw upon plentiful supplies of labour unless strikes were well co-ordinated and coincided with harvest time. Consequently, after initial successes the membership of the National Agricultural Labourers Union fell from a peak of 86,000 in 1874 to 10,000 by 1886. However, the experience increased the assertiveness of the labourers, and failure drove their leaders towards political solutions of which the first fruit was the county franchise of 1884. Like the Union's founder, Joseph Arch MP, the labourers' leaders greatly strengthened radical Liberalism in this period.

While great national issues like Home Rule remained somewhat remote, the rural radicals worked the villages with a mixture of demands for political rights (county franchise, county and parish councils, disestablishment, the burials question) and material improvements; the latter included eliminating duties on basic food items (the 'Free Breakfast Table'), provision of allotments and smallholdings, poor law reform, and the local veto on licensed premises. The vicar frequently appeared as an obstacle due to his prominent role in vestry meetings which controlled charitable endowments and lands that were regarded as a potential source of new allotments.[6]

Despite the radical upsurge of 1885 the Conservatives managed to retain the bulk of their territory especially in the Home Counties and Wessex, though it could no longer be taken for granted. Whereas their strength had its roots in agriculture, radicalism had to be sustained by penetration from outside; and the continual migration, or even emigration, of the most active and discontented village radicals steadily enfeebled their cause. It was assumed that the reservoir of rural radicalism could be tapped only when the labourer was made more independent of his employer by possessing sufficient land to feed his family; yet this required more drastic local government reform than was provided either by county councils – still often under landowners' control – or parish councils which were starved of resources. Conservative strength lay among landowners and farmers; Gladstone made some efforts to win over the latter by repealing the malt tax, by compensation to tenants for improvements, and by the 1880 Ground Game Act. However, this was overtaken by the more radical proposals of the mid-1880s pitched primarily at labourers. Finally, as we have seen, the Conservatives produced a constructive response to the challenge in the shape of the Primrose League which gave a new lease of life to landed politics.

Working-class Politics and Socialists

As the world's most advanced industrial society, Britain appeared to contemporaries to be certain to generate a mass working-class movement. In 1852 Marx had optimistically forecast that the introduction of universal suffrage in England would be 'a far more socialistic measure than anything which has been honoured with that name on the Continent. Its inevitable result, here, is the supremacy of the working class.'[7] Of course neither 1867 nor 1884 ushered in universal suffrage, but the reforms did make working-class voters numerically dominant in at least 89 constituencies with 95 MPs;[8] had they been at all cohesive they could rapidly have emerged as a substantial and discrete force like the Irish. Yet such expectations were regularly dashed. Not only was there no significant movement in Britain, even the emergence of an effective and independent political party for the working class proved to be a protracted affair. Why was this so?

One line of explanation grows from a recognition that in the past historians have exaggerated the impact of the industrial revolution on British society. Even in the late nineteenth century industry was organized on a surprisingly small scale, with the average workshop comprising only 29 men. Also, many workers found themselves in service occupations and highly dependent on the patronage of employers. By the 1890s trade union membership stood at only 1.5 million, though the figure rose towards 2.0 million, in a labour force of over 13 million. This was not such a large basis for an organized proletarian movement. Further, there is evidence that many British workers, though dissatisfied with their lot, were not basically alienated and entertained quite positive attitudes towards the political and social system. Some at least experienced the benefits of economic expansion in terms of free trade and rising real wages. Although the political system was weighted in favour of property and the legal system often biased against the working man, neither were impervious to change. Since 1858, when property qualifications for MPs had been abolished, it had been possible for a working man to stand for Parliament, though not until 1894 was the same true of poor law boards. In 1867 and 1884 several million working men won a parliamentary vote and from 1874 a handful sat as MPs. Those who were ratepayers also played a direct part in the fast-growing number of elective local authorities. Certain practical obstacles still hindered their participation. For example, polling stations were sparse and polling hours rather inconvenient (8.00 am to 8.00 pm after 1884), so that most men were at work when the booths opened in the morning and had to hurry in to vote in the last half hour at night. Most municipal authorities held meetings during working hours which made membership a serious burden. Even after the reforms of 1883, parliamentary elections were still expensive to fight, and MPs received no salary until 1911. This made it all but impossible for the working man unless he was subsidized by his union or could support himself by journalism and lecturing as Keir Hardie and Philip Snowden did.

However, the system at least remained open to pressure and reform on the part of those working men who were literate, politically aware and not worn down by poverty. Though the trade unionist was by no means typical of Victorian working men, he was sufficiently well entrenched in the traditional skilled crafts, in expanding industries like iron and steel and shipbuilding, and in textiles and coal to constitute a significant pressure group. However, this section has sometimes been regarded as a 'labour aristocracy' by which it is implied that the men were complacent and passive, and deficient in a sense of class-consciousness. Such men often placed a high priority on self-help strategies, such as providing friendly society benefits for their members, of which the middle classes approved. They also sought recognition by the employers with a view to establishing regular collective bargaining and arbitration rather than have frequent recourse to strikes. Some working men shared social, religious and political attitudes with employers; and the skilled artisan could still hope to emulate them by becoming a small entrepreneur himself. Yet these workers were also proud, independent and capable of asserting themselves in both industrial and political contexts. By 1868 they had established the Trades Union Congress as a pressure group monitoring and influencing industrial legislation and promoting its members' political interests through the Parliamentary Committee. By the 1870s the legal status of the unions had been much improved by the action of both political parties. Moreover, traditional ideas about the

damaging effects of trade unionism had been effectively challenged by
Liberal intellectuals like Henry Fawcett and John Stuart Mill who
argued that the free market would not operate satisfactorily without the
active participation of combinations of working men; the free pursuit of
higher wages was a wholly legitimate objective.

On the other hand the working class contained a tremendous range
of experience and attitudes which inevitably limited and complicated its
overall political impact. Between the skilled minority and the unskilled,
unorganized majority, between those enjoying a regular wage and those
condemned to casual labour, a major gulf still existed. The relative
comfort of, say, a blastfurnaceman earning £2 to £3 a week marked him
out from the casual labourer in London's East End or a Wiltshire farm
worker on 14s. Those involved in irregular or seasonal employment in
the low-paid or 'sweated' trades, or those who depended on employers'
patronage or charity were the least likely to generate independent political institutions or aspirations. Even among railway workers, for
example, contemporaries noticed a distinction between 'the goods side
and drivers and firemen not brought into touch with the public [who]
are Radicals, [and] passenger guards and porters who are also underpaid
but with funds augmented by tips and the patronage of the rich [who]
are Conservatives.'[9]

By the 1880s, however, change was under way. Realization that
British industry was losing its former dominance and an awareness of
extensive urban poverty shook prevailing attitudes. In this decade
socialism enjoyed a revival, though many of its early advocates were
middle-class men and women. If often proved a frustrating task for the
late Victorian socialist to wean the politically aware working man away
from his Gladstonian brand of politics; self-help and free trade appeared
to make more immediate sense than a new and vaguely understood philosophy. For some the route led via their existing religious principles
towards an ethical version of socialism rather than to an economic
creed. Nor was it yet obvious to many workers that state social policies
were desirable. Especially from the perspective of poorer families,
schemes of reform and improvement invariably appeared intrusive and
humiliating because of the interference, inspection or taxation they
involved. Government so often manifested itself in unwelcome forms
such as the poor law or the post-1870 educational innovations. The
latter led to loss of children's earnings, payment of fees at least until
1891, inspectors trying to enforce compulsory attendance, and, after
1907, medical inspection. Beneficial measures such as vaccination
against contagious diseases aroused much resentment; the stern
individualist Thomas Burt declared he 'did not intend to have my children treated as if they were cattle'.[10]

Nonetheless these negative attitudes should not be exaggerated. In time state intervention came to be seen as necessary and desirable, but it was not yet a practical basis for a major political movement even in the working class. The last 20 years of the nineteenth century saw a series of experiments among labour and socialist organizations before a new, viable strategy emerged. Most of the labour leaders regarded the really impoverished slum populations as too passive and dependent to respond to their relatively sophisticated appeal. As Ramsay MacDonald put it in 1911: 'It is the skilled artisan, the trade unionist, the member of the friendly society, the young workman who reads and thinks who are the recruits to the army of socialism.'[11] Yet for many years socialist parties met with little success. The Social Democratic Federation, founded in 1883, represented the nearest approach to a Marxist socialist party. By the late 1890s the SDF claimed only 10,000 members though its true membership has been put at 2,600; it was always crippled by its inability to win more than a derisory vote at parliamentary elections, although it scored some successes in municipal contests. Like most organizations that took their socialism seriously the SDF attracted articulate middle-class people, but men like H. M. Hyndman, H. H. Champion and William Morris tended to reduce the Federation to disputatious frag-ments all energetically defining their ideological position in numerous journals rather than converting the working class. It has been calcu-lated that no less than 800 Labour and socialist newspapers were pub-lished between 1890 and 1910, most of them with tiny circulations and very short lives. Even Keir Hardie's *Labour Leader* struggled against perennial losses. The only viable socialist paper, Robert Blatchford's *Clarion*, outsold all the rest of the socialist press put together with a circulation of 40,000. Blatchford's formula, not unlike that of other successful working-class papers, was a lively, readable blend of socialist radicalism combined with a vigorous, patriotic nationalism. It was Blatchford more than any of the politicians who articulated 'socialism' for the rank and file in pre-1914 Britain.

A far more realistic and pragmatic approach than that of the SDF was adopted by the Independent Labour Party founded in Bradford in 1893. Though socialist, the ILP displayed a certain flexibility absent from the SDF; for it espoused a shrewd mixture of radical Liberal causes and current trade union demands. Also its members reflected much more closely the working class of provincial England, and its leaders, especially Keir Hardie, spoke a socialism of a moralistic, humanitarian, revivalist kind. For some years the ILP-ers put their main emphasis on the local rather than the national sphere, working through municipal bodies, and also through trades councils which were often the most successful means of co-ordinating the efforts of the otherwise disparate elements in the labour and socialist movements. During the 1890s opportunities were seized, for example, in boards of guardians such as the one at Poplar in London to which George Lansbury and Will Crooks were elected; they were able to change policy locally by providing outdoor relief to the aged and fit working men temporarily unemployed, and even more importantly, to highlight the problems and thus concentrate the minds of the policy makers elsewhere. London was also the source of a notable triumph for ILP tactics in 1898 when West Ham Borough returned a majority of Labour members, who proceeded to improve the conditions of council workers by introducing two weeks' annual holiday, a minimum weekly wage of 30s, and a working day of eight hours. Although there was little co-ordination of labour and socialist action around the country, in practice a common platform did exist. This comprised essentially a demand for the municipalization of basic utilities like gas and waterworks where they were still in private hands (this was advocated on grounds of economy – an important consideration to a ratepaying electorate – as much as for fairness and improvement). The second basic proposal was to establish a works department so that the council could be a direct employer of labour; by this means it might both alleviate unemployment locally, and, by inserting a 'fair wage' clause into its contracts, stimulate improvements in the conditions of men employed privately. Often this was accomplished by means of co-operation with Liberals and Fabians as in the case of the London County Council Progressives, but it certainly gave the labour movement a coherent political programme pitched towards working men. In the long run this experience proved to be immensely important. Local government in Bradford, Glasgow or London provided an invaluable apprenticeship in elections and office-holding that was eventually built upon at the parliamentary level; indeed it left Labour's mainstream in the twentieth century with a pronounced municipal flavour, and probably compounded the neglect of ideology.

Yet despite this progress the ILP found it all but impossible to break into national politics. Though Keir Hardie was briefly the MP for West Ham (1892–5), the ILP's membership fluctuated around 6,000 to 9,000 by the end of the decade; financially starved and without access to trade union strength, the party remained a somewhat ramshackle and diffuse organization which, after the early successes, seemed to stagnate in the face of the trend to Conservatism during 1895–1900. However, the ILP leaders had grasped the fact that the key to effective independent labour politics lay in tapping the funds and organization of the trade unions; and the events of the later 1890s and early 1900s enabled them to translate their strategy into practice in the form of the Labour Representation Committee. The emergence of the LRC at the turn of the century has sometimes been explained in terms of an outflanking of the traditional craft unions by the more socialist and radical leaders of the 'new unions'. Undoubtedly several groups like the Gas Workers and General Labourers Union succeeded in extending industrial organization to many semi-skilled and unskilled men hitherto outside the movement. Moreover, the successful strikes of 1888–90 threw up many new trades councils, and leaders such as Will Thorne and Ben Tillett who were ardent exponents of independent labour representation and critics of the TUC. With their advocacy of the eight-hour day they took the initiative in the TUC away from Henry Broadhurst, the Parliamentary Secretary and champion of Lib–Lab strategy; by the 1890s the Lib–Lab MPs were not, apparently, achieving much except respectability for themselves. Broadhurst himself served as an under-secretary in Gladstone's last government, but neither this nor his work on industrial legislation impressed the younger working-class activists with political ambitions who did not enjoy similar advantages. Lib–Labbery worked well enough for the miners but this no longer seemed sufficient.

Nonetheless too much should not be made of the new unions. They remained comparatively weak and soon lost much of their membership; by 1900 in fact only 100,000 of the one million affiliated to the TUC were members of the new unions. Thus the emergence of what was to become the Labour Party in 1906 could hardly have occurred at that time but for the willingness of the well-established unions who still dominated the movement to indulge in an experiment. They had been much influenced by the experience of economic stagnation during the 1890s which exposed hitherto well-placed skilled men such as shipwrights, ironfounders, steel smelters and blastfurnacemen to 10 per cent unemployment rates. Further, the employers now displayed a tendency to take advantage of higher unemployment by combining for concerted action to curb union activity as in the case of the Shipping Federation and the six-month lock-out of engineering workers in 1897. On top of this the legal status apparently achieved in 1875 now appeared to have been undermined by a number of legal decisions notably the *Lyons* v. *Wilkins* case in 1896 and 1899 which infringed the right to picket. All this seemed to point to the need for unions to be represented in Parliament on a similar scale to employers; industrial weakness, in short, stimulated a characteristic turn towards political remedies. It was in this spirit that in 1899 the TUC approved by 546,000 votes to 434,000 a resolution of the Amalgamated Society of Railway Servants to establish a new and independent political organization. As a result 129 delegates representing unions and socialist societies met in February 1900 to set up the Labour Representation Committee. Its leading supporters at this stage included printers, boot and shoe operatives, gasworkers and dockers, and those like the railway workers who were trying to win recognition from their employers. Their purpose may best be defined as 'Labourism', that is, to achieve a greater degree of direct working-class representation than was possible within the scope of existing Lib–Lab arrangements. The chief authors of the strategy, Hardie and MacDonald of the ILP, recognized the futility of attempting to commit the LRC to any distinctive left-wing ideology lest they play into the hands of the many unionists who were anxious to 'bury the attempt in good-humoured tolerance'. Hardie contrived to obscure the inconsistency between a wholly independent party, which the LRC nominally was, and the relationship with Liberalism, which the bulk of the unions still desired. Thus the new organization was not in 1900 expected by most participants to differ dramatically from earlier experiments in labour representation. The LRC had to begin life as a loose federal organization with an executive of twelve, comprising seven trade unionists, two from the ILP, two from the SDF and one Fabian, and with an unpaid secretary in Ramsay MacDonald. The unions continued to hold on to their money and declined any ideological innovation. It was a modest start for a party that was to form a government only 24 years later.

Women, Politics and Labour

During the last 30 years of the century women impinged increasingly upon public affairs in Britain. They extended their range of employment in the expanding service sectors, notably as teachers, clerks, typists, Post Office employees and shop assistants; they also established a formal role both in the political parties and in local government. This process began to introduce a fresh element into conventional divisions along lines of social class and party ideology.

Although marriage and motherhood were seen as the inevitable lot of women, a high proportion of Victorian females remained single or became widows quite early in life. Working-class girls usually found themselves driven by necessity to paid employment at some stage in their lives. But most trade unionists regarded women workers as a threat because of their willingness to accept low wages. Working men used their growing foothold in Parliament to extend 'protective legislation' which was designed to exclude women from certain occupations. This conflict made women aware of the need for state intervention to impose minimum wages on the low-paid trades, as well as of the wider need for the vote. There are some grounds for thinking that women generally had a different view of politics partly because of the different experience in employment. Obviously they were much less likely to be members of trade unions than men; around 20,000 joined in the early 1870s, though there were 166,000 by 1906. This reflected the temporary nature of their work and also the type of occupations they held. They were strongly concentrated in domestic service and similar jobs where unions hardly existed and where they came into close contact with the middle class. There is some evidence that their attitudes and aspirations diverged as a result of this. Women clearly played a major role in giving their families 'respectable' status; they were more skilled at handling money; and were widely believed to be more interested in religion, temperance and other moral questions.

Gradually all this began to impinge upon the world of politics. In the 1880s new organizations like the Women's Co-operative Guild appeared which aspired to turn the concerns of ordinary housewives into political issues for the first time. The Women's Trade Union League provided a ladder by which young women like Margaret Bondfield began the long ascent to the cabinet. The political parties in the shape of the Primrose League, the Women's Liberal Federation and the Independent Labour Party made extensive use of women volunteers from the 1880s onwards. Some women, both middle-class and working-class, also gained a local government vote as ratepayers in 1869, and subsequently many were elected especially to the school boards and as poor law guardians. Apart from the direct implications for women's public role, this experience in municipal affairs had a broader significance. For in the late nineteenth century local government served as an important experimental field for novel social policies. Elected women played a major role in this, partly because as women they noticed and understood things which men neglected. Such innovations as school meals, modestly attempted in this period, were to become the subject of national policies during the Edwardian period.

Working-class Conservatism, Empire and Patriotism

Even today studies of voting behaviour suggest that around one-third of working-class voters consistently support the Conservatives. In the mid nineteenth century when voters were offered two parties drawn from broadly similar social backgrounds and eschewing a class appeal there existed no neat general relationship between class and party allegiance. Investigation has always been difficult because working-class Conservatism largely lacked organization, and therefore a record, and also because of the somewhat equivocal attitude of the party itself. While recognizing the division of society into ranks as natural and desirable, Conservatives feared the potential for class conflict in an industrial society; their leaders were thus anxious to avoid being drawn into a competition for votes by appeasement of material demands. As a result Conservatives approached the matter in two distinct ways. One involved appealing to working men as working men by cataloguing the beneficial measures enacted by Conservative administrations since Disraeli's time, and reminding them of how badly the Liberals fell down on their promises. This approach was typical of the National Union which printed huge quantities of literature on the theme. The alternative was that usually adopted by the leaders and the Primrose League, which amounted to an appeal to working men as patriotic Britons, as soldiers-of-the-Queen, as English workers and as Protestants. To Salisbury the drawbacks of the former approach were only too obvious. National Union conferences were regularly troubled with complaints by working-class delegates that 'the time had come when the Conservative Party should have its Burts and its Broadhursts'.[12] Yet James Mawdsley of the cotton spinners enjoyed a lonely eminence as one leading Conservative trade unionist: he ran in harness with Winston Churchill in the double-member constituency of Oldham in 1899. But in the absence of payment of members, which the party thoroughly disliked, this experiment was unlikely to be repeated.

Two kinds of explanation are usually advanced to account for working-class Conservatism. The first is in terms of deference. This implies a willingness by the voter to be governed by his social superiors who are equipped to rule by birth and training, and a tendency to iden-tify with the traditional values and institutions of his society, which invariably seem closely associated with the Conservative Party. This may well suggest the pattern for rural Conservatism; and is also consist-ent with the tendency noticed by some writers on local politics for Conservatives to do particularly well in both the wealthiest and the poorest wards.[13] There are signs of this in parliamentary elections too, notably in the East End of London, and in strong Conservative seats such as Bristol West which combined the wealthy with the dependent poor. The other explanation sees the Conservative working man as a pragmatic or secular voter whose choice implies some assessment that his self-interest is best served by supporting the Conservative Party. In the nineteenth-century context the deferential and the pragmatic element was combined in the concept of Tory paternalism in the sense of government by hereditary leaders fully alive to their obligations, material and moral, towards the lower orders of society.

Although deferential attitudes were widespread in the nineteenth century they did not automatically make for Conservative voting. For until the 1860s the natural ruling elite in Britain – the Palmerstonian Whig–Liberal combination – was more closely identified with the symbols of national pride than the sectional and peripheral Conservative Party. However, there is a strong prima-facie case for thinking that this changed during the Disraeli–Salisbury era as the Conservatives began to reap the benefit of association with patriotism and Empire. By his firmness over the Congress of Berlin, the Suez Canal, Afghanistan and South Africa Disraeli contrived to sharpen his disagreement with Gladstone, who could plausibly, if inaccurately, be accused of planning the dismemberment of the Empire and of weakness towards the United States and Russia when British interests were threatened. Thereafter Conservatives ceaselessly propagated their claim to be the party of national interests, and cast aspersions on their opponents' patriotism; they catalogued the radicals' failures in the 1880s – defeat by the Boers at Majuba Hill, abandonment of Kandahar, death of General Gordon – and pinned the label 'pro-Boer' indiscriminately on their rivals during 1899–1902. One conference speaker summed it up in 1905: 'in all those places where the enemies of England foregather, the advent of a Radical government would be hailed with undisguised rejoicing.'[14]

Some historians have gone to considerable lengths to exonerate the working classes from any sympathy with 'Imperialism', arguing that this was a sentiment of the lower middle and middle classes. However, this is tenable only if imperialism is fairly tightly defined, and if selective groups of working men are examined. The argument, for example, that the greater imperialism of the lower middle classes was manifested in their greater readiness to fight in the Boer War[15] is surely vitiated by the fact that, as in 1914, a huge proportion of working-class volunteers were rejected on grounds of physical unfitness to which others were less subject. There is more plausibility in the contention that working men regarded, or at least articulated, their patriotism in a different way, namely that they perceived a connection between vigorous imperial policies and material well-being. Such links obviously underpinned the popular Conservatism of centres like Woolwich, Newcastle and Sheffield where jobs depended on the fortunes of munitions manufacturers, and also in the dockyard towns of Plymouth, Chatham, Portsmouth and Southampton. However, Empire was hardly without its material advantages for other classes; and it would be rash to assume that the range of attitudes from patriotism to chauvinism was especially concentrated in any level of Victorian society.

In recent years the debate over the popularity of imperialism has been modified by the examination of a wider range of evidence. As a result it has become increasingly clear that ideas associated with Empire were very generally diffused by cultural rather than merely political mechanisms. For example, the growing body of children's literature typified by the *Boy's Own Paper*, the teaching of patriotic history and geography, the popular music hall songs, the Empire Exhibitions and the fiction, biographies and press accounts of British achievements in exotic parts of the world all familiarized the Victorian public with the idea of Empire. Moreover, the rapid growth of commercial advertising helped remind people of the close connection between many items of their diet and British colonial possessions. Many working-class families enjoyed personal links with the colonies to which they had dispatched their sons, and with the Royal Navy in which sons and brothers enlisted. Their feelings were heightened by the growing fear of other European powers and the threat of invasion which was so characteristic of the 1871–1914 period. Empire was clearly far from being a remote or abstract notion in late Victorian times.

However, it is still difficult to assess *how* important popular imperialism was in political terms. Much imperial sentiment seems superficial and thus liable to fluctuate sharply, as the evaporation of enthusiasm in the latter stages of the Boer War suggests. A good deal also depends on how and how far vaguely patriotic sentiment was focused in formal political ways. The great imperial crises and the general elections provided good opportunities, and organizations like the Primrose League maintained a steady stream of imperial propaganda for the Conservative Party.

Dislike of foreigners and defence of British interests formed complementary sides of a currency extensively coined by Conservative propagandists in the late nineteenth century at constituency level; they furnished the unifying theme behind the Irish Question, the aliens issue and the tariff. For example, it was argued that Home Rule would bring 'thousands of ruined and desperate Irishmen over to England to compete in our markets';[16] and much play was made with the common interests of the Irish Party, British Liberals and Britain's enemies. The pattern that had evolved in the Irish case was extended to the attack upon the immigration of aliens, usually described as 'pauper Jews' in the propaganda, who were similarly represented as undercutting wages, overcrowding accommodation and imposing a heavy burden upon the poor law authorities and ratepayers. The free trade in people was frequently blamed for conditions in the sweated industries; rather than advocating the imposition of minimum standards by law that would annoy small employers, Conservatives thrust the responsibility upon the influx of Poles and Russians.[17] That this struck a ready response even in radical working men is evident in Joseph Arch's disgust that Britain lost men through emigration every year while taking in immigrants who were 'the scum of their own countries, three of whom cannot do the work of one honest Englishman'.[18] When finally Balfour passed an Aliens Act in 1905 Conservatives continued to attack the new Home

"THE LIBERALS' PAL."

THE ALIEN EMPLOYER (to British Workman): "You can go now. Mine friend, who has just arrived, will do your work for half your wages."

Protectionist propaganda 1906 from the Conservative pamphlet 'Topical Tips for Typical Tykes'.

Secretary for not implementing it, and re-opening the door to 'the diseased and pauper aliens who are so dear to the Radical party'.[19]

Similar themes are evident in the tariff reform propaganda; material interests were articulated in the same emotive terms, namely the need to stand up for Britain by retaliating against the import of inferior foreign goods produced by cheap labour, which, owing to the spinelessness of the free traders, were depriving British workers of jobs. Protectionism characterized Conservatism locally well before Chamberlain's campaign was launched in 1903; in places like Sheffield where employment seemed threatened by imported German cutlery it became an integral part of the party's appeal and helped Conservatives to win three or four of the five seats throughout 1885–1914.

While these essentially nationalist themes provided the staple attack, more constructive elements were also included. Conservatives were keen to throw back at Gladstone the radical plea that Ireland blocked the way to reform by pointing to the combination of 'firm' government from Dublin with measures of improvement at home. Only a few of these produced tangible benefits, such as the elimination of elementary school fees in 1891, and the Truck Act of 1897 which placed limits on the much resented practice of paying workers in kind rather than in cash. On the whole, however, the Conservative Party stood to gain more by abstaining from too much costly improvement and allowing its rivals to provoke hostility to interference and regulation, particularly in the fields of temperance and education. Even apparently constructive measures like the 1875 Artisans Dwellings Act assisted the Conservatives indirectly; for where energetic municipalities like Liberal-run Birmingham availed themselves of the powers in the Act for slum clearance they fuelled working-class resentment against themselves.[20] Thus, for late Victorian Conservatives the key to their appeal lay in capitalizing upon the unchanging and unifying issues like Empire and the foreigner, while leaving the radicals to suffer the consequences of dashed expectations and disturbing innovation.

Three major conurbations became notable bastions of working-class Conservatism in this period. In Liverpool and west Lancashire generally the party's predominance was inextricably bound up with the working-class Protestant backlash against Irish immigrants as Catholics, aliens and rivals for employment and homes. As early as 1868 Gladstone's burgeoning interest in Ireland contributed to his ejection from a Lancashire seat. As a result the Conservatives enjoyed a popular and organized base in the working class; by the 1890s the Liverpool Workingmen's Conservative Association claimed 6,000 members, and under Archibald Salvidge they held seven or eight of the city's nine constituencies after 1885, the only regular exception being the Scotland division where the Irish comprised a majority. Nor was this sectarian pattern seriously shaken until 1945. Glasgow and western Scotland, also a point of arrival for Irish immigrants, displayed similar tendencies, though with the difference that more here were Protestants from Ulster; even before 1886 the Glasgow Conservatives had successfully brought the Orange Lodges under the party's umbrella where, in combination with the Liberal Unionists, they made a formidable force.

Another region conspicuous for its popular Conservatism was Birmingham and the west Midlands. This was not simply the result of the detachment of Chamberlain and the Liberal Unionists from the Liberals in 1886, for by 1885 Birmingham Conservatives had steadily raised their vote to 42 per cent. The party often ran working men and small tradesmen as municipal candidates and gained strength particularly in the poorer wards antagonized by the rule of the Chamberlainite machine.[21] Tariff reform won popularity among the west Midland metal trades, many of which were organized as small workshops where a close master-and-man relationship was more typical than large-scale production and unionization. After the amalgamation of Conservative and Liberal Unionist forces in 1886 Chamberlainite candidates were virtually unchallenged in every Birmingham constituency until 1929; and the west Midlands as a whole remained relatively resistant even to the Liberal revival of 1906. What is distinctive is the assertive, even populist character of Conservatism in both Birmingham and Lancashire.

By comparison the rural areas were more passive and deferential, as was the East End of London. In fact a formidable catalogue of poor East End constituencies elected Conservatives in the late nineteenth century: N.E. Bethnal Green, Walworth, Rotherhithe, Bow and Bromley, Mile End, Limehouse, Stepney, St George's (Tower Hamlets) and Deptford to take the best examples. Conservative strength here was, however, at least partly a reflection of Liberal and socialist weakness. London was notably irreligious, it was not strong on temperance, its workers were comparatively non-unionized; its population was quickly excited by the great imperial war-and-peace issues; and alien immigration from eastern Europe assumed considerable proportions from the 1880s. The poverty of East End workers was the result of the casual and seasonal nature of their employment, and of the abnormal role of the service industries which fostered an abject dependence upon middle-class patronage. Also much of the population were catered to by a wide range of charitable enterprises. All of this was apt to undermine any spirit of independence and self-help, and to leave the working population comparatively indifferent to politics. The small size of the East End electorate facilitated the survival of the older pattern of politics in which constituencies looked to candidates as providers of employment or as distributors of largesse. This made for a working-class Conservatism of a more passive and less consciously political nature than elsewhere, lacking a strong organizational base, and able to win by default. Thus in London, even more than in other regions, popular Conservatism turned out to be very vulnerable in the Edwardian period when the Liberals posed a vigorous challenge with free trade and social reform which raised the level of participation and swamped the limited Conservative vote.

The Lower Middle Class

In Britain it has been easy to overlook those who fall between the 'working class' and the 'middle class', possibly because they seem to have played a less dramatic role than elsewhere in Europe, or because of an assumption that such groups tend to diminish. No doubt the lower middle class is far from being a cohesive section of society, but for our purposes its members are defined by the very ambiguity of their situation, frequently working class by origin yet precariously clinging to the bottom ranks of the middle classes by occupation and attitudes. They were a key element in Victorian political evolution, and a rapidly expanding, not a declining, group from the 1860s. In occupational terms the lower middle class falls into two categories: first, the essentially pre-industrial group of small entrepreneurs, particularly shopkeepers, many of whom were hardly to be distinguished from the elite of craftsmen such as tailors and printers; second, the administrative, technical and professional occupations whose numbers were greatly augmented in a mature industrial society, notably clerks, civil servants, elementary school teachers, journalists, travelling salesmen, insurance and friendly society collectors, and policemen.

The political significance of what Victorians often called the 'shopocracy' is readily apparent. For not only did its members enjoy the time and independence for local political activity, they also comprised a large proportion of the pre-1867 electorate; even in industrial towns the shopocracy often formed 30–50 per cent of the total, with craftsmen making another 25 per cent.[22] In their ambitions and frustrations lay the seeds of formal political organization in boroughs. Municipal reform in 1835 presented an opportunity to challenge the exclusive control exercised by superior classes of merchants, landowners and lawyers. The basis of the controversy over parliamentary reform in 1866 lay in the Whig belief that, in view of the radicalism displayed by the urban shopocracy, the franchise had been extended as far as was safe, whereas Gladstone's proposal to lower the qualification from £10 to a £7 rental value was tantamount to a complete enfranchisement of small shopkeepers and craftsmen. Contemporary assumptions that they leant to radical Liberalism have been corroborated by evidence from surviving poll books for the mid-Victorian period which suggests that both shopkeepers and artisans supported the Liberals against the Conservatives by up to two-to-one, a markedly higher proportion than that of those immediately above or below them. During the 1870s local caucuses and the National Liberal Federation opened up further avenues of participation for them and for journalists and teachers who were quick to appreciate the moral fervour and individualist tone of Gladstonian Liberalism.

Although franchise reform in 1867 and 1884 rendered the traditional lower middle class less numerically significant, non-manual jobs increased from 2 million to 4 million in Britain between 1881 and 1914. In particular the number of clerks shot up from 100,000 in the 1860s to nearly 700,000 by the First World War; together with commercial travellers, teachers, and central and local civil servants they numbered approximately 920,000. Moreover, since they increasingly resided in distinct suburbs somewhat apart from working-class or solidly middle-class communities, they often became a major element in the single-member constituencies. Conscious of having risen just above the working class and existing frugally on yearly incomes in the £75–£150 range, Victorian clerks were distinguished more by a belief in respectability and social mobility than by higher living standards. Frequently teetotalers, active Nonconformists, and imbued with notions of self-improvement through individual industriousness and thrift, the new lower middle class was often as predisposed to Liberalism as the shopocracy. This is easily overlooked in the assumption that the urban clerk was typical of the sections detached from Liberalism in this period. There is, of course, a strong case for the view that their identification with their social superiors manifested itself in patriotic Conservatism and demonstrative loyalty to King and Empire on the part of those who volunteered to fight in the South African War. No doubt military service in such circumstances added zest and adventure to the lives of ambitious men confined to tedious jobs without prospects, just as it raised their status and self-regard. However, it remains unproven whether the lower middle class were especially prone to imperialism; and if the *Daily Mail* catered to the imperialists among them, the *Daily News* was read by their pacifists and Little Englanders.

Alternatively, lower-middle-class politics may have been determined by the pressures arising from a frustrating and ambiguous social position. Commercial salesmen were particularly vulnerable to economic fluctuations during 1875 and 1896. The supply of clerks and administrators, now beginning to be swollen by female recruits, was so plentiful as to make for stagnant wages and poor promotion prospects. Small shopkeepers, too, felt the competition of co-operatives and the rapidly spreading chain stores. These economic pressures coincided with an apparent loss of political clout as the organized working class claimed a growing share of legislative attention and ensconced their representatives in Parliament. Some occupations – teachers, clerks and railway clerks for example – were driven to form trade unions though they endeavoured at first to be professional associations rather than militant bodies; otherwise unionization was eschewed as a sign of non-middle-class status.

These pressures on income and employment manifested themselves politically in burgeoning complaints about high taxation and, especially, local rates. The activities of local authorities in urban improvement, education and coping with the pressure of poverty resulted in steep increases in rates by the end of the nineteenth century. However, this bore not upon the owners of land who were often very wealthy, but upon the occupiers of property, many of whom were householders or shop-keepers of modest means. Many Liberals and socialists saw the solution in terms of effective taxation of land values, but this was necessarily a long-term objective. The Conservative approach seemed more immediately attractive, namely, more grants-in-aid by national government. Lower-middle-class ratepayers were easily mobilized in opposition to schemes of improvement which required expensive loans. This was a recurring theme and it helps to explain the revival of municipal Conservatism in the Edwardian period.

However, the parliamentary loyalty of constituencies characterized by concentrations of lower-middle-class residents, such as Fulham, Hammersmith, Islington, Peckham, N. West Ham and Lewisham in London, and South Edinburgh, South Manchester and North Bristol is not clear. While these seats showed a shift towards Conservatism typical of the late nineteenth century, they also saw a reversion to the Liberals around 1906 as did most areas. In fact the three provincial seats mentioned above were more often Liberal than Conservative during 1885–1914, and South Edinburgh was never won by a Conserva-tive. In London, where Liberalism was markedly weaker, Fulham, Hammersmith and Lewisham had already become Conservative by 1885; and where, as in Lewisham, the lower middle class was mixed with middle-class residents, the Conservative lead seemed unassailable. However, the early Liberalism of the four Islington seats and N. West Ham re-emerged by 1906, and this casts some doubt on the idea that the lower-middle-class electors were fundamentally alienated by the Liberal abandonment of individualism in favour of collectivist reform. If some propensity for radicalism was retained this may have been due to their

Nonconformity, or may, alternatively, reflect their changing composition through constant recruitment. Literate, politically conscious young men and women rising into non-manual employment were often exponents of radical Liberalism and indeed of socialism, as figures like Ramsay MacDonald and Herbert Morrison, the son of a Lambeth policeman, indicate; already by the end of the century the Labour movement was drawing upon clerks, journalists and teachers for activists and municipal candidates much as Victorian radicalism had previously done.

Part Two
1895–1914

5

The Edwardian Crises

1895–1914

There are men who sit still with the fly-blown phylacteries of obsolete policies bound round their fore-
heads, who do not remember that while they have been
mumbling their incantations to themselves, the world
has been marching and revolving.

Lord Rosebery, Chesterfield speech, 14 December 1901

The Waning of Radicalism

By the mid-1890s radical Liberalism had lost the drive and purpose it
had displayed between 1867 and 1885. No doubt this was partly because
so many radical reforms had been accomplished; but it was also because
some reforms, notably the franchise, had not produced desirable results.
Gladstone's modest victory in 1892 by no means reversed the disaster of
1886; and in 1895 the Liberals won a mere 177 seats against 411 for the
combined Conservatives and Liberal Unionists, a performance that was
only marginally modified in 1900. It began to seem that the mass electorate, subject as it was to crude appeals to chauvinism and ephemeral
emotions, fell well short of the mature, informed body a stable democracy required. As a result many prominent Liberals felt disinclined to
transform the 1884 franchise into one-man-one-vote, not least because
this would now mean opening the pandora's box of women's suffrage.
Both older Liberals like Gladstone and younger ones like H. H. Asquith
often perceived women as the epitome of a mass electorate – politically
ignorant, emotional, vacillating. They took refuge in the argument that
since women were characterized by Anglicanism and were likely to
be enfranchised on a property basis they would inevitably lean to the
Conservatives. Yet they felt embarrassed in this illiberal attitude by the
pleas of the National Union of Women's Suffrage Societies, a rather

Liberal and moderate organization, and by the Women's Liberal Federation which steadily and successfully worked to convert the MPs to suffragism. It was fortunate for the anti-suffragists that the Conservatives also remained too divided to formulate a policy, and were, as a group, even more resolutely hostile to women's suffrage. Thus by the end of the century the great Victorian reform crusade was in danger of petering out amid the manoeuvres to block the women's claim.

Disillusionment became evident too in the new regard for the American system of government on the part of such 'radicals' as James Bryce. Once the model for popular radicalism, America now served to demonstrate the viability of stable, conservative democracy, characterized by devolution of power, legislative inertia at the centre, and a strong second chamber.[1] It was no accident that despite their difficulties with the House of Lords the Liberals were so slow to produce a scheme for reforming the powers and composition of the upper chamber. In the 1860s the anti-Liberal majority there had been 60-70; this widened steadily even before the withdrawals of 1886, so that in the 1893 vote on the second Home Rule Bill the Gladstonians found themselves outnumbered by 419 to 41. Much of the work of the 1892-5 administration was crippled by the peers, more so than in the past. Yet the obvious response, an appeal to the country, required a more popular cry than was provided by any of the rejected measures. Indeed an unreformed House of Lords constituted a useful insurance for voters who felt it safe to vote Liberal as long as Home Rule remained an impossibility. Thus despite much rhetoric from Rosebery, 1895 came and went without either a new issue or a determined plan to reform the chamber. Not until 1908 did the leadership think seriously about reform, and not until the budget of 1909 did the party risk linking a major social question with the constitutional issue. Meanwhile it seemed safer to accept the status quo than to challenge it; yet the consequence was to undermine the credibility of any Liberal social policies in the eyes of the electorate.

The electoral setbacks and inhibitions of post-1886 Liberalism have led some historians to argue that it was congenitally incapable of sustaining the role of a reforming party in a mass electorate. The grounds for such a view rest, first, on the party's inability to organize its following as effectively as its rivals, and secondly, on the individualism and rationalism that inhibited the Liberals from making the demagogic appeal required by an unsophisticated electorate.[2] This case appears convincing if based on the aloof, temperamental, parliamentary figures of Liberal Imperialism or on timid, faltering radicals like John Morley. However, it does tend to overlook the tough partisans such as Harcourt or Labouchere, the adept, manipulating whips such as Herbert Gladstone, J. A. Pease or the Master of Elibank, as well as the more obscure

TABLE 5.1   *Political loyalties of English daily newspapers*

	1868	1886	1900	1910
Liberal	26	66	71	57
Conservative	9	40	40	35
Independent	1	19	35	14
Neutral	8	13	25	15

Source: A. J. Lee, *The Origins of the Popular Press 1855–1914* (1976), p. 287.

organizers like J. Renwick Seager of the Liberal Registration Department. The legendary organizer Francis Schnadhorst remained secretary to the Liberal Central Association until 1893 though evidently well past his peak; and the activities of the Society of Certificated and Associated Liberal Agents indicate no less professional an attitude towards organization than that of their opponents.[3] The difference between the two parties lay not in attitude so much as in resources. By the 1890s far less money fuelled the Liberal machine, but this by no means indicated a revulsion from this aspect of politics. Similarly the party of Lloyd George and 'Limehouse' can hardly be suspected of eschewing a demagogic approach; what is true, however, is that in the period between the defection of Chamberlain and the emergence of Lloyd George the Liberals badly missed their former monopoly in popular platform oratory. The restoration of Liberal supremacy in all the coarser arts of politics by 1903–6 should warn us against portraying them as a special kind of party too encumbered by scruples to succeed. Their manifest weaknesses during the last 20 years of the century should not be mistaken for a congenital distaste or inacapacity for modern politics.

The attrition of Liberal strength may be discerned in the late Victorian press where the earlier predominance slipped somewhat. Many Liberal proprietors and editors no doubt liked to see their brand of political journalism as morally uplifting for the people while the Tories pandered merely to their baser emotions; radical papers were sometimes handicapped by proprietorial distaste for gambling and racing results which were a mainstay of the cheap evening press.[4] But the basic problem lay in the fact that it became increasingly difficult to sell strongly partisan newspapers of any variety by 1900 (see table 5.1). Moreover, the capacity of newer national newspapers to reduce their costs and draw a bigger circulation inevitably reduced the significance of the sober provincial press which had been disproportionately Liberal in sympathy; no major Liberal equivalent of the *Daily Mail* emerged. With its restricted audience and declining profitability the provincial radical paper stood in growing need of subsidies for survival; but at a time when commercial wealth was drifting further towards Conservatism this naturally meant a thinning out of the Liberal press in relation to its rivals. Yet although by the Edwardian period the Liberal advantage had been narrowed by comparison with the 1860s it had not been destroyed by any means.

In another respect the transition from the 1860s to the 1890s involved a more drastic curtailment of the Liberal lead over the Conservatives. When the Liberal Unionists withdrew in 1886 they took with them not only wealthy and influential Whigs in the counties, but, more importantly, middle-class men in the industrial areas who gave Conservatism in the north and Scotland vital infusions of business and Nonconformist, especially Wesleyan, strength.[5] With far fewer subscribers, constituency Liberal associations often had to neglect the costly annual work of maintaining the electoral register, and even to abandon contests; no less than 163 Unionists were returned unopposed in 1900 for example. Although local Liberal poverty was partly redressed after 1900 by infusions from central funds under Herbert Gladstone, the Edwardian party undoubtedly depended heavily for its finance on a small pool of really wealthy, progressive industrialists – Sir William Lever, Sir John Brunner, George Cadbury and Joseph Rowntree in particular.

A further consequence of the withdrawals was to leave the remaining subscribers in the constituencies with a greater influence over candidatures. The caucus system had never been as representative as its proponents had claimed; after 1886 it became increasingly a vehicle for the 'faddist' radicalism of the NLF which blocked the aspirations of working men to parliamentary representation. Usually a local caucus felt obliged to seek a candidate able to make annual contributions and pay his own election expenses; not only would a working man require support from the association, he would also be unable to administer the material assistance either to individual constituents or to the economy of the town itself which was expected of a middle-class politician. Hence it was often felt by working-class as much as by middle-class Liberals that a working man could not carry a radical constituency. The problem is well illustrated by Newcastle Liberalism. John Morley seemed an admirable candidate for this two-member seat in 1885; but as a journalist he had little money to devote to the association, which consequently succumbed to the temptation to adopt as his partner a wealthy but nondescript local businessman in preference to a working man like Arthur Henderson who would have widened the party's electoral appeal. Morley's defiant opposition to the eight-hour day compounded the alienation of organized workers thereby precipitating the loss of one of the Newcastle seats in 1892 and both in 1895.[6]

By contrast the concentration of miners in certain counties and the availability of financial support from the miners' federations facilitated the effective adoption of trade unionists by Liberal associations, especially from 1884 when miners benefited from the extension of the county franchise. In this way such seats could be economically secured for Liberalism; for the Lib–Lab members were much appreciated by Gladstone as sound radicals quite independent of the Chamberlainite caucus. However, though the Lib–Lab experiment was a novel and significant asset, by the 1890s it seemed incapable of extension beyond a handful of constituencies dominated by the miners. Paradoxically the weakness of the strategy lay in the ease with which the miners' leaders were absorbed into the party establishment. Elderly men for the most part, who had sat at the feet of Bright and Gladstone, the Lib–Labs breathed life into traditional Liberal individualism; indeed the aversion of men like Burt for state intervention (outside the mines) made them more rigid Liberals than many of the younger middle-class politicians of the 1890s. Thus, although they symbolized the common interest of working men and radicalism, and contributed positively to labour legislation, the Lib–Labs failed to make a significant programmatic or intellectual contribution to Liberalism; lacking a distinctive impact they were bound to be outflanked eventually by more radical Labour politicians.

These flaws in the infrastructure of radicalism were compounded by the absorption of the leading Liberals with in-fighting and the consequent vacuum in party leadership from 1894 to 1905. The adage that Gladstone became more radical with age has recently gained new support.[7] It is suggested, for example, that he perceived the Irish agitation as an aspect of the wider British working-class movement with which he increasingly sympathized. Certainly he deplored the suppression of workers' discontent in 1886 and 1887; but the Gladstonian defence of trade union liberties was individualist, and he could not embrace their economic demands as class representatives. Nor are there more than indirect indications of Gladstone's tentative sympathy for the radical social policies of graduated income tax and old age pensions. He strongly disapproved of Harcourt's Death Duties budget of 1894 and continued to hold that income tax facilitated extravagance and tended to the social disintegration of the community.

No doubt in the 1860s and early 1870s Gladstone had led Liberalism in a radical direction, but thereafter his energies were devoted more to restraining the forces he had unleashed; his tactics in 1886 obliged him ultimately to compromise with caucus politics to the extent of swallowing such previously unpalatable measures as Welsh disestablishment and land reform. But Gladstone's endorsement of the NLF's Newcastle Programme in 1891 was purely nominal. His reluctance to respond constructively to the social questions of the 1890s marked him as an essentially one-issue statesman who had become a liability to his party; and he found it hard to accept that he had been returned to power in 1892 *in spite of* Home Rule. Now growing deaf and tiring rapidly, Gladstone absented himself increasingly from the Commons and whenever possible avoided meeting his Cabinet, which made his sudden reappearances all the more trying for his colleagues. He took little interest in the development of policy beyond Ireland, and preferred to deal with a few individuals, notably Morley, with whom he felt at ease. But for his negativism and temperamental infirmity Morley might have been groomed as the next leader. Yet, to rest on Morley as Gladstone did was only to advance deeper into the cul-de-sac of mid-Victorian radicalism, not to face the industrial society of the future.

Gladstone's colleagues took his somewhat pitiful retirement over increased expenditure and naval rebuilding in 1894 with relief mingled with apprehension; for they failed entirely to compensate for the inspiration he had long provided for Liberalism. 'Neither Harcourtian iconoclastic crusades nor Roseberian grand panjandrum secretiveness will do any good,'[8] as one Liberal put it. Now the party counted the cost of losing its two outstanding radical statesmen: Sir Charles Dilke, ruined by a divorce scandal in 1885, and Joseph Chamberlain, soon to become Lord Salisbury's Colonial Secretary. No one adequately filled the vacuum. Rosebery, in many ways an attractive successor, rapidly proved congenitally unsuited to be Prime Minister and party leader; impaled upon a small, fractious Commons majority he did no more than inveigh ineffectually against the House of Lords in which he was himself incarcerated. In 1896 Rosebery threw up the leadership to spend the next decade exacerbating party divisions without making a determined attempt to regain his title. During 1896–8 Harcourt and Lord Kimberley shared the leadership in the two Houses; upon the former's retirement in 1899 Sir Henry Campbell-Bannerman attempted to consolidate a party rent by imperial controversies until he was rescued around 1904 by the discovery that he could win a general election. As a leader Harcourt was too narrow and negative, and too unpopular with his colleagues; Campbell-Bannerman and Herbert Gladstone were worthy but uninspiring; Morley and Bryce too detached, irresolute and pessimistic. Among the imperialists, apart from Rosebery, there was only Asquith, cold, remote and absorbed with his legal career; Grey, too dilettante; and Haldane, too much the intellectual and intriguer.

Liberal Imperialism

Absence of constructive leadership greatly exacerbated the discontent of young middle-class Liberals. For Herbert Samuel, Charles Trevelyan, Willoughby Dickinson and others of their generation the 1890s brought a heightened consciousness of the poverty and inhumanity of urban life. As sensitive young men growing to adulthood amid the dismal investigations of Charles Booth and Seebohm Rowntree they felt a certain guilt in the contrast between their own inherited wealth and privilege and the condition of the majority. Imbued with a Victorian sense of duty and public service many of this generation served a form of apprenticeship in social work connected with Toynbee Hall in the East End, or served on municipal councils, school boards and boards of guardians before entering the Commons. They admitted, too, the moral charge of socialism against the existing order of society even if they rejected its analysis and solutions. Moreover, they identified the danger of a mass electorate generating insatiable pressure for penal taxation and the confiscation of wealth, which threatened to reduce politics to a struggle between a party of property and a party of labour. Such a prospect was not to be avoided by Morley's dogmatic resistance or by faddism, but through the adoption of a constructive social policy. This explains why Rosebery was acclaimed and for years regarded as the white hope of younger Liberals; as the first chairman of the London County Council he seemed in tune with progressive politics and urban England.

Indeed Rosebery provided the link that bound up men like Trevelyan, Samuel and Runciman with 'Liberal Imperialism'. The label is a confusing one since the strength of Liberal Imperialism was by no means simply a reflection of imperialist sentiment; though it incorporated a right-wing element, it also included those who, rebelling against faddism, sought a positive social policy. This incoherence renders measurement of the number of Liberal Imperialists difficult. Analysis based strictly upon imperial issues indicates that in the parliamentary Liberal Party the Imperialists comprised one-eighth in 1892 rising to over a third by 1905.[9] This trend reflects the death, retirement and defeat of elderly Gladstonians and their replacement by younger men less committed to party traditions.

The Liberalism of free trade, self-help and non-interference did not drive them to open conflict, though it seemed an inadequate programme. However, the Gladstonian approach to foreign and imperial questions had always been contested, and it was this that crystallized the revolt. Strictly, Liberal Imperialism was a coherent force only at the top where it comprised essentially Rosebery, Asquith, Grey, Haldane, Sir Henry Fowler and R. Munro-Ferguson. They criticized Gladstone for his obsession with Home Rule, which was undesirable in itself and had led him to pander to NLF programmes. 'Mr G.', said Haldane, 'thoroughly demoralised the Liberal Party by the policy of sop-throwing in the two years before 1892.'[10] As a result, they believed, the party had alienated moderate middle-class support and forfeited its claim as the national party; it had degenerated into a rabble of protesters and faddists unlikely to inspire the confidence of the country as a whole.

Shaking off Home Rule and the Irish Party thus seemed essential; for even if the policy was right it remained inexpedient because it could not be forced through the Lords, and presented the Tories with a useful cry. To some extent, however, this split could be obscured by merging the Irish issue into a home-rule-all-round approach and a wider policy of imperial federation for the Empire. They regarded further British expansion as an inevitable consequence of the competition of the great powers, though they do not seem to have argued the economic virtue of this. The Liberal Imperialists shared with Chamberlain and many Conservatives a concern for drawing together the white colonies under an Imperial Parliament at Westminster so as to facilitate a closer defence policy. In the context of imperial federation the devolution of authority to Ireland would be less disturbing, while general devolution would enable Westminster to disperse many of the radical fads to the regions for settlement.

In foreign affairs the Liberal Imperialists desired continuity of policy between the parties. Although their disagreements with the Gladstonians began to manifest themselves during Rosebery's tenure of the Foreign Office in 1892–4, the split reached a climax only in 1899–1902 as a result of the Liberal Imperialists' support for Sir Alfred Milner in his negotiations with President Kruger; they adopted the somewhat naive view that the conflict was about defending the rights of British settlers in the Transvaal, from which it followed that the South African War was just. However, the 'pro-Boers' were so voluble that it seemed they would stamp their view upon the party in an election. To check this an Imperial Liberal Council was set up in April 1900 under Robert Perks MP, from which the frontbenchers stayed aloof lest they be charged with creating a faction. The Council claimed the allegiance of 109 MPs and 142 candidates, a considerable exaggeration. Most MPs adopted the compromise position that while the war had been forced on Britain, the government had been inept in diplomacy and negligent in its military planning. Until 1901 Asquith attempted to keep on the periphery of Liberal Imperialism so as to ease Campbell-Bannerman's task of holding the party together. He was dismayed, therefore, by the latter's celebrated speech in June of that year in which he condemned as 'methods of barbarism' Kitchener's use of concentration camps in South Africa. This seemed ominously to echo Midlothian and was interpreted as an abandonment of the middle ground by Campbell-Bannerman. When in September a Liberal Unionist candidate at the N.E. Lanark by-election was denied the party leader's support and that of other Gladstonians who preferred the ILP contender, they began to fear being squeezed out of the party. Their immediate response was to set up the Liberal Imperial League under Grey. However, only Rosebery could mobilize their strength in the country, and he now took another of his fitful initiatives in a speech at Chesterfield in December which contained a striking appeal for Liberals to adopt a 'clean slate' and free themselves of the 'fly-blown phylacteries' in domestic as much as foreign politics. Campbell-Bannerman responded to this clear challenge simply by inviting Rosebery to define his relationship to the Liberal Party. By establishing a new Liberal League in February 1902 Rosebery virtually admitted that he was outside the fold.

Although divisions seemed to be crystallizing as the South African War approached its end, Liberal Imperialism was in fact about to be submerged in the tide of Gladstonian revivalism. Asquith, Grey and Haldane did achieve high office in 1905, but the group had lost its coherence well before then. Rosebery finally parted company with his colleagues on account of their radical financial policies; but even before 1906 he had shown himself to be a handicap because of his steadfast failure to sustain his initiatives. At heart he had no desire to regain the Liberal leadership, preferring instead to lead a coalition; and for a time it was conceivable that the disintegrating Salisbury government and squabbling opposition would present him with the opportunity. However, the Liberal Imperialists failed to exploit the situation; always inept in the basic political arts they neither organized themselves in the Commons nor built up a grass-roots organization; remote and elitist they absorbed themselves with policy and office more than with in-fighting. Tactically the Liberal Imperialists sought the middle ground when the war was driving opinions to extremes; and their acquiescence in the policy of Milner and Kitchener proved genuinely offensive to Liberals who were not 'pro-Boers'. Nor did they compensate by launching a bold social policy; instead they conveyed only a distaste for programmes in general and Liberal fads in particular. Eventually they were wrecked by the ramifications of the war, particularly Balfour's 1902 Education Act which most Liberals attacked, and the revival of the free trade issue to which all rallied. Asquith in particular reworked his passage to Liberal affections by pursuing Chamberlain around the country. He appreciated that by 1902 the party was thoroughly tired of factionalism and anxious to unite on the causes presented by the Tories. Unity and revivalism swiftly made Liberal Imperialism irrelevant as a discrete force.

'National Efficiency' and Tariff Reform

The Liberal Imperialists were by no means alone in their attitude towards party politics, imperial and social questions. In a sense they simply represented a Liberal expression of the wider movement for 'National Efficiency' around the turn of the century which embraced Fabian socialists like Sidney and Beatrice Webb, as well as collectivist Conservatives like Milner, Chamberlain and, peripherally, Balfour. Though they sprang from every political tradition the enthusiasts for National Efficiency shared certain qualities and convictions. Fundamentally they were reacting to the perceived decline of industry and agriculture during the previous 20 years, and the corresponding enfeeblement of Britain as a world power, a process that appeared to culminate in the disasters of the South African War and subsequent revelations about the degeneracy of the British urban population in the Report of the Inter-Departmental Committee on Physical Deterioration in 1904. Apprehension about British decadence stimulated a variety of remedies including the improvement of secondary education, particularly technical and scientific, to enable Britain to compete with Germany. On the military side the critics fastened upon the crippling role of the Treasury, the lamentable amateurism of army officers and the inadequate training of their men; military training for civilians was commended for both its physical and moral advantages. Also typical of National Efficiency advocates was the bold application of state power in the field of social welfare, for Bismarckian rather than humanitarian reasons: a healthy population was a more efficient workforce and more stable politically.

The other unifying theme lay in the identification of the nineteenth-century system of parliamentary government as the underlying cause of Britain's decline. Critics argued that popular democracy had warped parliamentary politics by rendering it vulnerable to sectional pressures. Governments were run increasingly by amateurs adept at party warfare but incompetent in administration and the development of policy. They were obliged to indulge in sham conflicts on irrelevant issues that turned Parliament into an entertainment for a few partisans. 'Party is an evil,' declared Rosebery, 'its operation blights efficiency.' One striking consequence of this was held to be that too much authority had lapsed to the Treasury, whose narrow retrenchment philosophy killed both military innovation and social reconstruction; it also tended to eliminate the contribution of the expert and businessman to administration. This debilitating process was evident too at local level where specialists like doctors and engineers were losing out to the generalist and bureaucrat. In addition local government was hopelessly fragmented among 133 county, county borough, district and parish councils, 643 poor law boards, and 2,500 school boards. In short there were too many elected authorities with insufficient powers and expertise for coherent, efficient administration. But Balfour's Education Act and the Webbs' proposals for poor law reform in the famous Minority Report of 1909 were very much in accordance with National Efficiency thinking. Ideally it was hoped to bypass the lackadaisical, garrulous 20-member Cabinet by cabinet committees fortified with specialists and the practical wisdom of businessmen as a means of curbing party and Treasury influence. The cult of the expert found typical expression in the Committee of Imperial Defence established by Balfour in 1902 as a vehicle for the evolution of defence policy unimpeded by parliamentary interference.

Despite such notable initiatives along National Efficiency lines Balfour could not as Prime Minister (1902–5) avoid reaping the political whirlwind of the South African War. While attempting to sort out the problems bequeathed by his uncle he was overtaken by the tariff reform wave set off by Joseph Chamberlain in May 1903. His tariff reform campaign was designed in the short run to restore the initiative to a government faltering between the need to reduce high wartime taxation and to raise revenue for social reform. But it sprang from a long-term concern for national decline. During the 1880s and 1890s the remnants of Conservative agricultural protectionism had begun to receive infusions of support from industry, particularly steel and textile manufacturers subject to foreign competition. Whereas in 1860 only 5.5 per cent by value of British imports had been manufactured items, by 1900 this was 25 per cent.[11] Much impressed by what he took to be the effects of a protected domestic market upon Germany and the United States, Chamberlain argued that these powers were now using their system of mass production to dump goods so cheaply on Britain as to undermine our manufacturing sectors; unless checked the process would denude Britain of industry. Yet for Chamberlain the central virtues of a tariff policy was its contribution to imperial economic unification and its potential for the social regeneration of Britain. The first would be attained through preference for colonial goods in the British market and acceptance by them of our manufactured products; it seemed possible to make a start in 1902 by retaining the temporary levy of 2s a bushel on foreign grain but exempting Empire imports. The second object would be achieved through the increase in employment once the home market had been secured, but also through the application of the new source of revenue from tariffs to social welfare schemes. This desire for a constructive social policy reflected Chamberlain's long-standing belief that politicians must come to terms with the working class; yet while very many Conservatives were attracted by the commercial advantages of protectionism only a minority of imperialist–collectivists like L. S. Amery appreciated his wider vision and strategy.

However, this was the first time that the latent Conservative protectionism had been given a lead from the top, and it is no surprise that the bulk of the party fell into Chamberlain's lap after 1903, although ironically he himself was incapacitated by a stroke in 1906.[12] Before the election Balfour had attempted to hold a middle position between the free traders – 83 out of the 392 Conservative MPs[13] – and the protectionists on the basis of a retaliation policy, the idea being to force concessions from protectionist states and thus restore genuine freedom of trade. However tactically shrewd, this failed to satisfy the emotional forces unleashed on both sides of the debate; moreover, the two wings of the party soon became so unequal that any compromise proved irrelevant. For in 1906 the free trade MPs shrank to a handful; a few joined the Liberals, some were denied renomination and others perished in the electoral holocaust; meanwhile the 'Whole Hoggers' came to comprise a majority in the parliamentary party. By 1910 the free trade elements reluctantly accepted that the overriding threat was now the 'socialism' of Lloyd George; and to defeat it they acquiesced in a tariff policy. However, the rallying of the middle classes between 1906 and 1910 failed to compensate for the unpopularity of protectionism with consumers in the country. Thus after failing in the January 1910 election the Conservatives made frenzied efforts to reconcile their major constructive policy with the voters' apparent dislike of dear food. By December Balfour had decided on a pledge that no tariffs would be introduced without popular approval in a referendum, a tactic that probably produced a few gains in Lancashire, but left the party out of office and still badly divided. Indeed, Conservative realization that by staking everything on the tariff they had opened up the House of Lords, the Union with Ireland and the Welsh Church to radical attack led many to judge the whole campaign a mistake. Although Chamberlain had regarded a constructive social policy as integral to his strategy, neither Balfour nor Bonar Law, his successor in 1911, felt inclined or able to develop this. Instead they allowed themselves to be impaled upon a narrowly protectionist case closely linked in the public mind with the peers' revolt against Liberal taxation and welfare proposals. This misjudgement lay at the heart of the Conservative dilemma throughout the Edwardian period.

The Crisis of Conservatism

The origins of the notion that a crisis of dire proportions erupted
in Edwardian England lay in events during and after the First World
War. An apparent concatenation of more or less violent challenges to
authority before 1914 does convey an impression of a violent spasm in
which the consensus on which the social and political system rested
was disintegrating; it is tempting to see Edwardian governments rescued
from this prospect by the outbreak of war, which, however, only interrupted the collapse of the economic, social and political pillars of the
Victorian world. In order to substantiate such a thesis it would be
necessary to demonstrate, first, that the manifestations of violence were
in nature and in effect anti-parliamentary; and second, that they were all
symptoms of a common underlying malaise not just a series of coinci-
dental events. This has never, in fact, been done. Moreover, the thesis
has suffered from a prevailing assumption, the understandable result
of hindsight, that the Edwardian crisis was a crisis of Liberalism. Yet,
as one writer has wisely observed, it would be quite as appropriate to
discuss the period in terms of the crisis of Conservatism.[14]

The foundations of the Conservative dilemma were electoral, in the
sense that the party proved unable to dislodge from power the Liberal–
Labour–Irish alliance; and programmatic, in that the split over tariffs
simultaneously restored the unity and morale of the Liberals. It was
a misfortune for the Conservatives that their attempt to convert the
country to protectionism in 1910 coincided with a distinct economic
revival. No doubt this was a 'last innings' for traditional British staples
like coal and cotton: shipbuilding would have been in grave trouble
but for naval rebuilding programmes; and productivity continued to
languish. But the buoyancy of the Edwardian economy undoubtedly
took the steam out of protection and, incidentally, robbed it of its appeal
to labour.

Much the most ominous aspect of the crisis was Ireland. In particular
the appearance of private armies of Ulstermen and Nationalists and the
inability of the government after the so-called Curragh Mutiny of 1914
to use the army to enforce its policy in Ireland presented a severe challenge to an elected administration, especially in view of Conservative
connivance with the Ulster rebels. Yet there is a danger of swallowing
Unionist propaganda of the time. When the party disposed of Balfour in
1911 after his third election defeat, it took in Bonar Law a leader whose
strength was of a brittle kind. Not only did he lack the patronage of the
premiership, he enjoyed a status inferior to at least five colleagues in
terms of both governmental experience and social standing.[15] Merely a

compromise between Walter Long and Austen Chamberlain, Law had little hold on his party at first except as a vigorous debater on tariffs and Ulster. 'I shall have to show myself very vicious, Mr Asquith, this session: I hope you will understand', he told the Prime Minister privately in 1912.[16] His tough 'new style' was appreciated by the party as a welcome contrast to Balfour's elegant but ineffectual philosophizing. They rallied to him, but only because he was doing what they wanted. Pandering to the extremists had led his predecessor to disaster, and, given his failure to dislodge the Liberals from their Home Rule policy, it was likely to achieve the same for Law. By 1914 he and Sir Edward Carson were anxious chiefly to find a way out of the Irish problem without shattering the confidence of their followers.

Bonar Law's defeat was implicit in the Asquith government's persistence. It could not renege on Home Rule without destroying the hold of the Nationalist Party in Ireland upon whom it depended for its Commons majority. As Asquith put it, 'An ungovernable Ireland is a much more serious prospect than rioting in four counties.'[17] To some extent both party leaders had to consider the question through English eyes, in that both were playing to win the next general election. The Cabinet believed that by offering Lloyd George's ingenious compromise of a six-year exclusion for Ulster from the Dublin Parliament they had shown themselves reasonable to the English voters, who were antagonized by irresponsible Unionist interference with the army, and who viewed with relief the conclusion of the Irish Question at last. Hence they refrained from prosecuting Law, Carson and Captain James Craig since this would only be to rescue them from their dilemma. This impression is corroborated by the Unionists' own realization by 1913–14 that their attempt to stir the English constituencies over Home Rule was falling flat.[18] The Liberals were not to be caught out on a novel and perplexing policy as in 1886; they had long since lost what support they would ever lose on Home Rule.

Whether Bonar Law would have been rescued by a civil war can only be guessed at. However, one can look for connections between the Ulster controversy and the suffragette agitation or the industrial unrest. Comparison with the Women's Social and Political Union (founded in 1903 by Emmeline and Christabel Pankhurst) is illuminating, for while the authorities unhesitatingly used the law against the latter they treated the Ulstermen far more circumspectly. This reflected the inability of the women to mobilize mass support; by 1914 the Pankhurst militants represented no more than a shrinking rump of the women's movement increasingly isolated from potential adherents among working women and alienated from middle-class sympathizers.[19] Certainly the Pankhursts' antagonism to Labour and industrial action during 1911–14 runs against the idea of a general or connected revolt. The women's violence amounted to sporadic assaults upon property by a handful of activists designed to win publicity, which obscured the fundamentally conservative nature of the WSPU and the movement generally.

As for the wave of strikes, their basic causes lay in the price rises and stagnation of money wages after 1900. When to this was added the 1906 Trades Disputes Act which overthrew the Taff Vale judgement, and the increase in employment during 1910–14, it is clear that the major restraints on strike action had been removed. Much has been made of syndicalism as an underlying force at this time. While it is true that certain initiatives towards industrial unions and co-operation between unions, such as the Triple Alliance of coal, railway and transport workers, were consistent with a syndicalist strategy, the actual motives were of much more limited significance. Industrial unionism remained exceptional, and co-ordination of strikes was calculated to minimize the damage to the unions themselves; their objects in bringing pressure to bear was invariably to secure from employers recognition and a regular system of collective bargaining, not to undermine the parliamentary system in favour of industrial democracy. If the authorities had adopted a strategy of unmitigated coercion towards labour unrest and had declined to appease workers' demands, it is possible that the strikes could have developed into revolution. But neither government nor union leaders intended to allow this to happen. Although there were several explosive points, notably the shooting of two miners at Tonypandy in 1910 and the arrest of Jim Larkin during the Dublin transport workers' strike in 1913, these were exceptional. Frequently the unions found allies in ministers like Lloyd George and civil servants like Sir George Askwith of the Board of Trade whose object was to induce employers to engage in collective bargaining. In addition the Trades Disputes Act (1906), the Trade Boards Act (1909) and the Miners Minimum Wage Act (1912) demonstrated how Parliament could be used to further the aims of organized labour. The most striking endorsement of the labour movement's parliamentary strategy came in 1914 when all but three of the 63 unions that balloted on the question of a political fund associated with the Labour Party supported the proposal; this was hardly the action of men alienated from the parliamentary process. The leaders remained keen to take what the system offered in representation and legislation, in terms of employment under the Labour Exchanges scheme, and as approved societies under the 1911 National Insurance Act. This tendency to become integrated into the system rather than to undermine it was typical of the pragmatic approach of British trade unionism, which showed no sign of diminishing before 1914. The handful of syndicalists undoubtedly won a certain prominence in 1911–14 when the average union member was moved by the recent decline in real wages; but they in no sense led or directed the working-class movement, and enjoyed a fleeting eminence only while the special circumstances of 1911–14 lasted.

Thus, with the exception of Ulster the Edwardian agitations cannot be represented as effectively anti-parliamentary in nature; nor did they comprise a single or interconnected phenomenon, apart from a little rhetorical and stylistic imitation of the Ulster Unionists by the WSPU and some unions. Each remained a discrete movement. It is significant that the new light thrown on this period by oral evidence has tended further to undermine the apocalyptic view by showing how little sense of crisis the ordinary, obscure person had.[20] This underlines the point that the concept of catastrophe was essentially an upper-middle-class one, and even then, characteristic of the political 'outs' after 1906. Their exaggerated apprehensions about the arrival of independent working men in the Commons representing their class, and the general assertiveness of labour, were compounded by the demagogy of Lloyd George. Not since Chamberlain had attacked those 'who toil not, neither do they spin' in 1885 had they heard the upper class pilloried from on high. 'They are forcing a revolution and they will get it,' declared Lloyd George at Newcastle in 1909, 'the Lords may decree a revolution, but the people will direct it.'[21] However, it was not a revolution but graduated taxation and a modest redistribution of income that he intended; by preaching against the peerage he sought not to foment class conflict but to harmonize the potentially conflicting working class and middle class, for therein lay electoral salvation. Nor are there sound grounds for the old view that the people were in fact bored and disillusioned by the constitutional conflict of 1910. This is to miss the wider social dimension behind the constitutional argument; it also overlooks the actual evidence for turnout among voters: 86 per cent in January and 81 per cent in December 1910. Such figures have rarely been exceeded before or since; moreover, it is particularly striking that the second election of the year should have produced such a response, for a reduction of 4 per cent was the unavoidable result of the staleness of the register by December. The elections of 1910 can hardly be seen as other than notable indications of popular involvement in the parliamentary process. Though Bonar Law might claim that there were things stronger than parliamentary majorities, the experience of the Edwardian years belies such alien sentiments. Unlike the opposition who stumbled from one problem to the next, the government confronted each obstacle and ultimately imposed their strategy by the strength of representative democracy. They played the parliamentary game with indications of conviction because within the rules it was a game they invariably won.

6
Edwardian Progressivism

> British Liberalism is not going to repeat the errors
> of Continental Liberalism. . . . Let Liberalism proceed
> with its glorious work of building up the temple of
> liberty in this country, but let it also bear in mind that
> the worshippers at the shrine have to live.
>
> David Lloyd George, Swansea, 1 October 1908

Origins of the New Liberalism

The history of Victorian Liberalism has often been written as though it
is to be equated with *laissez-faire*. Clearly much of its drive derived from
an industrial middle class bent upon levelling the privileges of the aristocracy and eliminating restrictions upon individual enterprise. Yet
'economic liberalism' was always distinct from party Liberalism, whose
primary achievement was political democracy in Britain. In practice the
period from the 1830s to the 1880s was one of continuous experiment
with state intervention in the economic and social affairs of individuals
whose actions were restrained in the interests of the community; in the
process the Victorians laid the foundations for the huge central bureaucracy of the twentieth century. Particularly at the municipal level, where
Liberalism was often the party of expenditure and interference not
of retrenchment and abstention,[1] the notion gained ground that certain economic functions, ranging from water and gas to parks and li-
braries, were better performed by the community than by the private
entrepreneur.

Moreover the Liberalism of the Victorians was as subject as most
creeds to reinterpretation by its adherents; and the 1880s and 1890s
constitute an especially important phase of this kind. Reinterpretation
for politicians did not, however, imply any repudiation of essentials.

The primary concern of Liberalism continued to be liberty defined by the law. Confidence in the virtues of the free play of individual energies and talents was qualified by knowledge of the consequences and also by an appreciation that the terms of competition must not be too unequal; where they were, the state might legitimately adjust them even though infringing the rights of some individuals in the process. In the last 20 years of the century the elements of interventionism waxed steadily stronger, and not only in Liberalism. Why was this so? Undoubtedly the perceived difficulties of the British economy, now facing severe international competition and shrinking profits, eroded the attractions of industrial growth as a panacea for society's ills. Whereas in, say, 1851, it seemed likely that another generation of economic expansion would absorb unemployment and poverty, by the 1880s few could be so confident. Far from being eliminated, poverty, as the investigations of Charles Booth and Seebohm Rowntree suggested,[2] had remained at a depressingly high level. The consequences of advanced industrialism were minutely observed in London where society seemed to fragment into social classes by residence. Aware of the strains on their society, adherents of Liberalism tended to reaffirm their basic object of maximizing liberty as a means to individual moral improvement; some like Herbert Spencer sought to achieve this by advocating a reduced role for the state; others like T. H. Green, the Oxford philosopher, urged a greater and more positive use of interventionism. What is important historically is that by the 1900s it was those who thought along Green's lines who had come to typify active political Liberalism in Britain.

By the turn of the century an impressive body of academics and publicists were reinterpreting the Liberalism with which they had grown up. Green himself was no more than a representative, not the most advanced, of new Liberal thinking in the 1880s: while accepting the capitalist system as broadly consistent with social good, he justified state legislation in carefully limited areas to maintain the conditions for individual initiative. D. G. Ritchie, the collectivist radical, took a more emphatic view of the state as a positive agent of improvement. L. T. Hobhouse, the sociologist and journalist, argued that freedom was devoid of meaning to the victim of uncontrolled free enterprise, and urged collective action for mutual advantage. J. A. Hobson, perhaps the best-known propagandist for the 'New Liberalism', urged that the state should maintain a minimum standard of life for all its citizens and operate certain economic functions for the community as a whole. Hobson was most conscious of the link between social and political changes; the idea that 'politics had anything to do with industry or standards of living' was, he noted, somewhat novel. In his view, Victorian politicians had endeavoured to keep social questions out of politics by agitating alternative issues; but by 1900 the broad divide in politics corresponded increasingly with the social divide, with possession and property on the Conservative side.

However, thinkers are not usually politicians, and in Britain especially there is great scepticism about the connection between the realm of ideas and actual historical events. Yet links there were, if only in the shape of the 31 Balliol College men who sat in the Parliament of 1906, four in the Cabinet. Take the apparently unpromising example of H. H. Asquith whose ministerial career spanned the Gladstonian and the Edwardian phases. Tutored by Green at Oxford, Asquith was a typical politician in being rather uninterested in abstract ideas and not apparently afflicted by a social conscience. Yet he acquired an enduring scepticism about the traditional party platitudes and was unencumbered by ideological inhibitions such as *laissez-faire*; it was he who, as Chancellor of the Exchequer 1906–8, initiated the financial and social radicalism that antagonized traditional Liberals. However, the 'New Liberals' were usually more intellectually curious than Asquith. A typical example is Herbert Samuel who combined writing on Liberalism, investigation into social conditions and active party politics. Like William Beveridge and R. H. Tawney he had been at Oxford at a time when young undergraduates were urged to go out and discover why so much poverty existed in British society, and did so. Characteristically the first stop was work in London's East End, often at Toynbee Hall, before moving on to wider political activity. For those who chose to operate through the party system the intellectual basis of their action was twofold. First, it showed the continuity of Liberal thought, a matter of some importance to men like Samuel and Hobhouse, anxious not to repudiate their traditions. Second, it demonstrated the existence of a real alternative, both theoretically and practically, to 'socialism' to which many young middle-class men would otherwise have been driven. As it was they enjoyed a fruitful relationship with the Fabians, particularly Graham Wallas, the Webbs and Ramsay MacDonald. Indeed, much of what in twentieth-century Britain is termed 'socialism' is no more than the 'New Liberalism' of 1900.

The starting point for the 'New Liberals' of this period was a belief that, in the past, liberty, while a proper concern of Liberals, had been too narrowly defined in terms of legal, political and religious liberties; yet it was now apparent that for most men the chief restraint upon their liberty was economic or social in nature. Thus the individual's material welfare should be of equal concern to the state as his moral condition. In this way the New Liberalism came, for many, to imply drastic social reform. In the words of J. M. Robertson MP, 'Laissez-faire is not done with as a principle of rational limitation of state interference, but it is

THE PATIENT ASS.

From Punch, 18 April 1896.

quite done with as a pretext for leaving uncured deadly social evils which admit of curative treatment by state action.'[3]

However, New Liberals looked beyond the symptoms of distress to the underlying distribution of wealth. Did a redistribution of resources threaten the traditional Liberal commitment to private property? The reformers were clear that while the state ought not to infringe what rightly belonged to individuals, what did not rightly belong was a different matter. Wealth was so often the result not of individual enterprise but of community development that society could properly differentiate between earned and unearned income, and tax the latter more heavily for the benefit of the community at large. The death duties introduced by Sir William Harcourt in 1894 were a harbinger of this theme in radical policy which increasingly divided the Liberals from Conservatives. The best target for taxing the 'unearned increment' was, of course, land. For as a result of the expansion of towns and the needs of local authorities, the price of urban land increased spectacularly in the nineteenth century. To radicals, land was a monopoly of the privileged class which they had historically sought to 'free'. To levy a toll upon its increment, therefore, could provide resources for the state while leaving private ownership intact and stopping short of confiscation. In this way land reform provided both a practical expression for popular radicalism and a valuable bridge between Cobdenite traditions and New Liberalism.

New Liberalism also challenged the notion that taxation was inherently or necessarily an evil, and argued that the budget might become a positive instrument of social policy. This view was to be translated into practice by Asquith and Lloyd George as Chancellors in the period 1906-14, though Harcourt had pointed the way. Their policies offended orthodox economic wisdom which held that the uneven distribution of income in the community was both necessary and beneficial since its concentration in the hands of a few meant it would be channelled into future production; the effect of diverting it to the masses whose expenditure was held to be essentially non-productive would be detrimental to business activity. Now death duties were defended on the grounds that they tapped resources not normally available for investment. However, Liberals, notably J. A. Hobson, began to dispute the conventional financial assumptions fundamentally. Hobson claimed that the uneven distribution of income actually hindered the economy because it deprived the mass of the population of the capacity to consume goods while diverting the surplus into the hands of those who merely generated more goods for which there was an insufficient market. In short, the real weakness – underconsumption by the masses – could be remedied by a reallocation of purchasing power through taxation and social welfare; rising demand would stimulate economic growth. Underconsumptionist arguments enabled the New Liberals to justify their emphasis on social reform as a means of reducing the waste and inefficiency in society, for such expenditure need not be regarded as a cost or burden upon the productive economy. Thus the Edwardian governments were fortified by an assumption that one might helpfully raise the level of expenditure according to the condition of the economy and employment. It is not entirely accidental that in the 1920s Liberals were more inclined than their rivals to espouse Keynesianism.

Yet the New Liberals had to face the political implications of their ideas. Did not a programme of sweeping social reform and graduated taxation amount to a class policy at variance with the party's traditions? Some like Hobhouse frankly urged that the improvement in the conditions of the working class was now so overriding a priority that no party that claimed to represent national and not sectional interests could ignore it. Samuel argued that since any expenditure that raised the material condition of the poor was in the interests of the wealthy the latter should bear their share of the cost. This notion of a fair contribution from those best able to pay became a standard defence much favoured by Lloyd George during the controversy over his 'People's Budget' in 1909–10. By this stage the New Liberal orthodoxy held that the state must accept a wide responsibility for the welfare of the people financed by limited redistributive taxation; it broke with the traditional fondness for retrenchment and individual property rights; and it offended against the Gladstonian belief that taxation should not be a means of marking out different social classes or types of wealth. Even in Gladstone's time these principles had been infringed in special cases such as Irish land reform; and retrenchment had been gradually abandoned out of expediency. However, the New Liberals, fortified both by principle and by necessity, pushed financial and social policy unapologetically into its twentieth-century mould. Thereby they increasingly distinguished the Liberal Party from the Conservatives, who still favoured indirect taxation, objected to graduated taxation on principle, and preferred to restrict government expenditure to basic administrative functions.

Between the 1880s and the First World War the New Liberalism gradually came to occupy the mainstream of Liberal politics. The critical decade was the 1890s when the 'New Liberal' title began to be applied to various groups and individuals such as the Rainbow Circle whose members included Samuel, Hobson, Charles Trevelyan, J. M. Robertson and Percy Alden. They were absorbed both with social policy and with a political strategy of co-operation between middle- and working-class radicalism, such as that pioneered by the Progressives on the London County Council. By the turn of the century Hobson, Samuel, Robertson, Hobhouse and Charles Masterman, all prolific writers, had generated a coherent revision of their creed and a programmatic refurbishment for the party (see Guide to Further Reading). In 1896 the Rainbow Circle produced its own *Progressive Review*, but it enjoyed much wider support from radical editors such as C. P. Scott (*Manchester Guardian*), W. H. Massingham (*Daily Chronicle*), J. A. Spender (*Westminster Gazette*), and most importantly A. G. Gardiner of the *Daily News*, the cheap radical paper widely read by provincial activists which consistently promoted an alliance of Liberal and Labour forces.

Tension inevitably existed between the New Liberals and orthodox stalwarts among backbench MPs, local party chairmen, and municipal politicians who formed the warp and woof of the local party fabric. Impatient with existing organizations like the NLF 'merely reiterating its approval of the Newcastle Programme', New Liberals sought more direct approaches to power. Fortunately for them the electoral defeats of the 1890s and the withdrawal of some wealthy patrons left a vacuum for younger radicals: 1886 had prepared the ground; and by the 1900s those employers and other wealthy men who remained in the Liberal camp had generally accepted the need to come to terms with Labour.[4] Indeed among the keenest advocates of old age pensions, graduated taxation and state intervention were industrial magnates like William Lever and Sir John Brunner (the leading manufacturers of soap and chemicals respectively), who along with the Cadbury and Rowntree families continued to finance the party up to 1914. Industrialists like James Joicey, the north-east coal-owner, found radicalism excessive and quit the party; adherents of strict *laissez-faire* like Richard Holt, the Liverpool ship-owner, remained MPs until 1918 but had dwindled in numbers and influence. After 1900 the older generation of social radicals – Sir Charles Dilke, Francis Channing, Sydney Buxton – were joined by younger men in Parliament. In London where the field was wide open Charles Masterman, Christopher Addison, T. J. Macnamara and Percy Alden gained seats; here as elsewhere Herbert Gladstone played a vital role as chief whip (1899–1905) in placing radical candidates in winnable seats and often assisting them financially. In the north a similar role was filled by Charles Trevelyan, himself elected in 1899, who helped to place Samuel, Robertson and Runciman in radical industrial constituencies. The steady transformation of the personnel of Liberalism grew into a flood in 1906, for of the 401 Liberals then returned to the Commons, 205 had never sat in the House before.

This change was somewhat obscured by the aftermath of the South African War; none of the Liberal Party's leaders acted as midwife to the

New Liberalism as Lloyd George, Asquith and Churchill did after 1906. Indeed the war divided radicals like Hobson and C. P. Scott who condemned British policy, from men like Trevelyan and Samuel. After 1902 Liberal rhetoric was diverted towards such tempting targets as education, 'Chinese Slavery' and free trade, and propaganda took the negative line of reversing Toryism. This inevitable attempt to exploit the government's difficulties culminated in the revivalist campaign of 1906. However, this obscures the underlying trend. Examination of the 1906 campaign material shows the general commitment of candidates to old age pensions, graduated taxation, poor law and land reform, which was soon reflected in backbench impatience for legislation after the election. The governments of Campbell-Bannerman and Asquith turned out to be more radical than the campaign rhetoric had suggested. Retrenchment had been a useful stick with which to beat the Conservatives but it was rapidly abandoned by the incoming administration. Asquith's 1907 budget proved to be a key point in the overthrow of financial orthodoxy. He asserted the principle of income differentiation by retaining the rate of tax on earned income at $9d$ while raising that on unearned to $1s$ in the pound; he made compulsory personal declarations of every class of one's income; he forced the Treasury to accept the idea of a super-tax, and insisted that social reform obliged governments to plan for rising expenditure several years ahead. The widespread support for his non-contributory pensions scheme and the measures for the feeding and medical inspection of schoolchildren is some indication of changed attitudes in Britain; the individual was no longer seen as wholly responsible for his family's welfare; nor, significantly, was there any question of disfranchising the recipients of the new benefits as the recipients of poor relief were. In short the strength of the Liberals' position was that although they were reformers they were not dangerously in advance of opinion in the country. Similarly Lloyd George's 1911 National Insurance Act reflected Victorian self-help traditions in incorporating the contributory principle and by involving existing friendly societies and insurance companies in the scheme. His celebrated budget of 1909 embodied elements of redistribution in the shape of the £10 income tax allowance for children under 16, the super-tax on incomes above £5,000, the additional $2d$ on unearned income, the extra rates for death duties and the modest levies on land values; although the purchase tax increases on tobacco and spirits did bear upon poorer families. Of the £17 million deficit that Lloyd George intended to make up by these means £8 million arose from pensions, only £3 million for Dreadnought building, and the rest from a fall in revenue as a result of reductions in trade. The emerging strategy for dealing with an economy subject to serious unemployment involved three items: the Labour Exchanges of

1909; the attempt to replace the income workers lost through ill-health, unemployment or old age; and thirdly the Development Commission. In the 1909 budget the Chancellor set aside £200,000, with a promise of any surplus accruing to the Exchequer, for use by the Commission on experimental farming, forestry, rural transport and land reclamation. This reflected the thinking of radical industrialists in favour of state investment in those sectors of the economy that private enterprise failed to finance. Because fairly full employment returned from 1910 little use was made of the Development Commission, but it signified governmental intention to regulate expenditure as and when the state of the labour market made it desirable.

By the time of the campaigns on the 'People's Budget' in 1909–10 Lloyd George had reduced the New Liberalism to a tangible, popular form. He based his case squarely on a free enterprise economy under free trade. In this system, he contended, Liberalism represented the interests of those who created wealth, that is employers and workers, who were in conflict with a parasitic landowning class and their political agents. He often delighted to point to the wealth of the Liberal candidates on whose platforms he spoke, noting how much extra they would pay in taxation. What distinguished such men from their opponents, he claimed, was their willingness to shoulder a fair share of the cost of national defence and social reform, thereby proving the sincerity of their concern for the people's welfare, and also demonstrating that the Liberal Party was not bent upon the confiscation of wealth. Thus Liberalism served the vital function of unifying the social classes who worked for a living by seeing fair play between them in the national interest. The Liberal Party was the most efficacious vehicle for the working classes because it harnessed to their cause large sections of the middle class who would be frightened into reaction by a party based solely on labour. Here lay the political and intellectual rationale for the New Liberalism.

The Politics of the Pact 1903–1914

Though never an outstanding politician either as orator or administrator Herbert Gladstone became a pivotal figure particularly in the decade after he became chief whip in 1899. As heir to his father's 'Little England' views he greatly appreciated the rapprochement of Labour and Liberal forces as a result of the South African crisis. To Gladstone it was axiomatic that nothing of significance divided Liberals like himself from the mainstream working-class politicians: all parties, he believed, tended to develop a left, centre and right: the emergence of organized labour was thus essentially a natural expression of radical Liberalism whose inclusion under the Liberal Party's umbrella was both logical and necessary if progressive Liberalism was to be strengthened against the imperialist right now so much in evidence. To this end the Campbell-Bannerman–Morley–Gladstone leadership had declined to support an official Liberal candidate of imperialist views at the Mid-Lanark by-election of 1901 in favour of Bob Smillie the Independent Labour Party nominee. When another seat fell vacant at Dewsbury in 1902 they attempted, unsuccessfully, to secure the nomination of a working man, Sam Woods. In calling in the workers to redress the balance of middle-class Liberalism the party leaders clearly risked alienating their own local activists; however, without a large measure of common sentiment between Liberal and Labour forces in the country Gladstone's initiative in 1903 in seeking terms with Ramsay MacDonald, Secretary of the Labour Representation Committee, would not have been practicable at all. This appeared to be the lesson of three by-elections at this time. When the safe Liberal seat at Clitheroe fell vacant in 1902 it was filled unopposed by David Shackleton, a trade unionist of essentially Liberal convictions standing for the LRC, because of the approval of local Liberals. Similarly Liberals abstained at Woolwich, where they were weak, on behalf of Will Crooks (LRC) who gained the seat from the Conservatives. But it was the Barnard Castle by-election in 1903 following the death of Sir Joseph Pease that caused the greatest stir, for in a three-cornered contest the seat went to Arthur Henderson (LRC) by 47 votes. Although a Liberal defeat, the election's significance lay in demonstrating the vitality of Liberal–Labour sentiment among working-class voters. For Henderson won because he enjoyed the tacit support of the Liberal leaders; because as Pease's former agent he was well known locally as a *Liberal*; and because the local Liberal association blundered by nominating a tariff reformer at a time when free trade sentiment had been sharply aroused. Henderson, sound on free trade, was thus the best Liberal available. For Gladstone this underlined the dividends to be won by Liberal–LRC co-operation. For the elections did not indicate that the LRC was about to sweep the country in its own right. The Labour leaders appreciated this, though socialist activists often did not; at Norwich in 1904, for example, an ILP candidate obtained only 13 per cent while the Liberals gained the seat. This rubbed in the point that if socialists were unlikely to succeed as socialists, Labour candidates of Liberal views would flourish.

For MacDonald this was by no means an unwelcome reading of events. His own inclinations and record as a candidate led him to seek accommodation with the Liberals, but to do so from a position of strength. However, in 1900 the newly launched LRC had been too weak.

Only 376,000 union members had been affiliated (at only 10s per thousand) by 1901 although delegates representing 546,000 had voted for the creation of the LRC, and TUC membership was over three times this figure. However, the notorious Taff Vale judgement of 1901 which made the Society of Railway Servants, and therefore any union, liable for the financial losses arising from strikes, transformed the situation by stimulating union leaders to extend their political influence. By 1903, 861,000 had been affiliated, the fees had been raised, and a fund established to pay a £200 salary to MPs elected under LRC auspices thereby enabling the National Executive Committee to exert a degree of control for the first time.

As a result of these developments MacDonald found himself able to impose his strategy upon a labour movement now anxious to obtain rapid representation in Parliament, while at the same time he had something to offer Gladstone – not only votes, but the LRC's financial resources (this latter was important for hitherto a labour alliance had always appeared a financial liability to the Liberals). Thus by 1903 MacDonald and Gladstone had identified a common interest in victory over a crumbling Conservative government and the danger of jeopardizing it by splitting the Progressive vote. Later, when under attack from his own party, MacDonald tried to minimize his role in the pact by arguing that no formal bargain had been struck. But this was only because neither could guarantee to withdraw candidates in specific constituencies and both feared that a public announcement would provoke criticism. Gladstone's private papers show that there was nothing spontaneous about the pact; MacDonald made great exertions to kill Labour candidatures in Liberal seats not covered by the pact,[5] and, though he could not control the socialist societies he often emasculated their efforts by denying them the LRC ticket. For Gladstone it was relatively easy to secure a clear run for the LRC in derelict seats in Liverpool, Lancashire or Birmingham, and not difficult to share candidatures in double-member constituencies such as Preston, Bolton, Leicester, Derby and Newcastle, particularly as this was frequently marginal or Conservative territory. As a result 31 of the 50 LRC candidates in 1906 were unopposed by Liberals.

In retrospect the pact appeared an unnecessary mistake for the Liberals in that 24 of the 29 LRC MPs won by virtue of Liberal withdrawals, while the Liberals' own 401-seat landslide would not have been materially smaller in the absence of co-operation. However, in 1903 this had not been obvious. Labour had saved Gladstone a lot of money and tied the Conservatives down in all constituencies. Moreover, since the Labour members were for the most part 'sober, earnest Liberals' they reinforced the progressive drift of Liberal politics

admirably. The significance of this strategy is underlined by the availability of an alternative during 1903–5. For Chamberlain's tariff
campaign and the consequent hounding of free trade Conservatives from
their constituencies after 1903 presented the Liberals with a golden
opportunity to reverse the losses of 1886 by clawing back the centre
ground. They largely succeeded in doing this among the electorate, at
least temporarily, as their victories in southern and middle-class seats
show. Yet how much of the personnel and programme of the rebel
Conservatives should be absorbed? Those Conservatives who expected
free trade and retrenchment to provide an adequate bridge between
them and the Liberal Party were mistaken, as Trevelyan reminded
Winston Churchill:

> The Liberal Party is not a free trade party. It is only satisfied with
> Free Trade as an economic base to work from.... The whole
> raison d'etre of present day Liberalism is constructive reform....
> What I want to know is how much common ground can you find
> with reforming Liberals on economic and social questions? ...
> the reform forces in the party are vastly stronger than ten years
> ago and I am certain will never check themselves for the sake of a
> few Tory votes.[6]

As a result Liberal–Conservative co-operation in 1906 was limited to a
few exceptional cases; 12 crossed the floor before the election, including
Churchill and J. E. B. Seeley who won election in Manchester and
Liverpool respectively; others like Arthur Elliott (Durham City) and
Richard Cavendish (North Lonsdale) enjoyed a free run from the
Liberals. But the pact with Labour pre-empted any general arrange-
ment; Lancashire, the centre of free trade Conservatism, was already the
scene of the most widespread application of the Gladstonian strategy.

Faced with the bleak prospect of an overwhelmingly radical House
of Commons the tactics of the 157-strong Conservative opposition
were initially rewarding. By employing their majority in the Lords to
reject or emasculate legislation of concern to Liberal pressure groups
especially on education, licensing and land, they shrewdly maximized
discontent within the government's ranks. For while traditional radicals
became exasperated at the failure of their huge majority to overawe the
peers during 1906–8, the social radicals resented the time wasted on
bills that were clearly doomed. This feeling was exacerbated by unmistakable evidence that the peers were studiously accepting measures like
the Trades Disputes Bill and the feeding of schoolchildren for fear of
antagonizing the workers. So long as the government ploughed the
issues that left the country as a whole unmoved it deprived itself of the

option of a successful dissolution and exposed itself to attack from backbenchers and Labour for neglecting social questions; the loss of two by-elections to Labour at Jarrow and Colne Valley in 1907 appeared to underline the point. Thus so long as the Conservatives applied their destructive tactics judiciously they could oblige the Cabinet to soldier on while indirectly encouraging Labour to loosen its ties; by redividing the radical forces the opposition could reasonably expect to return to power at an election around 1911–12.

Unhappily for the Conservatives they had not thought out their tactics quite so rationally, nor did they apply them so precisely. So much emotion, fear and pride underlay their politics that they failed to resist the provocation offered by Lloyd George in 1909. There are now no real grounds for thinking that the Chancellor deliberately prepared his budget with a view to its rejection by the peers. His object was rather to use the budget as a Trojan Horse that would gain legislative entry for such items as land and licensing reform rebuffed in ordinary bills.[7] Yet when he perceived in the rising antagonism of the Tory Party the possibility of a first-class constitutional–social controversy he grasped it quickly. His budget in fact raised two matters of longer-term significance. The first was not the land taxes themselves but the consequent provision to undertake a valuation of all the land in the country, a necessary preparation for an effective radical policy for the land. To avert this more distant threat many peers felt obliged to reject the immediate proposals, modest as they were. Secondly, the increase in revenue demonstrated that social reforms could be paid for without abandoning free trade, and thereby knocked away a central prop of the tariff reform argument. Hence the particular prominence of protectionist Conservatives in the move to reject the budget. However, no one could be sure how far the Liberals would capitalize politically on the financial breakthrough, nor how soon. For the present their proposals were not self-evidently revolutionary in character; extra taxation could be justified by the need to pay for pensions, which the opposition dared not oppose because they were too popular, and the Dreadnought programme for which they had loudly clamoured. In throwing out the budget, therefore, they placed themselves in a dilemma exacerbated by the weight of constitutional precedent that heavily favoured the government. Had they stuck to their original tactics and left the budget alone, the Liberals would have borne the unpopularity for higher taxes, which fell upon all sections to some extent, without any immediate compensation. Instead, by assailing the innovations with great passion they invested them with a revolutionary significance, thereby burnishing brightly the progressive credentials of the government in the eyes of labour – the key to continued power. They enabled the Liberals to claim, with some plausibility, that their opponents were a lot of rich men trying to evade their taxes, and were intending to renege on old age pensions now that they realized the cost, a point which, significantly, Conservative candidates tried to refute at length during the 1910 general elections.

The opposition did derive some immediate gain from the constitutional crisis in that they obliged the Liberals to go to the country twice during 1910 and, in the process, removed the overall Liberal majority of 1906. However, the circumstances of the elections so greatly reinforced the 1903 pact as to keep the Conservatives more firmly out of office. Many a northern town that had not seen the landed aristocrat of radical demonology for years was now treated to the spectacle of elderly peers gracing the platforms of Conservative candidates; even Lord Curzon let slip the typically arrogant aphorism that 'all civilisations are the work of aristocracies', a remark that was endlessly repeated by gleeful radicals. The effect of all this on Labour was of crucial importance. It could not but welcome the government's initiatives as a step in the right direction; if the peers condemned the budget as red socialism MacDonald had no desire to dispute it. The Labour leaders' only doubts, justifiable ones, were whether the Cabinet would shirk the ultimate task of curbing the powers of the Lords permanently. Driven both by sentiment and by tactical necessity, therefore, Labour threw its efforts more strongly behind the Liberals, even to the extent of reducing its candidates from 78 to 56 between the January and December elections. Thus the triumph of Lloyd George's tactics in 1910 was a dual one; he dictated the terms of the debate by forcing the Conservatives into wild negativism and Labour into loyal acquiescence.

The Chancellor's achievement was not simply a short-term rhetorical coup, however. The New Liberalism had not begun with the budget of 1909, nor did it end with it; for the Cabinet could not cease to deliver social reform for fear of disappointing expectations aroused in the country. This undoubtedly made for certain difficulties in the short run. For example the 1911 National Insurance Act seemed to threaten so many vested interests[8] that the opposition exploited their fears effectively in the by-elections of 1911–12. By 1913, however, when the insurance benefits began to be paid out, the credit redounded to Lloyd George. Indeed, for all their vehemence in public some Conservative leaders had seen from the start that national insurance would only consolidate the Liberals' reputation, and by 1913 the most they could do was to promise to improve, not to repeal it. In order to counter the negative siege mentality that fell over the Conservative Party in the reaction from protectionism, prominent Conservatives like F. E. Smith established the Unionist Social Reform Committee in 1912. Yet it proved difficult to shift the party from its obsession with Ireland in these years. Perhaps there was truth in Bonar Law's characteristic comment that if the country wanted social reform it would not vote the Conservatives back into office. This prospect was enhanced because every stand the Conservatives took tended to compound their alienation from the bulk of the working-class vote which was what kept the Liberals in power. It is easily forgotten that even the Ulster question, on which the Labour Party remained as consistently nationalist as the government, helped to reinforce the electoral pact when it showed signs of breaking down. Hence the futility of a Conservative strategy that united their opponents instead of dividing them.

Despite this it is sometimes assumed that the New Liberalism was bound to destroy the Liberal Party by alienating the middle classes, or alternatively, that fear of a middle-class reaction would bring reform to a halt thereby losing the working-class vote. The electoral evidence bearing on this will be considered in chapter 7. Here it must be noted that the idea of a termination of social radicalism in terms of policy and programme around 1911 is largely theoretical; it is scarcely borne out by the empirical evidence. The budget of 1914 projected a record national expenditure of over £200 million; Lloyd George continued pushing out from the bridgeheads already established. Income tax relief for children was doubled; he introduced a graduated tax rising to 1s 4d in the pound on earned income over £2,500; super-tax now became payable at £3,000 instead of £5,000, and at steeper rates rising to a maximum of 2s 8d; and the scales for death duties were also increased to a maximum of 20 per cent on estates over £1 million. Also in 1914 a further instalment of radical social measures were introduced, including government grants for local maternity and child welfare clinics, £4 million in loans for local authority house-building, compulsory school meals, and proposals for minimum wages in agriculture.

These unmistakable signs of the government's intention to stick to its new course are all the more impressive in view of the criticism they continued to provoke in some quarters. Throughout 1906–14 there was evidence of middle-class protest against higher taxes and especially rates, which helps to explain Conservative municipal successes on the basis of ratepayers' revolts. Some industrialists also articulated their misgivings at the trend in policy; Alfred Pease, for example, explained his refusal to appear on a Liberal platform in Cleveland by his dislike of the

> disposition to multiply laws and restrictions. . . . The idea that the State can take from one class and give to other classes and take the place of individual enterprise is a very corrupting one.[9]

There was also a discernible feeling that too much legislation bestowed special advantages on labour. In 1908, for example, there had been pressure from colliery-owners and shipowners, reflected in Cabinet by Runciman, against minimum wages for miners as tantamount to 'truckling for miners' votes'.[10] However, the Liberal Party had already parted company with the Yorkshire coal-owners without, it transpired, impairing its grip on the Yorkshire constituencies. So long as sums of £5,000 and £10,000 at a time were donated by Lever and Rowntree the party did not need to fear the loss of the remaining Gladstonian businessmen.

However, the criticism made it all the more important not to neglect issues of traditional concern to Liberals: hence the time devoted to Welsh disestablishment, Home Rule and the franchise in 1911–14, in a shrewd attempt to balance the novel and the traditional elements in the programme. By 1912 the Cabinet was also well aware of the desirability of relieving the burdens of the lower ranks of the middle classes especially by sparing local rates from some of the cost of education, roads and the poor law.[11] This was one of the considerations that drove radicals and Lloyd George 'back to the land' in the last years of peace.

The Land Campaign, launched in October 1913, has often been misunderstood as an anachronism. Yet seen in all its ramifications it amounted to a drastic extension of social radicalism. Lloyd George capitalized on the widespread agreement that the previous 30 years had seen a disastrous weakening of British agriculture with serious social, economic and strategic consequences. His Rural Land Enquiry showed, as did official statistics, that 60 per cent of agricultural labourers earned only 18s or less per week, and that despite a reduction in the labour force housing conditions remained appalling since few landowners were now willing to invest in new cottages. Not only was it difficult for the opposition to deny the underlying case for action, but in addition land was an ideal means of arousing the enthusiasm of Liberals of all shades. Further, research into the distribution of wealth in Britain has undermined the old assumption that after the industrial revolution the chief source of great wealth was industrial in character; as late as 1900 the large fortunes in Britain were still to a remarkable degree concentrated in land, urban landholdings, and commerce.[12] In taking land as a target, therefore, the radicals were by no means mistaken. Finally, they expected to derive a considerable short-term electoral advantage in the shape of extra votes from labourers and farmers in many rural seats in the west and north narrowly held by Conservatives. This potential was underlined by the by-election successes scored in 1912 and 1913 by candidates who concentrated on land reform to the exclusion of all else (E. G. Hemmerde at N.W. Norfolk and R. L. Outhwaite in the urban seat of Hanley).

While Lloyd George publicized the campaign, much of the detailed preparation was undertaken by Runciman at the Board of Agriculture. Realizing that labourers tolerated low wages through fear of losing their cottages, Runciman planned for the construction of 90,000 houses by the state, each with up to one acre of ground to give the labourer a measure of independence. This was to be undertaken by a new Ministry of Lands and Forests which would also enjoy compulsory purchase powers to acquire undercultivated and waste land, thereby bypassing the county councils which had proved useless for the purpose. It was to appoint commissioners to fix the price of land and wages boards to fix fair minimum wages in each locality; farmers faced with higher wages would be able to appeal to tribunals for revision of their rent.[13] The government had already adopted such methods to regulate wages in the sweated industries under the Trade Boards Act and for the miners; the extension of the idea of establishing a 'minimum standard' restored the initiative in social policy to Lloyd George. Invited to join his Land Campaign, MacDonald and Keir Hardie admitted privately that land was the economic bedrock of reform, but feared a complete loss of their political independence.[14]

By the end of 1913 an equally important urban dimension had emerged partly due to the vociferousness of land taxers in Parliament, who wanted Lloyd George to offer precise policies for the towns. They urged in particular a national tax on land values so as to enable the government to relieve local rates; and also the rating of site values by municipalities instead of the levying of rates on the value of buildings and improvements. Lloyd George was evidently keen to respond to the pressure for relief of small property-owning ratepayers and small businessmen. He could claim with some justification that state-financed social policies had the effect of reducing the pressure of the poor on local rates; from 1911, for example, paupers were made eligible for old age pensions. During the winter of 1913 he committed himself to a measure of site value rating and promised the Town Tenants League compensation for small businesses faced with exorbitant demands by landlords for renewal of their leases. However, radical policies could not be implemented quickly – land valuation would not be completed until 1916. By 1914, therefore, Lloyd George had agreed to offer additional rate support from national taxation.

In short the Liberals embodied in the Land Campaign moves to shore up their exposed middle-class flank and simultaneously strengthen their standing with a number of working men. The expediency of this strategy is borne out by the Conservative reaction to it. After 1910 Austen

Chamberlain had warned his colleagues that unless they could offer alternative policies on land they would not win back the urban support they had lost. Tactically the Party Chairman, Arthur Steel-Maitland and the Chief Whip, Lord Edmund Talbot, believed it wise to avoid provoking controversy and thereby giving Lloyd George more credit over land reform. Indeed, Leslie Scott MP, of the Unionist Social Reform Committee, offered Conservative co-operation over his legislation if only he would not 'Limehouse' the landlords again.[15] But with the opposition at a disadvantage the Chancellor pressed on with the campaign, and there are few grounds for thinking that the New Liberalism had been checked on the eve of war in 1914.

Edwardian Labourism

With hindsight the evolution of the Labour Party is easily depicted in terms of a deterioration in ideological purity as the socialist inspiration of Keir Hardie gave way to the pragmatic leadership of Ramsay MacDonald. However, studies of both men and of the Labour movement generally have entirely revised such a picture. MacDonald was remarkably consistent in his views and objectives, while Hardie differed from him in style and temperament rather than in ideology or programme. The careers of both were characterized by a history of radical Liberalism and a practical grasp of electoral collaboration combined with persistent advocacy, vehement in Hardie's case, of independent political action by working men. As with most Edwardian Labour politicians the mainspring of their action lay in the social condition of working people, but the form taken by it was moulded by the ideas and institutions prevalent in the 1880s, notably the chapel, the trade union and the municipal council. A survey of the reading of the 29 Labour and 24 Lib–Lab MPs elected in 1906 revealed that hardly any had drawn their ideas from explicitly socialist sources; only two mentioned any knowledge of Marx, and only two had read the *Fabian Essays* of 1889. Much more widely read were Henry George (author of *Progress and Poverty*, 1879, a bible for land reformers), John Stuart Mill and John Ruskin along with the Bible, Dickens, Scott, Bunyan and Tennyson. Keir Hardie, while by no means unaware of Marxism, made no serious study of it; he found attractive the notion of the historic struggle of the working class and the prospective degeneration of capitalism prior to a co-operative, classless society; but he had no patience with the idea of a revolutionary overthrow of capitalism or of the growing immiseration of the workers. For him the object of political action in the British context was to take advantage of the available means for improving the lot of working people. This meant enacting social reform; adopting allies outside the Labour movement; and (what was most distinctive) increasing the direct representation of the working class by working men – in short 'Labourism'.

The economic ideas of Edwardian Labour were an amalgam of three main strands. First, they shared many of the Victorian assumptions about the economy, particularly the necessity for wage levels to be regulated according to the price commanded by the products of labour in the market. They shared enthusiastically the Liberal loyalty to free trade. This is a striking indication of the basic orientation of the movement, for while cheap bread had obvious attractions, free trade had not been an obviously desirable policy to the Chartists; nor would it have been a natural policy for a party seriously contemplating socialism. Indeed the Edwardian tariff reformers and right-wing apostles of National Efficiency were a good deal closer to advocating an economy operating on socialist lines than most Labour politicians. In addition the Labour Party espoused the radicals' predilection for graduated taxation and using the unearned increment of land to finance social reform. Henry George's *Progress and Poverty* seems to have stimulated Hardie as much as it did the young Lloyd George. 'Land Nationalization' was also used loosely as shorthand for compulsory purchase powers for local authorities; in 1892 Hardie referred to 'nationalizing the land by taxing land values' much as a radical Liberal would have done. Finally Labour politicians adopted a range of trade union demands for employers' liability and workmen's compensation for accidents, a shorter working day to spread the available employment, amendment of the Truck Act, and recognition of unions by employers. There was nothing here that looked out of place in the manifestos of Liberals in the 1890s.

Before the First World War the Labour Party never accepted state ownership and operation of industry as a general principle, and even limited forms of control like tariffs were automatically ruled out. Neither MacDonald nor Hardie had more than the haziest notion of the administrative implications of nationalization, or of the bureaucracy necessary for a comprehensive system of welfare services. Indeed the only grounds that some writers have found for justifying the description of Hardie as a 'socialist' is his advocacy of the nationalization of coal mines. Yet the significance of this was quite limited. He believed simply that state control would facilitate the achievement of union objectives, the eight-hour day and minimum wages, which he had found from experience in the Ayrshire coalfield difficult to win. In short, coal nationalization was not part of an analysis of how industry should be run, but a special case. Consequently while the Edwardian Labour Party undoubtedly had coherent ideas about economic affairs they were hardly *distinctive*; and any description of Labour as socialist must be modified by the fact that its 'socialism' had no basis in economics. At this time it meant essentially humanitarianism and fraternity, a generous-spirited belief in co-operative action for and by the disadvantaged which owed its inspiration to Christianity as much as to politics. The same tendency led Labour towards a pacific, anti-imperial, Gladstonian approach to international affairs. The South African War threw Labour and the radicals together in common outrage; hence J. Bruce Glasier of the ILP could say of John Morley, of all people, that he 'stood for much that [was] essential to a socialist state and international peace'.[16] In denouncing Kitchener's 'methods of barbarism' in 1901 Campbell-Bannerman rekindled the torch of Gladstonianism, and this was taken up by MacDonald in 1914 who stood thereafter as the heir to a common tradition.

While Hardie was not a systematic thinker, MacDonald gave Labour a more coherent, historical framework, and, perhaps confusingly, the language of socialism. Not only did he have no time for the class struggle; he never conceived of Labour as merely a working-class party. Not for nothing had he been secretary to a Liberal MP and an active member of the Rainbow Circle in the 1890s (as well as a member of the SDF in 1885, the Fabian Society from 1886, and the ILP from 1894). For him all that was wrong with the Liberal Party was that it had served its historic function and might obstruct the coming of the New Liberalism or socialism. Initially the ILP and later the LRC were seen by him as successors to the Liberal Party which would eventually take the form of a more effective alliance of middle-class and working-class radicalism. If there was a difference between him and Hobson or Hobhouse it was that he was trying to recruit the middle class and they the working class. Though MacDonald spoke of socialism it was not for him a policy but a vision that would evolve gradually rather than spring from the ruins of the present system. Society's progress in that direction was perceptible in small steps; when Balfour's government adopted the Unemployed Workmen's Bill in 1905, for example, this was worth having because it drove politicians closer to admitting an obligation to provide work or maintenance for every worker, and thus made Labour's own Right To Work Bill seem much less utopian after 1906. Despite his talk of socialism, MacDonald's own economic observations were apt to comprise a castigation of the dead weight of landownership and rent upon industry rather than an economic critique of capitalism. However, it has rightly been urged that the virtue of presenting socialism as an evolutionary growth from existing society lay in giving Labour its own objective which, if vague, did not frighten those who had to be won over; MacDonald's strength was a capacity to convey to radicals a reassuring sense of continuity and parliamentarianism and to Labour a comforting belief in ultimate, inevitable triumph.

Although MacDonald's approach clearly owed a great deal to his early Fabianism, it is significant that the Labour Party never availed itself of a Fabian programme before 1914. As a forcing house for investigation and ideas the Fabians inspired the respect of both Liberal and Labour politicians, but their claims to direct influence have been regarded as exaggerated by historians. The Fabian Society and the Labour Party were kept apart partly by the sheer elitism of the former, anxious not to waste time trying to build a new party based on what it saw as intellectually destitute trade unions. As a result, from the late 1880s much of the Fabian effort had been diverted into municipal affairs especially in London under the umbrella of the Progressives. The Fabian approach showed little of the humanity of the typical working-class politician but more of the hard-headedness of the National Efficiency school. Fabians believed that labour exchanges would facilitate the identification of shirkers; they criticized health insurance because it was wasteful to subsidize the sick; they welcomed the 1902 Education Act, which was generally condemned by Labour leaders; most of them supported the South African War and lacked sympathy with Home Rule and even with women's suffrage. They thus remained for long a middle-class pressure group largely isolated from the sentimental radicalism inherent in the working-class movement. However, this relationship began to change during the last two years of peace. Faced with the refusal of Lloyd George and Churchill to be guided by Fabian remedies as laid down in the Minority Report of the Royal Commission on the Poor Law and impressed also with the potential strength of the labour movement as demonstrated in the strikes of this period, Sidney and Beatrice Webb recognized that Labour could serve both as a vehicle and as a power base; the fruits of this were garnered during the war and afterwards.

Thus, what seems indisputable and central in the emergence of Labour as a separate party is not ideology so much as a struggle by politically conscious working men to achieve direct representation in Parliament. Consequently the MPs followed a course barely distinguishable from the Lib–Labs in the Commons before 1914 in that they threw their weight behind the Liberal causes and made a distinctive contribution only on strictly trade union issues. Hardie, despite the vehemence with which he sometimes attacked the Liberals, departed from the Lib–Lab approach only in seeking more seats for working men and in declining to take the Liberal whip. For most of the LRC MPs returned in 1906 the pact was perfectly consistent with long-held attitudes; they regarded the LRC as no more than a continuation of earlier efforts to elect working men so as to modify the law relating to them; few expected or wanted to transform the LRC's role as a separate pressure group into that of a governing party.

However, events conspired to eliminate the distinction between the Lib–Lab and the LRC contingents to the advantage of the latter. In the early 1900s the leading working-class politicians, John Burns, Ben Pickard, Thomas Burt, Richard Bell and Charles Fenwick, were Lib–Lab in sympathy but all elderly figures who had reached or passed their peak. Burns, the impassioned strike leader and SDF militant of the 1880s, had graduated by way of Progressivism on the London County Council and a parliamentary seat at Battersea from 1892 to an honoured position in the Liberal Party and cabinet rank in 1905. It is significant that when invited by Hardie to lead the LRC in 1903 Burns found it unattractive. Indeed before 1906 only two of the LRC MPs, Hardie and Crooks, stuck strictly to the independent line; Henderson, Bell and Shackleton became more or less identified with Liberalism. In 1903 there had been some danger that Lib–Lab forces would persuade the LRC conference to allow the affiliation of bodies like the National Democratic League, which would have stifled the independence of the LRC and kept it as a Liberal pressure group. However, attempts of this kind only provoked support for the ILP proposal for an extra levy on the unions to finance new candidatures. Yet in 1906 the Lib–Labs still numbered 24 in the Commons; but Burns, the symbol of the Liberal/working class alliance, spent his declining years complacently enthroned as President of the Local Government Board, an object of attack by Hardie for his reluctance to initiate remedial measures for unemployment. Meanwhile changes in leadership and militancy led the Miners Federation to seek affiliation to the Labour Party in 1908, a step that virtually ended Lib–Labbery as a separate body. In so far as the miners were incorporated into the Labour Party they tended to undermine still further its political coherence and minimize its distinctiveness from Liberalism.

Although specific aims and policies had been avoided in 1900 at the foundation of the LRC, nonetheless the typical Labour candidate of the 1900s offered the electorate a battery of proposals including the eight-hour day, reversal of the Taff Vale decision, employers' liability, old age pensions, poor law reform, the feeding of necessitous school-children, taxation of land values, free trade, Home Rule, nationaliza-tion of mine royalties, mines and railways, payment of MPs, curtailment of the powers of the House of Lords, and universal suffrage. There was virtually nothing in this that was not acceptable to the New Liberals, or to Gladstonians for that matter. Nor was this merely a tactic to win Liberal votes. The annual conference in 1906, for example, apart from reaffirming many of the items already listed, pledged itself to the Local Veto, condemned the Education Act of 1902, and welcomed the entente with France provided it was not used against Germany. It is only fair to note that at least one delegate protested at 'tinkering with the out-worn pledges of the Liberal Party'. Occasionally, as in 1908, a resolution calling for the socialization of industry slipped through without debate, apparently because it was not taken seriously enough to warrant the time, and served to encourage the socialists.

In the Commons, MacDonald demonstrated a clear idea of the appropriate tactics. 'Governments are not afraid of socialist speeches,' he observed, 'they are very much afraid of successful criticism in detail.'[17] This approach enabled Shackleton and MacDonald to play a useful role especially during 1906–8. The government proved quick to adopt Labour bills on trades disputes and the feeding of schoolchildren, and compromised on the Workmen's Compensation Bill. For Campbell-Bannerman, Labour thus helped the government in the direction in which it was already going. But it is not the case that the pensions scheme was the result of by-election losses to Labour in 1907, for their introduction had been carefully planned well beforehand by Asquith. What is true is that when Labour members voted for motions critical of the Cabinet on such matters as pensions they usually did so in company with larger numbers of Liberal backbenchers, all impatient to drive the Cabinet in the same direction. Unemployment provided the best issue on which Labour could distance itself from the Liberals by means of its Right to Work Bill and Hardie's dramatic interventions at Burns's expense. However, by 1908 the initiative was passing to the Liberals; after 1909 there were only occasional revolts by a handful of Labour members over the Insurance Bill and women's suffrage. Once the Liberals had lost their overall majority in 1910 Labour became nearly as reliable in the division lobbies as the Liberals: moreover, after the 1909 Osborne Judgement (which checked the rights of trade unions to use their funds for political purposes) Labour felt the need of cabinet help in changing the law. Eventually this concession was granted in 1913, and in 1911 Labour obtained payment of members.

Co-operation between the parliamentary party and the government naturally produced fierce criticism in the movement notably from Victor Grayson who had been elected as an Independent Socialist in 1907 and declined the Labour whip; there flourished a mutual antagonism between Grayson and the other Labour MPs who felt relieved at his defeat in 1910. A more persistent critic, the dockers' leader Ben Tillett, waged campaigns to make the parliamentary party responsive to conference, and published a famous pamphlet *Is the Parliamentary Party a Failure?* in 1908. Yet the leadership of MacDonald, Hardie, Snowden and

Henderson – 'softly feline in their purrings to Ministers', as Tillett put it – always carried the conference with them; from 1909 when he became chairman of the parliamentary party, MacDonald went a long way to establishing himself as leader in a traditional sense, and to confirming the right of MPs to make party policy.

The Workers and State Welfare

The evidence of so much common ground between Edwardian Liberals and Labour has led to the abandonment of the old assumption that a working-class party was bound to outflank its rival. However, some questions have rightly been raised about the new orthodoxy especially from the perspective of working-class reactions to policy innovations. For example, even if social reforms were welcome it is possible that workers placed a *higher* priority on such issues as wage rates and un-employment. Are we justified in assuming that reforms were generally poular in view of the suspicion with which they were often regarded in the Victorian period? Clearly this is a large subject still under analysis, but several general comments can be made. First, reactions do seem to have varied according to the type of reform; the unmistakable enthusi-asm for pensions did not extend to the medical inspection of school-children or to the Children Act which allowed children to be taken into care. Second, some innovations which were initially greeted with scepticism won acceptance in time. Unemployment insurance is a case in point. Another example is the labour exchange scheme. Workers were reassured that they were under no obligation to accept jobs at below union rates of pay or jobs that involved strike breaking, and by 1914 three times as many men were being placed in employment as in 1909. Third, the importance placed upon government intervention almost certainly varied within the working class. Lower-paid men, for example, were more likely to value health insurance because they often had no adequate existing scheme of self-help. Similarly unskilled men, and of course many women workers, had a greater interest in state inter-vention to fix minimum wages since they lacked the bargaining power to defend themselves; in chain-making, for example, the effect of the government's Trade Boards Act was to raise wages by approximately 50 per cent by 1913. It seems clear from the Land Campaign that Lloyd George was alive to the implications of all this.

7

The Electoral Struggle
1906–1914

Nothing has hampered our movement in the country
more than this false idea of independence, that only
Labour or Socialist votes should be given to Labour or
Socialist candidates. It is humbug.

J. Ramsay MacDonald, *Labour and Electoral Reform*, 1914

The traditional view that Edwardian politics was characterized by a
Liberal Party too ideologically rigid and rooted in middle-class radicalism to avoid being outflanked by a socialist party or to survive the
emergence of a working-class electorate has proved to be virtually
untenable. Yet the evidence that has destroyed the old view has also
generated an alternative interpretation whose strengths and weaknesses
will be considered in this chapter. Based upon the concept of 'Progressivism' this view entails a number of related propositions about the
nature of political change in the early twentieth century. It argues that
the increasingly national orientation of politics facilitated the regeneration of Liberalism in terms of both programme and personnel by 1914,
so that Liberal politics was directed by a set of professional politicians
and intellectuals propagating a synthesis of Liberalism and socialism
known as Progressivism, which restored its intellectual vitality and
popular appeal. The emergence of the Labour Party was less a sign of a
more radical type of politics than a reinforcement of Progressive Liberalism. This is borne out by the electoral revival based not on the
traditionalist reaction in favour of free trade and Nonconformity, but on
the social and economic issues characteristic of twentieth-century politics. A shift had taken place in the emphasis of political debate reflecting
a move away from the community and religious group basis of voting of
the nineteenth century towards the class-based voting of the twentieth
century, a change that had occurred substantially before the First World

War rather than after it. Thus the party divide began to coincide with fundamental social cleavages for the first time. These last two points are worth immediate clarification. The 1906 Liberal landslide was plainly increased by infusions of voters influenced by tariffs, education and other aspects of traditional politics; however, these fell away by 1910 as is demonstrated by the loss of Liberal gains in the southern residential and county constituencies. Yet the withdrawal of this middle-class support still left the Liberals in power because of their retention of the working-class vote, especially in the northern and industrial areas including Lancashire and London where Conservatives had formerly been very strong. Indeed in 1910 the Liberals were still gaining working-class seats not won in 1906. Thus the 'Progressive' interpretation amounts to much more than the view that Liberalism survived the Edwardian elections; it suggests that it adapted to the chief trends of twentieth-century politics, flourishing on the basis of its social–economic appeal to the working class. The implication is that there was nothing inevitable in the rise of Edwardian Labour as a governing party.

The Containment of Labour

If the general election of 1906 had stood in isolation as the last Liberal victory before 1914 it might be regarded as a freak; it would still be a formidable task to explain why a party capable of winning 400 seats was in fatal decline, but the suspicion would be there. However, the two elections of 1910, while far less spectacular victories, provided corroboration that 1906 was part of a longer-term change. Seen in perspective, 1910 was a more significant victory than that of 1892, for example, because the Liberal–Labour forces won a higher share of the poll, because they derived this more from the working-class seats, and because it was accomplished against the background of four years of Liberal government, whereas in 1892 they had enjoyed the advantage of having a Conservative government to attack (see table 7.1).

What was the relative position of Labour and Liberalism in the Edwardian period? Although the evidence is restricted by the very fact of their electoral co-operation, it is abundant enough to indicate relative strengths and a trend: 24 of the 29 Labour victories in 1906 were achieved in the absence of Liberal opposition under the pact; and the boost to Labour fortunes carried over into 1907 when the party gained seats at Jarrow and Colne Valley at Liberal expense. The year 1908, however, proved to be the turning-point, for the introduction of pensions in that year followed by Lloyd George's budget in 1909 restored

TABLE 7.1   *General elections 1892–1910*

	Conservative		Liberal		Labour		Irish Nationalist	
	% vote	No. of seats won	% vote	No. of seats won	% vote	No. of seats won	% vote	No. of seats won
1892	47.0	314	45.1	272	0.3	3	7.0	81
1895	49.1	411	45.7	177	1.0	0	4.0	82
1900	51.5	402	44.6	184	1.8	2	2.5	82
1906	43.6	157	49.0	401	5.9	29	0.6	83
1910 (Jan.)	46.9	273	43.2	275	7.7	40	1.0	82
1910 (Dec.)	46.3	272	43.8	272	7.2	42	2.5	84

the initiative to the government. Thereafter Labour experienced losses down to 1914. This is obscured by the affiliation of the Miners Federation to the Labour Party in 1909 as a result of which most of the Lib–Labs transferred to Labour giving the party a nominal total of 45 MPs; eight losses and three gains in January 1910 left 40 members. Common sentiment, stimulated by the challenge of the peers, made the two radical parties anxious to avoid splitting the Progressive vote in 1910; leading Labour figures like MacDonald, Hardie and Thomas had been elected in two-member seats with Liberal MPs and on the strength of Liberal votes, an arrangement they had no wish to terminate. As a result, despite an expansion of local organization between 1906 and 1910 the pact substantially held in that 78 Labour candidates stood in January, and only 56 in December, against 51 in 1906.

Moreover, among the voters the pact appeared to work even more effectively than in 1906; Labour candidates adopted all the Liberal issues and arguments, while the Liberal organization helped turn in the vote for them. Particularly impressive evidence for the effectiveness of the pact is provided by the cohesion of the Progressive vote in two-member constituencies such as Leicester. A negligible number of voters plumped for a single candidates only, the vast majority preferring to 'split' their two votes between Liberal and Labour and to ignore the Conservative (see table 7.2).

Thus within the confines of the pact Labour did well; outside it the party seemed to have a tenuous hold. In the 35 three-cornered contests in the two elections of 1910, its candidates came third in 29 cases, second in 6 and first in none. Attempts to break out of the pact against

TABLE 7.2   *Leicester: general election December 1910*

Result	Crawshay-Williams (Liberal)	13,238	elected
	MacDonald (Labour)	12,998	elected
	Wilshere (Conservative)	7,547	
Plumpers	Crawshay-Williams	728	
	MacDonald	574	
	Wilshere	7,245	
Splits	Crawshay-Williams/MacDonald	12,316	
	Crawshay-Williams/Wilshere	194	
	MacDonald/Wilshere	108	

TABLE 7.3   *Gateshead parliamentary elections*

1906		1910 January		1910 December	
Liberal–Labour*	9,651	Liberal	6,800	Liberal	8,763
Conservative	5,126	Conservative	6,323	Conservative	5,608
		Labour*	3,572		
	4,525		477		3,155

* The same candidate in 1906 and 1910.

Liberals met with failure except in two special cases (West Fife and Gower) where Conservatives withdrew in Labour's favour. In addition the Liberals displayed an alarming capacity to win back seats lost in by-elections (Colne Valley and Jarrow) and to recover seats like Gateshead 'lost' as a result of the miners' affiliation to the Labour Party (see table 7.3). The strictly independent Labour vote was, as yet, rarely sufficient to elect MPs who necessarily depended heavily upon tactical support from Liberals.

Although 1910 appears to undermine decisively any idea of an irresistible advance by Labour in the country, these elections were undoubtedly conducted in circumstances that militated against any effective initiative by the Labour Party. In order to elucidate a longer-term pattern, historians have scrutinized the various by-elections between 1911 and 1914, some discovering a decline and some an improvement in Labour strength. Mid-term by-elections naturally offered excellent opportunities for gains at the government's expense, but significantly it was the Conservatives not Labour who benefited. Clashes between

TABLE 7.4   *Huddersfield: Labour % poll*

1906	1906 (by-election)	1910 January	1910 December
35.2	33.8	31.6	29.0

Liberal and Labour candidates in working-class seats in this period do, however, shed light on their relative support. Vacancies in industrial constituencies coincided with severe industrial unrest and government unpopularity in 1911–12 over its National Insurance Bill. Labour also enjoyed the advantage of outside organization and abundant support from its MPs in most of the by-elections, which was not so freely available at general elections. However, despite this, Labour came bottom of the poll in each of the 14 industrial seats it contested, polling 10–20 per cent in six and 20–30 per cent in eight. The Liberals held on to almost all their working-class strongholds (though more marginal seats were lost to the Conservatives), and, as one study has concluded, in no contest did as many as half the miners vote for a Labour candidate.[1] Some results were, on the face of it, quite good for Labour, such as that at Holmfirth (a West Riding mining constituency) where the party's poll rose from 14.9 per cent in January 1910 to 28.2 per cent in June 1912. Whether this would have been repeated in the more difficult conditions of a general election is perhaps doubtful. The only valid comparison is with the by-elections of the previous Parliament when, especially in 1907, Labour had actually been able to gain seats. Further, the worst results for the party occurred in the four Labour seats to be defended, all of which were lost, one in a straight fight with a Conservative and the others in three-cornered contests where Labour came bottom of the poll (Bow and Bromley, Hanley, Chesterfield and N.E. Derbyshire); the worst was at Hanley which the Liberals regained reducing Labour to 11.8 per cent of the poll in the process.

If there is a pattern during the Edwardian period, these results suggest one in which Labour gained ground sharply in the early 1900s, reached a peak around 1906–7, and steadily, though not disastrously, fell back thereafter. Of course very few constituencies experienced regular three-cornered contests, but where there is a run of results the stagnation or decline of the Labour vote from around 1908 down to 1914 is fairly clear (see table 7.4). In short, there are no real grounds in the voting behaviour for believing Labour to have been poised to take over from the Liberals by 1914. On the contrary, without the protection of the pact the parliamentary party would have been reduced to a handful.

The Franchise Factor

Impressive as the evidence of parliamentary elections is, it may well be considered insufficient to support the argument because of its narrowness. For we have become conscious of how many men were excluded from the register before 1914: approximately four in every ten. By contrast the franchise reforms of 1918 produced an electorate equivalent to 95 per cent of the adult male population. In this structural change some writers have discerned the central explanation for Labour's ability to overtake the Liberals after 1918, and also the reason for their failure to dislodge the Liberal Party before 1914, the implication being that there was a large reservoir of working-class support that could not be tapped until the electoral law had been overhauled.

This is such an attractive and neat method of explaining the fluctuation in party fortunes over a long period that it is worth considering why it has not so far been demonstrated on the basis of evidence, and why it is almost certainly mistaken. The interpretation rests upon two assumptions; first, that the pre-war non-voters were working-class, and, second, that the working-class non-voters before 1914 were different from working-class voters in ways that made them more likely to support the Labour Party. However, these assumptions seem largely implausible. In 1911, a year in which the register was short because elections had recently taken place, some 42 per cent of adult males were excluded, but this figure comprised only 12 per cent who actually failed to meet one of the seven qualifications, and no less than 30 per cent whose names failed to appear only because the complications of the registration process and the residence requirement deprived them of their right to register as householders or lodgers.[2] Thus, the bulk of non-voters were not under permanent, legal disfranchisement, but would appear on the register from time to time according to their circumstances and the efforts made by the parties. Similarly the working men on the 1911 register could easily drop out next year owing to a change of address. One should not, then, exaggerate the difference between voters and non-voters, for their composition fluctuated constantly. The key to establishing the social characteristics of the electorate lies in an examination of the mechanisms by which some people were excluded and others included in the register. Certain causes of disfranchisement are well known. Men in receipt of poor relief, for example, were specifically disbarred; those who rented rooms below £10 annual value fell outside the lodger qualification; those who moved frequently, often because of inability to pay their rent, interrupted the 12-month residence requirement – and up to 30 per cent of families did move each year in some of the big cities; those who lived with their parents could not qualify as 'householders' themselves; and servants residing with their employers and soldiers living in barracks were subject to the same disqualification.

However, these circumstances surrounding disfranchisement were by no means simply a reflection of social class, but often of age, housing tenure and marital status. This becomes clearer if one approaches the question from the perspective of those who did qualify. Most men voted as householders. But achieving the status of head of household usually followed from marriage which typically came around the age of 30. Conversely, single men in their twenties were likely to live with their parents or to take lodgings and thus not to qualify. This affected middle-class men, who were even more likely to postpone marriage, as much as working-class men. Those occupations, in both classes, which required frequent moves in order to achieve promotion similarly kept some men off the register early in adult life. Dr Duncan Tanner has concluded from this that of the 4 million disfranchised men 2.5 million were unmarried including 450,000 middle-class men.[3] This leaves the working-class share of the electorate at a little under 70 per cent. This estimate should be compared with the working-class share of the population of around 80 per cent. This suggests that although some bias against working men existed it was not sufficiently great to constitute a serious handicap to the Labour Party.

This of course still leaves the question of whether the characteristics of those working men who were excluded from the register made them more likely to lean towards Labour. Both soldiers and domestic servants, for example, were taken by most politicians to be largely Conservative out of deference or personal interest; certainly such groups were isolated from the kind of political and social pressures that fostered Labour voting, or even Liberal for that matter. Again, those families constantly shifting between poor tenement accommodation or being forced onto the boards of guardians comprised the most impoverished section of the urban population whose vulnerability to charity, patronage and beer, and exclusion from the chief institutional pillars of radical politics, notably trade unions and Nonconformity, put them beyond the reach of the Labour movement. The Liberals drew traditional support from various poor immigrant communities particularly the Irish whose level of enfranchisement was abnormally low, and in the conditions of Edwardian Britain any increase in the Irish electorate would have helped them not Labour. Beyond this there are indications that much of the impoverished urban population lent support to Conservatism. Labour certainly found the problems of establishing an organization in such districts as Shoreditch, Whitechapel, Stepney and St-George's-in-the-East insuperable. As MacDonald put it in 1912: 'In places like the Potteries [of Staffordshire] where poverty and degradation is of the blackest kind, the Labour Party is bound to be weak.'[4] In contrast the Labour Party's ability to win and consolidate independent support in such areas as Colne Valley, Woolwich or Barnard Castle reflected a very different working-class population, one that was comparatively stable, skilled, highly unionized, affluent, literate and politically conscious. In many cases it was no doubt an advantage to Labour that the electorate was restricted to certain sections of the working class; for to have extended the electorate in, say, Bethnal Green, where only 42 per cent were voters, would have done little – in the circumstances – to improve the party's prospects.

This impression is corroborated by the attitude of both radical parties to the franchise. In 1911 the Liberal organizations through their feder-ations tendered confidential advice to the chief whip to the effect that one-man-one-vote by means of simplified registration and shortened residential qualification would give them a significant advantage, espe-cially if combined with the abolition of plural voting.[5] It is signifi-cant that exception was made to this only with regard to some parts of Scotland and certain Yorkshire seats (notably Bradford, Dewsbury, Colne Valley, Spen Valley, Shipley, Hull and Buckrose) where it was felt a wider franchise could give Labour extra strength from the younger voters. Generational differences may well have been the most promising aspect of the non-voters from Labour's point of view. For example, in the case of the miners 55 per cent enjoyed the franchise and it seems unlikely that the other 45 per cent had different political views, unless one takes into account that many of them were young men who may have been less wedded to Liberalism, more militant or more socialist than their fathers.[6] This may be reflected in the fact that although miners as voters appeared to remain loyal to Liberalism, the union leadership changed before 1914 and began to replace Lib–Lab collaboration with attacks upon Liberal seats. In general, however, the generation that grew to political consciousness amid the Edwardian phase of Lloyd George radicalism was likely to be captured by the Liberals.

Thus, the distinctions between voters and non-voters, so far as they existed, were not on the whole such as to facilitate drastic changes in party support at this stage. Indeed, Labour never behaved as though an extended franchise was the key to success; though committed to the principle of one-man-one vote the party never attempted to put pressure on the government on this question or to turn it into an issue. No doubt the Labour leaders appreciated that reform was not in their immediate interests; for their appeal was not as yet pitched to the amorphous collection of the disfranchised, nor did they yet possess the necessary organization to compete for them against the larger parties, Thus, although the non-voting working class may have been a potential source of Labour support, neither the political conditions prevailing before 1914 nor the party itself were favourable to the exploitation of this strength.

The Local, Municipal and Regional Dimension

By 1914 it was an open question whether the Gladstone–MacDonald pact, which lay at the heart of Edwardian politics, would survive the next general election, for it had been breached so frequently during 1911–14 as to raise the prospect that Labour was growing out of it. It is abundantly clear that for the voters and for the parliamentary leaders on both sides collaboration on Progressive lines represented a genuine and entrenched sentiment; however, its endurance at the intermediate level of party activists and local politicians appeared far more dubious. The strains were naturally greater at local, and perhaps regional, level. When in 1906 the politics of the pact were seen to operate nationwide, the effect on local Labour politicians, as one Liberal agent commented, was to make them see 'visions of themselves on the floor of the House of Commons, as they consider themselves as good as any Tom, Dick or Harry who are there at the present time'.[7] Instead of satisfying aspirations, except on the part of those actually elected, the arrangement showed the need for more pressure on the Liberals. However, Liberal associations saw no need for further concessions by 1910; and the result was a series of damaging three-cornered by-election contests beginning in November 1911 when Labour intervened in the Liberal-held seat at Oldham which the Conservatives consequently won. In July 1912 the Liberals triumphantly snatched Hanley from Labour, a humiliating result that provoked Labour retaliation at Crewe immediately afterwards. Altogether six Liberal and three Labour seats were lost as a result of three-cornered contests and many more were narrowly saved. Through the National Executive Committee the Labour leaders endeavoured to smother a number of potential Labour candidatures, but although they could withhold official sanction and money they lacked effective control over their constituency supporters. As a federal organization the party relied upon affiliated bodies, namely trade unions and socialist societies, to provide its steel frame in the country. In so far as the party possessed an electoral machine at all it comprised the branches of the Independent Labour Party who could not be prevented by the NEC from launching their own candidates occasionally. Only one

THE TRIANGULAR TEST.

LIBERAL WHIP. "MY COW, I THINK."   LABOUR PARTY LEADER. "MY COW, I THINK."

UNIONIST CANDIDATE (milking). "MY CHANCE, ANYHOW."

From Punch, 10 July 1912.

TABLE 7.5   *The Labour Party: affiliated constituency bodies*

1901	1902	1903	1904	1905	1906	1907	1908	1909	1910	1911	1912	1913
7	21	49	76	73	73	83	92	155	148	149	146	143*

* Sometimes given as 158 (85 trades councils and 73 LRCs) because some constituencies are counted twice.

constituency in ten had a Labour Representation Committee and then it was often inadequate as an electoral machine; the more numerous trades councils were frequently centres of Lib–Lab sentiment, reluctant in any case to run elections and preferring to rely upon the Liberals even in Labour-held seats.

For Ramsay MacDonald this posed an acute dilemma, heightened in 1913 when his supporters in Leicester demanded a fight for the vacancy arising from the death of the Liberal MP with whom he sat in harness. To the activists such by-elections presented a chance to prove that Labour MPs had not been elected merely by Liberal permission and an opportunity to demonstrate independence from the government, an attitude flatly repudiated by MacDonald as 'this false idea of independence'. In his view so long as the two parties had to combine at Westminster they must face 'actual Parliamentary conditions' in the constituencies too. Yet this strategy proved vulnerable to the charge of condemning Labour to a stagnant position, in view of Liberal obstinacy over seats. Though MacDonald had no intention of abandoning the pact, he accepted the desirability of putting pressure on the Liberals, but he believed this to be futile where organization was inadequate or where a candidature was frivolous and merely calculated to antagonize. In practice this often meant stopping candidacies of socialists from the ILP or British Socialist Party, whose influence within the party MacDonald was intent upon limiting. Yet he did not wish the party to be encumbered with the Lib–Lab elements whose primary loyalty was to Liberalism; and to this end he tried to manoeuvre them away from relations with Liberal associations and accepted also interventions by Labour in Liberal mining seats. He hoped he could hold his disparate forces together until the party was strong enough to resist the two other parties. But this was a long-term process dependent upon the development of a grass-roots organization; in fact the steady expansion in the number of affiliated constituency bodies up to 1909 had been checked and the slight decline was not arrested until wartime (see table 7.5). Like the electoral evidence this is inconsistent with the idea of a continuous or inexorable advance before 1914. Given this limited local base MacDonald determined to keep his bridges with Liberalism open until the time arrived when the radical rank and file would want to cross over to Labour and thereby convert a working-class pressure group into the non-class, national party he had always desired.

MacDonald's capacity for taking a long view was underpinned by the immediate pressure of Liberal retaliation. Their local associations had become alive to the disintegrating effects of having to withdraw candidates in favour of Labour. Twelve months after the Clitheroe by-election of 1902 the agent there, conscious, no doubt, of approaching redundancy, lamented: 'Our organization is falling to pieces like a rope of sand, our subscriptions have fallen to 25 per cent, and we cannot get a meeting together except, perhaps, with a view to winding up the business of the Association.'[8] Consequently, by 1914 there was a tendency to replace retiring Lib–Lab MPs with Liberals rather than to allow their seats to be filled by Labour; and even sitting members like Henderson and Hardie were threatened by Liberal opposition. The problem was that constituency activists often wanted to emphasize the differences between parties rather than maximize the common ground; a separate candidate was the best means of doing this. After 1910 the Cabinet was under pressure from radicals in the country to concentrate on the traditional reforms obstructed by the peers, and to show less indulgence to the trade unions. All this is not to say that the Progressive strategy was not feasible, only that it proved more difficult to sustain at the grass roots than in London, and that it hinged upon continued control of power by the Liberals at Westminster.

Historians are beginning to suggest a relationship between the municipal and the parliamentary pattern of politics in the Edwardian period. It has been argued that the municipal evidence runs counter to the Progressive strategy in several ways: for example, the signs of Liberal losses in local elections could be symptomatic of a grass-roots decline well before the First World War; and Labour advances threatened to drive the Liberals into co-operation with the Conservatives at local level, thus undermining their parliamentary tactics and effectively preparing the way for the widespread Conservative–Liberal collaboration between the wars. However, it is easy to attribute too much significance to municipal contests. In general, Edwardian local elections seem to have provided voters with an opportunity to punish the governing party at Westminster as they do today. In the early 1900s the Liberals gained from the reaction against Balfour, only to suffer losses after 1906. In a sense, then, such elections were an ephemeral indication of improving Conservative morale, and should not be mistaken for a fundamental Liberal collapse.

Yet in some ways municipal politics were altogether different from

TABLE 7.6   *Labour's municipal record*

	Candidates		Elected	Net gain/loss
	'Labour and Socialist'	SDF/ BSP		
1907	274	66	86	10
1908	313	84	109	−33
1909	422	133	122	23
1910	281	49	113	33
1911	312*	32	157	78
1912	463†	95	161	42
1913	442	52	196	85

* +23 undefined   † +38 undefined.

national. All three parties frequently avoided formal involvement; thus contests were sometimes between brewers or publicans, who were usually Conservatives, and temperance reformers, who were inclined to be Liberals. Conservative–Liberal co-operation in the shape of rate-payers or municipal alliances was not a novel feature in the 1900s but a continuation of the older attempt to win middle-class Liberal votes by harnessing Liberal Unionists to policies of retrenchment. Such tactics were an inevitable consequence of the local government franchise; by comparison with the parliamentary franchise it excluded certain working men such as lodgers, while including women who possessed a £10 occupation qualification. Consequently the concerns of small property owners, shopkeepers and the lower middle class generally, upon whom the municipal rates pressed hardest, were of central importance. In contrast to the parliamentary electorate, most of whom did not pay income tax, the municipal voters viewed retrenchment with a good deal of favour, and this obliged all parties to preserve the traditional cry of economy. This fact helps to explain long-term Conservative strength and also why radical Liberals and socialists saw national government as the more suitable vehicle for social policy; pending a thorough overhaul of local authority finance, they looked to Lloyd George to open up new sources of revenue by the taxation of ground values.

Labour's progress locally was surprisingly limited but more steady than in parliamentary elections. Table 7.6 shows, as one would expect, that 'Labour' locally was frequently represented by candidates of the socialist groups whose desire to drive a wedge between Labour and Liberalism was a long-standing objective. Whether this strategy was in decline rather than in the ascendant during the Edwardian years is still an open question. The nomination of known socialists usually alienated trades council support and tended to divide the Labour forces, which helps to account for the losses recorded in 1908. Following the success of Victor Grayson at Colne Valley, local socialists took the offensive only to find that moderate Labour and Liberal support had been antagonized. This was the basis of Labour allegations in 1908 that there had been Liberal–Conservative collusion in a number of towns to defeat its own candidates.[9] In cases like Bradford, Liberal–Socialist clashes were a traditional feature of municipal and parliamentary elections; in others, such as Bolton, Progressive co-operation prevailed at both levels. Where Labour did lose, as in 1908, this frequently reflected the temporary alienation of moderate Labour votes by socialists; in this sense the municipal pattern tends very often to complement the parliamentary alignment rather than to run against it.

However, it is evident that the Progressive pattern of politics had evolved more fully in some regions than in others. Lancashire and the north-west might be taken as the model in that it enjoyed the attentions of major exponents of the New Liberalism and the Labour alliance in C. P. Scott, radical entrepreneurs such as Sir William Lever and Sir John Brunner, and a prominent Cabinet exponent of social reform in Churchill. The traditional Liberal weakness in Lancashire facilitated electoral co-operation which produced no less than 13 Labour MPs in the region; by striking at working-class Conservatism the alliance delivered 47 of the 62 seats in 1906 and 42 and 35 in the two elections of 1910.

London provided a similar triumph for Progressivism in that the Liberals captured 49 of its 58 constituencies in 1906 and held 35 in December 1910, a dramatic reversal of the post-1885 pattern. London displayed most markedly the lapse of religious loyalties and the residential separation of the classes which had produced 38 seats with a working-class majority. Of these only two were Labour-held, for the structure of London's economy and the qualities of its working population made the capital very stony ground. Moreover, the entrenched tradition of joint Liberal–Labour action through the London County Council Progressives, and the concentration there of the New Liberal writers and MPs (notably Charles Masterman, Sydney Buxton, Christopher Addison, W. H. Dickinson and T. J. Macnamara) gave Progressivism a more commanding hold than in Lancashire.

Other major urban–industrial regions displayed some of the features of London and Lancashire, but less conspicuously and with significant

variations. For example the Midland coalfields of Derbyshire, Nottinghamshire, Leicestershire and Warwickshire were notable for their
profitability and relatively good industrial relations, which also made for
close political collaboration between owners and workers. It was here
that after 1910 Labour seats were melting away fastest – a reflection of
the Lib–Lab sentiments of the miners. Coal-owners like Sir Arthur
Markham were still prominent Liberal MPs, and this, together with
the presence of radical land reformers like Josiah Wedgwood, R. L.
Outhwaite and Edward Hemmerede, lent a more traditionalist tone
to radicalism in the Midlands and East Anglia. More advanced social
radicals were also present in the form of Francis Channing and his
successor L. C. Money in East Northamptonshire. Conversely the west
Midlands retained bastions of Conservatism still untouched by Progressive assaults.

In north-east England Lib–Lab attitudes were even more entrenched,
especially among the Northumberland and Durham miners who had
been pioneers of electoral participation but tended to maintain the partnership with the Liberal owners. The relative isolation of the region and
the long-standing predominance of Liberalism made for far less change
here during the 1900s than elsewhere. The MPs remained a mixture of
elderly trade unionists (Burt, Fenwick and Wilson) and local industrial
magnates (Palmer, Joicey, Furness), though by 1914 many of these men
had retired or were about to do so, to be replaced by career politicians
from outside the region. Though Labour had received Liberal support
in Sunderland, Newcastle and Darlington, the party had had to fight for
Chester-le-Street, Barnard Castle and Jarrow. Independent Labour and
socialist support was so weak by comparison with Lib–Lab sentiment
that the Liberals triumphed in three-cornered by-elections at Houghton-
le-Spring and N.W. Durham in 1914 and contemplated a counter-
offensive against Labour seats.

Wales has also been seen as an homogeneous region steeped in traditional Nonconformist Liberalism, or 'sunk in the politics of nostalgia'
in the words of Kenneth Morgan. Certainly Wales displayed fewer
signs of the New Liberal impact despite the presence there of Lloyd
George. This was largely a reflection of undimmed electoral success
since the 1860s and a strong feeling that MPs should be local men; it
also reflected the adherence of the South Wales coal-owners to the
Liberal Party, which eventually brought the industrial conflict into
politics with highly disruptive effects. By 1914 the great phalanx of
Welsh Liberalism was faced with widespread clashes with Labour
in Monmouth and Glamorgan, which up to that time had largely been
beaten off.

Yorkshire was another bastion of Liberalism even through the years of Conservative rule. However, the county had long been strong in ILP branches too, especially in the West Riding towns; the result had been regular conflict, for Liberals saw little need to concede seats to socialists. In fact the West Riding saw nearly as many three-cornered contests as straight fights in industrial seats, and only Leeds East and Halifax (the only two-member constituency) were willingly conceded under the 1903 pact. Nonetheless, though the activists feuded, the working-class elector-ate remained impressively loyal to the Liberals who retained 27 of the 38 West Riding seats in 1910. The vigorous Yorkshire Liberal Feder-ation enjoyed some notable Progressives as MPs – Charles Trevelyan, Herbert Samuel, Herbert Gladstone and Walter Runciman. The key to the strength of New Liberalism here lay in the radical, politicized working class which was not divided by anti-Irish and Conservative sentiment as was the Lancashire working class.

Some of these tendencies were present in Scotland where Liberal strength coincided with an early and ideologically devout socialist organ-ization, particularly in the west–central industrial belt. All but two of the eleven Labour candidates in Scotland in 1906 were considered by the Liberals there to be 'socialists' – an indication of trade union weak-ness and of an ideological divide which was absent in most parts of Britain. Hence the Master of Elibank (MP for Midlothian and later Liberal chief whip) warned against conceding anything to Scottish socialists,[10] described by Churchill, himself MP for Dundee, as an 'obscure gang of malignant wirepullers', for fear of undermining the morale of their own supporters. Thus no pact ever operated and Labour obtained only two seats in Scotland (Glasgow Blackfriars and West Fife) despite its considerable underlying strength. A particular feature was that Scottish Labour candidates seemed to draw as much support from Conservatives as from Liberals, and socialists displayed a tendency to vote Unionist in the absence of their own candidate. There are indications of this in the beneficial effect on Unionists of Labour withdrawals in N. W. Lanark and Leith in 1910, and in the Labour gain at West Fife after a Unionist withdrawal. Thus in Scotland the Progres-sive vote seems less of a reality than elsewhere in the country, and Labour stood much more on its own strength. If Scotland and to a lesser extent Wales were inconsistent with the Progressive pattern of politics, they were very much the exceptions; though some regions had obviously advanced much faster along the road to Progressivism they all exhibited a New Liberalism based upon working-class backing.

What emerges from a regional survey is that the advance of new ideas and personnel in the Liberal Party had taken place much earlier in regions like Lancashire and London than elsewhere, and that even in 1910 the New Liberals did not *dominate* the parliamentary party.

However, during the Edwardian period the candidates who replaced retiring MPs in traditionalist regions like the north-east and Yorkshire were
largely New Liberals. Thus, with the exceptions of the South Wales
coalfield and parts of Scotland, the party was evolving in one direction; the pace of change simply varied according to local circumstances.

When the Lights went out

By 1914 all parties had begun to prepare seriously for the general election which, under the terms of the Parliament Act of 1911, had to take
place by December 1915. There is sufficient evidence, without going
into the realms of speculation, to estimate the likely outcome of a dissolution in peacetime.

Any easy assumption of a Conservative victory finds surprisingly little
basis in the evidence. For example, the electoral trend has been deduced
from the constituencies that enjoyed a Liberal–Conservative contest
in December 1910 and in a by-election during 1911–14.[11] These show a
very definite and intelligible pattern of slight swings against the government in February–August 1911 (0.8 per cent), a heavy swing between
November 1911 and August 1912 (4.4 per cent), and a marked recovery
in the shape of a smaller swing against the government from November
1912 to May 1914 (2.1 per cent). This cyclical fluctuation of opinion was
of normal proportions, and indeed repeated the pattern of 1906–9 which
had culminated in a Liberal victory; by 1914 Liberal support appeared
to have returned to the level of 1909. Thus, there is no adequate electoral evidence for assuming a Conservative victory in 1915.

However, the political circumstances and issues of an election must
also be taken into account. The Liberals were endeavouring to create
advantageous conditions by means of a bill to abolish plural voting,
which on the outbreak of war required only its third and final passage in
the Commons; this move was calculated to deprive the Conservatives
of the three-to-one advantage they were thought to enjoy among the
500,000 plural voters and thereby deliver into Liberal hands 30 seats
won in December 1910. On policy the main initiative comprised Lloyd
George's Land Campaign which as we have seen equipped the radicals
with definite proposals on land-holding, minimum wages and house-
building – all designed to retain the initiative from Labour, label the
Conservatives as the party of privilege, recover support from small property owners in towns, and attract extra rural support among labourers
and small farmers. Taken with the government's other reform measures
this gave the Liberals a far wider appeal than the perilously narrow and
negative cry of their opponents.

It was not surprising, then, that some Conservatives, feeling that they had run out of ideas, apprehensively contemplated a fourth election defeat. Naval scares had lost their credibility. Fears about the National Insurance Act had subsided. Tariff reform still presented a dilemma because of the reluctance of Lord Derby, the Cecils and Lancashire and Scottish Conservatives to accept it. In November 1912 Bonar Law had decided to risk repudiating Balfour's pledge to hold a referendum before introducing tariffs, but the reaction against this proved so strong that he agreed to surrender the 'food taxes' for the sake of party unity. The effect was to dismay the farmers who had always expected to benefit from higher prices;[12] and the wider result was that by 1914 the party had little definite to offer the electorate on its central economic philosophy. This left Conservatives marooned on Ulster as their only chance of upsetting the government. As we have already noted, by 1914 the voters were a good deal less agitated about this than the politicians; and in so far as the issue had any novel impact it was as likely to harm the opposition (in view of their inclination to tamper with the army and jeopardize national security for party advantage) as to assist them. This somewhat desperate situation led several MPs including F. E. Smith and Leslie Scott to demand a more positive appeal, particularly to urban voters, with social and land reform; as Austen Chamberlain put it after 1910, without some proposals on land 'we have no chance of winning the towns back.'[13] However, by 1912–14 the party was in full retreat from the interventionist social policies advocated by the more advanced tariff reformers; it now seemed that their obsession with economic novelties had led the party into the disasters of 1910–11. So Bonar Law tried the strategy of ignoring Lloyd George's proposals, as far as possible, hoping thus to deprive him of a popular cry. Yet the danger was that the radicals, unchallenged, would win over voters who assumed Conservative opposition to reform. The one course from which the party shrank was outright attack upon the proposals – an indication that some lessons had been learned from 1910.

Thus the only development that seemed likely to upset Liberal prospects was widespread conflict with Labour. Yet the more the Conservative leadership played the Ulster card the closer they bound the Labour leaders to Asquith. It is easy now to overlook the overriding importance Ramsay MacDonald and his colleagues attached to maintaining Asquith in power so as to see Home Rule through to success. To this end in June 1913 MacDonald engaged in talks with two Liberal MPs, Josiah Wedgwood and Philip Morrell, on closer co-operation; it emerged that the idea of a firm alliance enjoyed the support of Snowden and George Barnes, the acceptance of even Hardie and W. C. Anderson, and the acquiescence of almost the entire parliamentary party who recognized that a formal alliance would be the logical conclusion of their position.[14] When, in March 1914, the government feared a rejection of the Annual Army Bill by the Conservative peers, Lloyd George offered on Asquith's behalf increased representation in return for Labour withdrawals in the constituencies, seats in the Cabinet and an agreed programme to follow an election.[15] Though this particular crisis failed to materialize it shows how MacDonald was under pressure to opt either for independence or for closer co-operation; by 1914 his predilection for the latter course threatened to dissolve the Labour Party into its main constituent parts, the Lib–Lab majority and the socialist minority.

By June 1914, according to Labour's chief agent, the party contemplated contesting 37 seats with sitting Labour MPs, another 18 where candidates had been sanctioned, 22 where candidates had been selected but not sanctioned, and 40 where candidates were possible but uncertain. Allowing for the fact that four of the Labour seats were also listed (significantly) among the 'uncertain' category this represented a total of 113. It is by no means obvious whether this was incompatible with a working arrangement with the Liberals. It can be argued that so high a total was incompatible with the maintenance of a working pact with the Liberals. Since we know that in 1918 Labour did indeed increase the number of candidates very greatly, it seems plausible that expansion forced by the grass roots was already under way by 1914. On the other hand careful examination of party organization and municipal performance in the areas apparently targeted has found no indication of a general advance during 1911–14, often a falling back; many of the proposed contests were essentially propagandist ones which could be sustained only at by-elections. Additional contests would, of course, have been feasible with trade union backing especially following the establishment of political funds. New research has, however, thrown surprising light on their actions. By 1914 the list of seats in which the unions were backing Labour candidates had *diminished* slightly over 1910. In some cases this was a reflection of rank and file members' reluctance to contribute to a political fund even though they had voted for it in principle; in others it reflected the leaders' feeling that there was no need to go beyond existing arrangements especially where this meant supporting propagandist candidatures whose only effect would be to damage the Liberal government.[16] This was reinforced by the NEC's refusal to be pushed into abandoning the pact too soon. By January 1915, when a general election seemed imminent, the party had sanctioned 65 candidates. This allowed for a little judicious expansion over December 1910 in seats dominated by the Tories and in some coalfields; but it clearly stopped short of the provocation which might have resulted in Liberal retaliation in the existing Labour constituencies.

The more the Edwardian evidence underlines the fact that the Liberals were in no imminent danger of decline, let alone eclipse, the more importance must, apparently, be attached to the First World War as the decisive factor in their downfall. Yet while a chronological explanation of this kind may be basically sound it surely cannot be made to run too far; for the war in no sense constitutes a sufficient cause, taken in isolation, for the dramatic disruption of the 1914–26 period. Indeed, the impact of wartime can best be understood in relation to pre-war problems; for the seeds of Liberal decline, patently present before 1914, developed mightily in the conditions of 1914–18.

What were the pre-war sources of weakness? Plainly the Progressive strategy tended to falter at the point where local activists came under pressure from parliamentary leaders; thus any growing apart of the two, such as began to occur after August 1914, was bound to be dangerous. Moreover, success hinged upon the Liberals remaining in office and delivering the full range of radical demands; the wartime collusion with the Conservatives from 1915, loss of office and of the radical initiative spelt disaster. In addition there were at least three areas of policy in which the pre-1914 Liberal government stood in danger of cutting itself off from its traditions; in each case they concerned not the social-economic purposes of Liberalism but its political–moral objectives, and in each case war fostered the conditions in which Labour could uphold these traditional Liberal causes.

First and most obviously, the drift of foreign and defence policy under Sir Edward Grey and the ex-Liberal Imperialists in the Cabinet during 1906–14 had offended Liberal sentiments reaching back to Gladstone and Cobden. Grey's obsession with the German threat had led him to cultivate the deeply detested regime of the Tsar, to pander to the cruel and corrupt policy of King Leopold of the Belgians in the Congo, to abet French imperialism in North Africa, and to instigate British military involvement on the Continent in their support. In their defence, ministers were driven ultimately to the Disraelian argument that national interest must take precedence over sentiment and morality. But however moribund Gladstonian economics were by 1914 the GOM's approach to foreign affairs remained very much alive on the left; radical MPs had often spoken out against Grey in the realization that their silence would present to Labour 'the whole honour of voicing the best traditions of Liberal foreign policy'.[17] The dilemma was obscured by the Prime Minister's success in out-manoeuvring the critics in July and August 1914 and by the paucity of the resignations; wartime eventually forced the radicals to develop a complete critique of Grey's policy and to adopt an alternative vehicle for its propagation.

Another area of politics in which the Asquith governments parted from Liberal traditions was the franchise question, particularly as it affected women. Forcible feeding of suffragettes and their reimprisonment under the 'Cat and Mouse' Act were felt to be deeply humiliating however much provoked by the Pankhursts; by 1916 when the tangled question of parliamentary registration reappeared Asquith's previous stubborn obstructiveness over the women was seen as the reason for the party's failure to rationalize the franchise when it had had the opportunity. More serious in the long run was the demoralizing effect of Asquithianism upon Liberal activists, especially women, in the country, who by 1914 had grown tired of being taken for granted by their leaders. The Women's Liberal Associations, torn between loyalty to suffragism and to party, were dwindling for lack of purpose, as members looked elsewhere.[18] 'Every bright and clever woman in my Liberal society has left us,' one complained to Mrs Lloyd George. 'Can you wonder at our intense gratitude to men like Philip Snowden and Ramsay MacDonald and labour associations who value their women?'[19] This discontent was in 1912 turned into electoral collaboration between the Labour Party and the National Union of Women's Suffrage Societies (the largest and non-militant suffragist organization led by Mrs M. G. Fawcett), whereby the latter provided money and organizers for candidates at by-elections and in seats presently held by Liberal anti-suffragists like McKenna and Harcourt.[20] In this way even before 1914 a number of middle-class Liberals in the NUWSS were being brought into regular contact with the Labour movement. This limited shift was to grow significantly during wartime as constitutional women suffragists joined with various anti-war groups in permanent alienation from Liberal politics in favour of Labour.

The third area where war exacerbated existing weaknesses concerns the trade unions. The Asquith government had not given adequate support to its own moderate adherents against their critics in the unions, as it shown by their handling of the Osborne Case of 1909. In this case the House of Lords had upheld the plea of a Liberal trade unionist who had challenged his union's right to use its funds for political activities. One colleague at least advised Asquith to allow the judgement to stand,[21] a view strongly reiterated by Scottish Liberal miners in 1910;[22] and nothing was done for several years, during which the Labour Party's income dropped by £20,000. However, in 1913 the Osborne Judgement was overthrown in favour of a system whereby unions were permitted to establish a fund for political purposes provided their members approved in a ballot and individuals were allowed to contract out. These safeguards failed to have the anticipated effect. Not only did most unions vote to set up the fund, but relatively few members opted out of the levy. Thus, whereas previously a union's contributions had had to come from general funds in competition with other expenditure demands, now very large sums were to be built up for the sole use of the Labour Party. Taken in conjunction with the payment of a £400 salary to MPs from 1911 this gave a solid foundation for a parliamentary Labour Party not previously available. Moreover, membership of unions affiliated to the TUC, which increased from 1.6 million in 1910 to 2.6 million in 1914, continued during the war, thereby facilitating the adoption of far more candidates than had previously seemed feasible.

In addition the government stood in danger of alienating itself from the rank and file by the authorities' handling of militant strike leaders, particularly Tom Mann and Jim Larkin. Although few workers were syndicalists they sympathized with Mann who was prosecuted in 1912 for urging troops not to shoot at men on strike.[23] In 1913 the leader of the Irish Transport Workers strike, Larkin, was sentenced to seven months' imprisonment for seditious libel, an act that Lloyd George immediately recognized as a political blunder;[24] for by casting itself, through the Attorney-General, as Larkin's prosecutor the government tended to divide and embarrass the moderate pro-Liberal working men.[25] This pattern was to be repeated during the war when unrest, particularly in the South Wales coalfield and among Clydeside munitions workers, had the effect of alienating Lloyd George from much of labour and resulted in the deportation of shop stewards. Though alive to the danger before 1914 the radical politicians entirely failed during the war to arrest their party's gradual severance from the organized working class which had been a pillar of its Edwardian triumphs.

Part Three
1914–1920s

8

The Impact of the Great War
on British Politics

> No man who is responsible [for embarking upon war]
> can lead us again.
>
> C. P. Scott to David Lloyd George, 3 August 1914

Disintegration of the Progressive Alliance 1914–1916

As if to prove the dictum that in politics the expected rarely happens
H. H. Asquith contrived to take Britain united into a major war in
August 1914 while preserving his Liberal–Labour–Irish alliance apparently intact and unscathed. This step was of such importance for subsequent developments that we must examine how it came about.

The traditions of Midlothian and the 'pro-Boers' were very lively on
the left in 1914. Ostensibly a formidable resistance to European wars
was entrenched in such bodies as the Liberal Foreign Affairs Group
under Arthur Ponsonby MP, which claimed the allegiance of several
hundred MPs; but in the crisis of July–August 1914 it could rely upon
no more than 20 or 30. Why did the opponents of war fail to stop their
own government? Over the years the radicals had been so concerned to
avoid the political menace and the financial burden of a large conscript
army that they had usually placed their faith in the Royal Navy as a
sufficient defence that was also cheap and non-aggressive. However,
naval innovation in the era of the Dreadnought and Von Tirpitz's Naval
Laws had made the 'Blue Water' argument a much more expensive one;
nevertheless radical complaints about the naval estimates had always
been contained because extra taxation had obviated any need to sacrifice
social reform for the navy. Similarly, Haldane's creation of the British
Expeditionary Force had been approved because he saved money
through reorganization and because the Force was originally seen in a
colonial context rather than in a European one. Grey and Asquith had

always been able to answer their radical critics by saying that Britain had given no undertakings to another European power for military support, which was true in the letter rather than in the spirit. For since 1906 both Foreign Secretary and Prime Minister had envisaged the prospect of a Franco–Russian war against the Central Powers in which Britain must participate because of the menace to her own security from the expected German victory. The creation of the British Expeditionary Force, the plan to convey it across to France (accepted even by the navy from 1911), the naval conversations with France, and the mutual reallocation of their fleets, all gave the government the immense political advantage of a precise strategy carefully worked out in advance.

Not only had the radicals failed to check the trend of foreign and military planning before 1914, they had also learnt to place confidence in Sir Edward Grey. His role at the London Conference of 1913 in settling the Balkan War, which could easily have involved the major powers, greatly reassured his critics about his desire and ability to keep the peace; hence in August 1914 it seemed to many that if Grey could not stop war it was indeed unavoidable. In fact during the vital week before Britain's declaration Ponsonby deliberately abstained from calling a meeting of the Liberal Party for fear of embarrassing the Foreign Secretary;[1] on his side Grey, by being conciliatory and ambiguous, kept the radicals waiting until the government was able to present the party with a *fait accompli*.

Further, one must remember that although in July 1914 half of Asquith's Cabinet of 20 were reckoned as opponents of British participation in a war, the ministers never gave a lead to the backbenchers. The most likely anti-war leader in the government, Charles Trevelyan, was trapped as an under-secretary, too junior to be privy to cabinet intentions yet obliged to be loyal until it was too late. Opposition to Grey at cabinet level had been more serious back in 1911 when Morley, Harcourt and Runciman led a revolt over alleged military undertakings given to France as a result of the Moroccan crises; this forced Asquith to establish a cabinet committee, including Lloyd George, as a guarantee that no British pledges would be given without specific approval by the Cabinet. Thereafter Lloyd George could not say, except in his memoirs, that he was either in ignorance of or basically in opposition to British foreign policy. Though he kept up pressure for naval economies and spoke publicly about improving relations with Germany these were merely token gestures; he never succeeded in altering policy. Indeed his personal weakness after the Marconi Scandal in 1912 left him unusually dependent on the Prime Minister who had saved him from resignation. Thus, although this was not always appreciated at the time, Lloyd

THE TRIUMPH OF "CULTURE."

From Punch, *23 August 1914.*

George had become a most unlikely leader of an anti-war crusade well before 1914.

In the absence of a lead from Lloyd George other ministers hesitated to throw away their careers and jeopardize the government. In the event there were only two cabinet resignations, those of Morley and Burns, both of them exhausted volcanoes by this time, neither of whom attempted to mobilize opposition in party or country. Asquith was extremely fortunate to escape so lightly, and it is a tribute to his patience and shrewdness in allowing events to make their impression that he kept the Cabinet together. Several considerations during late July and early August contributed to this outcome. An obvious one is the, to some, unexpected swiftness with which Germany implemented the Schlieffen Plan and marched into Belgium, thereby rapidly disabusing those ministers who had wanted to believe Germany basically a civilized power. This did not, of course, weigh with Grey, Haldane, Asquith or Churchill, whose case for British participation remained quite as strong if Belgium were untouched, but it helped weaken the resolve of their opponents. Further, it is now apparent from the diary of one minister, Sir Charles Hobhouse,[2] that they believed the German government deliberately kept its ambassador in London, Lichnowsky, in the dark about its intentions so that he would make a better job of convincing the British that their involvement was not called for; this sense of deception helped to close ranks. Secondly, it seems that some of the reluctant ministers (Runciman, Simon, Pease, Harcourt) were under the impression that war implied embarking upon an essentially naval enterprise in support of the French; had they appreciated how promptly the BEF would cross the Channel and how dramatically the continental commitment would grow under Kitchener's appeal for men, they would probably have stood out. Thirdly, there were important political considerations. If the Cabinet had failed to reach agreement Asquith, Grey and Haldane would have resigned thus breaking up the government. On 2 August Bonar Law and Lansdowne wrote to Asquith urging prompt support for France and offering 'our unhesitating support to the Government in any means they may consider necessary for that object'.[3] Asquith made a point of reading this to the Cabinet so as to underline the fact that they would be replaced by a Conservative or a coalition ministry. In short, a war was not to be avoided by a few Liberal resignations. Why should ministers, so recently battling to complete their legislation, surrender to the opposition what the electorate had denied them? Since war was expected to produce economic disruption and social distress it would enable the Conservatives to reverse the trend to social reform and make authoritarian innovations of all kinds. If there had to be a war, better that it should be a liberal one. In this way many Liberal and Labour politicians who on 3 August had prepared to join 'peace' meetings found themselves on the 4th reconciled to war by the consideration that Britain had done her best to keep the peace and could neither leave France in the lurch nor Belgium violated. This historic turnabout bears the hallmark of Asquithian statescraft. It would have been a blunder to have taken consent for granted. Given a short delay not only the Liberals but the Irish and Labour wings of the Progressive Alliance rallied strongly. The Irish leader, Redmond, astonished opponents and delighted allies with a bold speech backing Grey on 4 August. Given a short war and a Home Rule Bill on the statute book there was every reason for him to stick to Asquith and, by demonstrating Irish loyalty in England's moment of crisis, allay Unionist apprehensions.

Equally strikingly the Labour Party showed its patriotic instincts by voting to support the government and ousting its chairman Ramsay MacDonald in the process. Unlike most of his colleagues MacDonald seems to have perceived the significance of the war as a decisive interlude in which the Liberal alliance might be safely disrupted; but for the time being he had to make do with the ILP and the Union of Democratic Control[4] as bridges of anti-war sentiment by which middle-class radicalism would begin to cross to Labour. In retrospect the Great War provided Labour with a historic opportunity to cut adrift from the Liberal Party on a matter of Liberal principle. A similar opportunity might have been exploited during the South African War had not Labour been too young and ineffectual to forestall the Liberal recovery in 1902; 1914 proved to be different because the party was sufficiently established to seize upon the dilemma created by the Liberal leaders' decision to take Britain to war; but most were slow to see the new possibilities.

In rallying to the government the supporters of the Progressive Alliance shared a determination that this must not be a war of aggrandizement or one fought by 'methods of barbarism'. H. G. Wells's brilliantly pithy phrase 'The War to End War' stuck because it expressed what many wanted to believe. Men of intellectual weight like Gilbert Murray and James Bryce wrestled with their liberal consciences and concluded that this was a just war. Masterman, the minister initially responsible for propaganda, was able to draw upon the talents of the Edwardian literary world: Arnold Bennett, John Galsworthy, John Masefield, H. G. Wells and Thomas Hardy were among those who averred publicly that Britain was right to 'defend the rights of small nations, and to maintain the free and low-abiding ideals of Western Europe against the rule of "Blood and Iron" and the domination of the whole Continent by a military caste'.[5]

On the Conservative side, of course, all this dilatory manoeuvring for morally comfortable positions was regarded as irrelevant. The opposition responded to war with a single-minded patriotism unhampered by political scruples or traditions, and fortified by a conviction that they had been proved right in diagnosing the German threat. However, they soon realized that they were in an awkward tactical position. Conscious that their hour had come, the opposition believed that they ought to be running the war. The alternative was to join the armed forces, which some 98 Conservatives MPs had done by January 1915; their action strengthened the government's parliamentary position, and exacerbated the frustration of those remaining on the backbenches who became increasingly susceptible to scaremongering. It was all too easy to ascribe military failures to government's lack of determination and indulgence towards enemy aliens supposedly spying and sabotaging the war effort. If few leading Conservatives gave credence to the wild rumours that Prince Louis of Battenburg, the First Sea Lord, Sir Eyre Crowe of the Foreign Office, or Haldane the Lord Chancellor were Germany sympathizers, they did nothing to check them. For some months, however, the government's critics were held at bay by the inspired decision to appoint Kitchener Secretary of State for War. His reputation in the country made him hard to attack with any credibility, as the opposition soon discovered. The flaw lay in the fact that once appointed he proved difficult to remove, and that when victories failed to materialize it was his colleagues who were apt to bear the blame. This was the effect when Sir John French, casting about for an excuse for the failure of his offensive at Neuve Chapelle in 1915, blamed Kitchener for lack of high-explosive shells, though he had previously claimed to be amply supplied.[6]

The government's other temporary advantage lay in the 'party truce', which amounted to a suspension of by-election contests by the main parties and restraint by the Conservative leaders in Parliament. In fact Balfour, Bonar Law, Austen Chamberlain, Walter Long and Lord St Aldwyn were all involved, in Balfour's case quite closely, in official work by attending committees or giving advice. On the strength of this co-operation, government spokesmen were apt to claim that the opposition were informed of and responsible for the decisions made, an interpretation apparently well received in the country but highly exasperating to Conservatives who felt the Liberals were taking advantage of their enforced good behaviour.[7]

This situation exacerbated the tendency already manifested in 1910–11 for the Conservative backbenches to organize in defiance of their leadership. Up to a point it was useful for Bonar Law to be able to channel backbench energy into a body like the Unionist Business Committee; indeed he encouraged one of his rivals, Walter Long, to take the chairmanship, for it provided a forum for criticizing the government without actually breaking the truce or being unpatriotic. However, when in May 1915 the Unionist Business Committee threatened to force a Commons debate on the alleged shells shortage, Law could not stay aloof except at risk of splitting the party and jeopardizing his own leadership. Having established himself since 1911 by his abrasive style he found it dangerous to abandon what now seemed an inappropriate tactic. Yet if he failed to give a lead it began to look as though Curzon, Carson or Long would fill the vacuum.

By the spring of 1915 Bonar Law faced three unpalatable courses of action. He could simply join his followers in attacking the Liberals, which would have led to the general election due in December, and probably a Conservative government. He ruled this out because it would push much of the Liberal and Labour forces into opposition to the war as in 1899–1902 but with far more serious consequences; also the Edwardian industrial revolt seemed to compound Conservative doubts about their ability to handle an organized working class in a crisis. An alternative was to form a coalition with the Liberals, but this was rejected by Law and virtually all leading Conservatives as calculated to silence necessary criticism.[8] Thus Bonar Law stuck to the third option, the 'party truce', until May 1915. At this point the split between Churchill and Admiral Sir John Fisher, First Sea Lord, at the Admiralty combined with the launching of the 'shells scandal' in the press created pressure that was too powerful for Law to resist. Anxious to avoid being driven to censure the government he was pleasantly relieved to discover that Lloyd George and Asquith himself were offering him a coalition. However, because Law accomplished this largely in isolation from and against the wishes of many of his colleagues, the Conservatives failed to confront Asquith with agreed terms either on policy or offices. Asquith retained in Liberal hands all the key posts except the Admiralty, and Law, despite his obvious claim to a major role, was relegated to the Colonial Office because it suited his own rivals in the party to devalue his status. Yet this underlined for the Conservatives that it was not a genuine coalition but a triumph for Asquith.

In the short run the coalition served to put off the election which the Liberals expected to lose and kept Asquith in office until the end of 1916. In a longer perspective, however, it proved a crucial point in the disintegration of the Liberal Party. It would be far too simple to think that war placed an intolerable strain upon Liberal susceptibilities, for like all political parties they had a strong inbuilt tendency to hang together regardless of policy as August 1914 shows. We have already noted that the Cabinet's pre-war difficulties in the party over foreign policy, suffrage and labour militancy left them exposed to attack from the left, and wartime conditions exacerbated this. Well before the war the Cabinet had envisaged a wide-ranging Emergency Powers Bill. In 1911 they had introduced the Official Secrets Act, and they now enacted the Defence of the Realm Act, a sign that they were not inhibited by philosophical scruples from eroding individual rights. The crisis was held to justify other infringements of political liberalism: the Aliens Restriction Act, strict censorship, the National Register Act, and the protectionist element in McKenna's 1915 budget were further evidence of this. The point is that such measures were accepted in the emergency; they only became dangerously divisive when the party experienced the demoralizing shock of May 1915 when Asquith announced the end of the Liberal government without the slightest consultation or preparation even among his closest colleagues. 'The more I contemplate this Coalition, the more I revel in the new sense of freedom it gives us all,' observed one MP. 'No one on earth can pretend that we were elected to support this Government.'[9]

From this moment the Liberals and their leadership were fatally divided. Predictions that under Conservative influence the war would now be fought by something closer to Prussian methods appeared to receive confirmation in Ireland and in conscription. On the eve of war Home Rulers had been dismayed at the shooting of Nationalists in the south while the army was not apparently to be used against Ulstermen. The Home Rule Act went on the statute book but was suspended for the duration of hostilities. Thereafter the Irish alliance collapsed progressively. Redmond refused cabinet office in 1915 but Asquith took the odious Carson in as Attorney-General. Yet the situation did not become irretrievable for the Nationalists until 1916 when the Easter Rebellion was put down with calculated brutality by the army, who acted as though administering a lesson to a colonial people. The effect was compounded by the subsequent failure of the government to prevent the execution of Roger Casement. A rebellion that had begun with little support quickly gained retrospective sanctity with the result that by 1917 the country had thrown over the Nationalists for the Sinn Fein, and the Nationalist Party had become alienated from the Liberals. It was Asquith also who bore the blame for failing to obtain the acquiescence of Conservative ministers in Lloyd George's hastily negotiated settlement of the Home Rule question in the aftermath of the rebellion.

The drift to conscription had a similar effect. Asquith here prevaricated by opting for the Derby Scheme in October 1915 to give voluntaryism a last chance to produce sufficient men. When, inevitably, this proved inadequate he accepted conscription of single men in January 1916 and married men in June. His manoeuvring succeeded in keeping the government together. Yet the real strength of his position since 1914 had been that by continuing in office he provided the best guarantee against authoritarian measures; to retain that support he therefore would have had to make a stand on a matter like conscription which was so deeply offensive to many people. But instead his cleverness alienated so much support that by December 1916 most of the theoretically Asquithian forces resigned themselves to the Lloyd George Coalition on the grounds that the worst had already happened; there was no point in keeping Asquith as Prime Minister. Much of the confusion of First World War and subsequent politics arises from the fact that the right wing of Liberalism now looked to Lloyd George; while the left–centre had perforce to take Asquith for their leader. Bearing in mind his history of Liberal Imperialism, his sympathy for conscription at the time of the South African War, and his attitude to Grey's foreign policy, this was clearly a false position for Asquith; he was no 'quintessential Liberal', and thus never an effective leader in the circumstances arising out of the war.

Lloyd George and the Conservatives 1916–1918

For the Conservatives the real value of the 1915 Coalition, not apparent at the time, was that it solved the Edwardian dilemma by dividing the Progressive Alliance. More immediately, coalition had the effect of altering the relationship between Asquith and Lloyd George to the latter's advantage in that it gave him allies in Cabinet whom the Prime Minister could not ignore. For the strength of the Conservatives' position lay in the fact that the government's legal term would run out in December, and they agreed to no more than a bill prolonging Parliament's life for eight months. Consequently throughout the war the Unionist peers enjoyed the power of forcing a general election by declining to pass such a bill again. Through his skill in finding compromises Asquith lived with this situation until December 1916 when he made a major error of judgement. Appreciating Lloyd George's natural facility for responding constructively to immediate problems Asquith had rightly placed him at the new Ministry of Munitions. However, Lloyd George, conscious that he had to succeed, refused to be baulked by the obstacles to the manufacture of munitions; chief among these he identified the voluntary system of recruiting which deprived him of thousands of skilled engineering workers.[10] Though at the start of war Lloyd George had lent no support to Churchill's desire for conscription, he suffered no moral scruples over it, and proceeded to throw his weight behind those Conservatives who wanted compulsion.

Following Kitchener's death in June 1916 Lloyd George allowed himself to be manoeuvred into the War Office without any of the powers that he himself had helped to strip from the Secretary of State. Left thus with responsibility but insufficient control Lloyd George quickly grew frustrated and highly susceptible to schemes for reorganizing the machinery for running the war. His object in this was to eliminate the inefficiency arising from a dilatory Cabinet, civil servants and generals; though critical of Asquith he did not intend to drive him from the premiership, regarding him as essential for persuading the country to accept unpalatable measures – a view endorsed by Bonar Law. However, it proved difficult to bring pressure effectively to bear; he shrank from resignation which would leave him isolated and impecunious, and he feared Liberal hostility to him for scheming with the Tories. At first he found only Carson, who had left the Cabinet, and Sir Max Aitken, Bonar Law's *éminence grise*, to work with. Most Conservatives, however appreciative of Lloyd George's work at Munitions, had no desire to raise the untrustworthy 'little bounder' to the premiership. His strength came through Carson's role as leader of the 150-strong Unionist Business Committee. In November 1916 in a debate on the disposal of captured enemy property in Nigeria, during which the rebels demanded that it should be sold only to 'natural born British subjects' not to the highest bidder, Conservative MPs split 65 for Carson and 73 for Bonar Law, the minister responsible for defending the government's policy. Just as in 1915, the incipient party split obliged Law to act. For in antagonizing the tariff reformers of the UBC over the Nigerian issue he was offending his own staunchest supporters in the party. He therefore joined with Lloyd George and Carson to present Asquith with terms for a reorganization of the machinery of war. Basically this involved removing the running of the war from the traditional Cabinet to a War Cabinet of three members, not including the Prime Minister, who would be freed from departmental duties by their deputies and thus able to sit from day to day making rapid decisions.

Asquith had always made the mistake of taking Bonar Law for granted; given the connivance of the other leading Conservatives he believed it safe to relegate him to a minor position. However, after the Prime Minister's rejection of the Lloyd George–Bonar Law proposals the Conservative ministers met on 3 December and decided to offer their resignations; when communicated to Asquith by Law this decision induced him at once to reach a compromise with Lloyd George over a War Cabinet. Yet it rapidly emerged that Law, whether by accident or by design, had failed to convey accurately his colleagues' intentions. Curzon subsequently explained that the resignations would facilitate the reorganization of the government by Asquith, if necessary without Lloyd George; they were thus helping him against the manoeuvres of Law and Lloyd George. This changing interpretation of the Conservative ministers' motives was the major reason for a swift withdrawal by Asquith from the compromise, which in turn forced Lloyd George into an unwelcome resignation. Thereupon the Conservatives also resigned and the government collapsed. When Bonar Law declined the King's invitation to form an administration Lloyd George had his chance. He would have failed at this point had the Conservatives refused to serve under him. Their puzzling behaviour can only be put down to their own confusion. They probably feared that if they simply restored Asquith he might kill off any real reorganization of government which they thought essential; he was only the lesser of several evils. Some, like Curzon, who undoubtedly found Lloyd George repugnant, could not overcome the temptation to serve in any government; and Lloyd George might at least be more amenable to pressure.

That he could form a genuine coalition only became apparent when Liberal and Labour support materialized. A canvass of Liberal MPs by Christopher Addison revealed 49 firm supporters and many more who would be drawn by prime ministerial patronage. On the Labour side all the indications up to December 1916 were that the leading figures, Arthur Henderson and J. H. Thomas, preferred Asquith; yet he had exhausted his usefulness by now. After an entrancing appeal by Lloyd George, Labour MPs voted by 18 to 11 to back him, a decision confirmed by the NEC. Thus although Asquith had so recently seemed the indispensable Premier, there were sufficient elements of support in each party to make the new coalition feasible.

By his refusal to serve in the government Asquith became responsible in the first instance for the dire split in the Liberal ranks. For now the Liberals enjoyed two leaders, one the Prime Minister and the other Leader of the Opposition, along with two whips in the House. Though initially this was seen as a temporary and superficial division, it hardened during 1917–18 as MPs formed the habit of voting for or against the government. Though radicals and pacifists regularly attacked the illiberality of Coalition policies Asquith shrank from giving a lead, even on the question of British peace terms on which Lloyd George was very vulnerable. The sole exception was Asquith's intervention in support of General Maurice's allegations in May 1918 that the Prime Minister had lied to the Commons over the size of forces on the Western Front. Even here Asquith fumbled his opportunity by insisting on a select committee of investigation instead of accepting Bonar Law's rash offer of a tribunal of two judges. Though the Liberals' 98 to 71 split in favour of Asquith in the Maurice Debate seemed to formalize the division it only reflected a, by now, fairly well-established fact. There was little point in taking a risk over the Maurice issue if Asquith was not prepared to offer sustained, co-ordinated opposition. Instead he left it to backbenchers, protesting that he wished essentially to support the war effort, a claim whose credibility would have been greater had he not refused to join the government. This absence of strategy had a disintegrating effect on parliamentary politics. Like Joseph Chamberlain in

1886 Lloyd George took with him a few radicals like Addison and Montagu; but the bulk of his support came from the Liberal right and those attracted by his powers of patronage; for some of these coalition was to be a stage on the road to the Conservative Party in the 1920s. Conversely many of the radicals and pacifists were so dismayed by both Asquith and Lloyd George that they loosened their Liberal ties preparatory to a shift to Labour after the war. Many elderly, traditional Liberals drifted into retirement in 1918. Some Liberal critics of war such as Charles Trevelyan and Arthur Ponsonby fell out with their local parties and were not nominated at the next election. More commonly the links between MPs and their constituencies weakened and party organization deteriorated. To some extent this affected all parties; but the Liberals suffered much more, especially from 1916, from sheer lack of purpose and leadership. In contrast rank and file Tories saw patriotic war work as integral to the cause of their party, while for Labour the war provided additional opportunities for defending working-class interests. But for Liberals the war effort was at best a diversion and at worst a source of division.

The only feasible course for the Liberals after December 1916 lay in reasserting their leadership of the radical left by attacking the illiberality of the Coalition; Asquith's inability to do this not only in 1916–18 but until 1926 when he retired, doomed the party by leaving a vacuum for Labour. In particular the party lost the initiative on social questions during the second half of the war and the early post-war period. The New Liberalism was kept alive in the shape of wartime 'Reconstruction' and Lloyd George's house-building programme. However, this was strictly a Coalition initiative which, in any case, soon proved to be an embarrassment because the achievement fell short of the promises. Significantly, Liberals in local authorities proved very slow to implement the housing policy, and instead it rapidly became a central demand of Labour councillors. In this way Labour soon occupied the role played by Edwardian Liberals in social reform, while the Liberal Party itself moved to the right. It is in this sense that the war proved to be of crucial importance in changing the shape of British politics.

For the time being the future appeared to lie in the special relationship growing up between Lloyd George and the Conservatives which, remarkably, endured for six years. Recognizing the Conservatives as the chief prop to his government Lloyd George promptly elevated Bonar Law to be Chancellor of the Exchequer and Leader of the House. In that capacity Law, not the Prime Minister, would manage the backbenchers. He also took care to install in his War Cabinet two influential leaders of party opinion, Curzon and Milner, and to tie Carson down as First Lord of the Admiralty. By thus restoring a measure of power and dignity to the Conservatives, and reassuring them over his commitment to the 'knock-out blow' he made them more amenable than might have been expected. Law was never again in real danger of losing the loyalty of the party to a rival, and this was the essential underpinning to Lloyd George's Coalition.

Once committed to Lloyd George it seemed inconceivable to part with him, for the alternative was a renewed Asquith premiership that might lose the war or negotiate a humiliating peace. This prospect kept Conservatives loyal in the Maurice Debate when they rallied to Lloyd George despite a suspicion that he had been lying. Further, the original rationale for coalition in 1915, namely the difficulty of a purely Conservative government carrying the country during war, now seemed stronger. Much that occurred in 1917 underlined the point; industrial unrest, initially checked by the war, now began to rise sharply; the government, greatly fearing that the anti-war groups might infect industrial workers with pacifism, over-reacted by attempting to stop the activities of the UDC. With a man of Lord Lansdowne's stamp publicly urging a negotiated peace in November 1917 one can see why the danger of a collapse of the will to fight seemed to loom so large; Russia was going down in revolution, the French and Italian armies disintegrating in mutiny and defeat. In this situation Lloyd George's buoyant, well-publicized oratory seemed ideal for rallying the nation for further efforts.

For although the domestic situation looked precarious the war had created opportunities for repairing the Conservatives' connections with the workers. Addressing a rather critical special party conference in 1917 Bonar Law reminded them that in the past the opposition of organized labour had been fatal to Conservatism and tariff reform; but now, '"gentlemen, this war has shown us that among the Leaders of Labour there is a body which is national and patriotic" (Hear Hear and applause) "and feels these sentiments as strongly as we do."'[11] The implication was that certain concessions must be expected if a patriotic working class was to be harnessed to Conservatism. One means to this end was provided by Lord Milner's British Workers League established to provide working men with an alternative leadership to that of socialists or trade unionists. Designed to combine traditional Conservative policy with vigorous social reform the BWL furnished some 18 candidates in 1918 in industrial seats where the Conservatives felt they would have no chance, ten of whom were elected as the 'National Democratic Party'. Although the NDP soon lost credibility in the trade union movement once the war ended, it is significant as an indication of the Conservative mood during the last two years of war.

Milner was prepared to go to unusual lengths in terms of state intervention and social welfare to accommodate a wider social range of support; for a brief period in 1918–20 his colleagues paid what seemed a high price for mass backing. Yet before then the biggest gesture, and greatest risk, had already been made in the form of the Representation of the People Act which ushered in adult male suffrage. One of the most important manoeuvres of the fading Asquith Coalition had been the establishment in August 1916 of a Speaker's Conference on the franchise. Its report was inherited by Lloyd George in January 1917; with the firm backing of Henderson, Long, and an apprehensive Bonar Law he turned it into a bill. The Conservatives' fears were laid by various concessions, in particular the preparation of a scheme of postal and proxy voting designed to ensure that the men in the forces – on whose support they counted – would not be excluded from the election while the 'shirkers' and pacifists enjoyed the franchise. In addition they obtained a five-year disfranchisement of conscientious objectors, and a special franchise for 19-year-olds on active service. The modified redistribution would, they hoped, help them in rural seats and in Ireland, as would the extension of plural voting in some areas, a few extra university seats, and most of all, the promise (never fulfilled) of a complete reform of the powers and composition of the House of Lords so as to rectify what Conservatives regarded as 'one-chamber government' since 1911.[12] Even so, much of the party was highly disgruntled at being forced by its leaders to accept a huge electorate amounting to 21 million (of whom 8.4 million were women) in 1918 compared with barely 8 million before the war. Conservative Central Office had repeatedly warned that a majority of the new male voters would be working men, and in their twenties.[13] One must remember that politicians at this time felt acutely conscious of the immaturity of the young who lacked considered opinions and judgement and were liable to be swayed by emotional appeals; this was one reason for imposing a 30-year age limit on women voters. The most dangerous moment would come if and when demobilized troops returned to temporary unemployment and caused a landslide on the lines of 1906. Consequently for the Conservatives, alliance with Lloyd George clearly provided the safest means of effecting the transition from war to peace on the basis of a vast new electorate. He was pre-eminently the popular leader who could capture better than any of the staid and remote figures in their own party the support of the masses. With his Liberal and Labour followers Lloyd George would guarantee a popular majority for the Coalition, and the containment of the menace represented by an independent Labour Party. This was the electoral foundation of coalition strategy for the Conservatives until 1922.

Even in 1918 some right-wing Conservatives would have preferred to risk going it alone. Yet the leadership of the party would not let them do so. Working with Lloyd George became a habit; for Bonar Law particularly it proved an effective partnership; he shared with the Prime Minister relatively humble social origins and a lack of the grand panjandrum style of his colleagues. Balfour, Chamberlain and Birkenhead also relished the freedom from party cant that membership of a coalition gave them. Thus for rebel Conservatives separation of the party from Lloyd George would have been tantamount to separation from their own leaders.

Although by 1918 the prospect of American assistance and an improvement in food and shipping supply gave some confidence, it was generally expected that the Allies would have to fight on through 1919 for complete victory. It was therefore a wartime not a post-war general election that Lloyd George prepared for. Parliament was nearly three years beyond its proper term, and an appeal to the country for a mandate to finish the war would greatly simplify the government's work by purging the Commons of troublesome left-wing war critics. However, so much fuss had been made of the need to allow the troops to vote that an election was necessarily delayed until the autumn of 1918 when the new register was expected to be ready. But the real problem was to decide on what basis Lloyd George should appeal to the country. Though widely regarded as indispensable in wartime he had no real party, only a group of parliamentary followers. Characteristically Lloyd George did his best to keep his options open for as long as he could. He worked hard on polishing up his liberal and radical credentials, aided by the work of Addison on housing and Herbert Fisher on education; and by November he was able to hold out to Liberals the prospect of a fair peace settlement and a league of nations, and at home house-building, minimum wages, health and land reform, and even a reaffirmation of free trade and Home Rule. There was certainly an element of deception in this for he had already agreed a programme with the Conservatives that included some protectionist measures and a reform of the Lords; however he drew enough Liberals to him to serve his purpose which was to make him strong enough to bargain with the Conservative Party. As early as July 1918 his whip, F. E. Guest, had embarked upon detailed negotiations with Sir George Younger the Conservative party chairman for a mutual withdrawal of candidates to avoid dividing the coalition vote. By 20 July Guest had secured Bonar Law's agreement to a free run for Lloyd George Liberals in 114 seats, for Labour in 15 and for the NDP in 17.[14] In fact Lloyd George was still toying with ideas of making an independent appeal, and luring Asquith into his government as Lord Chancellor, when military events rapidly closed in. On 11 November the Armistice was signed, and on the 14th the Labour Party withdrew from the Coalition. He therefore fell back on the prepared plan of fighting in co-operation with the Conservatives, since if he did not win an election while his prestige was at its height the Conservatives would sooner or later wake up to the fact that they could manage without him. Consequently he and Bonar Law issued a letter of approval – dubbed the 'Coupon' by Asquith – to 374 Conservative, 159 Liberal and 18 NDP candidates, whose election would extend into peace the wartime Coalition government.

Labour's Change of Course

Superficially, Labour's divisions over the First World War mirrored those of the Liberals: a minority adopted outright opposition; the bulk concluded reluctantly that it was a justified war: and some, in a natural culmination of the strategy of 1903, went to the extent of serving in government from 1915 to 1918. However, these divisions were far less damaging to Labour, and we must consider why this was so.

By the end of the war Labour managed to rally around a new programme, achieve a clearer sense of purpose than its rivals and attain greater coherence than before. Fundamentally this was possible because the movement was still more than just a parliamentary force, and a split at that level was less vital than for, say, the Liberals. Also, for much of the rank and file, international affairs were still too remote to be acutely disruptive. Much of the credit for containment of the problem must be ascribed to Arthur Henderson's restraint; after succeeding MacDonald as chairman he made no attempt to purge the anti-war elements in the party. Nor did MacDonald wage his campaign primarily through the party, concentrating instead on the UDC and subsequently the ILP, which illustrates the advantage of the federal party structure adopted in 1900. Henderson, well attuned to the feelings of the average working man, simply supported the war effort by accepting a post as President of the Board of Education in 1915, and acted a a mediator between government and unions and a symbol of working-class co-operation. His inclusion had been expected to strengthen Asquith's hand against the Conservatives; for the voluntaryists, for example, had assumed that the labour movement would resolutely resist military conscription as tantamount to the direction of labour. This did not happen, and Henderson saw that on the whole the rank and file were too caught up in the war climate to worry much. He joined the new Coalition in December 1916 (as a member of the five-man War Cabinet) not because of any virtues of Lloyd George, but because working-class interests seemed, on balance, better served by working within the government than in opposition.

Nor was this merely a matter of collaboration foisted upon the movement by MPs. At its 1916 conference at Bristol the party's delegates representing 73 unions, 39 trades councils, 41 local Labour parties, two socialist societies and one branch of the Women's Labour League approved by 1.5 million to 600,000 a resolution pledging assistance to the government in waging war, and by a similar margin backed Labour participation in the Coalition. The next conference endorsed membership of Lloyd George's administration by a margin of six to one.

Nevertheless Labour had to perform a precarious balancing act. Participation by Henderson and others in government undoubtedly boosted the party's confidence and status; yet at the same time it had to keep intact its role as a pressure group for the working class. That this was possible may be ascribed largely to the activities of the War Emergency Workers National Committee which contrived to maintain the links between the party's obligations to its grass roots and its responsibility to government. Though originally conceived in August 1914 as a peace protest committee, the WNC promptly faced Britain's involvement as an inescapable fact and constituted itself as a body representative of the working class devoted to defending their immediate interests. From nine nominated and six elected members it grew to 40. Its secretary was Jim Middleton, the assistant secretary of the Labour Party. Among its prominent members were patriotic trade union leaders like Will Thorne, Havelock Wilson and W. J. Davis, TUC MPs like James O'Grady and C. W. Bowerman, and near jingoes like Ben Tillett, John Hodge and H. M. Hyndman. Patriotic Labour was no mere figment of the Conservative imagination. At the other end of the spectrum the WNC included ILP representatives Fred Jowett, H. Dubery, W. C. Anderson and Ramsay MacDonald, and more moderate critics of the war like Bob Smillie of the Miners Federation. Most, however, were of the 'sane patriotic' persuasion personified by Henderson who believed Germany must be beaten, but refused to enjoy the war. In this category were Fred Bramley, J. A. Seddon and Sidney Webb who was a patriot as in the South African War, but thought it a mistake to elevate the war into a dominant political question when it could be made to serve longer-term purposes.

Indeed most Labour critics tried to abstain from involvement in great issues over which they believed they could exert little influence. This disengagement from the war was sometimes deliberate; socialists like the young G. D. H. Cole, for example, were anxious not to discredit their cause by association with anti-war movements. Disengagement never had a demoralizing effect because Labour found an alternative in the form of concentration upon a defence of the interests of working-class families during wartime. At national level the WNC served admirably as the focus of this activity, vigilantly intervening with the authorities over prices, housing, rent control, and benefits and pensions for soldiers and their families. In this way it was possible to indulge in political work which kept Labour's basic purpose alive at a time when most forms of politics were suspended or disrupted. Its achievements should not be exaggerated; it probably only edged the government in the direction in which it was moving already, and it firmly declined to put itself at the head of unrest that threatened the war effort, or to risk a serious challenge on matters like conscription. It concentrated on winning compromises, yet avoided being sucked into the official machine: Smillie refused to become food controller; Henderson resigned from the Committee on becoming a minister.

Even more importantly the activity of the WNC nationally was complemented at local level by the work of trades councils. War generated all kinds of local bodies such as food control committees and profiteering committees for which trades councils and Labour municipal groups were called upon to provide representatives. They attempted, too, to resist pressure for retrenchment in local government, to maintain the real level of council employees' wages, and to see that the families of servicemen did not suffer.[15] Perhaps the most important single issue was housing; from 1917 Addison as Minister for Reconstruction attempted, through the Local Government Board, to persuade local authorities to prepare detailed plans for house-building. The response was very patchy, but Addison's initiative enabled Labour councillors, where already well represented,[16] to impose their housing policy, albeit temporarily. Thus from the Housing Act of 1919 until its abandonment in 1921 there existed a situation in which a Liberal minister's national policy was readily grasped by Labour locally; in this way Labour inherited the social reform tradition at grass roots and actually resuscitated Addison's measure in the form of Wheatley's Housing Act when in office in 1924.

At Westminster Labour's loyalty to the Coalition was not shaken until Henderson's visit to Russia in June 1917 which had been intended to encourage the provisional government of Kerensky to maintain the war effort. However Henderson, who welcomed the new democratic regime, soon recognized how precarious it was; to persist with the war was to invite overthrow by the Bolsheviks, and he came home convinced that Russia would have to move towards a negotiated peace to forestall another revolution. A means to this end was at hand in the shape of an impending conference at Stockholm of socialists from belligerent countries on both sides which Henderson believed should be attended by Russia and by representatives of British Labour. This episode demonstrates the dramatic effect upon such a pragmatic, unideological person as Henderson of removing him from the isolation of British domestic politics. He began to see the implications for Britain of the demobilization of disillusioned troops unattached to parliamentary democracy and open to anarchy and revolution. However, his new attitude towards Russia commended itself so little to his cabinet colleagues, obsessed only with military victory, that he was effectively sacked from the War Cabinet. Although George Barnes took his place, this proved to be a major blunder by Lloyd George, for it forced Labour into formal defiance of government policy for the first time. The Labour Party conference sanctioned British representation at Stockholm, and foreign affairs seemed suddenly to facilitate a rapprochement between middle-class socialists of the ILP and UDC and moderate trade unionists.

By September 1917 work was in hand on several key areas of Labour Party activity. A statement of 'Peace and War Aims', largely the work of MacDonald, Webb and Henderson, appeared in October; a new party constitution and a programme entitled 'Labour and the New Social Order' were ratified by a special conference in September 1918; and during 1918 Henderson devoted himself to preparing the party to fight a general election. All these changes, whatever their intrinsic significance, marked Labour's emancipation from the politics of the pact that had prevailed since 1903. Confidence and will to do this sprang from three sources. In the first place the parliamentary alliance had plainly ceased to exist, more by Liberal ineptitude than through Labour's intention. Henderson and MacDonald were conscious of the potential Labour support from middle-class radicals disillusioned and detached from their old party loyalty; Liberal organization had been deteriorating in working-class strongholds and many Liberal MPs would retire leaving opportunities for Labour. With no Liberal government in power all the pressures that had been effective in keeping Labour in tow before 1914 had lapsed.

The second factor was the expansion of the party's resources. Of course, payment of members in 1911 and the settlement of the Osborne dispute in 1913 had put the party in a stronger financial position. During the war total trade union membership rose from 4.1 to 6.5 million, and that of TUC-affiliated unions from 2.6 to 5.2 million. The intention of the constitutional reforms was to translate this latent strength into actual constituency machinery in the form of an organized party in every seat; the number of affiliated constituency bodies (LRCs and trades councils) grew as shown in table 8.1.[17] While their rivals were stagnating or collapsing Labour made up ground. The fairly static pre-war position changed significantly in 1917 and dramatically in 1918; the number of affiliated bodies for that year corresponds very closely with

TABLE 8.1   *The Labour Party: affiliated constituency bodies*

1913	1914	1915	1916	1917	1918
143	179	177	199	239	389

Labour candidatures at the election. The selection of candidates followed a similar pattern; the breakthrough was concentrated right at the end of the war. Although in January 1916, 30 candidatures were sanctioned, all but one of these were already on the list of 117 in 1914; by January 1917 four more had been sanctioned, though again two were on the 1914 list. Thus most of the 388 who fought in 1918 emerged in the closing stages. However, since 1914 the NEC had used two travelling organizers to tour constituencies to ascertain which should be fought, and this was stepped up in 1917 when 79 districts were visited.[18] Though the NEC adhered to the party truce, independent Labour candidates had appeared in by-elections at Salford North in February 1917 where a seat was gained from the Liberals, and at Wansbeck in May 1918 where the miners unsuccessfully contested Charles Fenwick's old constituency.

The third stimulating factor from the summer of 1917 was the realization by Henderson that the Cabinet would seriously press for the comprehensive electoral reform proposed by the Speaker's Conference. This was to assist Labour in several ways; by expanding the working-class vote at a time when the Liberals were in no position to exploit it; by limiting election expenses, which made the contest with the Conservatives less unequal; and by revising constituency boundaries, which in disrupting existing party organizations damaged the other parties more than Labour. In addition when Henderson contemplated fielding 500 candidates he did so on the assumption that the alternative vote (which prevents the election of a member on a minority of the votes), originally part of the Reform Bill, would obviate the danger of splitting the Progressive vote to Conservative advantage; it was not until February 1918 that the alternative vote was dropped from the Bill; but though worrying for Labour, this came too late to have a significant effect on the number of candidates. Thus the pact was dead and Labour with 388 candidates could bid to form a majority for the first time. In retrospect, the concatenation of a Liberal split, the war, and electoral reform created such obviously favourable conditions for a fresh strategy by Labour that it seems remarkable that the party was so slow to seize its opportunity. However much importance one gives to working-class political consciousness as the explanation for Labour's emergence as a major political party, the fact remains that the *timing* appears to owe far more to parliamentary politics. The potential for a governing party based on the working class had existed unrealized for decades, but there are no good grounds for thinking that Labour would have attained this status in the 1920s but for the decisions and blunders of 1914–18.

9

A Mass Electorate at War

No one can be really at peace in his own mind now
until he has in some way offered his life to his country.

Gilbert Murray to J. L. Hammond, 17 November 1915[1]

Impact on Civilians

The experience and response of the mass of people during the First
World War were of major importance in shaping the modern pattern of
British politics. The year 1918 saw the majority of the adult population
enfranchised for the first time, and produced an election that imposed a
pattern for the next half century. What is striking is that the immediate
impact of war seems to have been far less disturbing in Britain than in
other countries. The explanation for the comparative stability and
acquiescence of the population may be found first by considering the
material–social conditions of wartime, and second by examining how
attitudes towards the war were moulded and contained.

Against the immediate background of widespread industrial militancy
the authorities not unnaturally took at face value the threats made by
some socialist leaders to use the weapon of a general strike to stop international war. However, since the anti-war movement collapsed, on both
political and industrial fronts, this danger failed to materialize. Yet the
government greatly feared that a sharp rise in unemployment and an
increase in food prices, as a result of hoarding and the interruption of
imports, would generate mass disturbances; hence the need in the early
months for 'business as usual', as Churchill put it.

In fact the government's difficulties on the industrial front were to
arise not from a surplus of labour but from a shortage. The immediate
effect of the war was to reverse militancy: the 972 stoppages of 1914
dropped to 672 in 1915, and the number of days lost fell from 9.8

million to 2.9 million; there was a further fall during 1916 followed by successive increases in strike action in 1917 and 1918, when 5.8 million days were lost, and a fivefold increase during the 1919–21 period. By and large men were anxious to take advantage of opportunities created by the desperate need for coal, munitions and other war supplies to work a full week, and their leaders were drawn into co-operation by politicians stressing the crucial nature of their contribution to the war effort. Strikes in the South Wales coalfield led eventually to the state running the entire industry and conceding national wage agreements. Under the 'Treasury Agreement' of March 1915, later embodied in the Munitions of War Act in July, the engineering unions accepted temporarily a dilution of skilled labour and waived their right to strike in return for concessions over wages and profits. Inevitably the amenability of union leaders exposed them to challenges at local level, hence the emergence of a major shop stewards' movement in this period. The most serious disturbances were those led by the Clyde Workers Committee in 1915–16; however, this was a case in which a genuinely syndicalist leadership mobilized conservative craftsmen worried about the erosion of their position as skilled men but uninterested in a social revolution or in stopping the war. Clydeside was therefore of local importance, and untypical of the working population as a whole. The increase in strikes in 1917 reflected simply a desire to catch up with the price rises of the early part of the war. Walter Runciman, who had occasion to bargain with both sides of industry as President of the Board of Trade, concluded that the unions were far more susceptible to appeals to their patriotism than the employers who invariably insisted on guaranteed profit levels well above those of peacetime.

Since four-fifths of wheat, two-thirds of sugar and half of the meat consumed in Britain were imported, some price rises were inevitable; however, shortages and inflation during 1914–18 were never serious enough to have demoralizing effects upon the population. Although the rationing system of the last year of war seems to have been popular and successful, it was never applied to potatoes and bread because the authorities believed the industrial population must be well supplied with energy-producing foods. Both middle-class and working-class families were bombarded with instructions about economic eating, but the latter were quite resistant to this pressure. The Edwardian generation had grown up on an improved and varied diet in which meat made regular appearances on the tables of working-class families. Serious erosion of that standard was not necessary because the incomes of working-class families increased in real terms during the war. This was not primarily due to rises in wages rates, which fell behind price rises in the first two years, but to the movement out of low-paid employment such as domestic service into higher-paid jobs with plenty of overtime; women who had earned 10s as servants could earn from £2 to £5 in munitions factories. In addition many boys of 18 left home, freeing jobs such as running errands, delivering papers or selling from a barrow for younger brothers and sisters who absconded from school. Thus the labour shortage during the war stimulated the purchasing power of many families and built up a demand for consumer goods. Cheap items like black pudding were de-rationed because demand slackened, while luxury goods like pianos were bought by the thousand towards the end of the war. These manifestations of consumerism have much importance. They exacerbated the gulf between the civilian and the soldier who did not appreciate being told how lucky he was to be at the front. Also, in so far as civilian needs were satisfied there was no major build-up of discontent by the time of the 1918 election; only in the aftermath, 1919–20, when the civilian felt his gains slipping away, did he grow politically restive.

From the outbreak of hostilities the authorities had taken steps to persuade the civilian population that any hardships and sacrifices were well worth making. Initially they were unduly apprehensive about the panic and demoralization that news of military setbacks or zeppelin attacks might cause. They therefore adopted several techniques to maintain morale. Propaganda was directed from Wellington House by Charles Masterman, eventually superseded in 1918 by a Ministry of Information under Lord Beaverbrook; the Parliamentary Recruiting Committee flooded the country with posters and meetings; and the government, using its powers under the Defence of the Realm Act, censored closely all information pertaining to the war. However, the military reports emanating from the War Office and the Press Bureau were so bland and thin as to force the press to start bypassing the official machinery. There were absurd attempts to blot out outstanding events such as the German entry into Belgium on 3 August (reported in the *Daily Telegraph* but flatly denied by the Foreign Office), and the sinking of the *Audacious* by a mine (photographed for the American papers but censored in Britain). Yet there was a basis for official fears. Between 14 and 25 August the French armies had suffered no less than 300,000 casualties, a rate of 25 per cent; it was feared that knowledge of this would have shocked and possibly checked the flow of recruits.

However, when on occasion the truth slipped through – such as in *The Times'* report on Mons, headed 'Broken British Regiments Battling Against Odds' – the press were not very proud of their scoops. Most editors and proprietors wished to be loyal if only the authorities would feed them good rousing copy. This appears to have been widely reflected among their readers who often had no desire to read the unvarnished truth. *The Times* was denounced for its story on Mons, and the *Mail* and *The Times* were publicly denounced for criticizing Kitchener for shortages of shells in 1915. Therefore a compromise was devised in 1915 whereby a handful of journalists were allowed into France and had their articles censored on the spot and at the War Office before they reached their editors. The whole object was to protect the army from criticism and maintain domestic morale with unceasing streams of heroic tales. As one of the journalists later wrote:

> We identified ourselves absolutely with the Armies in the field. . . . We wiped out of our minds all thoughts of personal scoops. . . . There was no need of censorship of our dispatches. We were our own censors.[2]

Thus the press largely abdicated its function during the war, at least as far as military events were concerned; it soaked up the grotesquely inaccurate information about Haig's battles, and regaled readers with stories of troops who loved nothing better than going over the top.

The public were probably more inclined to believe what they read in the press than is the case today, especially when presented in photographic form such as the *Daily Mail*'s bogus official war postcards depicting 'Tommy' rescuing a comrade under fire. However, it must be remembered that to a large degree the troops co-operated by filling their letters home with reassuring platitudes about their good health and spirits in an effort to spare the feelings of their families. It was hardly surprising that when the men came home on leave they frequently found that an unbridgeable gap had opened up between them and the civilians, and they were often reduced to solitary brooding over their experiences.

However, as the lengthening lists of casualties appeared in the press during 1915 and 1916 telling a tale inconsistent with the official version, one might have expected signs of disillusion and questioning about the fight-to-a-finish. It may be that the sheer numbers of casualties were too difficult to take in, and that grief was concentrated on known individuals. Since so many families suffered losses their own grief could be partly assuaged in the general sense of loss; it soon became abnormal and humiliating *not* to have a close relative at the front. In these circumstances even to consider ending the war before the enemy had been defeated could seem a betrayal of those who had already died. This fear of disloyalty was instrumental in cutting off the anti-war organizations from most of the civilians who might have sympathized with them. Initially the flood of patriotism at home was so overpowering that the Union of Democratic Control (UDC), for example, feared even to make its views known to the public; this lack of any co-ordinated effort at opposing the policies connected with the war was never really overcome. Only when goaded by the right-wing press did the UDC articulate its interpretation of the war as a product of secret diplomacy, the arms race and the foolish pursuit of the balance of power. The implication that Britain was by no means blameless was treated with utter disbelief. To accept the UDC version of events would have been, for civilians and politicians alike, to admit that one had been wrong or deceived before 1914; and to concede the pacifists' argument would have been to allow them a higher moral standard than oneself. Although there was greater sympathy for bodies like the No Conscription Fellowship, social intimidation kept the number of applications for exemption by 'Conscientious Objectors' down to 16,000; even these were untypically middle-class, perhaps because the successful objector had to be articulate enough to face a tribunal keen to catch him out, and usually had to demonstrate pre-war membership of a group like the Quakers who were well known for pacifist sentiments.

The party truce in by-elections offered scope to independent candidates to mobilize discontent, but this was done successfully only by those who wished to push the government into more belligerent policies. When as a result of Keir Hardie's death in 1915 two 'Labour' candidates contested his old seat at Merthyr Tydfil, the pro-war C. B. Stanton easily defeated his anti-war rival. It was probably in 1916 that the anti-war movement began to make an impression. The appalling British disaster of the Somme involving Kitchener's volunteer armies reinforced doubts about the possibility and purpose of a complete military victory. The demise of the Asquith government released more left-wing politicians from an uncomfortable position. And in turning its attention to a negotiated peace and future methods of maintaining peace the UDC received indirect strength from similar pronouncements made in 1917 by President Woodrow Wilson and Lord Lansdowne. In April 1918 a peace-by-negotiation candidate polled a third of the votes at the Keighley by-election, a modest sign of a potential anti-war party in the country.

However, most people plainly regarded the origins of the war as irrelevant and the 'knock-out blow' as the only possible strategy. In the last resort this must be ascribed to the popular conception of the enemy. For the Edwardian generation had absorbed a diet of invasion literature and war scares fomented by the press, and by 1914 they were so highly susceptible to the idea that German spies and saboteurs were in their midst, especially among the alien population, as to accept suggestions that war critics were paid agents or sympathizers of the Germans. Moreover the circulation of atrocity stories served to transform the 'German' into a sub-human brute. Although quite without foundation, atrocity stories gained credibility partly by dint of repetition and partly by the authority given them by Lord Bryce's committee of investigation which pronounced thousands of 'atrocities' true, despite its failure even to interview witnesses. British propagandists enjoyed some factual basis to substantiate their view that German ways of waging war were inhuman; the execution of Nurse Edith Cavell, the sinking of the *Lusitania* or the use of poison gas were undeniable, though not without parallels on the Allied side. The arrival of Belgian refugees was for many sufficient proof of the inevitability of a fight to the finish.

The impact of wartime pressures upon political attitudes is not easy to discern, though certain features are clear enough. In the country party politics had been largely suspended as erstwhile opponents joined together on the recruiting platforms. At Westminster too, normal debate subsided with the result that the press stepped in to fill the vacuum. Right-wing proprietors and editors, though vociferously loyal to the war effort, attempted the systematic denigration of the Asquith governments, concentrating particularly on individuals like Haldane, Churchill and McKenna whom they presented as men of doubtful patriotism responsible for military and naval setbacks. By contrast the press tended to encourage the public to place its confidence in Kitchener and Haig, Fisher and Jellicoe; it is significant that many people refused to believe that Kitchener had gone down with HMS *Hampshire* in June 1916, so much did they need a figurehead. In addition, diaries and letters of the time suggest that many liked to see the guiding hand of the King behind the 'strong' measures like the Defence of the Realm Act; as one teenager put it in February 1916: 'We wish the King would turn all the Government out and give orders himself, and really beat the Germans properly.'[3] This naive longing for a leader is reflected in the enthusiasm of many middle-class people for the former radical menace Lloyd George. When he became Prime Minister in December 1916 his speeches on the 'knock-out blow' and his photograph were promptly pasted into the nation's scrapbooks – treatment usually accorded to soldiers but not to politicians.

Among the non-combatant population women were particularly vulnerable to the official view of the war. Private diaries written by women during the war, for example, tend to reflect the feeling that only as a man could one make a real contribution; this was relentlessly exploited by the recruiting campaigns and posters designed to challenge the manhood of the non-combatant male, and emphasize that the least, and most, that a woman could do was to ensure that her menfolk were dispatched to the front. Beyond this, officialdom approved most strongly of women as the bearers of the next generation of fighting men, hence the indulgence shown to mothers of the illegitimate 'war babies', offspring of thousands of Kitchener's volunteers in 1915. For middle-class girls, nursing was still seen as the appropriate wartime occupation, while working-class girls had to face resentment and prejudice when national necessity forced farms and munitions factories to take them on. This ran against the trend of half a century in which women were eased out of supposedly inappropriate heavy and dirty manual labour – except in the home. It is significant that where women who undertook male tasks during the war have left a record of their feelings they seem to have taken for granted that they were stepping in on a purely temporary basis, and they vacated their jobs at the end of the war without protest. This is not so surprising in view of the relatively conservative, middle-class nature of the bulk of the pre-1914 women's movement, which had largely confined itself to the narrow question of the parliamentary franchise and neglected the wider social objectives that the vote might help them to attain.[4] In this light the grant of the franchise in 1918 to women over 30 years of age who were either local government electors themselves or the wives of local government electors is explicable. Both the Speaker's Conference and Parliament were determined to keep women in a minority among voters, and to enfranchise only those who, as relatively mature, family women, seemed likely to constitute a stable, loyal section of the community.[5] Although the 8.4 million women voters comprised 40 per cent of the total electorate, they were not expected to form a distinct group pressing their own claims, but rather a loyal, patriotic body reflecting the politics of their husbands.

Thus the civilian population, if longing for peace, seems to have wanted victory first. Any disillusion evident from 1916 onwards was held in check partly by buoyant standards of living, by the absence of a credible alternative analysis of the war to resist official and press propaganda, and by a simple faith in the King, Sir Douglas Haig and Lloyd George.

Impact on the Troops

During the war many politicians adopted a comforting view of the men in the trenches as dedicated patriots; not only did they extend the franchise to them, but insisted on the need for their participation in a general election. However, much of this misplaced confidence stemmed from a confusion between the troops of 1914–18 and the regular army; in understanding their attitudes one must bear in mind the broad distinction between the regulars, the volunteers of 1914–15, and the conscripted men of 1916–18.

Among professionals and upper-class officers one finds the most evidence of an uncomplicated response to war, and, as might be expected, the least questioning or disillusion. Their observations are replete with sporting metaphors of war, with hunting at the front, and with war as a decent, honourable affair. This was characteristic of airmen whose favourite form of warfare – duels with enemy planes – appealed strongly to traditional, romantic notions. One of them protested against his sister's munitions work: 'if we can't win this war without our women coming down to manual labour of that description I'd just as soon we were licked.'[6] For such men war furnished an opportunity to prove their manhood and to simplify life's complexities; as Julian Grenfell, who had joined the army before 1914, enthused:

Isn't it luck for me to have been born so as to be just the right age and just in the right place – not too high up to be worried – to enjoy [the war] the most.[7]

Even in 1916 such men bore war's losses fairly stoically, followed their leaders uncritically, and interested themselves in simple patriotism and the status of their regiments. Indeed many felt only one doubt: 'I hope to God the politicians in England will not betray us and make peace before we have absolutely crushed our enemies.'[8]

On the other hand the vast majority of troops in 1914–16 were volunteers, 1,186,000 of whom came forward in the period from August to December 1914. By any standards this was a remarkable response. Although taught for a generation to expect an invasion and, since the early 1900s a German invasion, the bulk of the British people had remained stubbornly hostile to the idea of conscription. This reflected neither pacifism nor lack of patriotism, but status and pride. While the army was still associated with drunkenness, low company and exile, respectable working-class families were loath to allow their sons to join except out of dire necessity: 'I would rather bury you than see you in a red coat,' Field Marshall Sir William Robertson's mother had once told him. As a result even the Conservative Party, though agitating for extra expenditure on the navy, had declined to risk supporting Lord Roberts' National Service League in urging compulsory military training. However, hundreds of thousands of men in all classes found respectable forms of military participation in the Volunteer Force, the Territorial Army and the Rifle Clubs which were sharply distinct from both the regulars and from 'Prussianism'. Against this background of voluntaryism the response to Kitchener's appeal becomes explicable.

For many, of course, neither the personal nor the political implications of joining up involved much deliberate thought. Younger men often volunteered in a light-hearted way on the spur of the moment; for war offered a unique opportunity to get away from home to see foreign parts for a few months. For men without prospects Kitchener's army seemed a glamorous alternative. Yet although special factors such as the slump in the building trade during the summer of 1914 helped recruiting, it remains true that thousands left secure jobs as miners or engineers to join up.

Yet while September 1914 saw 450,000 volunteers come forward, October produced only 137,000; the first rush to the colours was already fading. In January 1915 the Board of Trade's Labour Department estimated that two-thirds of the males aged 17–45 were fit for army service, a total of 6 million; at this point roughly 2 million were already in the forces and at least 1 million working in vital industries, leaving perhaps 3 million possible recruits. During 1915 some 1.28 million men were taken, but it became more of a struggle to find them. In the months of July, August, September and December less than 100,000 volunteered, and the tone of the recruiting campaigns grew sharp and vituperative; the local press taunted the 'Shirkers of a National Duty'. In October, under Lord Derby's recruiting scheme, men were invited merely to attest their willingness to serve if required; significantly the Prime Minister's alleged promise at this point that all single men would be taken before married men prompted a sudden spate of marriages. Although the Derby Scheme may have stimulated the increase in October recruiting, by December the monthly figure had fallen to 55,000 compared with the 30,000 a week which some ministers were now demanding. After 16 months of war the pool of willing men had clearly begun to dry up. Now a man could calculate more coolly the costs and risks involved in going to war; it was plainly going to be a more protracted affair than originally thought; while casualty lists swelled ominously the attractions of greater employment opportunities at home increased. Consequently the authorities resorted to compulsion from January 1916, thereby squeezing out another 1.2 million in 1916, 820,000 in 1917 and 490,000 in 1918.

In contrast with the widespread disaffection and collapsing morale among the troops of France, Russia and Italy, the British appeared immune from mutiny or politically inspired discontent. This led many contemporaries during the war and inter-war years to characterize the troops as essentially passive, apathetic, shell-shocked and disillusioned but unable to articulate their feelings. More recently there has been a reaction against this approach to the effect that the British 'Tommy' was basically cheerful and stoical in temperament, a fact inexplicable to the educated middle-class sensibilities of the anti-war writers. However, this version, which is essentially part of the attempt to restore the reputation of Sir Douglas Haig and the war of attribution, is not well grounded in the source material. Certain aspects of the anti-war writers' case, for example the idea of the 'lost generation', have now been corroborated by research; while many of the features of war experience identified by Robert Graves or Siegfried Sassoon may now be studied in the contemporary records of ordinary, obscure men. In the long run, war experience was to have a disillusioning and a radicalizing effect for some working-class men and also for some middle-class men who found themselves closer to and in greater sympathy with the lower levels of society than they had ever been in peacetime. What concerns us here is how far the limited forms of discontent during 1914–18 had political implications.

It is perfectly clear that from the outset the spirit of the Kitchener armies was unusual; there was not the normal respect for the officers and only contempt for the training experienced in England. In the trenches keenness and discipline varied widely from one regiment to another. A common manifestation of discontent, recognized by the authorities, was for men to commit offences calculated to get them out of the front line to prison camps at base. In order to counter slackness and declining morale the army made great use of night-time patrols in no-man's-land, which the men often handled by sitting quietly and reporting 'all quiet', or even by mutual agreement with the enemy to ignore patrols. As one 21-year-old conscript wrote in August 1917:

> I'm doing properly whatever duty comes my way but I'm not going out of my way; I'm no longer interested in the Army; I'm only interested in finishing this ghastly war, and to that end I'll help.[9]

As for the cheerfulness shown by men going over the top, this was often the result of the very powerful rum ration or because of the greater chance of receiving a 'cushy' wound to send them home, as opposed to the likelihood of a fatal head wound in the trenches. There were also more deliberate manifestations of revolt, notably the mutiny by 10,000 British troops at the Etaples camp in the summer of 1917, an event concealed by the authorities at the time. Rates of desertion remained fairly high at around 10 per cent a year, worsening steadily after Passchendaele. Altogether there were 304,000 court-martial cases, of which 86 per cent resulted in conviction. The number of suicides and of men shot for cowardice in the trenches will never be known since they were officially recorded as deaths in action.

A major political implication of experience as a combatant was that the troops took a more balanced and relaxed view of the Germans than did most civilians. The army's intelligence broadsheets on atrocities were regarded as 'comic cuts' by men, who, while often bitter at the loss of friends and acts of cruelty, accepted that the behaviour of their own side was very similar. This helped to set them apart from the wild conceptions of those at home. 'Don't be harsh in your judgements on them,' one man reproached his mother, 'we who are up against them cannot be.'[10] Indeed coming home on leave was often the catalyst of disenchantment; when the men wanted only a good sleep their families were bent upon parading them before an admiring locality and discussing the one thing they wished to forget. It could be infuriating to be told how lucky one was to have a 'crack at the Bosche', to be handed white feathers when in civilian clothes, or to contemplate the profits being made out of the war to which Horatio Bottomley's *John Bull* magazine regularly drew the soldiers' attention. Alienated from home, men often found relief in rejoining their comrades who at least understood. Loyalty to comrades and to junior officers who shared the same dangers and privations was a major reason for the steadiness of the British troops. Even a man like Siegfried Sassoon, who ostentatiously quit the army in July 1917 in protest against the prolongation of the war, found himself driven back at his own wish in 1918. This underlines the important fact that the most dissatisfied soldiers were either isolated from a coherent alternative view of the war, or, like Sassoon, so antagonized by the pacifist spokesmen that no effective link was forged between critics at home and in the army.[11]

Consequently dissension tended to concentrate on specific material complaints such as poor boots, the pilfering of food on its way to the front line, and the 5s and 6s paid per day to colonial troops while the British received only 1s 6d. Some links grew up between these grievances and the Soldiers and Workers Councils in industry. In June 1917, for example, men in several southern county regiments formed the Home Counties and Training Reserve Branch of the Workers and Soldiers Council[12] and issued a number of demands such as examination by civilian doctors for wounded men before being sent back to the front; but they also made political complaints over their exclusion from citizenship, the failure of the government to indicate on what terms they would negotiate a peace settlement and the financing of the war by loans and the printing of money. However, although 'Soldiers Charters' were taken up by the ILP and some Labour politicians during 1918 there was never an effective attempt to harness the servicemen to the Labour movement let alone to the peace movement. Labour leaders often took at face value the confidence of the right wing in the troops, so that they suspected organizations of such men of being directed against trade unions, or even threatening the parliamentary system. Arthur Henderson's initiatives during the genesis of the Representation of the People

Act in 1916–17 and during the organizational extension of the Labour Party in 1917–18 reflected a profound apprehension about the consequences of several million ex-soldiers being unemployed and unattached to parliamentary politics. Political safety seemed to lie in demobilizing the soldiers as quickly as possible so that their aspirations might be tackled as workers rather than as soldiers. It would be fatal, Herbert Morrison told the ILP, to attempt a unionization of the armed forces which would 'lead to the army being looked upon as a respectable profession'.[13] In this way the political potential of military discontent was never exploited during the First World War.

The Coupon Election 1918

The Coupon Election of 14 December 1918 in which no less than 21 million soldiers and civilians enjoyed the right to vote, proved to be a watershed in twentieth-century politics. It ushered in the inter-war era of Conservative dominance; it dealt the Liberals a blow from which they never fully recovered and thereby gave Labour the chance to become the parliamentary opposition.

The victory of the candidates of the Lloyd George Coalition in 526 seats out of 707 left it in a remarkably strong position, particularly in view of the failure of the largest opposition group, Sinn Fein, to attend Westminster (see table 9.1). Like most elections the 1918 result had been broadly determined well in advance of the campaign. It is difficult to interpret the landslide other than as a long-delayed eruption of Germanophobia which could only redound to the benefit of the Conservatives. Not all government candidates actively stirred such emotions for it was unnecessary to do so. Lloyd George can be defended from the charge of intending to fight the election on a policy of making Germany pay 'until the pips squeak', for he had begun by speaking of a sanely negotiated peace and domestic reform. But he was too sensitive to audience reaction to stick to unpalatable topics, and it was not surprising that he ended the campaign pandering to popular desires for vengeance instead of using his prestige to counter them; on 11 December he put prime ministerial approval on the notion that Germany should pay the uttermost cost of the war and on an absurdly high estimate of what that was.

Candidates were made to feel that their soundness on this issue was under scrutiny; in London, for example, candidates received telegrams from the editor of the *Evening News* demanding:

For the guidance of your constituency will you kindly state whether if elected you will support the following (1) Punishment of the Kaiser (2) Full payment for the war by Germany (3) The expulsion from the British Isles of all Enemy Aliens.

In a competition of this kind the Conservatives enjoyed a head start, for Liberal and Labour candidates, even those who had been staunch supporters of the government, could have their pre-1914 record thrown back at them. In Shoreditch Christopher Addison, despite having the coupon and his wartime ministerial record, found his Conservative opponent pointing to his votes against the naval estimates: 'It has not taken a war to teach me my policy.'[14] Since very few candidates were prepared to repudiate or question the cause or conduct of the war, the Conservatives could simply adopt the stance of men who had been proved right by events. Most politicians contrived to capitalize on their personal contribution preferably by military service; by way of compensation women were photographed with husbands in uniform, while older men drew attention to their part in the South African War or to their sons' role in the present one. It is not without significance that the only seat gained by an uncouponed Asquithian Liberal was at Leith where William Wedgwood Benn was able to quote from General Hamilton's dispatches on actions in which he had taken part.[15]

Some opposition politicians tried to turn the obsession with the forces to their advantage by widening the issue to the welfare of the troops

TABLE 9.1 *1918 general election*

	Coalition seats	Vote %		Opposition seats	Vote %
Con	335(374)*	32.6	Lab	57[†](388)	22.2
Con			Lib	28[‡](258)	12.1
Uncouponed	48(75)	6.1	S Fein	73 (102)	4.5
LG Lib	133(159)	13.5	I. Nat	7 (60)	2.2
Nat Lab	10(18)	1.5	Others	16 (197)	5.3
	526			181	

* Figures in brackets denote number of candidates.
† Also Independent Labour at Anglesey and Aberdeen N., Co-operative at Kettering and National Socialist Party at West Ham (Silvertown) give the total of 61 sometimes quoted.
‡ 37 were elected as Liberals without the Coupon, but 9 of these took the government whip subsequently.

and their families. They often criticized Lloyd George for effectively disfranchising the men by rushing into an election while they were still abroad. C. P. Trevelyan warned against the maintenance of conscription after the war, and his 'Soldier's Fourteen Points' included rapid demobilization, state maintenance for discharged men, an increase in privates' pay to 6s and higher weekly pensions. But with his UDC record Trevelyan polled a derisory 5.6 per cent (admittedly as an independent against three party candidates); perhaps the most impressive poll by a 'pacifist' was Arthur Ponsonby's 22.6 per cent against Coalition Liberal and Labour at Dunfermline.

Our understanding of the outcome of the 1918 election is enhanced by comparing it with another landslide, that of 1945, which shows that the association of an election with a war does not necessarily produce a move to the right. In both cases the party in office at the start of the war proved highly vulnerable to blame for lack of preparation or of determination in conducting the war. Moreover in 1945 there was no question of branding the Labour opposition as unpatriotic, for the Conservatives were, if anything, more exposed because of their pre-war weakness in the face of the dictators. There is a further element of difference that bears strongly upon the results. During the Second World War it could be confidently assumed from 1943 onwards that Germany could not win, which relieved the people of much concern. There followed two years in which the sacrifices imposed upon civilians grew more irksome; in the process thoughts of revenge faded and attention turned towards domestic conditions after the war. Thus by the time of the election the issues of social reform in which the voters were primarily interested were precisely the issues that the Labour Party could most effectively exploit.[16] No such considerations applied in 1918. As late as the spring of 1918 the war was very nearly lost by the Allies, and it was assumed that hostilities would go on through 1919. When during the summer of 1918 the military tide suddenly began to turn, the Armistice and the general election followed rapidly while the emotions of wartime were still high. Thus the timing of the Coupon Election was vital; had it been postponed, however, until 1919 or 1920 it would instead have caught the angry mood of disaffection and produced a result far more favourable to the parties of the left.

While the underlying mood determined that 1918 would be a Conservative victory, it does not fully explain the scale of the victory. Naturally the result represented a distortion of the voting in that the Coalition won 74 per cent of the seats for 54 per cent of the poll. In the absence of the Liberal–Labour pact the opposition forces were bound to throw away much of the territory held in 1910. What perhaps requires consideration is why the one factor that might have been expected to tell in favour of the non-Conservative parties, the vastly increased franchise, did not apparently help.

To consider first the forces vote, it is evident that the government went to considerable lengths to allow them to participate in the election. This complicated and prolonged the preparation of the new register; men in Belgium and France were granted postal votes with a two-week delay in the count to give them time to reach the returning officers, and those further afield voted by proxy. Yet there are good grounds for doubting whether the soldiers' vote was a loyal government one. Out of the total electorate of 21 million, service voters numbered 3.9 million; of these 2.7 million were sent ballot papers but only 900,000 actually voted in the election. This low rate of participation reflected the physical difficulties and a certain isolation from politics in general and from local constituency conditions in particular. From what we know of the troops' resentment against domestic propaganda they were bound to find the Coalition's case less plausible than the civilians did, but the main factor was simply the difficulty of mobilizing their support in the chaotic conditions of 1918. Observers at the count noticed that soldiers had sometimes expressed their feelings by inscribing 'demobilize first' on the ballot, and that a high proportion of absent votes went to Labour candidates.[17] The private papers of a number of prominent pacifist politicians certainly contain letters from soldiers wishing them success and endorsing their views on the war.[18] And well before the election the UDC organizers had reached the conclusion that discharged men provided the most receptive material.[19] Thus there are indications that, as in 1945, the troops would in fact lean to the left. However, it must be stressed that this was a latent tendency not fully realized in 1918; too many had to vote while still abroad, and the direct connections between politicians and soldiers such as Sassoon's work for Philip Snowden at Blackburn were very much the exception.

The evidence, impressionistic as it is, tends to suggest that civilian voters, particularly the women among them, were far more the backbone of the Coalition's majority. Isolated from the real war they were apt to want to prove their loyalty to the men who had fought by voting for a tough peace settlement; this was their vicarious blow against Germany. Candidates themselves formed the impression that women voters leant strongly to the Coalition,[20] voting as they believed their husbands or brothers would wish. This seems credible in the light of the finding of later studies that women as a whole give a consistently higher Conservative vote than men. If so, this is important because of the large role of women in 1918. For their effective part was rather greater than their 40 per cent share of the electorate suggests. Women frequently acted as proxies for sons and husbands who comprised one-third of the

3.9 million service vote. Also the overall turnout of only 59 per cent conceals wide differences; at York, for example, it was found that 75 per cent of home electors had voted, but only 40 per cent of absent voters. Thus women as part of the domestic electorate seem likely to have had an effective ratio of 50:50 with men in 1918.

Inevitably the coupon arrangement attracted much contemporary comment, particularly from those who ascribed their defeat to the misleading effect it had had on voters. However, there are good grounds for thinking that the coupon was a handy excuse for those who would have been defeated in any case. Although 133 of the 159 Liberals who received the coupon won seats, this was because in most cases the coupon deterred local Conservative associations from opposing them; it was the free run that guaranteed success. This is corroborated by the successes of Conservatives who stood without the coupon: 25 of these were Irish Unionist MPs, but in Britain 37 Conservatives stood uncouponed with success in 23 cases. A number of these were in hitherto unfavourable constituencies; for example Barrow was gained after 12 years as a Labour seat; and Liberal seats fell at Bury (where the Liberal had the coupon himself), Rotherham, Derby, Salford West, Forfarshire and East Fife (Asquith's seat). It looks very much as though Conservatives were doing equally well with or without the coupon. It may, however, have been decisive in tipping the result against prominent Asquithian ex-ministers who were within reach of victory, notably Runciman at Dewsbury, Samuel at Cleveland and McKenna at Pontypool. Here Conservatives won simply by maintaining their pre-war share of the poll while the non-Conservative vote was evenly split between Liberal and Labour. These are distinct from the really disastrous Liberal performances such as Sir Charles Hobhouse's 7.6 per cent at East Bristol or McKinnon Wood's 8.2 per cent at Glasgow (St Rollox), which reflect a widespread collapse of party organization during the war, deteriorating relations between MPs and local associations, and a failure to keep in touch with a vastly expanding electorate in these crucial years. The Asquithians had created a hopeless tactical position for themselves. By declining to attack the 'knock-out blow' approach to the war they cut themselves off from one section of opinion; yet by refusing to participate in Lloyd George's Coalition government they only emphasized their position as the men who could be blamed for the early failures. This was an untenable position simply because the public found it hard to understand.

In many ways the Labour Party's performance in 1918 is the most interesting. The total of seats won, 57, is significant only by comparison with the pathetic performance of the Asquithian Liberals, for it represented only a modest advance on the 42 seats won in 1910. Moreover to a considerable extent the same ground was being held in the two elections: solid mining constituencies. There was a similar concentration of Labour MPs in Lancashire together with an expansion from bridgeheads already established in the coalfields of South Wales, the North-East and the Midlands. Here the redistribution helped the party by increasing the number of seats dominated by highly unionized working-class communities. Of the MPs in 1918, 51 had been nominated by trade unions, 25 of them by the Miners Federation. In terms of seats, 1922 was to be the real point of breakthrough for Labour.

The other factor contributing to the successes of 1918 was the patriotic attitude adopted by many trade unionists. Prominent Labour figures like J. H. Thomas, who won comfortably against Conservative and Liberal opposition, and J. R. Clynes and Vernon Hartshorn, who were unopposed, took a line very similar to Lloyd George's over reparations and Germany. Conversely, candidates attempting to propagate the views of the UDC or ILP usually met overwhelming rebuff even in working-class seats, and local Labour parties did their best to avoid association with the ILP for fear of damaging their chances. Anti-war MPs, though not surprised at losing, were astonished at the scale of their defeat; at West Leicester MacDonald won only 23.6 per cent in a straight fight, while Snowden achieved 19.7 per cent at Blackburn in a three-cornered contest. Thus, the socialist/trade unionist rapprochement on foreign policy from the summer of 1917 appears not to have penetrated from the national to the local level. In the country Labour chose to present the war as a triumph for the working classes and made only token gestures towards ILP views of past and future foreign policy by talking vaguely of international co-operation in place of secret diplomacy. MacDonald and Snowden, like Ponsonby and Trevelyan, had been misled by audiences which 'listened spellbound' in private meetings or ILP gatherings. It proved difficult to translate their enthusiasm into an efficient canvass of a mass electorate. As MacDonald's agent explained: 'the root cause of lethargy among ILP'ers was the *fear* of personally defending an unpopular candidate. I mean having to encounter opposition on the doorsteps.'[21]

In the long run, of course, the seats won in 1918 were of less significance than the size of the Labour vote – 22.7 per cent of the total. This cannot be assumed to reflect the effect of the expanded franchise; it reflected the number of candidatures, now 388 compared with 56 in December 1910. Comparisons between the pre- and post-1918 franchise are complicated because in most cases both the constituency boundaries and the number of candidates also changed. An analysis of the performance of all Labour candidates in relation to changes in the size of the electorate in 1918 has found that the *higher* the proportion of new voters in a constituency the *less* well the party did.[22] In part this reflected the tendency among female voters to favour the Conservatives. Clearly the 1918 election results provide little evidence that Labour achieved a dramatic breakthrough as a result of a new reservoir of electors. By contrast, in the municipal elections of 1919 and subsequent years Labour did make sweeping gains especially in the London boroughs. Interestingly, however, most of the new male parliamentary voters were still not qualified to vote in local government which was based on a franchise very close to the pre-war parliamentary electorate.

Thus the key to Labour's strength lay in taking over in 1918 part of the support and strength of the Liberal Party. Since for 707 seats there were only 258 Asquithian Liberal candidates compared to 388 Labour ones it is obvious that many former Liberals were obliged to choose between a Labour and a government candidate or stay at home; 1918 broke the habit, and thereafter the number of Liberal candidatures fluctuated wildly from one election to another. Both Liberal and Labour candidates in 1918 commented on the numbers of ex-Liberal constituency activists now running Labour campaigns.[23] Arnold Rowntree pointed out that those who had previously voted Liberal 'for traditional reasons but are not specially interested in policies' often went for the Coalition, while radicals, pacifists and the more politically involved were opting for Labour in 1918. This loss of local activists, which crippled Liberal work at constituency level in the inter-war years, was really the most dire consequence of 1918, for it meant that subsequent national Liberal revivals could never be made to survive at the grass roots. This development was less the result of the coupon itself than of Asquith's earlier abandonment of the pre-1914 Progressive Alliance from 1915 onwards. Because at the time relatively little canvassing was done and because voters were sometimes reluctant to proclaim their alienation from their old party, the full extent of the leakage was not apparent until the count when candidates often blamed the coupon for the result. But the underlying importance of 1918 lay in a shift of existing Liberal support to Labour, and, of course, to Conservative candidates; in so far as the newly enfranchised made an impact it was probably to strengthen the Coalition government.

10

Party, Ideology and the State
in the Great War

... the substitution of public service for private profit
is no new ideal for me who was brought up by my
Father to believe in the Municipal Socialism of the
London Progressive Party.

William Wedgwood Benn to A. Munro, 25 January 1927

The Myth of Laissez-faire and Interventionism

There is a pervasive notion that the politics of the Great War in Britain
took the form of an ideological struggle between the forces of *laissez-faire*
and those of interventionism and collectivism in which the former
was decisively, and inevitably defeated; December 1916 when the rigid
adherents of economic liberalism were displaced by the Lloyd George/
Conservative Coalition is usually seen as the turning-point in this
conflict.[1] Now it has long been obvious that this interpretation of 1916–
18 is particularly difficult to square with the economic attitudes of
governments of all kinds during the inter-war period, especially the
1920s, which hardly reflect conversion to collectivism by the experience
of the war. Moreover, now that we are aware how far *laissez-faire* had
already been abandoned by the Liberals before 1914 we can only be
thoroughly sceptical of writers who assume that the prevalence of this
doctrine accounts for the difficulties encountered by the governments of
1914–16.

The truth is that every main political school found interventionist
ideas acceptable in certain respects but repugnant in others; sections of
every party had already moved towards the modern conception of the
state; and the collectivist policies practised in the 50 years after 1918
were essentially extensions of those principles established before 1914.
Liberals had characteristically come to see the state as a humanitarian

agency of social welfare and a redistributor of surpluses for the benefit of society, but drew the line at protectionism and confiscation, and sought to make free enterprise work effectively rather than to eliminate it. The Labour Party shared these attitudes; it espoused state ownership of one or two special industries, but shrank from a state that threatened freedom of labour or freedom of trade, and was innocent of the role of a sophisticated modern bureacracy. Socialists, while being clear about the superiority of the common good, ranged all the way from Fabian confidence in a benevolent state to the Guild Socialist and syndicalist suspicion of it. Conservatives were willing enough to bow to state control in the civil and military spheres when pressing national interests required it, but in economic affairs they accepted the paraphernalia of control on a strictly temporary basis and retained intact their belief in minimal government and minimal taxation; while the bulk of the party had shifted closer to *laissez-faire* they had made trade a special exception, and one school of imperialists had embraced a Bismarckian concept of the state. The First World War did not so much modify any of these attitudes as rearrange the places of those who held them.

Up to 1914 it was the Liberals who, because of their restoration to office in 1906 and because of their relatively rich intellectual heritage, had done most to shift Britain away from nineteenth-century economic doctrines. Thus, hostility to state interventionism was not a major problem for them during wartime. Just as the government was prepared to play fast and loose with its political principles, so too it proceeded largely unencumbered by traditional economics. The Asquith Cabinet had in fact considered in advance of war what kinds of steps would be necessary to save the economy from collapse in time of war. Having identified food supply and disruption of internal communications as major problems they had prepared to intervene in the fields of railways and shipping insurance despite Treasury advice to the contrary; and they were quick, of course, to underpin the whole financial system in 1914. Hence there was no hesitation in using their powers under two Acts of 1870 and 1888 to impose control on the railways in August 1914. This was done by co-operation between the railway company directors and civil servants through the Railway Executive Committee, a typically pragmatic step that set the pattern for many subsequent extensions of control during the war.

In so far as the government's approach was governed by principle at all it was derived not from economics but from a military conception of the kind of war Britain would fight. If one started from the assumption that the careful pre-war plans based on a modestly sized Expeditionary Force and the Royal Navy were Britain's chief contributions, then it followed logically that there would be no radical disruption of the economy and little need for additional controls beyond those already mentioned. The War Office would be able to rely upon its existing arrangement with the arsenals and with private munitions manufacturers to supply the army without imposing great strains upon the resources of the economy.[2] Nor was this contrary to military views; it was in fact underpinned by the government's military advice as to the quantity of ammunition required by the army; despite the experience of the South African War the experts continued to regard the artillery as basically a supporting weapon, and were content to use shrapnel rather than high-explosive shells, although the latter were later found indispensable on the Western Front.[3] Thus when a 'crisis' blew up in 1915 over a shell shortage the situation was the result of the government having acted on certain military judgements by military men, not because it was inhibited by economic doctrines.

The underlying reason why the Asquith government got into difficulties was that it allowed, almost unthinkingly, the original basis of its war policy to be drastically altered by Lord Kitchener's vast extension of the size of the armed forces. By January 1915, when some 2 million men had enlisted, business could no longer be run as usual, even with the navy keeping the trade lanes open, because of the huge demands made on our economic resources by the needs of the troops for supplies of all kinds, and because of the shortages of skilled labour particularly in mining, engineering and agriculture. An alternative strategy was articulated by Maurice Hankey, Secretary of the War Council, by ministers like McKenna and Runciman, and by civil servants like Hubert Llewellyn Smith of the Board of Trade; the latter argued in January 1915 that of the 3 million fit men of the right age still remaining at home no more than 1.1 million could be taken for the army without crippling British industry.[4] The implications of this were that Britain's best policy lay in using her industrial base to support the Allies, making maximum use of the Royal Navy militarily and economically, and restricting her offensive role on the Western Front. For reasons that need not detain us here this strategy was not followed; Kitchener's mass volunteer armies gave way to conscription and to a greater and greater British participation in the land war. What is important is that although these alternatives were hotly disputed, the disagreements sprang not from economic beliefs but from differing politico-military conceptions about how to fight the war.

The empirical evidence tends to show that even those who believed in a 'small' war were flexible and opportunistic in adopting appropriate policies; indeed it was a matter of trial and error with forms of intervention and control for all governments during the war years. A characteristic and important example of this is food supply. At the outset of the war the Asquith government stepped in to purchase wheat from the USA and Argentina and sugar from the West Indies, to control Indian wheat, and to secure an agreed scale of maximum retail prices with shopkeepers. This policy grew bit by bit until by 1918 no less than 80 per cent of Britain's food was passing through the government machine and subject to price control. The palpable intention of Asquith's government was to interfere with the free market by cutting out the middlemen, whose competition raised prices, and by releasing their own supplies onto the market so as to keep the price level down. Thus, for example, a Board of Trade index that showed a 15 per cent price rise at the beginning of August 1914 showed a 5 per cent fall at the beginning of September.[5] However, not only was this activity done secretly, it was even denied by Walter Runciman, the President of the Board of Trade in the House of Commons;[6] the reason was the fear that private traders might be deterred from bringing in goods if they thought the government would undercut them. Thus official statements about the virtues of 'business as usual' should not mislead historians as they often did contemporaries as to the real policy being pursued.

In other spheres intervention came as and when a particular problem was identified. Politicians were not slow to involve themselves in the munitions question: as early as October 1914 Kitchener had a 'Shells Committee' forced upon him; in March 1915 a new cabinet committee known as the 'Treasury Committee' was given authority by Asquith to override the Secretary of State for War; under the Defence of the Realm (Amendment No. 2) Act 1915 the government armed itself with wide powers including the right to control factories for the production of munitions; and in May 1915 a fully fledged Ministry for Munitions was established under Lloyd George. Under its auspices during 1915 and 1916 the government imposed control over 250 factories and mines, and regulated prices and profits; the needs of migrating munitions workers helped produce the Rent Restriction Act; strikes in the South Wales coalfield led to control there in November 1916 which was extended to the whole coal industry in 1917.

This system of controls grew continuously throughout the war; there is little justification for seeing December 1916 as marking a particular shift from *laissez-faire* to interventionism. Lloyd George was, of course, not by nature moved so much by ideological considerations as by an appreciation of immediate problems. He certainly accepted certain aspects of the McKenna–Runciman approach to the war, particularly their view that there was a limit to the number of men who could safely be taken from industry; hence his concern to bring skilled men under conscription back from the front. He persevered with well-established

experimentation; for most of the key decisions involving state intervention in the economy had already been taken before he became Prime
Minister. What Lloyd George did was to dramatize the policy; for
example the system of County Agriculture Committees devised in 1916
was incorporated in the 1917 Corn Production Act under which production targets were imposed upon farmers with the threat of losing
their land if they failed to co-operate. Similarly he highlighted the food
question by appointing a food controller. Lord Devonport, the first
appointee, made little impact but his successor, Lord Rhondda, did
advance policy a stage further by a cautious experiment with sugar
rationing, which was greatly extended in the closing stages of the war.
On balance it would be hard to argue that Lloyd George's government
was either more or less prone to approaching its problems from a coherent view of the state's proper role. The conventional picture of Lloyd
George's arch-opponents McKenna and Runciman as doctrinaire exponents of *laissez-faire* is a gross caricature. It is significant that while Lloyd
George himself was no radical as wartime Chancellor of the Exchequer,
McKenna was responsible for a drastic increase in the income tax in
1915, broke with free trade in October 1915, and introduced the Excess
Profits Duty at 50 per cent.

None of the wartime governments erected their system of controls
deliberately in the sense that they thought out the principles involved.
Policy developed in a piecemeal fashion as one sector of the economy
came under strain and an *ad hoc* solution was found. Wartime intervention was a matter of expediency rather than of ideology; and because
there was little sense of conversion on the part of the politicians of
Lloyd George's Coalition, so, once the crisis had passed, there was
correspondingly little inclination to preserve and perpetuate what had
been erected in wartime. The immediate sequel was therefore a swift
collapse of the elaborate apparatus of economic controls; and the framework of social reconstruction was no sooner erected than dismantled.
For an explanation of these events we must look further at the Conservative Party and at the 'irregulars' brought in to man the machine
of government by Lloyd George.

Conservatism, Capitalism and the State 1914–1922

Not only has the Conservative Party been much less studied than its
rivals, but such work as exists tends to look more at leadership and
organization than at ideology; and it is easy to make the assumption that
the Conservatives, whether out of patriotism, through sheer pragmatism

or from an inherent collectivism, responded positively to the wartime phase of interventionism. A limited empirical basis for this assumption does exist in the party's keenness for conscription and various forms of control over civilian life in which their attitude contrasted with that of many Liberal and Labour figures. However, it would be a mistake to translate this political stance into the realm of economics and to project the Conservatives as natural interventionists. In the generation before 1914, as we have seen, the tendency had been for Conservatives to adopt the arguments of nineteenth-century economic individualism, and the struggle over tariffs had left the party very hostile to almost all forms of interventionism by 1914.[7] There must be some doubt whether this was really reversed by the First World War. In the Edwardian era the party had been in one of its periodic bouts of ideological in-fighting over protectionism; the other issues that really mattered to Conservatives at the time were Ulster and the House of Lords. That the tariff issue remained alive throughout the war was largely a reflection of the vigour of the Conservative backbenches. This was by no means new, for since 1903 the 'other ranks' had been seizing the initiative, and in 1911 the party unceremoniously removed its leader, a tactic that became a habit for Conservatives during the twentieth century. But the war years certainly increased the scope for backbench activity particularly through the Unionist Business Committee, established in 1915, and the Unionist War Committee in 1916; the former pursued trade matters relentlessly and the latter agitated any question on which the government, and by implication the Conservative leadership, showed slackness. Part of their power arose from the leadership the two committees enjoyed by Long and Carson respectively which made them difficult for Bonar Law to ignore. The trend culminated in the famous party meeting at the Carlton Club in 1922 which killed the Lloyd George Coalition and bequeathed to the party a permanent organization in the 1922 Committee. In the last two years of peace Law had been checked on food taxes by a revolt of his free traders, and so it was by 1914 an open question what a Conservative government would attempt beyond a measure of imperial preference; thus the battle to push the party to a frank acceptance of protectionism was still to be won. Now wartime created fresh opportunities for protectionism, as the UBC quickly saw. German colonial and overseas markets became available to British enterprise, while the elimination of industrial imports from the Central Powers stimulated new developments at home. The Balfour of Burleigh Committee on Commercial and Industrial Policy in 1917 endorsed the view that at the end of the war Britain's infant industries would require full protection. These possibilities stirred some sections of industry to exert pressure on the Conservative Party. In certain respects private industry's experience of wartime co-operation with the state had proved reassuring; many firms received large contracts and often abnormally high levels of profit; they were shielded from the usual competition and to some extent from the pressures of their labour force. These cushioning effects stimulated some industries actively to seek government help in the form of tariffs and subsidies, co-operation with the civil service and amalgamations designed to control the market.[8] The object was to extend such advantages into peacetime while sloughing off the high wartime levels of taxation and direct government intervention on prices and operations.

During the war attempts were made to stiffen the somewhat shaky Conservative commitment to protectionism, now apparently compromised by the entanglement with Lloyd George. However, the Federation of British Industry, not all of whose members saw great advantages in tariffs, tried to avoid a strong line on protectionism or close association with political parties. Consequently a new organization, the British Commonwealth Union, sprang up in December 1916, determined to prolong economic warfare with Germany and inspired by fear of socialism and revolution. The BCU promoted 24 Conservative candidates in 1918 of whom 18 were elected, although its influence through key figures like Sir Robert Horne was much wider than this suggests. By 1918 it was saying what most Conservatives thought, for the one essential condition for the preservation of the Coalition at that time was the inclusion of protection for key industries and anti-dumping legislation in the manifesto. In this sphere at least the new government attempted to live up to its promises with the Safeguarding of Industries Act of 1921 which imposed a $33\frac{1}{2}$ per cent duty on goods imported largely from Germany.

The general theme of Conservative policy arising from the war was that business must be set free – with a special exception for trade. Any consideration of the impact of the war on the party's attitude must take account of the fact that every aspect of control apart from trade protection had been dismantled by 1922 to vociferous approval. Food rationing lingered longest because of apprehension in 1919–20 about unrest among demobilized men and the trade unions; and the Ministry of Food proved itself by keeping supplies moving during the railway strike of 1919. But by the second half of 1920 when world food prices began to fall the government gladly ceased subsidies, scrapped the rationing apparatus, and abolished the Ministry itself in March 1921, followed by the sugar and wheat commissions. Less popular forms of control had been dismantled from 1919, and by 1921 Munitions, the Coal Control Department and the Railway Executive had all closed. Sir Eric Geddes, the Transport Minister, produced a plan to nationalize the railways in his 1921 Act, but the Cabinet rapidly dropped it in the face of backbench hostility, and the most he could achieve was amalgamation of the existing companies into four groups. On coal, where the war had generated some support for public control, the government prevaricated by appointing the Sankey Commission, but ignored the verdict of a majority of its members in favour of some form of nationalization, and proceeded to decontrol the industry in 1921, earlier than planned.

Such an emphatic and rapid reversal of wartime innovations reflected the absence of any intellectual conversion by most of the politicians concerned. There did exist a degree of support among some of the civil servants who relished a new and constructive role. For example, the pre-war use of trade boards and minimum wages by the Liberals was extended during the war to agricultural and munitions workers, and some 63 trade boards had been established by 1921. However, the move towards a general minimum wage was decisively checked in 1921 because the administration of trade boards conflicted with the Treasury's view that money spent on public purposes deprived productive industry of investment, and with its conviction that a minimum wage policy would hinder the downward movement of wages believed to be essential for a return to full employment.[9] In short, the Treasury, especially when led by the highly orthodox Austen Chamberlain, still held the whip hand over younger innovatory ministries like Labour, and managed to have centres of economic heresy like the Ministry of Transport abolished by 1922. In the absence of strong political support the new ministries that embodied interventionist thinking proved highly vulnerable.

Superficially the creation by Lloyd George of the Ministry of Reconstruction in 1917, which gave way to the Ministry of Health in 1918, represented a bolder commitment than Asquith's Cabinet Committee on Reconstruction. However, the new Ministry under Dr Addison suffered from the Cabinet's habit of delaying its plans, particularly for housing, throughout 1917–18 so that they ran into the post-war inflation; but Lloyd George's basic blunder lay in denying the Ministry executive powers and obliging it to persuade ministries like the notoriously unconstructive Local Government Board under the Conservative Hayes Fisher to accept its proposals. That the two outstanding social reform schemes were the responsibility of Liberals – Addison for housing and H. A. L. Fisher for education – exposed them to much Conservative carping and obstruction. Conservatives came to resent not simply the large number of new ministries and departments spawned by Lloyd George, but his predilection for insinuating into them all kinds of 'experts' and businessmen from outside party politics whose virtue indeed was supposedly their freedom from party shibboleths. The most reviled were the press barons, Northcliffe, Harmsworth and Beaverbrook; Sir Joseph Maclay, the Shipping Controller, held Parliament in such low esteem as to refuse to sit in either House. Conservative politicians were not alone in feeling both worried and insulted; for the new ministers, as the personal creations of the Prime Minister, added to his patronage and power while sapping that of the party and Parliament. Not surprisingly there was a severe reaction against these practices after 1918. Even fairly liberal-minded Conservatives like Stanley Baldwin were inclined to assume a necessary connection between the extension of government controls and corruption; the dynamic figure of Lloyd George so personified economic interventionism as to make them recoil for some years from a repetition of wartime policies.

The introduction of experts and businessmen into the Coalition represented the culmination of the earlier movement for National Efficiency. Now this approach did involve certain Conservatives, notably Lord Milner and his flock of disciples, many of whom were ensconced in Lloyd George's personal secretariat in 1917 – another form of prime ministerial government to its critics. While other Conservatives sometimes lent support to an extended role for the state, for example Salisbury over housing and Selborne over agriculture, Milner was the only major figure who consistently identified *laissez-faire* as an evil because it precluded full employment and social reform. In describing himself as a 'National Socialist' Milner implied the use of state power in a Bismarckian sense to regenerate Britain's industry and population. It is significant that when in August 1920 the Cabinet considered the preliminary verdict of the Sankey Commission on the coal industry only five ministers supported nationalization – the two Liberals, Addison and Montagu; the two Labour men, Barnes and Roberts; and a solitary Conservative, Milner. Yet he was too isolated from the mainstream of Conservatism now bent on a return to nineteenth-century freedom. Among the younger men there was a strong echo of Milnerite radicalism in Sir Oswald Mosley, elected as a coalitionist in 1918. Imbued with a similar determination to raise the standards of the working people he sought to take the tariff policy to its logical conclusion in an economically united Empire under a strong benevolent state. Yet to mention Mosley is to move to the periphery of Conservatism in the 1920s, and to remember that he had abandoned the party as hopeless by 1922. It is significant that a number of those prominent Conservatives who joined Labour during the 1920s – Mosley, Lady Cynthia Mosley (daughter of Lord Curzon), Lord Sankey, Oliver Baldwin and Stafford Cripps – had been moved to a strong policy of state action by their sympathy for the lower classes engendered by wartime experience. They are very much the exceptions that tend to prove the general Conservative trend in the 1920s.

Finance and taxation were at the root of Conservative post-war attitudes, particularly in the reversal of the promise to build half a million 'homes for heroes'. As a central aspect of policy in 1918, housing shows clearly the ideological limitations of official thinking. In the first place the government would not consider building the necessary houses itself, preferring to leave it to local authorities to settle quotas, buy land and offer contracts to private builders. As a result of the Cabinet's tardiness the housing programme was eventually launched amid a post-war boom in which builders were undertaking more profitable work than local authority housing; as a result the government reluctantly offered them subsidies to make it worth their while. In defence of the government it has been argued that it was inconceivable to have imposed controls on the costs of the building industry at this time;[10] this of course is to overlook the fact that in 1918 the government had been doing precisely that in a vast range of industries.

By 1920 the subsidies had made the housing programme far more expensive than originally envisaged and it ran straight into the demand for retrenchment which was already growing loud by the end of 1919. For the 'anti-waste' campaigners within and without the Conservative Party, housing was seen as a prime cause of the high rate of income tax, still at 6s at this point. Led by Chamberlain, a very retrenchment-minded Chancellor, the government managed to reduce the tax to 4s, and in 1921 appointed the Geddes Committee to recommend cuts in expenditure. Its report in 1922 effectively put paid to major reforms in education and housing, while the strength of backbench feeling on the subject drove the Prime Minister to defend his Minister of Health by referring to his 'unfortunate interest in public health'![11] The interpretation of contemporary critics like Keynes of these reversals as the result of pressure by narrow and blinkered businessmen-in-politics does have considerable basis in the evidence. We have already noted the well-established means by which Conservative backbenchers exercised their strength, and how a government bill on transport could be routed by its own supporters on the floor of the House of Commons. Research into the composition of the party has shown that the newly elected MPs, of whom there were 168 in 1918, were drawn more from the middle class and less from landed backgrounds than those sitting in 1914.[12] While the change in this direction predated the war it received a boost in 1918; over two-thirds of the entire parliamentary party were businessmen (39 per cent) and professionals (31 per cent), while those whose connections were with the traditional occupations – the land (15 per cent) and the services (15 per cent) – were a small minority.

The understandable groundswell of opposition among the rank and file to both pre-war and wartime taxation and intervention was not checked by a coherent economic philosophy among its leaders, who, in the case of men like Austen Chamberlain, seem to have shared the prevailing conviction that the economy would right itself once the burdens and obstacles imposed upon it were lifted. Bonar Law, a fairly timid wartime Chancellor, had indicated sympathy for a levy on capital designed to lift the crushing burden of national debt payments; but when the idea was pronounced suicidal by the party chairman, Sir George Younger, Law promptly dropped it.[13] Even the comparatively liberal Stanley Baldwin, who had supported social reform before 1914, bowed to retrenchment as a member of the Geddes Committee. He went along with the capital levy to the extent of imposing a personal one on his own fortune when Financial Secretary to the Treasury in 1919; but as President of the Board of Trade he took his part in decontrolling the coal industry in 1921. Thus as the party approached the 1920s it seems to have been struggling to return to *laissez-faire* rather than move away from it, apart that is from its tariff policy which the war helped to strengthen. But beyond this the experience of 1914–18 appears to have produced a negative reaction against interventionism which had profound effects upon government handling of economic problems in the inter-war years; not until the 1930s was Conservative faith in the role of the state partially rekindled.

Labour's Socialist Commitment and the Liberal Inheritance 1914–1929

Up to 1914 the relationship between the Labour Party and socialists had been one of mutual suspicion. While trade unionists often resented socialists as middle-class people who were merely milking them of their funds, socialists despaired of the absence of ideological coherence and the prevailing parliamentary 'opportunism' of the party's leaders. The First World War by no means destroyed these objections on either side. However it did provide an institutional means, through the Workers National Committee, for more constructive participation by socialists in the activities of the party than previously. The fact that middle-class socialists like Sidney Webb and R. H. Tawney supported the war facilitated their absorption, especially under the aegis of Henderson who pronounced himself keen to 'enlarge the bounds of the Labour Party and bring in the intellectuals as candidates'.[14] Because wartime collectivism produced a proliferation of committees requiring labour representation and joint boards of managers and workers such as the Whitley Councils, it seemed to the Webbs the ideal opportunity for the transmission of their ideas to the machinery of the state. In the long run the close involvement of Fabians in the party meant that when, a generation later, socialist programmes of nationalization became practical politics it was the Webbian brand of socialism that was adopted. However, in the short and medium term the process of wartime collectivism alarmed socialists like Cole and Tawney who considered that it merely bolstered capitalism by making profits secure and by tightening the relations between business, civil servants and government. This pre-empted genuine socialism in the sense of greater control by workers in industry; and as a result many socialists were by 1918 more anxious to dismantle the controls of an autocratic state than to extend them.

On the face of it the Labour Party constitution of 1918 marked a major shift to a coherent left-wing position, including as it did the commitment in Clause IV to 'secure for the producers by hand or by brain the full fruits of their industry, and the most equitable distribution thereof that may be possible upon the basis of the common ownership of the means of production'. Yet this claim has been strongly refuted by a number of historians in view of the party's record in the inter-war period; some argue that ideas are far less important than class and organization, others that statements of principle like Clause IV should not be taken literally.

The significance or insignificance of the socialist commitment becomes clearer if it is seen in the context of the other changes in the structure of the party centrally and locally at this time. Almost from the start of the war a distinct right-wing and patriotic reaction directed particularly against the ILP had manifested itself within the movement. By 1916 a group of union leaders under Havelock Wilson of the seamen were attempting to launch a strictly trade union Labour Party. In January 1917 these elements narrowly succeeded in persuading the party conference to modify the procedure for electing the National Executive Committee; whereas under the original constitution the unions and the socialist societies had chosen their own representatives separately, the new proposal was for selection by conference as a whole, thereby throwing the choice effectively to the big unions. This move was followed later in the year by Henderson's plans to harness middle- and working-class supporters to the party by means of a framework of constituency parties and ward branches based on individual membership (again a departure from the original federal pattern of 1900 involving predominantly indirect membership of the party through affiliated bodies). These innovations won the support of the TUC Parliamentary Committee in September 1917 as a realistic response to the expansion of the franchise. Now this reform of membership and constituency bodies also commended itself to socialists in some ways; individual membership was likely to draw in many middle-class recruits, and the 500 candidates envisaged by Henderson both implied a complete break with the Liberals and presented excellent opportunities for middle-class candidatures. In practice, however, the structural reforms did not always have this effect. In so far as the Labour Party created individual membership and proper constituency parties it deprived the ILP of the special role it had hitherto fulfilled in the movement. From 1909 to 1918 the ILP lost membership and suffered a breakaway to the British Socialist Party founded in 1911. Although the ILP picked up some new middle-class members after 1918 it was a much enfeebled body (in 1918 only three of the Labour MPs were nominated by the ILP whereas its members had dominated the 1906–14 party). But the clearest sign of the ILP's slackening hold had come in the conference decision in January 1918 to abolish the right of socialist societies to elect their own representatives to the party executive; instead the NEC was to comprise eleven trade union, five constituency party, and four women's section representatives all chosen by the entire conference.

In view of this tendency for power to shift to the right wing, one is bound to question the importance conventionally attached to the adoption of a socialist line in foreign policy statements and in Clause IV of the constitution. Clearly most unions regarded the constitution with some suspicion, and it took someone of Henderson's reputation to reassure them that were not committing themselves to a radically new departure in policy. Since Clause IV was not translated into a precise or comprehensive socialist economic programme, they were no doubt justified in thinking of it as, in substance, no more than the 'collectivism' of social reform and the 'socialism' implied in the nationalization of mines and railways which had been approved before the war; it did not imply centralized economic planning and particularly not of labour itself, which must, they thought, remain free to bargain. Party policy, as expressed in 26 resolutions of conference in 1918 and as put to the country in December, emphasized the development of social welfare, minimum standards of health, housing and education, extension of the unemployment insurance scheme to occupations presently omitted, consumer protection and attacks on profiteering, resumption of free trade generally and trade with Russia in particular, the restoration of civil liberties and complete industrial freedom, graduated taxation and a levy on war profits to pay off the national debt, Irish Home Rule and a just peace settlement. Apart from these traditionally radical policy pronouncements, the unions were reassured in their control of the party by a further concession proposed by the miners, the textile workers and the dock workers after the conference debate in January 1918: this raised the union representation on the NEC from 11 to 13. Thus on everything that mattered – policy, organization and electoral machinery – the unions saw no threat, and could afford to regard with some indulgence vague statements of ideology embodied in the constitution.

On the other hand, if the socialist commitment cannot be taken literally, it should not be regarded as being devoid of meaning. For it was at least an emphatic way of underlining the permanence of the party's break with Lloyd George in 1917, and its intention to become a truly independent party with a simple yardstick to distinguish it from Liberalism. It has been credibly suggested that the function of Clause IV was to provide the kind of political myth that most political movements cherish and around which they may rally. 'Socialism' both showed the party faithful where they stood in relation to previous historical development, and generated a necessary sense of inevitable progress towards a better state of things. Certainly MacDonald, by articulating this theme, endowed Labour with a formidable optimism and sense of purpose during the 1920s. Like 'Empire' for late nineteenth-century Conservatives, 'Socialism' was for Labour a symbol sufficiently vague to be impervious to mere day-to-day policies and events.

This idea of 1918 as a symbolic change rather than one of substance for Labour is certainly consistent with the empirical evidence that we have about the many recruits won by the party after the war. We have already noted the tendency for local Liberal activists to defect to Labour in 1918 and for Labour to champion social reform in local council chambers in 1917–18; an equally pronounced infusion of first- and second-rank politicians (particularly from Liberal but also to a lesser extent from Conservative backgrounds) took place between 1918 and 1929. Often people of middle- and upper-class status who were accused of betraying their class, these men and women palpably transformed Labour into the kind of national representative party that MacDonald had long envisaged.

In considering their impact intellectually upon the party one must bear in mind that the chief stimulus causing them to sever relations with their old party was the war, either its origins or its consequences. MPs such as E. T. John, H. B. Lees-Smith, Josiah Wedgwood, R. L. Outhwaite, Joseph Martin, Arthur Ponsonby and Charles Trevelyan had severed relations due to disagreement with their constituency parties before the Coupon Election, which they fought largely as independents or ILP members before joining the Labour Party. Others waited to be defeated as Liberals before switching allegiance, notably Percy Alden, Sydney Arnold, Noel Buxton, Willoughby Dickinson, Edward Hemmerde, Joseph King, L. C. Money, J. D. White and R. C. Lambert. In general they rebelled against what they saw as a mandarin elite at the

Foreign Office, which under Grey had foisted the war upon Britain, and also against the uses to which victory was being put, notably repression in Ireland and India, resistance to the new revolutionary regimes in Europe, exploitation of Germany for the benefit of a few capitalists and the defeat of trade unions at home. The disclosure by the Bolsheviks of the secret treaties demonstrated, in their view, how little British policy had been based on respect for self-determination and how much on cynical manipulation of territory in the interest of power politics.[15] Trevelyan, one of the most articulate, justified his transition to Labour by drawing a comparison with the moral leadership of Liberalism by Cobden and Bright after the Crimean War, which was taken over later by Gladstone; like most of the recruits Trevelyan plainly saw Labour continuing this tradition in foreign affairs.

Through their participation in Labour's Advisory Committee on International Questions, Liberal and pacifist recruits rapidly made foreign and defence matters salient within the party. Their role in MacDonald's two governments was also significant. In 1924 they included Trevelyan (Education), Haldane (Lord Chancellor), Josiah Wedgwood (Chancellor of the Duchy of Lancaster), Noel Buxton (Agriculture), Ponsonby (Under-Secretary for Foreign Affairs) and Sir Patrick Hastings (Attorney-General). In 1929 Trevelyan again served at Education with Addison (Agriculture), Wedgwood Benn (Secretary of State for India), Arnold (Paymaster-General), William Jowett (Attorney-General), Lees-Smith (Postmaster-General), and Ponsonby in two successive under-secretary-ships and the Duchy of Lancaster.

Since all these apart from Addison, Haldane and Wedgwood Benn seem to have been prompted to change allegiance primarily by foreign affairs, one must consider how far the recruits were in tune with Labour on social and economic matters; did they inhibit or strengthen the demand for a left-wing economic policy? In many respects they plainly reinforced the existing tendencies of their new party, particularly Labour's predilection for free trade. They argued for the morally beneficial effect of free trade on international relations, and sought the re-opening of commercial relations with Russia. They also believed that competition, which had been one means of checking the power of capitalists, had been curtailed by wartime protectionism and cartels; many ex-Liberals preferred state control to protectionism for private industry. Their conviction that Labour was a better champion of the free trade cause on which the Liberal leaders had reneged was confirmed by Snowden's 1924 budget which removed the McKenna duties. Other ideas received a strong boost from the recruits. The capital levy owed its conception to Sydney Arnold among others, and was regarded by J. A. Hobson as an important factor in his switch of loyalties. With the

WNC's support for the 'conscription of wealth' Labour seemed the party most likely to adopt the levy. Though party conferences did indeed approve it, MacDonald and Henderson made it clear well before 1924 that they would not attempt to put such an 'extremist' policy into operation. A similar cause was land taxation which brought a vocal band of ex-radicals including Wedgwood, Trevelyan, Hemmerde, Outhwaite and White into the party, arguing that Lloyd George had betrayed them and that Asquith was useless. Although in 1925 conference endorsed their views and although there was strong support in the party for nationalization of the land, there was little chance of the 1929 government taking up either policy.

If there is any doubt about the heterogeneity of Labour's social and economic ideas in the 1920s, Josiah Wedgwood provides further confirmation. A thoroughly old-fashioned radical–individualist moved by concern for Indian, Irish or aliens' oppression, he abhorred state interference: 'By Socialism, I suppose you mean Social Reform and inspecting babies' hair. By Socialism I mean a land (or a time) when we shall not need policemen.'[16] Wedgwood's immense popularity in the Labour Party – he was made vice-chairman of the parliamentary party – is a testimony to the strength of Gladstonianism there.

However, a number of men can be said to have seen in social questions a positive reason for joining Labour: for example, Leo Chiozza Money, the Liberal–Fabian, who, having served as an under-secretary in the Coalition, resigned in disgust at the rush to decontrol industry. Others such as Lord Haldane and Percy Alden were also appreciative of collectivism on Fabian lines; Haldane's enthusiasm for administration by a trained elite made him a willing nationalizer of the coal industry. In some ways the most central figure in Liberal–Labour politics proved to be Christopher Addison. When he broke with the Liberals in 1923 he identified in justification three areas where Labour's claims were superior: social reform (particularly housing and education), free trade, and disarmament.[17] What Addison termed 'Practical Socialism' involved state intervention to raise standards where private enterprise was inadequate. In housing Labour adopted his policy of subsidizing council house building from national taxation. In agriculture he effectively wrote Labour's programme in the 1920s to reflect his desire for a system of agricultural marketing boards that would eliminate middlemen and offer guaranteed prices to producers. In support of this policy Addison attempted, though without success, to persuade the 1929–31 Labour Cabinet to abandon free trade in favour of import quotas on food imposed by the boards.[18] If a recruit like Addison was more accurately a collectivist than a socialist, nonetheless his Agricultural Marketing Act demonstrated a better grasp of the legislative route to socialism than any minister except Herbert Morrison. Though not likely to push the party much beyond the limited nationalization already contemplated, Addison and the other recruits strongly reinforced the predilection for socialistic progress through social welfare which typified mainstream Labour opinion. In this he personified the continuity between New Liberalism and Labour. 'All social reformers', as Trevelyan put it, 'are bound to gravitate, as I have done, to Labour.'[19]

One of the few who considered economic as distinct from social questions was William Wedgwood Benn, who, when he joined in 1927, declared that he had for some time questioned 'the theory of private enterprise and free competition';[20] as competitive industry failed to revive in the 1920s and relapsed into combinations of capital, he increasingly saw workers' control as an alternative form of industrial organization; he saw this as a natural development from the municipal socialism of the late nineteenth century. Even among those like Trevelyan and Wedgwood Benn who were attracted by ideas there is no sense of dramatic conversion or any indication that the change of party implied a new position on economic and social policy. When Trevelyan referred to the 'minimum socialist programme' in the 1920s he included a package of the 'living wage', public works especially housing, nationalization of mines and railways, a levy on land values, a capital levy and free trade. In so far as there was an underlying theme it was the Hobsonian one of increasing the power of consumption of the mass of the people.

Thus Labour's transition from minor to major party status between the First World War and the 1920s provides a singular example of the continuity that underlies political change. For the Liberals did not collapse during the 1920s because of their addiction to discredited doctrines of free trade, social reform, Irish Home Rule, Gladstonian views on armaments and international morality, civil liberties and self-determination in India; on the contrary they collapsed because Labour now enjoyed a stronger claim as champion of all these Liberal traditions than did the Liberal Party. Transition to Labour involved a reaffirmation of one's political principles rather than a surrender or infringement of them. Ultimately the war entailed not an intellectual or programmatic outflanking of one party by the other so much as the inheritance by Labour of the broad ground of pre-1914 Progressivism.

Part Four
1918–1939

11

The Elevation of Labour and the Restoration of Party Politics

1918–1924

The Labour Government's main weakness is vanity; they are all . . . delighted with the good impression they are making on the middle class.

Diary of William Wedgwood Benn, 19 March 1924

Fragmentation of the Coalition

In view of the critical state of the war in 1916 the establishment of Lloyd George's Coalition was not surprising; what is more remarkable is that it survived until 1922. As hostilities drew to a close Lloyd George seemed unshakeably ensconced in the premiership, an impression later reinforced by his pre-eminent role in the peace settlement and the subsequent international conferences. However, domestic affairs, where he relied upon his agents (first Bonar Law and then Austen Chamberlain), proved to be his undoing. After four years of peace the Prime Minister embodied the irregular, interfering spirit of wartime too well to be widely acceptable, and in the absence of any permanent institutional supports he proved vulnerable to the reassertion of party feeling. Lloyd George fitfully perceived the unlikelihood of the Conservatives settling down permanently as his supporters, or, had he wanted such a thing, of their making him their leader, which left the alternative of launching a new centre or national party. Rearranging the political kaleidoscope to produce new combinations was a favourite pastime for politicians in the immediate post-war years because so many of them enjoyed a tenuous attachment to party. Lloyd George might therefore reasonably have hoped to draw from the Conservatives the ex-Liberal Unionist Chamberlain, those like Milner, Balfour, Birkenhead or Worthington-Evans who were apt to disparage the party and who relished the conditions of coalition government, and the ambitious and opportunistic like Curzon who would enrol with the dispenser of patronage. From the Labour ranks J. H. Thomas and J. R. Clynes were optimistically believed likely to join Lloyd George, while the Coalition Liberals furnished him with administrative talent, if little political inspiration. However, in normal times such a collection could not cohere, as the government of coalitionists, businessmen and experts had done during the wartime emergency. Politicians need a common basis of sentiment or objective if only because without it they cannot maintain organization and loyalty in the country; this is why it is futile to study modern politicians purely as a group seeking power without reference to their ideology and popular following. In the absence of a coherent programme or philosophy the 'centre party' proved a chimera.

The insufficiency of power alone is demonstrated by the disintegration of Coalition Liberalism after 1918. The essential justification for their participation had been the reconstruction programme. Yet by 1921 reforms in housing, education and agriculture had been curtailed or abandoned for the sake of retrenchment. The Safeguarding of Industries Act of 1921 with its $33\frac{1}{2}$ per cent tariff on certain goods provoked over half the Coalition Liberals to vote against their government or abstain. Even more offensive was the recruitment of the 'Black and Tans' to subdue Sinn Fein, a policy presided over by a Liberal minister, Sir Hamar Greenwood. The only other Liberal influence lay in Indian policy as directed by Edwin Montagu: he pledged self-government in 1917 and pushed through the Montagu–Chelmsford reforms in 1919, while Conservatives roared their approval of repressive measures like the Amritsar Massacre carried out in India itself. Montagu's reward was bitter vilification which drove him to resignation in 1922. Christopher Addison had been obliged to give up as Health Minister in 1921, which served to underline Lloyd George's unwillingness or inability to stand by his Liberal ministers when they pursued a progressive policy. Thus by 1922 the Coalition Liberals, seeing no future in saving the Prime Minister from his reactionary colleagues, began to resolve their embarrassing dilemma by making overtures to the Asquithians for reunion; although some, such as Winston Churchill and Sir Alfred Mond, shifted towards a formal Conservative allegiance. This imminent disappearance of coalitionism had been heralded by electoral vulnerability. Between 1919 and 1922, when the Asquithians made five by-election gains, the Coalition Liberals lost nine seats, seven of them to Labour, a significant indication that their role as bulwark against the left was played out.

That the Coalition survived, despite this, for four years of peace reflected Conservative appreciation of the Prime Minister's positive achievements. He had been persuaded to take a strong line towards both Sinn Fein and the Bolshevik regime in Russia; by 1921 he had been led to financial retrenchment by pressure of the anti-waste campaigns; most importantly, he had managed to steer a course through the intense industrial militancy of 1919-20 culminating in the collapse of the 'Triple Alliance' of miners, railwaymen and transport workers in March 1921, and to do it by judicious concessions; for example he set up the Sankey Commission on the coal industry but resisted its majority recommendation for nationalization. By 1922 industry had been returned to private control with a measure of tariff protection.

Against this some Conservatives felt that the government merely prevaricated over tariffs and assistance for agriculture. Nor did the National Union feel it had been fairly treated over reform of the House of Lords, a Conservative objective since 1911, and a condition for acceptance of franchise reform in 1917. Despite investigation by the Bryce Committee and a pledge of reform by Bonar Law and Lloyd George in 1918 nothing was done to restore the powers or change the composition of the Upper House. From the start, the core of criticism of the Coalition had been the 42 MPs dubbed 'Diehards' who were for the most part typical of the landowning and Ulster elements of the party, not of the business elements as were the coalitionists; and as elderly men unlikely to serve in government they enjoyed secure representation in safe Conservative seats;[1] on both counts therefore, they felt little need of coalition. The Diehards were specially antagonized by Indian reform, the Irish settlement and the reversal of policy towards Russia, all of which smacked of Bolshevik influence in public life.

However, only 58 MPs voted against the Irish Treaty, and Diehard opposition is by no means an adequate explanation of the overthrow of Lloyd George. By the time of the Carlton Club meeting, disillusion extended well beyond mere items of legislation. Many backbenchers had never ceased to dislike Lloyd George as much on personal as on political grounds. Once the pressure of national crisis was lifted, their resentment at his irregular methods of government resurfaced. They believed that he undermined both the Foreign Office and the Treasury through his personal secretariat, and that he exploited incidents like the Chanak Crisis of 1922, when Britain almost went to war with Turkey, to perpetuate a presidential style of government. Though the War Cabinet and the non-political ministers had disappeared, he remained associated with unsavoury characters such as Sir William Sutherland and Maundy Gregory through whom honours were lavishly dispensed at inflated prices. Though the Conservative Party also benefited from the sale of honours, in the debates of 1921 critics chose to foist the guilt upon the

Lloyd George fund. Thus it was in generalized fears about methods of government and corruption that a determination to sever relations festered; when Stanley Badwin spoke of the 'morally disintegrating effect of Lloyd George on all whom he had to deal with', he reflected widespread Conservative sentiment.

In addition some Conservatives contemplated the cost of coalitionism in terms of their own careers. Since May 1915 the party had always been denied a share of office proportionate to its numbers. Even during 1919–22, when there were in total 21–2 cabinet seats, Conservatives occupied only 10–12 of them.[2] This was most irksome for the rising junior figures whose promotion was blocked; it has been estimated that some 40 individuals were deprived of office in this period; notable among them were Lord Selborne and Sir Arthur Steel-Maitland, the former party chairman. Junior ministers outside the Cabinet, including W. C. Bridgeman, R. A. Sanders, Sir P. Lloyd-Greame, Edward Wood and L. S. Amery, also comprised a centre of opposition to the Coalition in 1922.

The New Strategy 1922

By 1922 these fears had been crystallized by the realization that it was no longer politically necessary to subject the Conservative Party to Lloyd George. For the tactical rationale behind coalitionism consisted in the assumption that the advance of Labour could best be checked by using Lloyd George to harness Liberal and new, unattached voters to Conservatism. Between 1919 and 1922 this assumption broke down decisively in the eyes of most Conservatives. The coupon arrangement of 1918 had left Coalition Liberals defending working-class seats vulnerable to a Labour resurgence which swept Spen Valley and Dartford in 1919, Norfolk South, Heywood and Radcliffe and Southwark S.E. in 1920, and Leicester East and Pontypridd in 1922. Altogether Labour made thirteen gains, including five from Conservatives, in these years, clear evidence that they rather than the Asquithians (five gains and one loss) were benefiting from the unpopularity of the Coalition. Hence the growing acceptance that the party must accustom itself to Labour as the permanent opposition party.

For a time right-wing resentment towards the government was harnessed by independent Conservatives fighting on a retrenchment platform led by Horatio Bottomley and Lords Rothermere and Northcliffe. By 1920 candidates of the 'Anti-Waste League' were snatching safe Conservative seats on a policy most Conservatives wished to make their own. Thus, not only was Labour's advance not being blocked, but the Conservatives seemed unable to unite in the face of the challenge. If the party continued to tie itself to Lloyd George, the argument ran, he would reduce it to the divided and demoralized condition in which he had left the Liberals. Such considerations induced weightier figures like Lord Salisbury to initiate the People's Union for Economy which was designed to absorb the retrenchment sentiment and unite working- and middle-class support thus avoiding a sharp polarization along class lines between Labour and the rest.[3] In the short run Salisbury lent respectability to the rebellion, while facilitating a shift in policy towards retrenchment; by the end of 1921 the electoral threat of the Anti-Waste League had been contained by the adoption of their platform by official candidates.

Once the Labour gains had undermined the Prime Minister's credibility as a radical leader the acceptance of him and his policies grew not merely irksome but futile in Conservative eyes. That he could be dispensed with was dramatically underlined by the by-election at Newport in October 1922. Here a Conservative, intervening in a Coalition Liberal seat, emerged top of the poll in a three-cornered contest. Newport thus reinforced those who argued that safety now lay in abandoning Lloyd George in favour of a straightforward appeal by an unencumbered Conservative Party; for if seats like Newport could be won they were well within reach of an independent majority. This emboldened Conservative associations to adopt candidates in Coalition Liberal seats, thereby forcing them to seek a return to the Asquithian fold.

March 1921 proved to be decisive in breaking up the Coalition in that Bonar Law's resignation through ill-health provided the rebels with an alternative Prime Minister 18 months later. Law's successor as party leader, Austen Chamberlain, wholly failed to conciliate the disgruntled Conservatives. Aloof and remote, Chamberlain treated the junior ministers somewhat contemptuously; with his Liberal Unionist origins he never felt as acutely as Law the strain of coalitionism on the party. Out of stubbornness and loyalty Chamberlain declined to give any indication that the premiership would not remain indefinitely in Lloyd George's hands.

Conscious of the danger, the Prime Minister contemplated snatching a quick election early in 1922 so as to enable him to create a new ministry and a new centre party on the strength of a full five-year term of office. However, the hint of this in January drew a sharp reaction from a phalanx of leading figures outside the government – Salisbury, Derby, Selborne and Law – as well as from Baldwin, Curzon and Griffith-Boscawen. But the party chairman, Sir George Younger, took the lead in announcing his refusal to stand as a coalitionist at a general election. However much Lloyd George might declare he would not be bullied by a 'second-rate brewer', he was deterred by Younger's initiative which stimulated local parties to adopt candidates in Coalition Liberal seats thereby confirming Law's and Baldwin's fear of an imminent split in the party caused by Lloyd George. He thus let slip an opportunity to quit his allies on an issue of his choosing, relying instead upon Chamberlain who, after consulting his colleagues about the next general election, consented to summon a meeting of the parliamentary party at the Carlton Club on 19 October.

Of the 286 MPs present at the Carlton Club only 86 voted to maintain the Coalition and 187 against. Analysis has suggested that a majority of the Chamberlainites not only held office but also represented somewhat marginal constituencies vulnerable to a loss of Liberal support.[4] In the absense of these pressures the bulk of the party failed to respond to Chamberlain's offer of an election without coupons but with co-operation. By failing to voice his own reservations about Lloyd George he played into the hands of Baldwin who condemned the Prime Minister as a divisive and demoralizing force. By holding out the prospect of fighting under a separate party programme Chamberlain could have kept the Coalition going for some time, but by adopting a tough response to a moderate motion he alienated himself from the moderate mass of the party who now took confidence in the presence of Bonar Law, clearly available as Conservative Prime Minister. Without him many of the rebels would have shrunk from cutting adrift from Lloyd George for fear of losing office altogether.

The consequences proved to be immense and long-term in nature. Within hours Lloyd George had resigned office, and the next day Law was elected party leader just before forming a new administration. He followed this up with a vital decision – to dissolve Parliament at once, the upshot of which was a comfortable Conservative victory with 344 seats out of 615. By quickly plunging into an election so recently resisted by the party Bonar Law shrewdly caught his opponents unprepared. Lloyd George, barely alive to being out of office for the first time in 16 years, could not quite decide whether to attack the Conservatives for having ejected him, or to attempt to keep open the option of a new coalition with the Chamberlainites who stayed aloof from the new government. Though designated simply as a Liberal he found himself proscribed as an alien by most Asquithians. All seemed suddenly anxious to dissociate themselves from him. By ditching him now that he was an electoral liability the Conservatives avoided the unpopularity they otherwise risked as the governing party; the left, too, was deprived of much of the momentum generated since 1919. Speed, in short, was Law's best weapon in 1922 and he used it to the full.

However, the real significance of the Conservative decisions in 1922 concerned long-term strategy. As in 1918 they sought to contain the emergence of organized labour under the widened franchise, but they adopted a different method. Instead of relying on Lloyd George they now hoped to destroy him along with the Asquithians by squeezing their support between themselves and Labour. By concentrating the debate on Labour and building it into a major force they would shake out enough right-wing and moderate Liberal support to give them a comfortable lead over Labour. The 1922 election demonstrated the feasibility of this strategy.

Baldwin and Normality 1923

No one grasped the new strategy more eagerly or exploited it more deftly than Stanley Baldwin who had emerged from the relative obscurity of the Board of Trade to the Exchequer in October 1922, thence to the premiership on Law's retirement in May 1923. For him, practical wisdom in politics consisted, first, in so arranging matters as to exclude Lloyd George from office, and second, in keeping his party calm about the prospect of a Labour administration. He was wholly responsible for the next crucial decision that determined the political pattern of the 1920s, namely the plunge into a general election in November 1923 only a year after the previous contest with a fresh majority still intact. Ostensibly the reason was Baldwin's wish to introduce tariffs designed to reduce unemployment; but he was hampered by the pledge given by Law not to introduce them without the nation's express approval. Since the consequence was to turn the 344 Conservative members into a minority of 258 and to precipitate the first Labour government the whole exercise appeared to many contemporaries an unforced error of grave proportions.

This, however, was a superficial and short-term view. Any notion that the need for protectionism had grown so urgent as to permit no delay may safely be dismissed as an explanation for Baldwin's conduct. He had, if anything, become more lukewarm about tariffs during his term at the Treasury[5] and his willingness to offer the Chancellorship to McKenna in 1923 provides corroboration that it was far from the forefront of his mind. Baldwin's action had less to do with the economic merits of protection than with the political implications of its adoption. For he remained obsessed with the need to complete the restoration of normal party politics initiated by Bonar Law. So long as Chamberlain, Birkenhead, Balfour, Horne, and Worthington-Evans stood outside a Conservative Cabinet the prospect of a revived coalition could not be ruled out. Baldwin also recognized the palpable inferiority of his Cabinet by comparison with the team Lloyd George might still field; with a worsening economic situation and no clear policy he felt reluctant to stumble on while the critics waited confidently for the 'second-eleven' Cabinet, in Churchill's phrase, to collapse in discredit.

By announcing his wish for a mandate on tariffs in a speech at Plymouth on 25 October, Baldwin at once polarized politics. Since the Liberal Party was bound to declare for free trade, Lloyd George could not escape an unequivocal stand, nor is there any good evidence that he had intended to opt for protectionism. For Baldwin the advantage consisted in the fact that Lloyd George, in nailing his colours to the free-trade mast, thereby facilitated Liberal reunion and simultaneously isolated himself from the Chamberlainites – permanently as it turned out. This served Baldwin's real purpose of restoring party unity, for regardless of the result of the election it emerged that the former coalitionists would now serve under him in a future Conservative government. But although he consciously placed his majority in jeopardy in 1923 Baldwin did not realize how great was the risk; though the tariff issue appeared suddenly it was hardly a novel proposal, and since the party had carried it through five elections there was no reason to anticipate catastrophic losses; the Conservative majority was expected to be reduced rather than destroyed.

When, on the contrary, a strong reaction in favour of free trade and cheap food produced 107 Conservative losses and only 18 gains the gamble was seen to have failed lamentably. Yet there was no great upsurge in favour of a coalition to check the dreaded advent of Labour to office. Baldwin certainly suffered much criticism for his miscalculations, but very few challenged his underlying strategy. Instead of being deprived of the leadership he was retained as a bulwark against men like Birkenhead who were so unpalatable to the rank and file. Thus Baldwin was able to steady the party while it came to regard Labour's entry into minority government as a safe and temporary experiment between two Conservative ministries. Such conclusions reflected the parliamentary arithmetic of 1923 in that the 258 Conservatives faced 191 Labour and 158 Liberal members. Labour could not govern for long alone; nor could they even take office without a measure of outside support. Therefore instead of resigning promptly after the election Baldwin remained in office to meet the new Parliament in January 1924, as he was fully entitled to do as Prime Minister and leader of the largest party. In this way he focused attention upon Asquith who was obliged to take the deliberate step of voting the Conservatives out of power, thereby earning the responsibility for putting MacDonald in. Had Baldwin quit immediately he would have given the King a measure of choice between MacDonald and Asquith. As matters turned out the arrival of a Labour administration, which squeezed Liberalism more drastically and rapidly than any alternative, served to advance the new strategy to Baldwin's ultimate advantage.

The 1923 election epitomized the failure of the Liberals to seize their opportunities through internal division and the absence of firm and constructive leadership. With Asquith out of Parliament from 1918 to 1920 Lloyd George could have had himself elected leader or chairman, but at that stage there must have seemed little point in attaching himself to the shattered remnants. As early as February 1919 some Liberal MPs, reflecting the feeling of the rank and file, began to hold meetings designed to lead to reunion of 'Wee Frees' and coalitionists. However, the Asquithians, still outraged at the Coupon Election, feared absorption by the more numerous Lloyd George supporters and declined all offers of the government whip. Asquith himself gave no impetus to the move for party unity; 'the old man is stoical to the point of indifference', as McKenna put it. Unfortunately he displayed little beyond stoicism. After a remarkable by-election triumph in the working-class constituency of Paisley in February 1920 he failed to take any initiative either on policy or on reunion until, in 1926, the leadership of a much-enfeebled party finally slipped from his palsied hand. By 1920 the split within the party had worsened in that every coalitionist Liberal seat was now regarded as a legitimate target for independent Liberal candidates. Although the coalitionists published their own *Lloyd George Liberal Magazine* and set up their own local organizations, their position was extremely shaky in the country. In 1922 their 150–60 candidates contrasted with the Asquithians' 320; moreover their seats were very vulnerable. Of the 116 Liberals elected in 1922 only 47 were coalitionists and of these only 4 had won against a Conservative. With the renegades thus humbled Asquith should have shown magnanimity for the sake of the party and worked for reunion before it was too late. Instead he did nothing to check the factionalism of Lord Gladstone, Simon, Runciman, and others who professed to regard Lloyd George as an incubus upon the party. Their antagonism was only sharpened by the realization that they desperately needed subsidies from his political fund. In the surge of enthusiasm over free trade in 1923 Lloyd George did dispense £160,000 to the party, but thereafter he held on to his money as his one major bargaining weapon; rather than pour it out to help an organization under Asquithian control he chose to wait for his older rival's inevitable retirement. Having lost his seat at Paisley in 1924 Asquith carried on from within the House of Lords for no other purpose than to prevent the party succumbing to Lloyd George. He thus largely prevented the rejuvenation of Liberalism until after 1926, by which time too many radicals had been lost to Labour to permit even Lloyd George to restore the party's old strength.

Factionalism caused the Liberals to let slip their big opportunity in 1923, when all the leaders, except Churchill, apparently agreed on giving MacDonald his chance to become Prime Minister. Disintegrating tendencies were inherent in the situation, for in the country Conservatively inclined Liberals would inevitably blame the leaders for putting a Labour government in office, while left-wing Liberals would equally have resented any attempt to maintain Baldwin in power. Lloyd George's remark that 'if Ramsay were tactful and conciliatory I feel certain that the Party as a whole would support him in an advanced Radical programme'[6] looks particularly naive in view of the fact that MacDonald was very prickly towards the Liberals, had no such radical programme, and was not offered detailed terms in return for Liberal support. But it was characteristic of Lloyd George to think of constructive programmes while remaining blind to the effect of his proposal upon his party. As a party the Liberals' only viable strategy in 1923 lay in declining at once to vote for a MacDonald administration, thus obliging the King to summon Asquith rather than risk a third general election. Many Conservatives would have voted to keep Asquith in office for a short period as an acceptable alternative to Labour until they had regrouped. It would have been a risky course, but infinitely less hazardous and destructive for the party than the inept choice actually made. This was the last chance to restore Liberalism as an independent governing party, and it is still puzzling that such shrewd politicians missed it. The best explanation lies in their personality and recent history. Lloyd George, so recently ousted from the premiership, would not go out of his way to return too quickly, especially to his pre-1916 role as junior to Asquith; and Asquith had had too much experience of the Welshman's machinations to want to preside again over a ministry that included his rival.

The MacDonald–Baldwin Axis 1924

In the immediate aftermath of 1918 the Labour Party seemed unsure how to reap the benefit of its newly won position. In the eyes of MacDonald, temporarily in the wilderness, those who had survived the electoral holocaust were an uninspired set of trade union leaders who had not yet grown out of their subordinate relationship with Lloyd George; the party, he said, 'must forget the purple bondage and the flesh pots of Egypt which were its reward for the sorry part it played in the war'.[7] Though moved by bitterness MacDonald had a point; under William Adamson the parliamentary party conducted itself less like an opposition – and government-in-waiting – than as a pressure group seeking minor concessions from the rulers. As a result the parliamentary party tended to lose control in the movement between 1919 and 1922.

Yet these were vital formative years in several ways. As the reaction against the war and traditional diplomacy began to gather strength the Labour MPs were seen to have failed to offer serious opposition to the Treaty of Versailles. To the socialist and pacifist critics stolid trade unionists had nothing to offer on great moral issues; yet MacDonald both understood and could articulate their views. In addition this period saw a continuation of the dramatic wartime expansion of the industrial side of the movement and an outburst of militancy which reached a peak in 1921. Moreover, the success of many strikes tended to raise the prestige of the industrial as compared to the parliamentary movement. The alternative to the parliamentary strategy was cast not in terms of syndicalism but of 'direct action' which won the approval of party conference in 1919 and took practical shape in the Triple Alliance of miners, railwaymen and transport workers. Direct action claimed its greatest success in May 1920 when the dockers refused to load the *Jolly George* with arms for use in Poland against the Bolshevik cause. The government's retreat gave some grounds for the belief that they had compelled it to abandon its interventionist policy. In fact there was nothing revolutionary in the objectives of the union leaders; direct action was no more than a means to limited, material objectives. In April 1921, when two elements in the Triple Alliance withdrew to leave the miners to strike alone, direct action crumbled and thereafter the parliamentary leaders regained the initiative. Although MacDonald had been highly apprehensive about direct methods in 1920 he kept on the right side by saying that the country had been saved from another war – a widely acceptable view of this episode.

Many politicians defeated in 1918 assuaged their pain with the thought that this was a good parliament to be out of; for Ramsay MacDonald this was not untrue. His exclusion left him free to articulate the sentiments of Labour activists in the country and served to emphasize his patent superiority as a parliamentarian to those presently encamped uneasily on the opposition front bench. Indeed his attraction as leader during the 1920s was strikingly similar to Gladstone's for the Liberals in the 1870s; outstanding in the Commons, he appealed outside as leader of moral righteousness; because of the ambiguity of his politics the various elements within the party could look to him as their own spokesman. Thus MacDonald furnished a unifying force able to harness to the Labour cause the socialists of the ILP, the prickly idealistic ex-Liberals and the dour, respectable unionists. The later repudiation of MacDonald fostered the view that for the Labour Party an individual leader was less important than the ideology or class unity of the movement. Yet the party clove to MacDonald as a substitute for a clear philosophy; moreover, as a working-class party it exhibited remarkable fondness for its leaders, especially those drawn from the higher social classes, as the election of the radical baronets Sir Charles Trevelyan and Sir Oswald Mosley to the National Executive Committee suggests; conference always felt immensely flattered at the presence of such recruits.

Of course MacDonald's re-establishment in the leadership did not occur suddenly. Initially he seemed an electoral liability and his narrow defeat in a by-election in the Labour seat at Woolwich in February 1921 was cited as proof that his war record remained a bar. However, after Woolwich there appeared little mileage in scurrilous attacks on his patriotism, and in 1922 he was returned comfortably to the Commons for the South Wales mining seat of Aberavon. Further, MacDonald enjoyed a great advantage over his rival J. R. Clynes, whom he defeated 61 to 65 for the leadership after the election; he had a clear idea of the strategy appropriate for the party. Although Labour led the Liberals in Parliament by 142 to 116 their popular support was equal and there could be no certainty in 1922 that the Liberals would not succeed in making Labour again the third force in a two-party system. The new leader had no doubt of the urgency of keeping Labour's claims upon radicalism to the fore, and taking advantage of the factionalism in the Liberal camp. Hence his refusal, unlike Clynes, to be conciliatory over occupation of the opposition front bench which he declined to share with the Liberals. This was symptomatic of his intention to polarize politics around a Conservative–Labour struggle; an objective wholly shared by Baldwin and substantially realized during 1923–4.

In this task MacDonald derived an early advantage from the prominence of foreign affairs in 1922 and 1923. The crisis over the French occupation of the Ruhr and the incubus of reparations tended to vindicate left-wing criticism of Versailles and strengthen MacDonald's authority. In addition the Labour leader was a keener student of foreign affairs than either of the Conservative Prime Ministers and could handle them on relatively equal terms. In particular Baldwin's government, worthy but mediocre, served to undermine any notion that Labour was not in the same league.

When the election of 1923 made Labour, with 191 MPs, the second largest party, MacDonald, though surprised at the sudden turn of events, grasped his historic opportunity without hesitation. He appreciated that if Labour failed to produce a ministry at this point the Liberals would probably do so, thereby forcing Labour off the opposition front bench in favour of the retiring Conservatives. He therefore proceeded to form his administration as though he enjoyed a majority and a full term of office ahead of him. Since he could at any moment be voted out by the Conservatives if the Liberals merely abstained, the logic of the parliamentary arithmetic called for formal co-operation with Asquith. Yet the latter asked for no agreement, while MacDonald for his part resolutely avoided any understanding. This was in part a reflection of personal vanity and sensitivity; he had no governmental experience and thought his opponents were waiting for him to make a fool of himself. However, it was also deliberate policy to kill the client relationship with the Liberals; any deal with Asquith would have antagonized the left, and it was actually advantageous to preserve his minority position as an excuse for the absence of socialist legislation. This was indeed necessary, since MacDonald had no idea of a socialist programme and intended simply to demonstrate a capacity to run the administration quietly, so as to explode the myth that Labour was either 'unfit to govern' or dangerously radical.

Agreement with the Liberals would have tied MacDonald to office for much longer than he really wished to hold it. He certainly had no desire to invite immediate defeat, as some ILP members urged, by offering Parliament a full socialist programme; that would only have proved the critics right about Labour. It would also, in view of the King's reluctance to grant a third general election, have deprived MacDonald of a dissolution and led to a Liberal government. The Labour leader intended to govern the country for a short time, and then find a way out before basic economic and social questions had to be faced. In this sense MacDonald was always seeking a defeat, but not too soon; he managed to achieve this with the tacit co-operation of Stanley Baldwin.

In pursuit of respectability and reassurance the new Premier strengthened his Cabinet with experienced figures from Liberal backgrounds – Haldane as Lord Chancellor, C. P. Trevelyan at Education, Noel Buxton at Agriculture, Josiah Wedgwood as Chancellor of the Duchy of Lancaster – and from the Conservative ranks – Lord Parmoor as Lord President of the Council and Lord Chelmsford at the Admiralty. The rest of the posts were filled by known moderates apart from Health and Works which went to two socialists, John Wheatley and F. W. Jowett. In so far as the Prime Minister faced pressure over posts it took a personal rather than a political form. Somewhat sobered by the magnitude of events the party felt reluctant to insist upon the claims of any particular groups or individuals. The overriding objective was to launch the government, and the more it conformed to prevailing notions of a proper administration the better the party liked it. MacDonald's rigid insistence on the wearing of court dress by his ministers and the eagerness of the new ministers' wives to be coached by Beatrice Webb in the behaviour appropriate to their role, were trivial but telling symptoms of the desire to win acceptance.

RAMSAY THE UNRUDDY.

Sir Despard Murgatroyd—Mr. MacDONALD   *Mad Margaret—SOCIALISM.*
    D. M.   "I ONCE WAS A VERY ABANDONED PERSON—"
    M. M.   "MAKING THE MOST OF EVIL CHANCES."
    D. M.   "NOBODY COULD CONCEIVE A WORSE 'UN . . . ." [*Dance.*
    M. M.   "THAT IS ONE OF OUR BLAMELESS DANCES." —*Ruddigore*, Act II.

From Punch, *20 February 1924.*

Matters of policy also reinforced the strategy. As his own Foreign
Secretary, MacDonald succeeded in improving relations with France
as a necessary prelude to French withdrawal from the Ruhr and a
reduction of reparations under the Dawes Plan. No one could fault this
any more than they could attack Snowden's cautious free-trade budget

or Wheatley's Housing Act based on Addison's earlier measure. The flaw lay in the absence of ideas on unemployment; Snowden granted a placatory £28 million for public relief works in July while MacDonald endeavoured to restore trade with Russia by granting recognition to the new regime.

For the most part the Conservatives remained content to grumble at Baldwin for his part in causing the advent of Labour to office, but were deprived of any sense of trauma. By avoiding anything controversial MacDonald facilitated the Conservative leader's desire to allow the new government a short period of office. As Neville Chamberlain observed, 'it would be too weak to do much harm, but not too weak to get discredited.'[8] Consequently there was no effort to turn Labour out, a fact obscured by Baldwin who launched himself on a series of speeches in the country during the summer of 1924, thereby conveying to his supporters a gratifying impression of a great ideological battle which bore little relation to the actual situation in Parliament. In fact Baldwin both liked and trusted the Prime Minister; he approved the continuity in foreign policy and continued to receive a selection of Foreign Office papers during the year.[9] In the Commons, of course, the 191 ministerialists theoretically stood in dire danger of defeat by the 258 Conservatives; however, government defeats on relatively minor matters helped to maintain the illusion that Baldwin was fulfilling the opposition's job, while on major issues there was sometimes a suspicious closeness between the government's margin and the number of Conservative members absent and unpaired. By keeping MacDonald in until September Baldwin hoped to allow time to reorganize and arouse his supporters in the constituencies; since the spring the party had been under instructions to work on the basis of a November election. Thanks to the common interest of the two leaders polling day was 29 October.

By September the Conservatives were ready to censure the government over the withdrawal by the Attorney-General of a proposed prosecution of a Communist editor, J. R. Campbell, under the Incitement to Mutiny Act; meanwhile the Liberals, patience exhausted at MacDonald's refusal to co-operate, put down a motion criticizing the Russian Treaty negotiated by MacDonald. His reaction was a mixture of delight and relief:

I am inclined to give the Liberals an election on it if they force it. I have no intention of deserting a post of difficulty but the conditions of office perhaps bribe me to take this chance of ending the present regime.[10]

As a private note in his diary, this shows MacDonald's eagerness for speedy release. He particularly welcomed an attack upon the Russian Treaty because it lent a general political significance to the challenge and therefore justified a dissolution. Baldwin took a similar view; it was better to secure their defeat on the Treaty than over the Campbell case.[11] So determined was MacDonald not to let slip the opportunity for his government's defeat that when the Liberals put an amendment to the Conservative motion asking merely for a select committee of enquiry, he insisted on treating it as a resignation issue. This was quite unnecessary, and he knew that Asquith wanted to find a way out of the confrontation; nonetheless MacDonald secured his own defeat by 198 to 364 votes!

Yet there were entirely sound reasons for taking this course. After nine months his own supporters had grown increasingly unhappy both about rising unemployment and about the government's willingness to declare a state of emergency and use troops in the dock strike and in a London Underground strike. MacDonald could not go on much longer with so little of substance to show; nine months was sufficient to prove Labour's competence to the undecided voter. By surrendering office at this stage he lent plausibility to the view that lack of a majority had prevented him from tackling basic economic questions; that he perished defending left-wing causes like the Russian Treaty and the Campbell case also served to deflect criticism within the movement. The impression of reactionary forces ganging up to eject Labour was greatly reinforced by the so-called Zinoviev Letter during the election campaign. This document purported to be an incitement to class war in Britain from the President of the Communist International in Moscow. A gift to Conservative propaganda, released on the weekend before polling day for maximum effect, the Zinoviev Letter probably made no more than a marginal contribution to the Conservative victory; its importance lay rather in strengthening Labour's own impression that it had been deprived of office by capitalist conspiracies, and thereby helped to divert attention from the ideological shortcomings of the government itself.

It may be objected that no Prime Minister risks an early general election, let alone courts one, if he cannot be confident of winning it; yet that was not really an option for MacDonald, since a Conservative victory fairly soon was inevitable. By-elections during 1924 reassured MacDonald that his own support would not collapse; Labour held Burnley and gained West Toxteth (Liverpool). More significant was the Liberal loss at Oxford to a Conservative through Labour intervention and the attrition of the Liberal vote at Glasgow Kelvingrove from 18.1 per cent to 4.9 per cent to Conservative advantage. Such results confirmed the shakiness of the swollen Liberal poll of 1923, and the prospect that Conservatives would recover many seats narrowly lost to the Liberals in that year. That the Conservatives were bound to be the major beneficiaries in the short run mattered little to MacDonald. For his main concern was the relative strength of Labour and Liberalism; while his party dropped from 192 to 151 seats in 1924, the Liberals' 158 shrank to 42; Labour candidates rose to 512 while the Liberals fielded only 340; consequently their respective share of the poll stood at 33 per cent and 17.6 per cent. In this way the 1924 election completed the joint objectives of Baldwin and MacDonald by squeezing out the Liberal Party and raising Labour to the status of government-in-waiting on a permanent basis. The return to two-party politics after the confusion of wartime was almost complete.

12

Origins of the Conservative
Electoral Hegemony

1918–1931

It is not surprising that the desire to put an end to this
plague of annual elections should be uppermost in the
minds of many voters.

The Nation, 1924

Although the most striking feature of the 1920s was the sustained surge
in popular support for the Labour Party, this should not obscure the
Conservative preponderance which so characterized the period. Indeed,
during 1918–39 the Conservatives formed or predominated in governments after five of the seven general elections, and were consistently
the largest party except during the 1929–31 Parliament. How was this
hegemony established and maintained at a time when the terms of the
electoral battle had changed drastically and in ways that might have
been expected to present the advantage to a rival party claiming to stand
for the working-class majority? How far, if at all, was the political
struggle modified as a result of the introduction of a new element of
uncertainty in the shape of the female electorate? In this chapter we
shall attempt to isolate the chief elements both in Conservative success
and in Labour's growth which proceeded apparently unchecked until
1931.

The Impact of the Electoral System

It would be erroneous to assume that the Conservative parliamentary
majorities of 1918–39 reflected their transformation into a natural
majority in the country. A glance at the voting figures shown in table
12.1 indicates that the victories of the 1920s were attained on a fairly
narrow basis, usually a bare two-fifths of the poll. It can be argued that

TABLE 12.1

	Conservative		Liberal		Labour	
	% Vote	Seats	% Vote	Seats	% Vote	Seats
1922	38.2	345	29.1	116	29.5	142
1923	38.1	258	29.6	159	30.5	191
1924	48.3	419	17.6	40	33.0	151
1929	38.2	260	23.4	59	37.1	288

TABLE 12.2 *Unopposed returns*

	Conservative	Liberal	Labour
1922	42	10	4
1923	35	11	3
1924	16	6	9
1929	4	–	–

Conservative strength is in fact underestimated by the figures because of the number of strongly Conservative seats not contested by the other parties and therefore omitted. It is true that Conservatives enjoyed a disproportionate share of unopposed returns, largely in Northern Ireland and south-eastern county divisions. However, the numbers were not large and were diminishing (see table 12.2). In fact the net loss of Conservative votes arising from this source is insufficient to make more than a marginal impression on their share of the poll even in 1922.[1] In that year only 483 Conservatives stood and a portion of the party's support must have gone to National or ex-Coalition Liberals. But their share is also inflated by the smaller number of candidates fielded by the Liberals whose absence in 1924, for example, from 275 of the 615 constituencies, served to boost the Conservative share. One may generalize by saying that the Conservative–Liberal–Labour share changed from 4–3–3 in the early 1920s to 4–2–4 by the end of the decade.

That such a division generated comfortable Conservative majorities may be ascribed in the first instance to party relationships and the electoral system. Single-member systems invariably produce highly unrepresentative results in which slight shifts in votes lead to exaggerated changes in representation; but the effect is notoriously erratic when three, rather than two, evenly balanced parties are in competition. Whereas before 1914 the Lib–Lab pact had resulted in straight fights in five seats out of six, during the 1920s three-cornered contests became usual. Consequently the division of the Progressive vote between Labour and Liberal gave the Conservatives a major advantage. This was dramatically demonstrated in 1922 when the comfortable Conservative majority of 345 (out of 615) was based on a percentage poll five points *below* that obtained in the disaster of 1906 which had yielded 157 seats (out of 670)! By contrast the Liberal and Labour parties managed 58.6 per cent in 1922 compared with 54.9 per cent in 1906, yet returned only 258 members instead of 430. In 1922 they divided the vote virtually evenly between themselves, though the seats fell out to Labour's advantage because the greater concentration of its vote in certain industrial counties and conurbations brought its candidates more frequently to the head of the poll. The erratic operation of the electoral system left a major impact on politics during the successive general elections of 1922, 1923 and 1924. Labour came to power with only 191 seats following the 1923 election when a modest loss of Conservative votes precipitated a net loss of 87 seats largely to Liberal candidates in constituencies where Labour did not stand. The bizarre logic was reversed the following year in that Labour's increased strength facilitated Baldwin's return to power; for the rise in Labour candidatures from 422 to 512 occurred largely in seats won by Liberals in 1923, thereby producing many of the 107 Conservative gains from Liberals. Labour itself won substantially fewer constituencies in 1924 despite an increased share of the poll.

The long-term effect of the electoral system emerges from a comparison between the 1922 and 1929 elections. Although the Conservative vote was similar in each case they won 85 seats fewer in the latter year. The reason for this lay in a realignment of the non-Conservative vote during the decade. For whereas in 1922 Labour and the Liberals took 29 per cent each, by 1929 they stood at 37 per cent and 23 per cent; despite their party's 'revival' during 1926–9 many erstwhile Liberals regarded Labour as the more probable or desirable winner against the Conservatives. The disproportion in seats – 288 to 59 – was far greater than previously.

Why did the non-Conservative politicians not attempt to deprive the Conservatives of their built-in advantage either by means of proportional representation using multi-member seats or by using the alternative vote in single-member seats? Before 1914 the Liberal Party, though tempted by the alternative vote, had neglected such innovations so long as the pact held. All parties tended to interpret Edwardian elections as meaning that the bulk of Liberal and Labour voters would use their second preferences to mutual advantage. Therefore when

PR and the alternative vote were debated under the Representation of the People Bill in 1917–18 most Labour and Liberal MPs favoured the alternative vote while the Conservatives resisted both schemes. Although the radical parties still retained a majority in the Commons at this time, they lacked leadership on this point, and in deference to Conservative objections Lloyd George induced sufficient coalitionist Liberal and Labour members to reject all varieties of reform. Thus they missed their best opportunity to break out of the traditional system. After 1918, since the Conservatives were unyielding, the Liberal Party hoped to obtain reform from the minority Labour governments. At the Speaker's Conference of 1930 the Liberals proposed PR in urban areas and the alternative vote elsewhere, a formula that seemed likely to maximize their advantage; for they would gain Labour second preferences in rural counties while limiting Labour's clean sweep of industrial regions. Unlike many in his party MacDonald had always disliked PR, but in view of the vulnerability of his government he gave consideration to the alternative vote. Now according to the party's chief agent, if this had been applied in the 313 constituencies whose MP had been elected on a minority vote in 1929 the representation would have been substantially modified: the Liberal total would have risen from 41 to 88, Labour's from 120 to 135–43, and the Conservatives fallen from 152 to 67–82.[2] Yet for MacDonald this would not have been an unmixed blessing; for the advantages of curtailing the Conservative strength were outweighed by the disadvantages of boosting the Liberals. Moreover the agent's calculations had to be made on the assumption that each party's first preference votes would remain the same. However, the likelihood was that the new system would have encouraged wavering radicals to vote Liberal instead of backing Labour in order to keep the Conservatives out, and also relaxed the pressure on 'moderates' to vote Conservative rather than Liberal to stop Labour. Already the Liberals under Lloyd George's inspiration were dangerously near to a breakthrough; their 5 million votes in 1929, against 8 million for each of the other parties, threatened a return to three-party politics. MacDonald's whole strategy in the 1920s consisted in using the logic of the first-past-the-post system to drive the Progressive vote into Labour's camp, as the Liberals had used it before 1914. To allow the Liberals a guaranteed parliamentary base of between 100 and 150 members – the inevitable consequence of electoral reform – would have been to destroy the prospect of a majority Labour government which was now within sight. A bigger Liberal representation would have led to coalition which, especially with Lloyd George's participation, foreshadowed a restoration of the Liberals as the senior partner in government. Thus although MacDonald humoured Lloyd George even to the extent of introducing a

TABLE 12.3   *Estimated result of December 1910 election under 1918 boundaries*

	Actual result December 1910	Effect of 1918 boundaries
Conservative	272	306
Liberal/Labour	314	322
Irish	84	79

bill for electoral reform, he relied upon the Conservative peers to delay and destroy it for him; it was a reasonable assumption that his government would not last long enough to have to fight for the measure. The establishment of a National Government in 1931 killed off any prospect of reform, and also undid the Liberal revival of 1929 by shifting the Liberals into a closer relationship with the right, thereby completing the vacating of the left for occupation by Labour. Conservative predominance between the wars was, thus, for Labour a necessary price to be paid in the medium term for maintaining its own elevation as the major alternative at the expense of the Liberals.

The Conservatives and the Constituencies

The second key element in the Conservatives' success is to be found in the reorganization of the constituencies in 1918 and the Conservative response to it. The previous redistribution back in 1885 had left plenty of anomalies such as seats like Kilkenny with 1,700 voters, and the shifts of population since then had only exacerbated the disparities. By 1918 the average English constituency had twice as many electors as the average Irish seat and somewhat more than those in Wales and Scotland. This over-representation told against the Conservatives, though it was to some extent balanced by Conservative command of many small boroughs in England.

It seems obvious that the growth of population since 1885, especially in suburban areas around London, Birmingham, south Lancashire and Glasgow, would inevitably have produced Conservative gains under any redistribution that moved towards equal constituencies. One historian has estimated that if the 1918 redistribution had operated at the previous general election (December 1910) it would have had the effect of adding 3 to Liberal strength, 5 to Labour and 34 to the Conservatives (see table 12.3).[3] However, this calculation of a net Conservative gain of

26 should not be seen simply as the effect of equal constituencies. If one sets aside the 6 net gains in Ireland – for Ireland's representation was exempted from the general provisions in 1918 – one has 20 gains in England, Wales and Scotland; this includes 4 university-seat gains (also exceptions to the population rules), which leaves 16. The key to these in fact lies in the overall increase in the Commons to 707 members rather than to any strict application of the principle of equal constituencies. None of the parties had objected in principle to equalization at the Speaker's Conference in 1916; existing borough and county seats were to retain separate representation only if their population reached 50,000 and new ones were to be formed for every 70,000 and for remainders of 50,000. The redivision of residential constituencies, particularly in London, Middlesex, Surrey, Warwickshire and Lancashire, certainly generated additional Conservative seats. Before 1914, 9 of the 13 largest seats had been Conservative, of which 7 were in London (Croydon, Ealing, Enfield, Harrow, Lewisham, Wandsworth and Wimbledon); Wandsworth, for example, became 4 separate seats in 1918 each returning a Conservative. However, much of this was offset by the disappearance of many small Conservative boroughs like Salisbury, Winchester, Windsor, Taunton, Canterbury, Hereford and Bury St Edmunds, which were merged into the surrounding county constituencies. These modifications had a special significance within the party for they eroded still further the natural parliamentary base of the landed elements while extending that of the commercial and urban sections, a process discernible by 1900 but greatly speeded up in the twentieth century.

In fact the principle of equal constituencies was circumscribed in ways calculated to assist the Conservatives, such as the increase in university representation from 9 to 15,[4] which the party had expected to lose altogether.[5] In addition the rules for constituency size were always interpreted flexibly because of the assumption that parliamentary boundaries should coincide with administrative ones. In 1918 the Boundary Commissioners' room for manoeuvre was significantly widened by a Conservative amendment to the instructions to the effect that they should avoid creating constituencies of an inconvenient size or character.[6] This could not save sparsely populated (Liberal) counties like Caithness and Sutherland or Radnor and Brecon from amalgamation; but it did allow a number of English agricultural seats to be given the benefit of the doubt where their population was not too far below the limit laid down in the Act. According to private Conservative estimates at least 17 county seats, which on a strict interpretation should have been abolished, were thus preserved.[7] This was possible only at the cost of inflating the membership of the Commons from 670 to 707, something that the House, though very critical, was prepared to tolerate on the assumption that before very long the Irish element was bound to shrink as a consequence of Home Rule. Thus, so far as England, Scotland and Wales are concerned, the 1918 redistribution gave the Conservatives a modest gain, not so much through the application of equalization as by certain judicious modifications of it.

Ultimately, however, their major gain came from Ireland, where Conservatives had long been anxious for redistribution, in view of the huge Nationalist preponderance. In fact in 1918 the total of Irish seats was raised by two to 105 with a slight internal rearrangement. But since the 73 Sinn Fein members elected in 1918 refused to attend Westminster, the Irish element was for all practical purposes removed at this point. After 1922 the separation of the Irish Republic left Northern Ireland with only 12 Westminster MPs, not more than two of whom were ever other than Unionist. Thus, whereas before 1918 the Conservative Party had normally suffered a handicap of around 65 (that is 84 minus 19) from Ireland, after 1922 they usually enjoyed an advantage of 8–12. Herein lay the real gain; the virtual disappearance of the Irish factor from Westminster in itself made it far more difficult for the non-Conservative forces to obtain a majority than previously.

If one turns to consider the regional distribution of Conservative support in the new constituency system one finds considerable continuity of strengths and weaknesses between the wars. A comparison based on the proportion of Conservative seats held in each region in the 1892–1910 period with that in the 1922–35 period points to an enduring pattern in which Wales, Scotland and the four northern counties and Yorkshire continued to be the party's weakest areas, and the counties south of the Wash–Severn line the strongest.[8] What modifications there were are best brought out by comparing the elections of 1900 and 1924 when, for England, Wales and Scotland, the party won 67 per cent of the seats on both occasions. If these victories are broken down into six broad regional groups it is clear that southern England, London and the Midlands remained the strongest and Wales, Scotland and the north the weakest (see table 12.4). By 1924 Conservatives had grown even more reliant upon southern and midland England. Their tightening grip on the south reflected, first, some spread of middle-class residential population beyond London (hence a drop in their share within the capital itself), and second, the Conservatives' ability to take up the slack resulting from Liberal decline in East Anglia and the south-west, both areas in which Labour found it difficult to inherit fully the old radical vote.

Inevitably any regional perspective somewhat exaggerates the fundamental north–south divide; on the other hand if one looks at the spread

TABLE 12.4 *Seats won by Conservatives in 1900 and 1924 (%)*

	London	Southern England	Midlands	Northern England	Scotland	Wales
1900	86.4	79.4	68.2	63.6	51.4	17.6
1924	62.9	90.9	73.6	50.1	50.7	25.7

TABLE 12.5 *Distribution of Conservative seats in 1924*
(England, Scotland and Wales)

Total	Middle class 20% or more	Middle class 10–19.9%	Middle class under 10%
409 (602)	169 (200)	236 (356)	4 (46)

Source: M. Kinnear, *The British Voter: an Atlas and Survey 1885–1964* (1969) pp. 122–4.

of Conservatism socially, the impression is more one of a nationally based party. On the basis of the occupational categories in the census of 1921 it has been found that 200 constituencies had a middle-class element of 20 per cent or above in their occupied male population.[9] Of these 200 the Conservative Party invariably won 130–80 during the 1918–31 period. While this was a valuable base it was by no means the key to their post-war electoral hegemony, for the middle classes had plainly shrunk as a proportion of the electorate. What was therefore vital for the Conservatives during the 1920s was their capacity to supplement their basic 130 with a further minimum 130 in the seats where the middle-class element fell below 20 per cent, thereby making an irreducible minimum of around 260 in the Commons, which rendered it difficult for any other single party to obtain a majority. What is remarkable is that, apart from 1923 and 1929, they usually held another 100 on top of this from the less middle-class areas. A breakdown of the Conservative victory in the 1924 general election illustrated in table 12.5 shows that the party's massive command of the Commons rested upon successes in more than two-thirds of the constituencies where the middle-class element fell between 10 per cent and 19.9 per cent or, to put it another way, where the working class comprised 80–90 per cent.

The corollary of this spread of Conservative seats was dependence upon fully mobilizing their support in each social group by means of an efficient and comprehensive electoral machine. The traditional skill in doctoring the register of voters naturally became redundant under the new simplified system in which the bulk of the work was done by town clerks and clerks to the county councils. Registration gave way to a new emphasis, particularly on increasing the number of volunteer workers; this followed from the curtailing of expenditure and introduction of one-day polling in 1918 which threw most constituencies upon their own organizational resources on polling day. The party activist's role as intermediary between politician and voter became still more important as a result of the increase by two and a half times in the size of the electorate. Many were young voters whose loyalties were less deep or less rigid than those of pre-war voters; one indication of the difficulties this posed is the fall in turnout to 70–6 per cent during the 1920s against the 81–6 per cent in Edwardian elections. There are certainly grounds for thinking that the Conservatives responded more effectively to the challenge presented by this larger, relatively uncommitted electorate than either of their rivals. While the Liberal agents disappeared and Labour made do with union organizers, the Conservatives improved their existing system of training and examinations for agents, some 352 of whom, together with 99 women organizers, received training between 1924 and 1937.[10] Regular attention by professional staff enabled the party to get to grips with the new system of absent voting established in 1918 for those whose occupations kept them away from home; the routine, meticulous work of tracking down such people and ensuring postal votes for loyal supporters probably came more naturally to the clerically minded Conservative organizations than to their Labour rivals.

A new emphasis was also placed upon fund-raising activities and upon raising large numbers of small subscriptions. Indeed Conservatives from Baldwin down were now heard to criticize the party for relying too much on candidates wealthy enough to relieve constituency associations of any need to finance elections. Rather than widening their choice by adopting impecunious but able candidates, as Baldwin urged, it seems that some constituencies relieved their MPs of bills they normally paid; even this process did not go very far, for only a quarter to a third of local associations appear to have become financially independent by the 1930s.[11]

Labour's Grass Roots 1918–1929

Between the First World War and the 1930s the Labour Party turned itself from the rather loose federal structure it had originally been into a substantial parliamentary party supported by a strong central organization and a comprehensive framework of regional and local organization and membership. Much of the credit for this achievement must be ascribed to Arthur Henderson who held tight control over head office, the National Executive and its sub-committees until 1924 when he temporarily surrendered the party secretaryship. He was helped by the new national agent, Egerton Wake, who in 1918 appropriately replaced Arthur Peters, a man whose sympathies with Liberalism rendered him a hindrance to the expanding party. Central to Henderson's dominance was his co-operation with the trade unions whose financial contribution nationally and locally underpinned the whole structure. During the 1920s the union membership affiliated to the party – which was based very approximately on the number who paid the political levy – rose to 3.5 million, though the figure fell sharply to 2 million between 1927 and 1928 as a result of the Baldwin government's Trade Disputes Act which introduced the practice of 'contracting in' for the levy.

At constituency level union branches or trades councils were often instrumental in fighting election campaigns and selecting candidates. On the whole union-sponsored candidates held the safer seats, and even in difficult rural constituencies the key trade union frequently determined the choice. Dependence upon strong union branches explains the patchy but continuous growth of constituency organizations during the 1920s. The number of affiliated constituency parties rose year by year from 397 in 1918 to 626 by 1924, though the latter figure is inflated by some double affiliations. The three general elections in 1922–4 clearly provided a stimulus in that the 140 constituencies lacking a Labour party in 1921 had shrunk to 19 by 1924. Yet there remained a shortfall of up to 100 between affiliated parties and parliamentary contests, which reflects the inability of young organizations to sustain expensive campaigns in the absence of strong union branches. Nevertheless the pattern of continuous expansion which began around 1917 was virtually complete by 1929 when the Labour Party fought on almost as broad a front as the Conservatives. The party's steadily rising share of the national poll is a direct measure of the additional candidates fielded; the average poll per contest, which hovered around the 40 per cent mark, reflects additional candidatures in weak constituencies in 1924 and 1929 which depresses the average figures (see table 12.6).

The dramatic interruption in this pattern of growth in 1931 diverted attention from the flaws in the party's organizational base during the 1920s and it is to these that we must now turn. In the first place it is clear that many constituency parties were little more than nominal, and that the pattern of individual membership projected in 1918 always

TABLE 12.6   *Labour growth at general elections*

	1918	1922	1923	1924	1929	1931
% total poll	22.2	29.5	30.5	33.0	37.1	30.6
Candidates	388	411	422	512	571	515
Average % poll per contest	–	40.0	41.0	38.2	39.3	33.0

remained an elusive goal rather than an achievement. Frequently local Labour parties comprised simply the delegates of local union branches plus some socialist societies' representatives. After 1918 in the industrial north-east, Lancashire, Scotland and Wales the old trades councils had frequently adopted the title of 'Divisional Labour Party'; consequently at local level the party remained an umbrella organization outside the real centres of power as it had been before 1914. It is not surprising that the desired mass membership was rarely attained. In 1928, when separate figures became available, individual party membership stood at 215,000; though no doubt a considerable improvement on pre-war strength, this suggests a constituency average of around 350 only. Even this must be qualified by the knowledge that 1928 was a buoyant time for Labour – now anticipating victory over a fading Baldwin administration – and that all parties' official figures tend to exaggerate real membership. Although Conservative figures were not published, local evidence suggests a massive advantage in membership; by 1929 the Glasgow Conservatives, for example, enjoyed an average of 2,000 per constituency. A brighter sign for Labour was the recruitment of women; some working-class towns like Woolwich and Barrow claimed around 1,000 women members by 1924, though these had been unusually well-organized localities before 1914 and remained exceptional in the 1920s; at this time individual membership was often far more female than male in composition. Also among the seats with over 200 women members were mixed industrial and middle-class towns such as York, Colchester, Gloucester and Newport, in each of which Labour either won or ran the Conservatives very close in 1929; they were in fact the crucial battleground if the party's total of 288 seats in 1929 was to be turned into an overall majority of 308. In this struggle the disproportionately middle-class Labour women's sections had a vital part to play in taking on the Conservative organization on more equal terms.

It may be thought that individual membership was insignificant in view of the huge affiliated union membership and that the unions somehow endowed Labour with all the apparatus of a mass political party; yet this was by no means the case. For one thing the affiliation to the party of an arbitrary number of union members meant much less, in terms of individual commitment, than taking out direct membership; indeed recent studies suggest that many of those who pay the political levy are unaware that they are doing so. Also, although total union membership reached a peak of over 8 million in 1920, thereafter until 1934 it steadily declined to almost half that number, so that it was a wasting asset for much of the period. What is most important is that although a trade-union-based organization was perfectly adequate for mobilizing voters in overwhelmingly unionized working-class constituencies, this could guarantee only a hard core of MPs; for a party whose path to a majority necessitated winning the more mixed seats this could never be a satisfactory substitute for the efficient machine built up by the Conservatives. Moreover, although the unions were a vital source of funds they remained somewhat inflexible about how the money was deployed. Henderson, who was acutely aware of the need to channel resources through headquarters into needy and marginal areas, never obtained the funds he believed to be necessary. Against the opposition of a number of union leaders he managed to persuade Conference in 1920 to raise the levy from 2d per member to 3d, and this produced £40,000–50,000 a year. In 1923 he resurrected the fighting fund to assist impecunious constituencies, which had been abolished in 1919. Although some £20,000 was thereby paid out in 1924 this still fell short of Henderson's objective of equalizing the expenditure of the richer and poorer constituencies. Seats fought by the miners, for example, spent on average 50 per cent more on elections in the early 1920s though they could have managed on less than most. Because the trade unions felt reluctant to allow headquarters unlimited powers to redistribute the movement's resources Labour continued to enjoy abundance in its safest seats but failed to make good the deficiencies in areas where it had to make gains. A crucial consequence of this failure to tap resources fully was the poor provision of full-time agents. In 1920 the number stood at 112; it rose to 133 in 1922 and tailed off to 113 by 1924, though it was supplemented by 20–30 agents employed largely by the Miners Federation. By 1929 a maximum of 169 had been recorded, but this fell back to 136 by 1935. Again these agents were concentrated largely in safe seats. Only a total of 300–400 full-time professional agents would have placed the party on an equal footing with its rival.

In many ways, however, the most positive aspect of Labour's advance was in municipal politics which provided the opportunity to defend working-class living standards even though the party only briefly held national office. In the first post-war elections in November 1919 the change of mood since the Coupon Election became clear. Outside London Labour gained 400 seats; and in the London boroughs its candidates were elected for 572 out of 1,362 seats. These gains were not only of a far higher order than pre-war ones, they were also improved upon in nearly every subsequent year between the wars. Much of the ground was won at Liberal expense; indeed the Liberals' inability to survive at the local level was underlined by a steady fall in the number of municipal candidates which continued even when the party was enjoying revivals in parliamentary elections. It was the London Labour Party under Herbert Morrison's leadership which demonstrated the most effective approach to party organization. Here the strategy was characterized by the channelling of funds from the Transport and General Workers Union to the central control point, and by less reliance on major meetings and more on the thorough doorstep canvass in which women members came into their own. Even in some most unpromising seats the LLP established effective organizations, and claimed high membership figures – 2,000 in the case of South Poplar for instance. Mastery of the canvass, which was particularly appropriate for the huge suburban housing estates around London, was regarded as a key factor in the remarkable Labour gains in such places as North Camberwell in 1922 and Mitcham in 1923. 'The new school of Labour politicians is a scientific school', Morrison claimed, 'It knows that noisy tub-thumping does not make up for careful organization.'[12]

Morrison's hyperbole did highlight another characteristic of Labour's approach to elections during the inter-war years. After 1918 Henderson made great use of regular regional conferences and rallies, and for these, as for parliamentary elections, he relied heavily upon obtaining star speakers. The price was unduly heavy speaking engagements for Henderson himself (who thought nothing of giving a two-hour oration at a by-election) but also for MacDonald. The party's reliance upon the Victorian radical techniques of inspirational rallies and whistle-stop tours, at which MacDonald undoubtedly excelled, is all of a piece with the relative neglect of individual mass membership and efficient local machinery. For although Conservatives also held big rallies this was never such a central part of their approach to the electorate. Their leaders, usually less proficient with the Gladstonian oration, showed, especially in Baldwin's case, considerable facility with the quieter technique of the radio broadcast; and their larger membership, and efficiency with transport, the canvass and the postal vote were far better calculated to mobilize their support from among the enlarged electorate of relatively uncommitted voters than was Labour's traditional radical revivalism. This has sometimes been lost sight of by writers who attribute the Liberal decline to an inherent inability to master the techniques for mobilizing the post-1918 mass electorate, inhibitions from which the more democratic Labour Party should in theory have been free. Yet if there was a basic division in approach it would seem, in practice, to have been between the Conservative Party on the one hand, and, on the other, the Labour and Liberal Parties whose strengths and weaknesses betrayed a common Victorian origin.

Women in Inter-war Politics

In 1918 women comprised just under 40 per cent of the total electorate; by 1924 their share had risen to 42.8 per cent, and by 1929, following the introduction of equal suffrage, to 52.7 per cent. Only recently has this new majority in the British political system begun to attract the scholarly attention it deserves. This may reflect an assumption that the political impact of women proved to be slight and that the feminist movement entered upon a decline after 1918. No major women's party emerged as some politicians had feared, and only a handful of women became MPs. After Nancy Astor's breakthrough at a 1919 by-election, two were elected in 1922, eight in 1923, four in 1924, fourteen in 1929, fifteen in 1931 and nine in 1935. Some of the former suffragists and suffragettes eschewed any attempt to enter Parliament because they felt none of the parties were yet willing to treat women equally; Eleanor Rathbone, however, sat as an Independent MP for a university seat from 1929 to 1946. Many activists had been Liberals, but the declining fortunes of their party severely hampered their chances between the wars. A number of very able women chose to pursue a political career within the Labour and Conservative Parties, but for most this meant accepting the orthodox priorities of the party rather than promoting feminism.

Nonetheless women made an impact in several ways. Each party felt obliged to overhaul its organization after 1918, to recruit new members, to establish formal representation for women in the party machine, to create a professional hierarchy for women, and to address propaganda to them. The two main parties showed the same recruitment pattern; women's membership rose to a peak in the late 1920s – one million for the Conservatives and 250,000 to 300,000 for Labour – followed by a slight decline in the 1930s as the early enthusiasm wore off.

The concern felt by politicians over the new voters may also be charted in the fluctuating proportion of candidates who made specific appeals to women in their election literature: 46 per cent in 1922, 39 per cent in 1923, 63 per cent in 1924 and 67 per cent in 1929. This reflects the fact that initially Labour were more inclined to bid for female votes, whereas the Conservatives feared that this would be divisive. But the defeat of Baldwin in 1923 was widely attributed to women, especially as the debate over tariffs and free trade had pushed food prices to the top of the agenda. Thereafter Conservatives gave much more attention to women. This was reflected in the pattern of political debate and legislation during the 1920s. The combination of adult male suffrage and the rise of the Labour Party consolidated the Edwardian trend towards giving such questions as standards of living, unemployment and social welfare a high priority on the agenda. Women's entry into the system simply strengthened that trend. Thus the parties competed with one another to offer women essentially the same policies: widows' pensions, equal suffrage and local maternity clinics financed by the state. During the 1920s a large number of measures for women were enacted. But by 1929 the politicians had had sufficient experience of female voters at five general elections to know where they could draw the line. No more feminist reforms were now on their agenda; women's politics could be confined essentially to domestic questions and their interests treated as though they coincided exactly with those of their children and husbands. Thus during the 1930s women's politics appeared to have been contained, though the domestic approach was yet to reach its culmination in the form of the welfare state after 1945.

One of the most important questions, though difficult to answer, is, for whom did the women vote at inter-war elections? Naturally there is a good deal of propagandist and impressionistic evidence here. In 1918 candidates in all parties judged that women had reacted very patriotically and voted for the Coalition government. On the other hand the announcement of equal suffrage in 1927 led the right-wing press to warn that young women were highly susceptible to socialism. Certainly the Tories attributed their setbacks in 1923 and 1929 in part to vacillating females. However, the objective evidence suggests that they were probably wrong to do so. Studies of several elections between 1918 and 1931 have found an *inverse* relationship between the level of the female vote in a constituency and the level of Labour support; in other words women as a group leaned a little towards the Conservatives.[13] This is consistent with other evidence for the inter-war period. Conservatives clearly mobilized more women within the party than Labour. The experience of working-class women in the field of employment may have played a part in this. Many women were in service occupations, in which trade unions were very weak; even in industry female workers were far less likely to join a union than their male colleagues. Consequently they seldom underwent the same process of political socialization which cemented the loyalty of growing numbers of working men to Labour.

From Punch, *15 November 1922.*

This has been underlined emphatically in a local analysis of politics in Preston, where, after Labour's advance in 1918, the party lost support. This appeared to reflect the character of the local party which was dominated by male trade unionists who had emerged from the war rather hostile to the employment of women. They opposed municipal and national spending on welfare for women, and discouraged the organization of women within the party. The loss of votes from women forced some modification of these attitudes, but after the policy failure of the second Labour government women proved slow to return to the party even in 1935.[14]

This does not mean that Labour was not gaining support generally among working-class women during the 1920s. The 1924 MacDonald government made the reduction of taxation on food items one of its priorities, and the party placed great emphasis on widows' pensions and improved maternity services. But it was probably more difficult to win over the women's vote than the men's. Consequently by 1929 this was the more vulnerable part of Labour's support, and this manifested itself after 1931 when the party lost votes heavily among women electors.

The General Strike and the Realignment of the Working Class

In the past it was assumed that the central feature of popular politics between the wars was the emergence of social class as the basic determinant of political allegiance, a development that in itself would account for the replacement of the Liberals by Labour as the party of the working class. As a broad description of what happened this sketch has much to commend it, but as an explanation it does not take us very far. We have already considered the strong empirical grounds for thinking that the shift to a class-based pattern had already occurred before the First World War. Even for the inter-war years an interpretation of the role of class depends very much on the perspective adopted, whether, for example, one studies the Labour vote in terms of its class origin, or whether one examines the total working-class vote in terms of its party loyalty. In the former instance, studies of post-1945 voters suggest that among Labour supporters 87 per cent were working class and 13 per cent middle class; however, of the working-class electorate only slightly over 60 per cent supported the Labour Party in the 1945–51 period.[15] During 1918–39 the proportion must have been considerably lower than this. For what actually happened in this period was that Labour progressively pushed up its share of the total poll so that by 1929 it had reached 37 per cent, falling to 30.5 per cent in 1931, and returning to a similar level (38 per cent) in 1935. It has been rightly pointed out that the pattern was something less than a sudden and complete breakthrough resulting from the incorporation of millions of new voters in 1918;[16] such drastic transformations can occur, as the near eclipse of the Irish Nationalists and the rise of Sinn Fein from none to 73 seats during 1916–18 shows. Yet in Britain the working class, markedly less monolithic than the middle class after 1918, failed to conform at all neatly to a pattern of class allegiance.

An estimate of working-class support for the Labour Party may be obtained from the 1929 figures if one makes an assumption that 76 per cent of the 22,648,000 who actually voted were working class; this leaves 17,212,000 as against a Labour poll of 8,389,000. One cannot be sure what proportion of Labour votes were middle class, but if 13 per cent is taken as a maximum and none at all as the minimum, then Labour's share of the working-class vote would fall within the range 42–8 per cent in 1929. At other inter-war elections, except for 1935, the proportion would of course have been lower. It must be doubtful, in the light of such (admittedly approximate) calculations, whether Labour was any more effective in winning the working-class vote after 1918 than the Liberals had been before 1914. Since the Liberals had been able to draw more strongly on the middle-class electorate they had been more successful, on occasion, in obtaining overall majorities.

Thus we have more than one problem to explain. Why was there a steady and impressive rise in Labour support? And why did it stick at a fairly low ceiling around 37 per cent even after recovering from the check administered in 1931? We have argued earlier that there was so much continuity between pre-war Liberal and post-war Labour support that the explanation for the replacement of one party by the other must be essentially chronological–historical. An alternative approach would involve adopting a structural explanation, namely that while pre-1914 Liberal voters largely continued to support their old party, Labour's new strength was derived from newly enfranchised and, by implication, different, working-class voters. However, these approaches are by no means mutually exclusive. Elements of each are combined in the idea of the political generation as an explanation for the pattern of political change. Clearly the regular arrival of a fresh set of young voters and the removal by death of older ones constitutes a structural transformation of the electorate; but the chronological–historical element is also implicit in that each new generation experiences a different set of political circumstances; young voters have been found to be less set in their loyalty to party than their elders and more impressionable in the face of events. The formation of their political attitudes, therefore, tends to reflect the political conditions that are paramount in the years when they are growing to adulthood and political consciousness.[17] One study of voters alive in 1960 has highlighted the fluctuation between political generations by isolating the allegiance of those who voted for the first time in 1935, of whom 45 per cent supported Labour, those who voted for the first time in 1945, of whom 61 per cent supported Labour, and those who voted for the first time in 1955, of whom 48 per cent supported Labour.[18]

Which were likely to have been the critical formative influences making for political generations between the wars? Those born around 1900 – and consequently voting for the first time in the early 1920s – experienced a traumatic political apprenticeship in the First World War and post-war chaos, which, in view of the sorry conclusion of Lloyd George's Coalition in 1922 may well have disrupted Liberal allegiance more severely than among the older generations. The generation born around 1914–18 grew to political awareness in the late 1920s and early 1930s; it is a matter for speculation whether for them the discrediting of MacDonald's second government weighed more or less heavily than the fact that by this time Labour was plainly the only real alternative government.

In what sense did national events and trends help to mould a generation relatively predisposed to Labour sympathies? We have noted already the groundswell of trade union membership which doubled from 4 to 8 million between 1914 and 1920, and the accelerating industrial militancy during the latter half of the war. In 1917 the number of working days lost in strikes doubled to 5.8 million; but the real explosion came in 1919, with 21 million days lost, in 1920, with 35 million, and in 1921, with 86 million. What stoked up this outburst was the maintenance of full wartime employment by the post-war boom until the summer of 1920, and the abandonment of compulsory arbitration procedures by the government. At this stage, workers sensed that although wages were higher than before the war they had missed the real fruits of victory. Union leaders felt that their patriotic restraint had not been fully reciprocated by the employers who had reaped vast profits, and so they now declined responsibility for holding back their members' demands. These were years of rising expectations which, during 1920–1, suddenly seemed unlikely to be fulfilled. Though few can be said to have been directly influenced by the Russian Revolution, the comparison did serve to highlight a belief that Britain alone was slipping back into the status quo. The hurried Coupon Election soon came to be regarded as a tactic to hamstring the workers' new power; and the impression of the Coalition as a conspiracy of employers to deceive the workers gained credence from the neat defusing of demands for public ownership by timely wage concessions and the Sankey Commission. By the summer of 1921 unemployment had leapt to 2 million or 18 per cent of the insured workforce, and union membership soon began its inexorable downward slide as long-term unemployment took its toll. This turn of events was significant in several ways; it induced an embattled defensiveness in the labour movement which lasted until the Second World War; and in the short run it generated a sense of betrayal which spilled over into the 1922 general election.

The fusion of Conservative and some Liberal forces in the Coalition after 1918 drove many working men to see Labour as the natural alternative for them; indeed during 1915–22 Lloyd George had established himself in the eyes of their leaders as an enemy more dangerous, because cleverer and more unscrupulous, than the Conservatives, an interpretation vociferously reinforced by the Liberal recruits to Labour. Meanwhile the independent Liberal Party became bereft of those politicians most in tune with labour aspirations, and seemed to have nothing of relevance to say; in so far as it won back the coalitionists it appeared less congenial to labour. Though it developed constructive industrial policies along the lines of the wartime Whitley Councils, no policy was likely to be as effective electorally as an attitude; and in a period of sharply rising unemployment and dashed expectations the Liberal stance of impartiality between the two sides of industry inevitably appeared evasive and insincere. In this way the 1920s were an instrumental phase in severing the Liberal Party from its traditional working-class base; indeed the years from 1918 to 1924 were possibly more important in this respect than 1914–18, which is usually taken as the decisive period. In this process the significance of the Labour government of 1924 cannot be overestimated; for however brief its life, it made the Liberals redundant at a stroke for the working classes.

In some ways the General Strike of 1926 stands out as the key stage in the evolution of politics in the 1920s. There was nothing revolutionary in either the motivation or the methods behind the strike. It was essentially a defensive measure against an imminent threat of general wage cuts in industry. Under the leadership of people like Ernest Bevin and Margaret Bondfield the union movement was wedded to the parliamentary system; they hoped that the threat of a general strike would encourage Baldwin to intervene again in the coal industry, or that he would be driven to hold a general election. Although MacDonald and his colleagues felt apprehensive about the likely effects of the strike on Labour's fortunes, in the event the failure on the industrial front had the effect of strengthening his political position.

In the short run the nine-day strike appeared to be a triumph for Baldwin. But he derived no real advantage from it. This has been obscured by most traditional accounts of the strike written from the perspective of the London leadership. As a result of local and regional studies it is now clear that working-class backing for the strike was remarkably solid; people were keen to join and not at all ready to return to work after nine days. This inevitably had a destabilizing effect on the loyalties of working-class Conservatives. Similarly Liberal supporters were torn between the views of Sir John Simon and Asquith who considered the strike illegal, and Lloyd George who dissociated himself from his leader. Lloyd George's credentials were by now too besmirched for him to restore his standing with organized labour, however. After 1926 the Liberals continued to lose ground in working-class constituencies even when enjoying a national revival under Lloyd George's leadership.

The General Strike, after all, gave the working class a strong motive for rallying around the unions and the Labour Party. The Baldwin government promoted this by its trade union legislation in 1927 which made general strikes illegal, prohibited certain workers from joining unions, and substituted the practice of contracting in for the political levy for contracting out. In the event it is true that the prohibition on sympathetic strikes was never invoked. And although the new rules had the effect of reducing the Labour Party's income from the levy by about one third, this was purely temporary. But if the direct consequences were marginal, the 1927 legislation nonetheless served as an important symbolic grievance. It helped to unite the industrial and political wings of the Labour movement around the objective of re-electing Labour to office. After the experience of 1924 unity could not be taken for granted because serious doubts had arisen about the wisdom of taking office without the power to implement a radical economic programme. However, after 1926 MacDonald succeeded in fending off his critics in the ILP. His task was rendered easier by the apparent drift of Baldwin's government on the economic front. After 1926, industry's costs were not significantly reduced, export markets were not fully recovered and unemployment continued to mount to 1.1 million by early 1929. The Cabinet attempted to gain the initiative by a set of proposals designed to stimulate industry, including de-rating, safeguarding by means of tariffs, and Empire development. However, neither politicians nor voters evinced much enthusiasm and the 'Safety First' strategy fell flat. Labour appeared as the party most likely to tackle unemployment, and its vote went up from 33 per cent to 37 per cent which produced 287 MPs, only 21 short of an overall majority. The one worrying feature of 1929 for Labour was the Lloyd George Liberal revival which pushed up the party's proportion of the vote to nearly a quarter. However, this was essentially the result of a big increase in the number of candidates financed by Lloyd George. At the grass roots, Liberal organization was still falling back. As the Labour organizers observed, the 'revival' was essentially an ephemeral phenomenon puffed up by the publicity attaching to the arrival of Lloyd George's 'circus' in certain favourable areas rather than a firmly entrenched gain.[19] At the general election in 1929 only 24 of the 43 existing Liberal seats were held; 33 of the 35 gains were at Conservative expense, while 17 of the 19 losses went to Labour. Thus the slide away from the Liberals in working-class areas manifested in municipal activity was repeated in the parliamentary contests notwithstanding a revival.

This working-class realignment was partly a cause and partly a consequence of the collaboration of middle-class Liberals with Conservatives in anti-socialist pacts which took such forms as a Citizens Party in Bristol, a Municipal Association in Hull, or a Progressive Party in Sheffield. While such combinations checked Labour's attainment of majority control in many cities during the 1920s, they left Liberals holding working-class wards which were highly vulnerable to Labour, and merely turned the Liberals into a Conservative force in the long run. For the party could not be sustained by an appeal for cautious, Conservative votes at the municipal level and for radical anti-Conservative votes at the parliamentary level. The confusion was compounded by the growing fluctuations in the number of candidates, which had the inevitable effect of breaking the habit of voting Liberal and obliging erstwhile supporters to make an alternative choice. Radical Liberals were often antagonized by the appearance of ex-coalitionists as Liberal or National Liberal candidates in 1922–3, while the more right-wing and traditionalist supporters withdrew into the Conservative camp in great numbers in 1924. Each subsequent revival began from a lower level and never recouped the losses of 1918. The attrition of the traditional Liberal constituency culminated in 1931–5 when the Liberal MPs – apart from Lloyd George and his family – were absorbed into the National Government, in the case of the Simonites on a permanent basis. After a short interruption Labour then resumed its absorption of the remnants of industrial Liberalism.

The 1920s were also a formative period for other elements within the electorate such as the Irish, hitherto a pillar of the Liberal vote. Though largely working class the Irish had displayed a reluctance to vote Labour. Yet the war shattered the Liberal–Nationalist alliance, and as early as 1919 the leading Irish politician in Britain, T. P. O'Connor, had begun to urge Irish voters to back Labour; the new alignment was formalized in 1924 when MacDonald made him a privy councillor. On O'Connor's resignation from his Scotland (Liverpool) constituency his successor simply received the Labour nomination. Wherever the Irish were numerous, as in Liverpool or Glasgow, they came to be a bastion of Labour strength – but as Catholics rather than simply as working men. For the transition from one party to another occurred during the early 1920s when Labour was a staunch Home Rule party free of association with the Easter Rebellion or the 'Black and Tans' policy; Labour could thus inherit one role within the traditional sectarian pattern of politics which in places like Liverpool and Glasgow still had much life in it.

Similarly there was no sudden collapse of 'Nonconformity' but rather a political realignment of many Nonconformists to Labour's advantage. Ever since the settlement of certain Nonconformist grievances in the 1860s there had been a gradual drift from radicalism to Conservatism especially among Wesleyans; and by 1914 groups like Quakers had grown so high in the social scale and so close to the establishment view as to be largely patriotic volunteers despite their reputation for pacifism. Conversely those Nonconformists whose sympathies were engaged by the anti-war movement and who had been ardent social reformers often migrated via the ILP to the Labour Party afterwards. By 1924, 86 Labour parliamentary candidates were Nonconformists (as against 120 Liberals) and 45 Labour MPs were Nonconformists (as against only 21 Liberals).[20] However, Liberal support among middle-class Nonconformists did remain relatively firm, so much so that the relationship was still discernible in 1960.[21] The big shift occurred in the working class. One modern study of voters alive in 1960 who had reached voting age before 1914 suggests that whereas working-class Anglicans of their generation were evenly divided between Conservative and non-Conservative allegiance, working-class Nonconformists split 4:1 against the Conservatives.[22] Although this pattern had largely died out among new voters after 1945, for inter-war voters religious traditions remained politically relevant. In County Durham, for example, the smoothness of the transfer of loyalties from Liberal to Labour after the war owed much to the pervading Methodist tradition common to both. A generation before 1914, Durham Methodists had adopted both the secular ideology of radicalism and the institutionalized politics of the miners' lodges. Their mobilization in the post-1918 Labour Party therefore involved little perceptible 'conversion'; for adherence to Labour did not imply adopting socialism except in the general ethical sense in which they were already socialists.

What such shifts did imply was a certain moderation in objectives and methods which characterized the labour movement in general, not just the Nonconformist element in it. It has been rightly observed that notwithstanding the grievance of unemployment, manual workers during the 1920s and 1930s displayed remarkably little predilection for a drastic soak-the-rich policy, but tended rather to compare their own situation with that of other workers.[23] Their apparently limited aspirations were surely of a piece with their politics; for their characteristic claim – faithfully reflected by the Labour Party – was that the working man was entitled to work, and failing that, maintenance, not that the distribution of wealth in society should be fundamentally altered. Essentially the party appealed to the self-respect of the working class rather than to any militant sense of class consciousness. This is consistent with Labour's steady accumulation of support up to 1929 which nevertheless fell short of two-fifths of the total vote. Despite its stance as, in essence, the party of the working class at a point in time when the working class came into its own electorally, Labour failed to overturn the existing pattern of approximately class-based loyalties; the persistence of substantial working-class Conservatism ensured that. What Labour did accomplish was the inheritance of one sector within the pattern of political allegiance that had been established before the First World War.

The Election of 1931

The break-up of the second Labour government over the measures designed to deal with the economic crisis led to the formation of a National Government under MacDonald in August 1931. Three months later the new administration called a general election which it won with 67 per cent of the vote and 554 MPs. Labour found itself reduced to a mere 52 MPs; after a decade of progress its share of the poll had dropped to 30.5 per cent.

How are we to understand this dramatic turning-point in electoral politics? In the first place, with only 52 MPs returned in 1931 Labour's voters were grossly under-represented. The net loss of 236 is explicable if one remembers that in 1929 the system had worked in the party's favour in giving it more seats than the Conservatives for slightly fewer votes; four out of ten Labour seats had been won on a minority vote and often by very slender margins. In these circumstances a slight shift of votes was bound to be disproportionately damaging. Second, it seems almost certain that even without the extraordinary events in which Labour's leader along with senior figures like Philip Snowden and J. H. Thomas joined with their opponents, the party was heading for defeat. The by-elections of 1929–31, in contrast to those of the first MacDonald government, brought substantial falls in the Labour poll, a reflection of its inadequate response to mounting unemployment. However, the scale of the defeat was clearly exacerbated by the peculiar circumstances of the 1931 election. In this connection it is often stressed that the effect of withdrawals by Liberal candidates – down from 513 in 1929 to 173 – was to leave Labour facing far more straight contests than in 1929. Around three-fifths of former Liberal voters seem to have supported National Government candidates and only one-fifth supported Labour. In addition there are grounds for thinking that the Labour leaders, notably Arthur Henderson, made inept attempts at playing what was, admittedly, a weak hand. Before the election Henderson largely gave support to the new government's proposals, thereby exposing the ambivalent position of many former Labour ministers, and creating some confusion in the party. The opposition never managed to put forward a convincing alternative economic policy or shake off the charge of having run away from the crisis.

There is, however, a strong tradition to the effect that, although the National Government achieved its victory by means of special arrangements and stratagems, Labour's own support remained loyal. This does not seem to be borne out by the evidence. In the 49 constituencies which saw a straight Labour–Conservative contest in both 1929 and 1931, Labour's vote fell by almost a quarter. Nationally its poll dropped from 8,389,000 to 6,649,000 despite an increase of a million in the electorate and a turnout of 76 per cent, which was as high as in 1929. However, it is conspicuous that Labour did well in South Wales, where it held almost all its seats in Glamorgan and Monmouthshire. By contrast in north-east England, a very similar region in many ways, the party fared much worse, losing 14 of the 16 seats it had held in County Durham and Tyneside. Such regional variations have not so far been explained.

Finally, it is of some importance that Labour had expected to blunt the impact of the National Government's attack on their record by playing the free trade card. There were, after all, several precedents to suggest that the electors punished Conservatives whenever protection was made a priority, as it was in 1931. For the first time, however, the voters failed to react, perhaps because after such a serious and prolonged depression free trade seemed an inadequate policy. This is corroborated by the experience of the Samuelite Liberals who, though part of the new government at this stage, vigorously advocated free trade. They suffered as great a loss of votes as Labour candidates. Thus 1931 marked a new post-Victorian era in which protectionism would be taken for granted. Yet for Labour there was a silver lining to this particular cloud. For 1931 represented a worse result for the Liberal Party which was split exactly in half and whose decline continued in 1935. Labour, on the other hand, remained the alternative party of government, and was quite capable of effecting a recovery from the débâcle, as the 1930s were to show.

13

The Eclipse of the Extremes
1931–1939

... you are following the very traditions of Disraeli himself adapted to the present day.

Stanley Baldwin at Cambridge, 1924

Labour, Socialism and Keynesianism

Whereas during the 1920s the Labour Party under MacDonald had generally been regarded as moderate and respectable, in the 1930s it enjoyed a largely undeserved reputation for extremism and irresponsibility; it was even accused of harbouring undemocratic, totalitarian tendencies in view of the admiration for the Soviet system of centralized planning shown by some socialists. Ironically the party devoted considerable energy to dissociating itself from Marxism and purging Communists from its ranks. In reality the Labour movement remained characteristically parliamentarian – perhaps deferentially so – in approach. Its objective was not to challenge the basis of the political system or the economic structure so much as to master the machinery of government with a view to securing the maximum concessions for working people. As I have said, the Labour Party placed upon the state a general obligation to provide work, or failing that, maintenance for those in need of it, but it was for years unclear about whether this entailed drastic and comprehensive economic controls by the state. Though the movement had always included a large part of British socialism it was not socialist as a whole, except in a limited sense; and despite the frequent use of the fashionable idea of 'planning' in Labour circles during the 1930s, the gradual evolution of a coherent Labour economic policy owed as much to Keynesian and Fabian thinking as to socialism.

In the immediate aftermath of 1918, even socialists often regarded wartime controls as a unique experiment rather than as a pointer to future strategy; libertarian socialists like C. D. H. Cole and Clifford Allen were convinced that state collectivism had merely helped to shore up a decaying capitalism, and therefore looked more to workers' control than to centralized state planning. However, by 1923, in the face of mounting unemployment, the ILP was in retreat from Guild Socialism, and began to concentrate upon techniques for managing the economy. The ILP's *The Socialist Programme* of 1923 displayed an under-consumptionist approach in the emphasis it laid upon raising and stabilizing the demand for the products of industry by a more equal distribution of incomes. Indeed the ILP had already begun to study Keynesian ideas to some effect: it identified a scientific credit policy as the means of moderating the fluctuations in the economy;[1] and unemployment was ascribed basically to inadequate purchasing power which was itself a consequence of insufficiency of bank loans. Thus state management of banks and credit seemed to the ILP crucial for economic planning; and the extension of control over other industries was similarly seen in the light of what each would contribute to costs, prices, production levels and so forth.

This is worth stressing because it was at variance with the woolly imprecision of official Labour Party thinking at the time. For notwithstanding the 1918 constitution and *Labour and the New Social Order* the party had yet to think out the implications of economic planning or even the mechanics of imposing control. However, throughout the 1920s the ILP and other critics failed to push the party into formulating a more definite economic policy. If anything, Labour backed away from precise, radical notions such as the capital levy, for example, as being inconsistent with its electoral appeal. As a result MacDonald arrived in office unexpectedly in January 1924 without an economic strategy, except in so far as he shared with other governments of the 1920s a conviction that the solution to unemployment would be found in the restoration of the export markets for British capital and staple industries; this required a stabilization of the world economy and a return to a high level of trade. This was, of course, hopelessly flawed, for even when international trade did climb back to pre-war levels Britain could not reclaim her former share. Moreover, Britain's capacity to stimulate world trade and to counter the general drift to protectionism and international indebtedness was severely circumscribed. While the United States declined to play this role the most that British governments could do was try to whittle down German reparations, and MacDonald enjoyed some success in this with the Dawes Plan of 1924.

Despite the common ground that existed between the various

governments in Britain the political debate was increasingly, and quite misleadingly, cast in terms of 'capitalism' versus 'socialism'; the House of Commons even treated itself to a debate on this theme in 1923; yet this was a choice that was never in fact available. The real alternatives were between the more orthodox capitalist solutions of restoring British trade and balancing the budget, and the ideas of the reformist, radical capitalists. The latter were not the property of a single group, but influenced a miscellaneous collection of people including Keynes, Lloyd George, Sir Oswald Mosley, the ILP and Political and Economic Planning (PEP). They offered various mixtures of public works schemes funded by budgetary deficits, devaluation of the pound, cheap money policies, and tariff protection, all of which were designed to reduce unemployment by increasing the demand for British-made goods. Placing the emphasis on stimulating the domestic market, they effectively abandoned futile attempts to manage the world economy. In marked contrast MacDonald and Philip Snowden remained rooted in an optimistic nineteenth-century belief in maximizing commercial intercourse. As Chancellor in 1924 Snowden produced a model Gladstonian budget in which he devoted a modest surplus to reducing duties on food items, and subsequently permitted himself only a niggardly grant towards public works schemes. For nine months the Labour movement was too awed and delighted at the spectacle of a Labour Chancellor as orthodox master of the Treasury to challenge effectively the basic policy pursued.

However, once in opposition again the party ventilated its doubts as to the wisdom of accepting office without a parliamentary majority sufficient to enact a radical economic programme. Remarkably, the party leaders managed to escape any such commitment, or being tied to any definite economic strategy before their return to office in 1929. In accomplishing this they were helped by the manner of their departure from office in 1924 which fostered the illusion that capitalist conspiracies had ejected a socialist administration. However, much the most important means of deflecting criticism was provided quite fortuitously by the General Strike of 1926.

The crucial decision to entrust the General Council of the TUC with the responsibility for a general strike strategy had been made during the absence of several of the moderate leaders who were involved in MacDonald's government. However, the moderates were willing to risk a general strike even if they hoped it would be unnecessary in the last resort. The explanation for this lies in the reaction of men like Ernest Bevin, leader of the Transport and General Workers Union, to the fall of the Labour government. They now anticipated widespread conflict with the employers, who would be backed by a Conservative government. This diagnosis was soundly based, in that the decision in 1925 to restore the pound to its pre-war level of $4.87 could be sustained only if there followed a general reduction of costs, and therefore of wages, in British industry. This appraisal led Bevin to approach a general strike as a defensive measure against the expected attack on workers' wages generally, and not simply as an unselfish act to stand by the miners. This is why 1926 saw both a general strike *and* a miners' strike. The wider objective of checking general wage reductions was at least partially attained. Fortunately for both the General Council and MacDonald, who gave no effective support to the strike, the immediate outcome did not produce a reaction against the moderate leadership as might have been expected; if anything it strengthened their hold by discrediting the advocates of industrial action, and helped to concentrate the energies of the trade unions into parliamentary channels.

In an industrial sense the General Strike was not of great significance, for it marked the end of a long period of declining militancy; union membership had been falling steadily for five years *before* 1926 – a reflection of substantial long-term unemployment. On the other hand, the strike had a considerable political significance in uniting the Labour movement and deflecting criticism of the first Labour government. Thus, when the ILP began to flourish its proposals in *The Living Wage* in 1926, MacDonald merely condemned its authors as extremists – a singular demonstration of the authority now attaching to the leader. Similarly when Sir Oswald Mosley (Labour MP for Smethwick) urged him to adopt a clear and precise economic programme, he too was swept aside in preference for the usual general statement of party attitudes.[2] Quite the most serious threat to MacDonald's lofty generalities was represented by Lloyd George who succeeded in making unemployment the major issue in 1929 – though to Labour's benefit rather than his own. Since 1926 Lloyd George had been rebuilding his bridges to radicalism. Old colleagues like Charles Masterman, Manchester radicals like E. D. Simon, Ramsay Muir and Ted Scott, and an important collection of radical economists and academics including Hubert Henderson, Walter Layton, J. M. Keynes, William Beveridge and J. A. Hobson had pooled ideas through the Liberal Summer Schools and Lloyd George's Liberal Industrial Enquiry which generated the famous Liberal Yellow Book *Britain's Industrial Future* in 1928. This document bore the Keynesian imprint in its proposed use of the Bank of England's control of credit to stimulate trade and in its proposals for major schemes of public works supported by deficit financing. What was impressive, apart from the intellectual underpinning, was the detail with which the proposals had been considered. It was calculated that every £1 million invested in road-building would generate 5,000 man-years of employment. In the first year some 350,000 extra jobs were to be created by such means. This was the basis of Lloyd George's claim that he could reduce unemployment, which stood at 1.1 million in June 1929, to normal proportions within a year.

Thus in complete contrast to MacDonald, Lloyd George had a definite idea of how he would proceed if returned to office. Why was Labour's response to Keynesianism so ambivalent in the 1920s? Some swallowed uncritically the Snowden–Treasury arguments against deficit finance. Some thought of public works in terms of the traditional efforts of local authorities – both inadequate and humiliating; they had not yet grasped the scale of Keynes' proposals or the underlying justification. Moreover, it was comfortingly easy to dismiss them as palliatives designed to shore up a system in fatal decline; socialists correctly saw that in so far as Keynesian methods could create full employment under private enterprise they would undermine a central part of their own case. In the long run, Labour was in fact to opt for Keynesianism rather than socialism, but the process was a gradual one and somewhat obscured by the trauma of 1931. For the time being it was sufficient to adopt MacDonald's line, partly out of conviction, but also as a matter of tactics, and dismiss the Liberal campaign as a typical stunt by a man notorious for unfulfilled promises. Yet the basic vacillation and confusion were evident in the party's 'Appeal to the Nation', which boldly promised to deal with unemployment by schemes that 'have been before the country for years before the Liberal Party – in the hope of reviving its declining fortunes – appropriated some of them and proclaimed them as original'; the real position was given away in the lame admission that 'the most important attack upon unemployment is to restore prosperity to the depressed industries.'

MacDonald's eloquent exposition of socialism for years before 1929 only served after 1931 to reveal him to his erstwhile colleagues as a humbug. Yet he can be defended, partly on the grounds that the Labour movement itself willingly placed its confidence in him, as his triumph over his critics at party conferences as late as 1928 shows;[3] and partly on the grounds of the continuity of his political thought and objectives over 20 years which mitigates any charge of unprincipled opportunism. For MacDonald, socialism had always been a distant conclusion to the eventual transformation of society which he never expected to see; it was as much spiritual as political. In so far as he envisaged a governmental route to socialism he believed, not as a Marxist, that it would emerge from the crisis and collapse of the existing system, but as a Fabian, that it would grow from the steady evolution, even success, of the system. Meanwhile the Labour Party was the proper vehicle for guiding society to socialistic solutions with the consent of both workers and the middle classes.

MacDonald, however, left himself exposed to periods of economic depression in which the only practical justification for holding office lay in the party's capacity to protect working people from the effects of unemployment. The absence of a short- to medium-term policy for handling unemployment itself proved to be the fatal flaw. Both in 1924 and 1929 the lack of a parliamentary majority was adopted as an alibi for the failure to attempt any steps towards socialism; but this could not entirely conceal the fact that neither government had such intentions. Nor is it plausible to argue that MacDonald's actions were entirely circumscribed by the magnitude of the economic problem facing him when he entered office in 1929. Unemployment was 1.3 million in November 1929, 1.7 million in April 1930, and 2 million by July 1930. Yet the Prime Minister, finding foreign affairs more congenial, divided responsibility for economic matters between Snowden at the Treasury and J. H. Thomas, who as Lord Privy Seal held a brief for unemployment but was denied real executive powers and civil service backup. MacDonald only compounded this original mistake by proliferating extra committees such as his Economic Advisory Council. Only Mosley, a junior minister under Thomas, supplied the government with a coherent programme in February 1930 in a memorandum that envisaged deliberate expansion of purchasing power, restrictions upon imports, and public control of banking so as to finance industrial development. Although it seems that MacDonald had grown privately sceptical of Snowden's faith in balanced budgets and free trade, he did nothing to check the Cabinet's endorsement of the Treasury view: public works schemes would take a long time to bring into operation; they were inherently uneconomic, and since no idle reserves existed, they would only damage private industry by robbing it of investment. Mosley resigned, and Thomas escaped to the Colonial Office to be replaced by Vernon Hartshorn, upon whom the Prime Minister showered pathetic letters entreating him to do his job and put 'pressure on industries to put themselves in order'.[4]

Yet another economic and political strategy was available to MacDonald in seeking the co-operation of Lloyd George, who could marshal both the extra votes in the Commons and the intellectual artillery to cope with the Treasury – in return for a sustained attack on unemployment. Since the election Lloyd George had been constantly on the Prime Minister's doorstep bearing ideas and proposals, anxious to mould his policy. It is now clear from MacDonald's own papers that he played Lloyd George shrewdly by keeping him and his advisers involved in protracted negotiations on relatively trivial matters with no intention of reaching an overall agreement on economic management;[5] even the Bill to reform the electoral system by introducing the alternative vote, which was seen as contrary to Labour's interests, was emasculated safely by the Lords before the government fell.[6] All this served the purpose of keeping Lloyd George from alliance with anyone else. Natural caution and pride made MacDonald hesitate to allow the Liberal leader into his government on any terms.

It has been argued that the Keynesian remedies of Lloyd George or Mosley were not valid alternatives in view of the failure of similar policies in the United States to overcome the depression there. This is, however, to overlook the fact that the slump in America was of far graver proportions than that in Britain; in fact the substantial reduction in unemployment achieved by President Roosevelt suggests the possibilities open to British governments for stimulating an economy that was comparatively lightly affected.

Thus for various reasons MacDonald missed his opportunities until in August 1931 the collapse of international banking faced him with a real crisis at last. In accordance with the Treasury view that the priority was to restore confidence and avoid a devaluation, Snowden drew up a list of reductions in expenditure totalling £78.5 million, including a 10 per cent cut in unemployment benefit, so as to balance the budget. Although the Cabinet accepted this reluctantly by 12 votes to 9, the General Council of the TUC flatly rejected the proposals; this led to a retreat by the waverers, notably Henderson, who perceived the danger of alienating the industrial wing from the politicans. As a result the government broke up on 23 August, but was replaced immediately by a National Government with MacDonald as Premier and Snowden as Chancellor.

Inevitably, MacDonald's severance in 1931 from the party he had done so much to build up produced a reaction against his style of leadership; and some critics like Stafford Cripps and Harold Laski cast doubt on the possibility of ever achieving socialism through a parliamentary system. However, it was not Parliament that had blocked socialism. Nor was the alternative strategy of mobilizing working-class power to overawe Parliament seriously proposed; the trade unions would have been the last to lend themselves to such a course. Instead the party kept its reappraisal within the gradualist, parliamentary framework, but sought a more precise and feasible left-wing policy than before.

In the long run the chief effect, supported by the union leaders, was to shift the party towards Keynesianism as the most satisfactory way of managing or 'planning' the economy. Even before the fall of the government the TUC's General Council, led by Ernest Bevin, had adopted the Keynesian view that attempts to defend the exchange rate were futile;

they declined to accept the necessity of waiting for capitalism either to collapse or to recover its heath as a precondition for socialism; instead they sought ways of creating jobs in the short to medium term; and in rejecting retrenchment and further deflation they had been fortified by the conviction that alternatives did exist. By 1933 this approach had crystallized in a specific commendation by the TUC of the New Deal programmes of President Roosevelt as worthy of emulation.[7] Its priorities were now a programme of public works financed out of national credit, a 40-hour maximum working week, the raising of the school-leaving age to 16 and the prohibition of labour by those under 16. This was seized upon by socialists as proof that the unions, lacking a theoretical framework, had been seduced by reformist capitalism. Many on the left now grew less flexible than they had been in the 1920s; for the emergence of fascist regimes out of the ruins of European capitalism fostered a conviction that economic strategies like the New Deal were merely doomed attempts to stave off fundamental change. However, the bulk of the party's leaders appreciated the significance of the Rooseveltian revolution in radically extending the power of the state at the expense of private capitalism. Although they often took to describing their policy as 'socialist planning' they meant by this Keynesian techniques for managing an economy in which only limited sectors would be under public ownership; in *For Socialism and Peace* (1934) nationalization proposals included coal, gas, electricity, water, transport, agriculture, iron and steel, shipping, shipbuilding, engineering, textiles, chemicals, insurance and banking. Attacks by political opponents and the eloquence of the socialists gave this lengthened list undue prominence; but between 1935 and 1939 the party concentrated upon a small selection of public utilities and ailing industries where opposition to public ownership from vested interests would be slight. Nationalization remained a matter of limited attempts to staunch the worst wounds in the system, leaving four-fifths of industry in private hands. The extent of the nationalization proposals was thus less important than the evolution of a definite procedure for taking over and running industries. The chief architect of this was Herbert Morrison, the one minister of 1929–31, apart from Addison, to have demonstrated a real grasp of the practicalities. His London Transport Bill established the principles of compensation for the dispossessed private owners, and the operation of publicly owned industries by small boards of experts and businessmen selected by the minister and responsible to him rather than to Parliament or the employees. Although the exclusion of workers' participation and trade union representation drew severe criticism from Bevin both in 1930 and subsequently, Morrison's blueprint survived without serious amendment as a guide to Labour's nationalization programme after 1945; it was a form of state collectivism inspired by the need for efficient servicing of a mixed economy and represented a return to the ideas of the Webbs.

The National Government and Liberal Toryism

The National Governments of 1931 to 1940 have figured so prominently in left-wing demonology that one tends to overlook the outrage of the far right at having what they regarded as an effete liberal administration foisted upon them when a proper Conservative one was easily attainable. A true interpretation of the period requires an appreciation of both perspectives. There is no question that these governments were, in policy and tone if not in personnel, thoroughly Conservative; the point is that they represented the triumph of a particular type of Conservatism. In this fact lay the reason for turning what was originally intended as a temporary expedient into a long-term fixture.

In accepting the royal invitation to form a coalition in August 1931, MacDonald, Baldwin and Sir Herbert Samuel, then acting Liberal leader, all appear to have contemplated co-operation for a matter of weeks or months only in order to undertake unpopular measures necessary to balance the budget and restore confidence; they would fight the next election separately. However, this expectation collapsed with extraordinary speed. In view of the perfectly adequate majority in the Commons, the three-year term still remaining, and the demoralized condition of the opposition, the decision to hold a general election on 27 October 1931 was an unnecessary diversion from the new government's task. The obvious explanation is that the circumstances provided the Conservatives with an irresistible opportunity to take advantage of Labour's disarray, and that MacDonald was unable to resist being used by them for a national appeal as Lloyd George had been used in 1918. However, this is less than a complete explanation. For one thing MacDonald himself does not seem to have required such encouragement. Although he told Samuel on 18 September that there was no justification for a dissolution, he had been encouraging Baldwin to that course for some time before:

> How long can this Government continue? My own impression is, not very long, and, indeed, if we could get such a state of financial stability as would bear what undoubtedly would be the shock of an election, I would not stand in the way of a Dissolution.[8]

By 14 September he was confessing to the King his fear of going to the country after taking the necessary economic measures, for 'the feeling of national unity will ebb away.'[9] Since Baldwin was under pressure to ditch MacDonald at the earliest opportunity it was clear that unless the special arrangements of August were put on a permanent footing his career might end abruptly. MacDonald was not ambitious any longer; he simply had nothing to live for now but politics, and no effective role in politics except within Baldwin's alliance.

On the Conservative side many were appalled at the prospect of another coalition. Indeed Baldwin seems to have been reluctant initially to contemplate one because it might provoke another revolt against him by his right wing. He anticipated that on the collapse of MacDonald's Cabinet he would himself be invited to form a government. However, the pressure of the King and the willingness of Samuel for the Liberals to establish a coalition made it very difficult for Baldwin to refuse to co-operate. Once the case for a temporary National Government had been accepted Baldwin soon found compelling reasons for keeping it alive. For despite his role in destroying the Coalition in 1922 Baldwin actually liked coalitions – provided that Lloyd George had no part in them (he must have thought it divine intervention that immured the 'Goat' in hospital with a serious operation during the formation of the National Government in 1931). In harnessing MacDonald and the Liberals to the 554-seat landslide for the government Baldwin executed more than a short-term electoral manoeuvre: he imposed his control over the Conservative Party by emasculating his own right wing. For the massive increase in Conservative MPs from the 258 of 1929 to the 471 of 1931 radically altered the composition of the party. It has been estimated that 100 MPs owed their seats directly to withdrawals of Liberal candidates.[10] At least 150 were unlikely to have been elected on a purely Conservative ticket; their capacity to survive at the 1935 election, as many of them did, rested very much upon the credibility of a national policy in the eyes of erstwhile Labour and Liberal voters. While Conservatives could have governed without winning all the industrial working-class constituencies captured in 1931 and 1935, without them Baldwin would have been deprived of support for his liberal, Disraelian brand of politics. Thus the origins of the National Governments lie in Baldwin's attempts during the 1920s to lead his party from slightly to the left of its centre; the relative security of his position during the 1930s is a measure of his success.

Baldwin was particularly well equipped to ease the Conservatives through a period when their chief opposition came from a party claiming to represent the working class. A wide range of Labour politicians recognized him as a man separated from them more by background than by principles. His own son, Oliver, joined the Labour Party in 1923; and Baldwin's own experience of harmonious industrial relations in the family firm contributed to his relaxed attitude towards the working class. He not only displayed a greater willingness than most of his colleagues to treat Labour MPs as equals, but even reproached his own party for restricting its choice of candidates to the small proportion of the population wealthy enough to finance their political careers. By comparison, all the alternative Conservative leaders in the 1920s – Austen Chamberlain, Curzon, Birkenhead, Balfour, Churchill – were remote and aloof. Neville Chamberlain, implored by Baldwin in 1927 not to address the Labour members as though they were dirt, replied: 'the fact is that intellectually, with a few exceptions, they are dirt.'[11]

Yet Baldwin's 1924–9 premiership had shown how difficult it could be to stick to the relaxed relationship with working-class leaders which he favoured. In 1925 he had had to use a prime ministerial veto in Cabinet to kill a bill prepared by MacQuisten, a backbencher, which attacked the unions' political levy. Similarly he had deliberately used a subsidy to maintain miners' wages in 1925 while the Samuel Commission was at work; the cabinet papers now show that this was not because of any unreadiness to meet the emergency, for the machinery was virtually complete in 1925;[12] it was a political decision to buy nine months in the hope of avoiding a general strike altogether. When this failed Baldwin seemed to pass the peak of his influence; and gave way to the pressure for restrictive legislation on trade unions in 1927.

The other major element in Baldwin's brand of Conservatism was represented by the catalogue of social reforms enacted by Chamberlain while at the Ministry of Health: the 1925 Widows, Orphans and Old Age Contributory Pensions Act, the Unemployment Insurance Act and the Local Government Act of 1929, which abolished the poor law unions and introduced block grants for local authorities. This at least reversed the negativism of 1920–2 and gave the Conservatives a constructive position in social matters which they had not had since the 1870s. After 1931 there was no reversal of the Baldwinian approach, despite the impression of financial severity cultivated by the National Government. After embarking on a strategy of orthodoxy and deflation the government devalued in 1931 and actually ran modest budget deficits from 1932 onwards; by 1934 the expenditure cuts necessitated by the crisis had been removed; and the Chancellor, Neville Chamberlain, deliberately promoted low interest rates – to reduce national debt charges – which stimulated the boom in house-building during the 1930s. Doctrinaire reliance upon market forces was most conspicuous in shipbuilding, where capacity dropped dramatically; in iron and steel this was masked by the establishment of new plant; and in coal many inefficient mines were kept in operation by means of a quota system for production and fixed prices. Positive intervention in the economy went beyond the protective tariffs of 1931 and 1932, so that three-quarters of all imports paid duties. For example, use was made of Labour's Agricultural Marketing Act to fix quotas for imports, and production was bolstered by subsidies and marketing boards which cost £100 million per annum by 1934. In contrast a niggardly £2 million was made available for public schemes under the 1934 Depressed Areas Act, though in 1937 the Chancellor introduced remission of rent, rates and taxation for companies moving into such areas. The willingness of Baldwin's ministers to impose rationalization through the state where private enterprise seemed inadequate or inappropriate was shown in the creation of the Central Electricity Board in 1926 and in the granting of a charter to the BBC in the same year. This approach continued under the National Governments, which revived Morrison's plan for a London Passenger Transport Board in 1933 and merged the private airlines into a public body, the British Overseas Airways Corporation, in 1939. All in all these measures of empirical nationalization, of piecemeal social welfare, and of economic pump-priming effected a steady shift in the Conservative position during the 1930s so that it was separated from that of the Labour leaders more by emphasis and rhetoric than by substance. Its performance fell well short of the expectations of bodies like Political and Economic Planning set up in 1931, and the Next Five Years Group of 1935; representative of elements within all three parties they continued to propagate the Keynesian strategy for operating capitalism with high economic growth, full employment and social welfare. While there was no intellectual acceptance of their proposals by Neville Chamberlain, they ensured that the inheritance of the younger Conservatives such as R. A. Butler and Harold Macmillan would be broadly similar to that of their Labour rivals after the Second World War.

Baldwin's ability to reassure rather than to provoke was also calculated to win over the relatively uncommitted elements among the voters, notably women who, as a result of the Equal Franchise Act of 1928 (another of Baldwin's liberal successes in the teeth of cabinet opposition) now formed 52 per cent of the electorate. For the new voters, male and female and less politically committed than the smaller pre-1918 electorate, Baldwin was an ideal leader, radiating a wholesome, non-political appeal. A more distinct element, perceived as vital by Conservative tacticians, was the regular Liberal voter and those apt to surge back to the Liberals in the elections of 1923 and 1929. Attempts to attract wavering Liberals took various forms. In the first stage the entire parliamentary Liberal Party, except Lloyd George and his family group, joined the National Government in 1931. When in 1932 the Samuelites resigned over tariffs, Sir John Simon retained about half the MPs, who fought the 1935 election at National Liberals. Simon's only virtue as Foreign Secretary in 1931–5 was as the embodiment of Liberal influence on the government. While there is no evidence that the politicians believed the voters to be pacifists, they did try to court popularity from disarmament and the League of Nations, both symbols of the will for peace; hence their fear of being blamed for the failure of the Disarmament Conference at Geneva, chaired by Arthur Henderson,[13] and their concern to stay on terms with Lord Robert Cecil and the League of Nations Union which urged voters to support candidates most likely to back the League.[14] Rightly or wrongly Liberals were thought to be especially keen on the League and disarmament. Therefore Baldwin took care to advance the popular and seemingly liberal Anthony Eden to the status of cabinet minister with responsibility for League affairs; and when Simon was replaced it was to Sir Samuel Hoare, a Conservative with relatively liberal credentials, that the Foreign Office fell. The success of all this was marked by the willingness of the Samuelites to vote for the government's defence estimates in 1935. Yet the price had to be paid in terms of criticism from the right who intensely resented Simon for his apparent willingness to sacrifice British sovereignty through the League of Nations and for allowing the Soviet Union to join in 1934. This demeaning pursuit of the League was, in the critics' view, practised by both Hoare and Eden whom they accused of abandoning Britain's vital interest in good relations with Mussolini as a result of his invasion of Abyssinia. In addition, if the National Government's liberal tendencies were ever in doubt, Winston Churchill vociferously reminded Liberals what a real Tory policy on defence or India should be. Everything, in short, served Baldwin's purpose of entrenching him on the middle ground from which neither the Liberals nor Labour could dislodge him.

Baldwin's liberal credentials were most severely tested by controversies over imperial affairs. Indeed he could well have been overthrown but for the division of his right-wing critics between the Indian cause and the United Empire Campaign, both of which dogged him throughout the late 1920s and early 1930s. In retrospect Baldwin emerges as the key figure in leading the Conservatives away from their traditional role as defenders of Empire, and in this sense his leadership represented a sharp break with that of Bonar Law which had been so closely associated with resistance to Irish Home Rule. Though an MP before 1914 Baldwin had been too obscure to be associated with that desperate stand, and like Hoare he simply could not share the sense of trauma at losing Ireland. It was Baldwin who dropped the 'Unionist' tag in referring to his party; and he expressed his patriotism infrequently in imperial terms, preferring to cast it in the form of a romantic celebration of all things English.

In the case of India, Baldwin took up where the Lloyd George Coalition had left off. Those Conservatives who were most closely involved in Indian policy – Edward Wood (Lord Irwin), Hoare and Baldwin himself – largely shared the liberal assumption that western-educated Indians ought not to be excluded indefinitely from government, because their active collaboration was necessary both to the maintenance of British rule and to eventual self-rule. The Montagu–Chelmsford reforms of 1919 had already created in India an electorate of 5 million with powers over certain reserved topics at provincial level. These reforms were due for revision in 1929, but Baldwin anticipated this by appointing a Commission under Simon in 1928. Unfortunately Indians were not included in the Commission, whose usefulness was completely destroyed by the famous Civil Disobedience campaign launched by Gandhi. In order to regain the initiative Lord Irwin, now Viceroy, issued an important declaration in October 1929 to the effect that dominion status was 'the natural issue of India's constitutional progress', and initiated the first of the Round Table Conferences. Irwin provoked a storm of protest from the Conservative right wing, especially when his policy culminated in the Gandhi–Irwin Pact of 1931 – a demoralizing blow to the morale of the British administrators. At home the Secretary of State, Hoare, followed up with the massive dose of reform (the 1935 Government of India Act), which extended virtual self-government at provincial level and created a franchise for 30 million people. It was this approach that decisively alienated Churchill from Baldwin after 1929, and led him to resign from the shadow Cabinet in January 1931 so as to be free to attack official policy. Although the critics attracted only 40–50 votes in the Commons, their support in the party was much more widespread and open. At a meeting of the National Union's Central Council in February 1933 the Cabinet's policy was challenged and upheld by only 189 to 165 votes; and it was flatly repudiated by both the Conservative women and the Junior Imperial League. At the 1934 party conference the India rebels lost the vote by only 543 to 520.

Baldwin managed to live with such a bitter and long-running controversy partly because the leading India rebels failed to combine with the protectionists under Lords Rothermere and Beaverbrook. Since the party's defeat in 1929 they had waged a campaign for 'Empire Free Trade' in their newspapers, in the party organization, and even at by-elections. A decisive clash occurred at the St George's (Westminster) by-election in March 1931 in which Baldwin's candidate, Duff Cooper, triumphed over his Empire Free Trade rival. Although Rothermere contributed financially to the India Defence League (a backbench Churchillian group), there was little chance of the rigid free trader, Churchill, reciprocating by lending support for protectionism. The greatest danger to Baldwin was probably Neville Chamberlain whom the press barons offered to back as alternative leader in 1931. The same motive led Rothermere to adopt Sir Oswald Mosley as a suitable battering ram in the early 1930s, also without success.

Thus, in the light of the controversies through the 1925–35 period, Baldwin's distaste for a purely Conservative administration is entirely explicable. His centrist, liberal, conciliatory brand of politics, which had been initiated in the mid-1920s, checked in the later 1920s, and nearly destroyed along with his own leadership during 1929–31, was continued under the aegis of the National Governments. Only by effecting a modification in the balance within the party could Baldwin hope to lead Conservatism in the way he wanted. Consequently, as early as 1932 he began to present the National Government as Britain's long-term bulwark against dictatorships of right and left – an increasingly credible picture now that Europe was falling under totalitarian regimes. By 1934–5, with the financial crisis clearly over and the economy showing signs of recovery, Baldwin had no difficulty in rallying his party to the 'national' strategy if only as the best means of preserving the country's stability from a resurgent left.

The Threat from the British Union of Fascists

By deliberately seeking the central ground of politics Baldwin ran the risk of driving his opponents in the party to an alternative leadership outside the National Government. In the early 1930s the most compelling and coherent alternative was that offered by the British Union of Fascists under Sir Oswald Mosley. Not only did Mosley appear to have a bolder grasp of economic and social problems than the conventional politicians, he and his movement also posed a dire electoral challenge to the National Government, and thus for some years threatened to undermine Baldwin's entire strategy. With hindsight it is comfortingly easy to assume the inevitability of the BUF's failure, and to attribute its loss of momentum after 1934 to the public reaction against the anti-semitism and the violence associated with the notorious BUF really at Olympia in June of that year. Yet the underlying reason for the BUF's decline almost certainly lay in the modest economic revival in 1934. It was this that gave the government the confidence to risk a general election in November 1935. Fascism was only likely to succeed as a revolutionary movement if it enjoyed the opportunity to step in to save a collapsing and discredited capitalist democracy from communism, but by 1935 this was clearly not going to materialize in Britain. However, since there was scarcely time for the BUF to reorientate itself around a parliamentary strategy before the general election, Mosley decided to abstain, and the National Government escaped unscathed.

Yet it was not until 1936 that the government felt confident enough that the fascists were losing public sympathy to take legislative action to curtail their activities by means of the Public Order Act which banned political uniforms and empowered the police to ban marches for three-month periods. Up to that time the politicians were in fact highly apprehensive of Mosley's capacity to win adherents right across the political spectrum; and it is the threat he posed to the conventional party system which must be explained. In particular the reaction of those on the right of British politics to the apparent rise of fascism in Britain was more complicated than might be supposed. In the Commons debate on Mosley's Olympia rally in June 1934 Conservative, not Labour, members were the most prominent contributors; and despite the reputation of this debate as a turning-point in BUF fortunes relatively few of them actually expressed total disapproval of the BUF. In fact a number of Conservative and National Labour members readily admitted to some sympathy with Mosley as a man who had to 'sow his wild oats'; some condemned him but made a point of praising 'the thousands of young men who have joined the Blackshirt Movement. They are among the best elements in this country.'[15] Conscious of the vulnerability of urban, working-class seats won in 1931 to be defended at an election a year or two away, they felt alarmed at seeing large numbers of younger people going over to the BUF 'in shoals'. Research on fascist grass-roots support is limited and BUF membership figures are still unavailable; therefore the claim that 500 branches existed by 1936 may considerably exaggerate fascist strength. But something of significance may be discerned from the distribution of the parliamentary constituencies the BUF planned to contest by 1936–9: 39 in and around London, 16 in Lancashire, 12 in Yorkshire, 6 in the Midlands, 3 in Wales. Fascist campaigning in the northern towns was designed to win over traditional working-class Conservatism by a nationalist–protectionist appeal; in areas of declining industry this must have seemed a potent threat to the Conservative Party and to Baldwin's strategy in particular; it serves to remind us that the impression of the BUF as an East End of London anti-Jewish movement is only part of the picture. Certainly the politicians were torn between resentment of Mosley as an electoral rival who could deliver their seats to Labour, and admiration for his capacity to hold meetings in areas where, they claimed, left-wing disruption normally made it impossible for them to do so. Thus Olympia actually confirmed the truth of Mosley's boast that he could conduct political rallies anywhere; the possibility that he would continue to gain ground made for a hesitant response as yet by the party. In the event their fears were not realized because Mosley, evidently deterred by the poor showing his infant New Party had made in 1931, decided to abstain from the 1935 general election.

Those close to the Conservative establishment were more suspicious of Mosley as a divisive force exploited by his patron Rothermere. They shared with many politicians a deep distrust of a man who could change his party allegiance as often as he had done in a rather short career, especially when he had 'betrayed his class' by joining the Labour Party. In addition there existed an ideological deterrent. While some shared Mosley's anti-democratic sentiments and despaired of the effete Baldwinian leadership, they saw no great need for an extra-parliamentary force so long as the pillars of society, particularly the monarchy, the Church, and to a lesser extent even Parliament, remained intact. Economically much of what Mosley had to say was an extension of tariff reform and imperial development perfectly congenial to Conservatives. Yet there was a radical edge to his ideas. He sharply distinguished between those capitalists who manufactured goods and those who were devoted to finance, insurance and trade. He often attacked the latter on the grounds that they helped Britain's competitors and imposed the bankrupt policies of nineteenth-century liberalism on Britain in their own narrow interests. His willingness to exploit the power of the state at the expense of private enterprise further alienated Conservatives, especially as the economy showed distinct signs of climbing out of the depression; Britain had escaped the inflation that had devastated middle-class savings elsewhere and thus opened them to radical economic alternatives. Mosley's wartime experience and his six years in the Labour Party had not been for nothing; they had left him with a conviction that the pathetic conditions of life of most British people could be improved if the resources of society were brought fully into play. This radicalism would only be acceptable on the right when the only alternative was the radicalism of the far left.

This quality in Mosley's thinking which enabled him to address himself coherently to the central question of unemployment largely accounts for the appreciation of him by some socialist politicians such as Aneurin Bevan and James Maxton in 1930, who saw him as a complete contrast to the ineffectual MacDonald. John Strachey and the ex-Labour MP John Becket even followed him after 1931. However, the bulk of the Labour movement was alienated by Mosley's abrupt abandonment of the party after failing to carry the conference with him in the autumn of 1930 and by his intervention in the Ashton by-election which cost Labour the seat. Thereafter he had to contend with systematic opposition wherever Labour was strong. After Hitler's rise to power the trade unions, hitherto inclined to regard the BUF simply as an unofficial arm of the National Government, increasingly identified it as part of an international phenomenon; noting the tendency of fascist regimes to suppress trade unions they threw their weight against any attempts to win over working men in areas of declining industry.

In the final analysis the inability of the BUF to become a major force at the expense of the existing parties may be ascribed to three causes. First, the relatively light impact of the depression upon Britain which spared the middle classes from inflation and permitted a rising standard of living for many working-class families. This left the main institutional pillars of society, enhanced by victory in the First World War, resilient and popular, at least by comparison with most of the rest of Europe. Secondly, the timing was unfortunate. In 1931 the New Party was too young to mount an effective challenge, and in 1934–5 economic revival checked a slide towards the BUF; the uncommitted voters and the neglected lower middle classes were swept up by the National Government thus depriving Mosley of his natural constituency. Thirdly, Mosley's thesis that Britain should concentrate on a self-contained Empire leaving the inward-looking Nazi Germany to do the same in east–central Europe, while attractive at the start of the 1930s, had waned by 1939 and left him exposed as a potential agent of Hitler by that time.

The Left, Rearmament and Public Opinion

After the trauma of 1931 the forces on the left of politics gave way to fissiparous tendencies with the result that they largely failed to rally an effective opposition to the National Governments, despite the fact that the dominant problems, unemployment and defence, ought to have worked to their advantage. At the centre of the Labour Party in this period lay a leadership vacuum. Of the founding fathers only Henderson, Clynes and Lansbury still occupied prominent positions in the movement, though this facilitated the emergence of three men from the second rank, Herbert Morrison, Ernest Bevin and Hugh Dalton, who were to become key figures for the next 20 years. In the Commons after the electoral holocaust of 1931 the party numbered a mere 52 members (including the ILP), of whom 26 represented the Miners Federation; for the most part they had been loyal to MacDonald and were still too confused to give a strong lead now that he had gone. Only three MPs had any ministerial experience, and so Lansbury by default became party leader and Clement Attlee his deputy. When in 1935

Attlee succeeded to the leadership his modesty and inconspicuous efficiency seemed qualifications enough. Though from a middle-class background he had no history except within the Labour movement; having worked his way up through local government in London, Attlee was a safer choice than the more brilliant figures or the intellectuals recruited from other parties. Hence Herbert Morrison (who was his senior as a minister and his superior as party organizer and public speaker) was passed over. The small size and mediocrity of the parliamentary party robbed it of the dominance it had enjoyed through the National Executive Committee since 1918; whereas on average 16 of the NEC's 23 members had been MPs in 1918–31, only three were MPs in 1931–5. Consequently with each major institution of the party – NEC, parliamentary party and the National Joint Council – dominated by cautious, defensive trade unionists it proved difficult to come to terms with both the socialists and the rebellious movements among the rank and file.

Union defensiveness was caused by the continued drop in membership to 4.5 million by 1934. Although this left a huge slice of the working class outside union organization they were not recruited in substantial numbers by rival bodies such as the ILP, the Socialist League or the Communist Party; membership of the latter did rise from 2,500 in 1930 to 6,000 in 1931 and to 18,000 by 1939, but this reflected middle-class concern about fascism rather than working-class allegiance. The most serious threat to the unions came from Wal Hannington's National Unemployed Workers Movement, which at its peak in 1931–3 managed to mobilize 50,000 men; even this must be set against the total of almost 3 million unemployed among the insured population at this time. Despite the apprehension of the orthodox leaders of labour, the methods of the NUWM tended to be limited to hunger marches and petitions, and its objectives to be confined to the restoration of the cuts in unemployment benefit and abolition of the means test. In neither sense, therefore, was it really radical, let alone subversive; what violence accompanied its meetings was half-hearted and unorganized, and the movement fizzled out in 1933 in an anti-climax reminiscent of Chartism. It is a tribute to the political apathy of the 1930s, or perhaps to the cushioning effects of welfare benefits and falling prices, that the Labour Party could afford to shun the NUWM without danger to itself. Loss of working-class support to the National Government was a much more serious concern.

The party leaders bore even more lightly the severance of ties with the ILP in 1932, after which the latter went into headlong decline. However, the split led some ILP members to join the new Socialist League, a small but vigorous intellectual elite including G. D. H. Cole,

Sir Stafford Cripps, Harold Laski, Sir Charles Trevelyan, R. H. Tawney, D. N. Pritt, Ellen Wilkinson and Aneurin Bevan. Though designed as a research and propaganda group within the Labour Party, the Socialist League rapidly ran into the same problem as the ILP of developing a rival programme to that of the party. It also became embroiled from 1933 in attempts to persuade the party of the virtues of a united front strategy against fascism incorporating the Communist Party, which from 1935 was seeking affiliation to the Labour Party. These efforts were decisively rebuffed by annual Labour conferences.

In fact the only effective challenge to the centrist leadership in the 1930s – the Constituency Parties Movement – emerged outside the conventional left-wing forces. This was essentially a spontaneous expression of rank and file frustration at their effective exclusion from power in the party since 1918. In the original constitution the constituency activists had enjoyed a certain role through the generous representation of the ILP on the NEC. However, the ILP had gradually ceased to play a prominent part. Moreover, the reforms of 1918, while allowing the constituency parties to nominate candidates for 5 of the 23 places on the NEC, left the choice to the vote of the whole conference, which in effect meant the block votes of the larger unions. Yet the constituencies were now the one expanding section of the movement; individual membership rose to 419,000 in 1935. At this point, a campaign for constitutional reform led by Ben Greene emerged particularly in the southern constituencies. As a body of loyal party workers at the heart of the movement the Constituency Parties Movement could not be brushed aside like the socialist societies even though much of its strength was concentrated in areas where Labour representation remained slight. In 1937 conference agreed to raise constituency representation from five to seven and to allow them to be elected separately. Although this coup had not been engineered by the left, the movement had enjoyed, to its embarrassment, the support of Cripps since 1936; certainly its immediate effect was to strengthen the influence of the left, since Cripps, Laski and Pritt were among those elected from the constituency parties to the NEC.

Thoughout the inter-war period the controversies between the left and the leadership were largely fought in the realm of defence and foreign policy with the left gradually losing the initiative. During the 1920s Labour had been strongly placed to criticize those who had imposed a punitive settlement on Germany at Versailles for the satisfaction of France. In adopting the view that it was a blunder to fix 'war guilt' upon Germany and to squeeze reparations from her, and in condemning the armaments race as a major cause of war in 1914, the party was well within the mainstream of British thinking. In principle

Labour went somewhat further in that it advocated a drastic revision of the Versailles Treaty on the ground that it had been an imperialist peace that deprived Germany of colonial and economic assets and flouted the principle of nationality where it would have worked in Germany's favour as on the borders of Czechoslovakia and Poland. However, in practice Labour and Conservative governments operated a bi-partisan policy during the 1920s involving strictly limited steps towards the appeasement of German grievances – a downward revision of re-parations, assistance with the currency, persuading the French to quit the Ruhr, and an early evacuation of the Rhineland. Appeasement thus stopped well short of accepting the right to racial unity of all Germans, or of permitting Germany's re-establishment as a major military power.

One consequence of their attitude towards Versailles was an initial hostility by many Labour politicians to the League of Nations on the grounds that it was a vehicle for the victorious powers to apply sanctions to preserve an advantageous status quo. Pacifists, both Christian and socialist in inspiration, urged unilateral disarmament as a surer way to permanent peace than embroilment in League affairs. This position was never accepted by the parliamentary party although its members regu-larly voted against the defence estimates, and the party conference in 1922 and 1926 passed resolutions opposing any participation in wars. However, these decisions represented the high-water mark of left-wing pacifism which progressively gave way to the more pragmatic approach of Henderson, Bevin, Dalton and Attlee who argued in favour of 'collec-tive security'; this meant elevating the League of Nations to a place of central importance in foreign policy and through it applying sanctions – economic and if necessary military – against aggressor states; therefore for Dalton and Bevin there were strict limits to British disarmament and a point where rearmament would become necessary. In spite of the impression of fundamental differences of principle between the pacifist left and the Conservative right, the position of the Labour leaders closely approached that of the Conservative and National Governments. By 1922 expenditure on the armed forces had been cut back to £110 million – from £600 million in 1920 – and remained around that level until 1935 when both parties decided that rearmament was necessary.

The pace of disarmament and appeasement has sometimes been explained in terms of an all-pervading pacifism in inter-war British society. This involves demonstrating first that the public was pacifist and second that the awareness of this moulded official policy. Certainly the late 1920s and early 1930s saw some striking manifestations such as the anti-war publications, notably Robert Graves's *Goodbye to All That* (1929) and Vera Brittain's *Testament of Youth* (1933). No doubt the success of such volumes a decade after the war tells us something about the mood of the 1920s and 1930s; but they do not point to a general pacifism so much as to a repudiation, particularly by some of the middle classes, of the kind of appeal that had been used to justify war in 1914–18. A similar significance may be placed upon the famous Oxford Union debate in 1934 on the proposition that 'this House will in no circumstances fight for its King and Country'; in condemning politicians' manipulation of the people in one set of circumstances they did not necessarily indicate a refusal to fight when a proper cause arose, as it did for many when the Spanish Civil War broke out. Nor are the findings of the more important Peace Ballot of 1934 to be interpreted as proof of pacifism. The immediate background to the ballot was Germany's withdrawal from the Disarmament Conference in 1933. This called into question the effectiveness of the League of Nations which had been widely, if vaguely, regarded as the best means of avoiding war. To demonstrate support for the League and collective security the League of Nations Union therefore conducted a poll in which 11.5 million people voted. While an overwhelming majority favoured the reduction of arms by international agreement even to the point of their elimination, they were also prepared to face a situation in which the reverse occurred. Some 6.7 million voted for applying sanctions including military ones against aggressor states who flouted arbitration by the League; only 2.3 million opposed this. Thus support for the League ought not to be equated with pacifism; there clearly existed public support for resistance to the dictators in the early 1930s, as was strikingly demonstrated by the extremely hostile reaction to the Hoare–Laval Pact of 1935 which offered a partition of Abyssinia to the advantage of Mussolini.

Indeed any idea of the National Government being tightly constrained in its foreign and defence policy by the public's adamant refusal to contemplate war and rearmament is a travesty. The classic piece of evidence used to substantiate this view was the East Fulham by-election of October 1934 when a Conservative majority of 14,000 was turned into a Labour majority of 4,800 supposedly because disarmament was offered by the latter and 'warmongering' by the former.[16] However, this interpretation has been largely discredited by critical examination of the evidence. In the first place the constituency was far from being a safe Conservative seat: the 14,000 majority reflected only the special circumstances of 1931; in 1929 East Fulham returned a Conservative by 1,700, and in 1935 by 1,000. It was therefore by no means remarkable that it fell to the opposition in a mid-term by-election. Nor was the by-election fought primarily over defence, but rather on domestic economy and housing questions which were ably exploited by an attractive, middle-of-the-road candidate who apparently won over the bulk of the

Liberal vote in the absence of a Liberal candidate. Moreover, even if East Fulham could be interpreted as a pacifist vote, it would have to be set against the comfortable Conservative victories in seats where their candidates frankly espoused rearmament, such as Basingstoke and Twickenham in 1934 and Aberdeen South in 1935.

In any case there appears to be no good evidence that the government was sufficiently impressed by the election at the time to allow its defence policy to be determined by fear of public opinion. Endowed with the massive mandate of 1931 the Cabinet had already displayed a willingness to disappoint expectations on the economic front, and it seems unlikely that they would have shied away from a vital policy merely because it would bring unpopularity. In fact the chief restraint on defence in the early 1930s and after 1935 when rearmament began was imposed by Neville Chamberlain as Chancellor of the Exchequer; and his central arguments were the economic ones of the Treasury. He refused to allow his nearly balanced budgets to be jeopardized by a major increase in defence spending; the expansion of one sector would inevitably weaken other sectors of the economy and would force the government into massive borrowing. In 1934 the report of the Defence Requirements Committee urged that Germany not Japan should be regarded as the most likely enemy, and the army and air force expanded with that in mind. Under Chamberlain's influence the Cabinet opted for building up the RAF as a deterrent force, thereby restricting the proposed expenditure increases to £59 million rather than £97 million as originally suggested.

In the same hesitant way and at much the same time the Labour leaders also moved into a position of cautious support for rearmament. Despite the leadership of the elderly Lansbury the pacifists were steadily undermined from the early 1930s – initially by Japanese aggression in Manchuria which led both the TUC and the NEC in 1933 to advocate an economic boycott. The advent of Hitler to power also altered attitudes by putting fascism firmly into an international framework. Hitherto much had been made of the unwisdom of putting arms into the hands of the National Government, a view that received short shrift from men like Bevin. In 1934 Henderson carried the conference by 1.5 million to 670,000 on a resolution favouring collective security through the League. This led to the resignations of Cripps, of Arthur Ponsonby as leader in the Lords, and finally of Lansbury. However, the outbreak of the Spanish Civil War in July 1936 was to have the most powerful effect of all in that it led many of those usually most opposed to intervention, such as Trevelyan and Cripps, to demand active support by Britain for the Spanish Republicans. By 1937 the party had abandoned opposition to armaments to the extent of ceasing to vote against the defence estimates. By 1939 opposition and government had reached a common view of the war against the dictators as a justified one.

The General Election of 1935 and its Aftermath

Although the 1930s were undeniably dominated by the National Government, the new coalition did not appear very secure, particularly in the period before 1934 when unemployment grew worse and fascism was gaining support. Nor should it be forgotten that this coincided with a very marked recovery by the Labour Party. This was especially notable in municipal elections; in 1932 the party gained 458 seats to attain a higher level than in 1929; progress continued in 1933 and culminated in the capture of the London County Council in 1934. Individual membership rose by 100,000 during 1933 when it reached 380,000, but the momentum was hardly sustained in 1935 when it levelled out at 419,000. By-elections showed the Labour poll returning to and sometimes exceeding the 1929 level. However, two gains in 1932, two in 1933 and four in 1934 represented rather limited successes amid 40 by-elections in which the government held on to the bulk of its vast 1931 gains; spectacular losses like East Fulham were not indicative of a general trend of opinion. When the depression reached its nadir in 1932–3 the opposition should have reaped the electoral dividends; yet they were the opposition precisely because of their inability to cope with the depression. In addition, by July 1935 when unemployment fell below 2 million the growing sense of recovery deprived them of a central line of attack. The government pointed to the construction of one million houses since 1931, the restoration of the 1931 cuts in salaries and unemployment benefits, and the tax relief in Chamberlain's 1935 budget; and during the election he took the opportunity to announce extra funds for road-building to offset attacks upon his parsimony towards the unemployed. On only one occasion had the government run into serious opposition from the unemployed. In 1934 it decided to remove unemployment assistance from the Public Assistance Committees and administer it on a uniform basis through a central body, the Unemployment Assistance Board; when in January 1935 it became clear that the new uniform scales would reduce the income of many families there arose a rare display of outrage throughout the country. Thereupon the new scales were promptly dropped; and Baldwin took care to get the election safely out of the way well before revised scales were implemented in 1936. In so far as there was a safe time for an election it was the autumn of 1935 only a few months after the King's jubilee. Still saddled with the charge of having run away from the financial crisis in 1931 the Labour leaders found it difficult to erase the impression that if they returned to office the crisis would return with them; it seemed unwise to jeopardize the modest improvements achieved under Chamberlain's unimaginative management.

The only alternative line of attack for the opposition lay in questions of peace and rearmament. Now some historians, usually as part of a defence of Baldwin's handling of rearmament, still insist that the general election of 1935 was fought on foreign and defence policy, and thereby might be held to have furnished the Prime Minister with a 'mandate' for rearmament.[17] Yet this has never been demonstrated. An explanation on these lines would argue that the Labour Party benefited from its anti-armaments stance in 1934 but failed in 1935 because public opinion had veered round to support of rearmament. We have already seen how dubious the first part of this argument is. To say that rearmament was an issue in 1935 is to assume that the main parties adopted clear and opposed views that could be perceived by the voters; for no item of policy, however intrinsically important, becomes an issue that turns votes unless the parties manage to articulate it clearly. While we know that substantial differences did exist between, say, Churchill at one extreme and Cripps at the other, the views of Attlee–Bevin–Dalton and Baldwin–Chamberlain–Simon were never far apart and had been steadily converging on one another. Far from unequivocally exhorting the electors to accept a rearmament programme Baldwin insisted that 'there will be no great armaments' and that the Cabinet intended only to 'repair gaps in our defences'. Both sets of party leaders were striving to edge their followers and the country towards a modest rearmament programme; neither wished to make a point of advocating it, but they would not go out of their way to resist it. They sought to express what seemed to be the generally acceptable view that Britain must possess whatever weapons were necessary to enable her to play an effective part in collective security through the League. Indeed in so far as any clear message emerged from the 1935 election it was the central importance attached to the League, which of course united the political parties. Instead of trying sharply to differentiate their views on defence, leaders of both parties preferred to concentrate on domestic questions. Thus rearmament never grew into an issue in 1935, and no mandate was either sought or given. In a thickening international atmosphere the public were doubtless not alarmed by limited doses of rearmament, and took refuge in confidence in the League.

The Labour Party devoted much of its effort to rebutting charges of extremism in domestic and economic affairs which had been sedulously cultivated by National Government supporters. It was easy to point to connections between British socialism and some of the policies of Stalinist Russia whose economic planning was frankly admired by the Webbs and others. At the election the Communist Party exacerbated matters by publishing its manifesto on the same day as Labour and emphasizing that all its candidates but two had been withdrawn so as not to jeopardize the return of a Labour government. Since 1934 the Labour Party had gone to the lengths of organizing a series of 'Peace and Freedom' meetings to emphasize its commitment to parliamentary democracy and to dispel fears of totalitarian sympathies. Unfortunately the prominent resignations of Cripps, Lansbury and Ponsonby so close to the election drew more attention to the left. The death of the re-assuringly moderate Henderson in 1935 robbed the party of a familiar face; and Attlee had too short a period as leader and too faint a person-ality to make a useful impact before or during the election. It proved difficult to present the party as an effective ruling group while MacDonald remained to call into question the fitness of his former colleagues to govern. Fitness in office was thus a far more damaging cry in the 1930s than it had been in the 1920s.

There are grounds for thinking that the popular reputations of the rival parties had been moulded by the mass media well before the election. Apart from sporadic right-wing criticism the only consistent opposition the National Government had to face in the press came from the radical *Daily Chronicle* and the Labour *Daily Herald*; not until 1938 when the *Daily Mirror* swung to Labour did the balance shift significantly. Perhaps more important were the cinema newsreels which by the 1930s catered to a huge working-class audience; these were in-variably calculated to foster an optimistic, patriotic view of current events in which ministers received the bulk of the coverage for their gallant efforts against the odds; the tendency to minimize the contro-versial aspects of current affairs would have hampered any opposi-tion whatever its complexion. Similarly analysis of the newsreels, programmes and personnel of the BBC during 1932–5 suggests a distinct bias in favour of ministerial achievement and neglect of oppo-sition views.[18] The gradual effect of all this upon the public perception of politicians is to be distinguished from the direct and immediate advantage that probably accrued to the government from Baldwin's mastery of the technique of reassuring radio broadcasts in contrast to the more formal and stilted messages delivered by Attlee.

In these circumstances the comfortable survival of the National Government, still allied with the Simonite Liberals and National Labour remnants, is quite explicable. With a net gain of 94 seats in 1935 the Labour total reached 158, almost three times its 1931 figure, but nowhere near the 287 of 1929. Despite an average swing of 9.4 per cent to Labour the government held 435 seats, 388 of which were Conservative. In areas like the West Riding, Durham, Northumberland and southern Scotland, barely touched by economic recovery, the swing exceeded this; but in the buoyant west Midlands it was only half the national average. In Birmingham where 6 of the 12 seats had fallen to Labour in 1929, none did so now. Many industrial working-class constituencies – all three in Salford, all four in Newcastle – returned National Government candidates; even Jarrow was but narrowly recovered by Ellen Wilkinson. The true extent of Baldwin's success may be discerned in the 40 seats that enjoyed a straight Conservative–Labour contest in 1929, 1931 and 1935; here the swing away from Labour between 1929 and 1931 had been 15.1 per cent and the swing in their favour between 1931 and 1935 only 9.9 per cent, so that roughly a third of the lost support continued to adhere to the National Government. In the 32 seats with a three-cornered contest in the three elections, Labour candidates almost recovered their 1929 vote; however, the redistribution of part of the Liberal vote in favour of Conservative and National Liberal candidates kept the government's supporters well ahead. This underlines Baldwin's key achievement in claiming the middle ground. Although the Labour share of the national poll (38 per cent) narrowly exceeded that of 1929 (37 per cent) it brought 130 fewer seats because of the concentration of non-Labour votes on National candidates where previously they had been more evenly divided between Conservative and Liberal. Having been boosted by the electoral system in the 1920s Labour was thus seriously under-represented by it in the 1930s.

Between 1935 and the outbreak of the Second World War there were no clear indications of a major change in the status quo. During 1936-8 the government suffered swings to Labour in by-elections but they were usually below 10 per cent, which suggests a certain stability in partisan allegiance. The growing polarization of opinion for and against appeasement, which was to manifest itself in the emergence of 'Popular Front' candidates opposing the Munich settlement, had evidently not yet been translated into party terms. Such candidates challenged unsuccessfully at Oxford in October 1938 and at Bridgwater in November where a hitherto safe Conservative seat fell. However, these seem to have been special cases, and as yet no consistent trend against Chamberlain's conduct of foreign affairs had emerged. The chief division was within the Conservative ranks; for example the Duchess of Atholl resigned her seat to fight a by-election in December only to lose narrowly to an official Conservative who backed Chamberlain. Opinion polls which were now being conducted by Mass Observation indicated a certain bewilderment among voters on foreign policy questions with inevitable fluctuations in attitudes towards the government, but no substantial movement in favour of one party; the chief effect of the undoubted public concern at the approach of war was to raise turnout on both sides.

Thus on the available evidence one is bound to conclude that any general election held up to 1939 would have resulted in a further term for the National Government. This curiously unexciting conclusion to a decade marked by trauma and extremism reflects the skill of both Conservative and Labour leaders in emasculating their respective radicals, isolated on the peripheries; and further, the success of one of the two schools of moderation in outmanoeuvering the other on the central ground of British politics.

Epilogue

Between the outbreak of war in September 1939 and the general election of July 1945 political fortunes in Britain changed drastically in favour of the Labour Party. As early as 1943 the opinion polls – a novelty that most politicians disregarded as yet – pointed to a huge Labour lead of 16 per cent. And despite the prestige of the Prime Minister, Churchill, this advantage was only narrowed to a comfortable 6 per cent on polling day which gave Labour 393 seats and an overall majority for the first time. The 1945 election thus decisively ended the chronic imbalance in the party system in which the Conservatives had been so dominant since 1918. The result was essentially a defeat for the Conservative Party rather than Churchill; for Conservatives were still widely labelled the 'Guilty Men'[1] whose pursuit of appeasement had left the country unprepared for war. By the summer of 1945 the public seemed interested chiefly in domestic matters, especially housing and social welfare which the Beveridge Report had crystallized and publicized two years earlier. In fact politics in the post-1945 era was to revolve more than ever around questions of social policy and economic management. In 1945 this gave Labour the inestimable advantage of being able to speak with greater credibility and conviction on precisely the topics which the voters believed to be most important. Moreover, the Labour Party could no longer be written off as dangerous or unfit to govern as in the 1930s. Its leading figures, particularly, Attlee, Morrison and Bevin, had served with distinction in the wartime coalition since 1940. Although their economic and social policies had not changed significantly between 1935 and 1945, they were no longer regarded with apprehension, partly, perhaps, because of the reassuring wartime experience with state organization and the feeling for equality of sacrifice engendered by the emergency; in short the mood of 1945 was very close to what one historian has called 'Mr Attlee's Consensus'.[2] In addition the electorate itself had changed considerably since the last election in 1935. As many as one in five electors were voting for the first time, and of these 61 per cent are estimated to have supported the Labour Party – a reflection, no doubt, of their education during the depression and the rule of the National Governments. Thus long-term trends as well as immediate pressures worked strongly in the party's favour at this time.

The 15 years after 1945 marked the apogee of the political system which had evolved gradually from late Victorian politics. By this stage the need for fundamental change appeared to have come to an end. By 1928 the political system had managed to absorb the bulk of the adult population as citizens without becoming unstable, and it had been tested in the depression without succumbing to anti-parliamentary forces. Subsequent modifications, such as the elimination of the university franchise and the remaining business voters, or the enfranchisement of 18-year-olds, proved to be relatively uncontentious by comparison with the great Victorian reforms. By 1945 this parliamentary democracy had produced a system characterized by two evenly balanced parties, one broadly representative of labour and one of property. To most Victorians this would have sounded an alarming recipe for instability; yet in most respects change had been so heavily masked by continuity and consensus that this was by no means a justified fear.

In the institutional sphere the period witnessed a steady but not spectacular diminution in the role and authority of ordinary MPs and of Parliament, and a tendency for power to be concentrated further in the Cabinet, in cabinet committees, and in the Prime Minister, his personal entourage and leading civil servants. In this respect Lloyd George's premiership was probably a turning-point; for although none would confess to emulating his methods, his successors invariably repeated his habit of creating independent sources of advice and extending the powers of patronage. One might have expected that the rise of a party whose roots lay outside Parliament would have led to drastic modifications in the system. In practice, however, Labour was a guardian of parliamentary tradition except in so far as it tended to undermine the House of Lords. In principle Labour's policy was the policy of its Conference; but in practice the relationship of leaders and followers was not far removed from that between the National Liberal Federation and the parliamentary Liberals in the late nineteenth century. Once in office a Prime Minister like Attlee was hardly less powerful *vis-à-vis* his party than his Conservative equivalent. The difference was that Labour showed much less respect towards its leaders but was nonetheless very loyal and indulgent to them, while the Conservatives, though more deferential, were consistently ruthless in disposing of leaders who were felt to be beyond their useful life. In terms of personnel the two parties, though rather different, grew more alike. In the parliamentary Labour

Party the proportion of working-class members shrank steadily after 1945. On the Conservative side the middle classes also advanced as the landed aristocracy faded imperceptibly. The latter had begun their prolonged retreat from national government back in 1889 by opting for county councils as a more congenial sphere of activity. After the Parliament Act of 1911 and the rise of the Labour Party they inevitably acquiesced when Lord Curzon was passed over in 1923 despite being the obvious choice as Prime Minister.

In policy and administration the post-1945 era also witnessed a surprising coalescence between the parties. For while the Liberal Party came near to dropping through the trap-door of history, the governments of both major parties tended to reflect the influence of two Liberals – J. M. Keynes and William Beveridge. Conservatives made no attempt to dismantle the social reforms that came to be known as the 'Welfare State'. And both parties had emerged from the war in agreement with Keynes's premise that a comprehensive welfare system depended upon the maintenance of fairly full employment by the government; nor did they have to contend with a recalcitrant Treasury in applying Keynesian methods of economic management. The maintenance of employment helped to blunt socialist objections to the economic system, as did the Attlee government's nationalization programme. This proved much less controversial than expected because it left 80 per cent of industry privately run, relieved business of a number of unprofitable utilities, gave compensation to the dispossessed, and involved a system of running public industries that Conservatives found broadly acceptable.

Perhaps the chief architect of mid-twentieth-century Conservatism was Stanley Baldwin, though he is unlikely to be generally regarded as such for some time. Yet it was during the 1920s that he prepared his party to surrender the imperial cause which had been the pillar of late Victorian Conservatism, a process that culminated in the rapid dismantling of the Empire in the 1950s and 1960s and Britain's application to join the European Economic Community. After Baldwin Conservatives invariably chose their leaders from their more liberal or innovating figures like Sir Anthony Eden, R. A. Butler and Harold Macmillan, or Edward Heath and Reginald Maudling.

Finally there is the electoral dimension to political change that has figured so prominently in these pages. In retrospect the displacement of the traditional Liberal Party by Labour as the major governing party on the left during 1914–29 proved to be a remarkably smooth one. This was a consequence of the intellectual and electoral overlap between the two. By the Second World War Labour had emerged as the standard-bearer of the key elements in radical Victorian politics: it incorporated the Gladstonian tradition in foreign affairs; it was a party of causes;

it maintained libertarian principles; and it propagated improvement through social reform. Equally significant is the social–geographical distribution of Labour strength in the country after 1945. Though relying on its large working-class vote Labour had not come near to extinguishing working-class Conservatism; by 1945 the party had won over sufficient middle-class and suburban support to make it a national party on the Liberal model. Just as 50 years earlier non-Conservative representation was concentrated in Wales, Scotland, the four northern counties and Yorkshire; London and, to a lesser extent, Lancashire were still the major volatile regions which each party had to win for an overall majority. The only real difference between the nineteenth- and twentieth-century patterns is that Labour was a more urban party than the Liberals, and could not recapture the old radical strength in south-west England, the Scottish highlands or East Anglia, though it often did in rural Wales. With these qualifications, however, modern elections provide a striking demonstration of the continuity of appeal by the parties of Attlee and Asquith.

Notes

CHAPTER 1: *Party and Participation 1867–1900*

1 Brian Harrison, *Separate Spheres: the Opposition to Women's Suffrage in Britain* (1978), pp. 59–64, 71.
2 J. R. Vincent, 'The Electoral Sociology of Rochdale', *Economic History Review*, 16 (1963–4), pp. 79–81.
3 N. Blewett, 'The Franchise in the United Kingdom 1885–1918', *Past and Present*, 32 (1965), pp. 33–4.
4 ibid., pp. 46–7.
5 R. J. Olney, *Lincolnshire Politics 1832–85* (1973), pp. 158–81.
6 G. E. Mingay, *The Gentry* (1976), pp. 79, 172, 177; F. M. L. Thompson, *English Landed Society in the Nineteenth Century* (1963), p. 342.
7 T. J. Nossiter, *Influence, Opinion and Political Idioms in Reformed England* (1975), pp. 48–9.
8 ibid., p. 53.
9 J. Howarth, 'The Liberal Revival in Northamptonshire 1885–95', *Historical Journal*, 12 (1969), pp. 90–1.
10 Countess of Warwick, *Joseph Arch: the Story of his Life Told by Himself* (1898), p. 329.
11 P. F. Clarke, *Lancashire and the New Liberalism* (1971), p. 251.
12 Charles Roberts, *The Radical Countess: the History of the Life of Rosalind Countess of Carlisle* (1962), p. 85.
13 Before decimalization in 1971, three monetary units were in use: the pound (symbol £), the shilling or *s* (one-twentieth of a pound) and the penny or *d* (one-twelfth of a shilling).
14 Patrick Joyce, 'The Factory Politics of Lancashire in the Later Nineteenth Century', *Historical Journal*, 18 (1975), pp. 533–41.
15 ibid., pp. 541–3.
16 Nossiter, *Influence, Opinion and Political Idioms*, pp. 125–8.
17 Surviving two-member boroughs were Bath, Blackburn, Bolton, Brighton, Derby, Devonport, Halifax, Ipswich, Leicester, Newcastle, Northampton, Norwich, Oldham, Plymouth, Portsmouth, Preston, Southampton, Stockport, Sunderland, York, Merthyr Tydfil and Dundee.

18 Derek Fraser, *Urban Politics in Victorian England* (1976), pp. 115–24.
19 L. Kitchen, 'The 1892 Election in the Tyneside Area' (Newcastle M. Litt. thesis, unpublished, 1979), pp. 268, 284.
20 Leeds Liberal Federation Executive Committee Minutes 1894–1924; Keighley Conservative Association Minutes 1885–1904.
21 J. A. Garrard, 'Parties, Members and Voters after 1867: a Local Study', *Historical Journal*, 20 (1977), p. 151.
22 NUCCA Conference Minutes, 1897.
23 Quoted in the *Campaign Guide* (1892) published by the Conservative Party.
24 W. L. Guttsman, *The British Political Elite* (1965), p. 104.
25 R. Pumphrey, 'The Introduction of Industrialists into the British Peerage', *American Historical Review*, 65 (1959–60), p. 7.
26 H. H. Asquith, *Memories and Reflections* (1928), vol. II, p. 105.

CHAPTER 2: *The Evolution of the Gladstonian Liberal Party 1867–1895*

1 In full, the Society for the Liberation of Religion from State Patronage and Control.
2 Henry Pelling, *America and the British Left* (1956), pp. 16–27.
3 C. Harvie, *The Lights of Liberalism: University Liberals and the Challenge of Democracy* (1976), pp. 112–14.
4 Robert Spence Watson, *The National Liberal Federation 1877–1906* (1907), pp. 3–4.
5 D. A. Hamer (ed.), *Joseph Chamberlain: the Radical Programme* (1971 edn), pp. xxii–xxv.
6 T. W. Heyck, 'Home Rule, Radicalism and the Liberal Party 1886–95', *Journal of British Studies*, 13 (1974), p. 69.
7 Michael Barker, *Gladstone and Radicalism 1885–94* (1975), p. 24.
8 P. C. Griffiths, 'The Caucus and the Liberal Party in 1886', *History*, 61 (1976), p. 192.
9 Barker, *Gladstone and Radicalism*, p. 75.
10 Quoted in D. A. Hamer, *John Morley* (1968), p. 236.

CHAPTER 3: *The Conservative Revival 1874–1900*

1 *The Times*, 6 June 1865.
2 Balfour to Salisbury, 27 August 1891, J. P. Cornford, 'Parliamentary Foundations of the Hotel Cecil', R. Robson (ed.), *Ideas and Institutions of Victorian Britain* (1967), p. 296.
3 *Conservative Annual Conference Report*, 1867, fol. 3–4.
4 NUCCA Conference Minutes, 23 July 1880.
5 NUCCA Conference Minutes, 14 November 1882.
6 R. E. Quinault, 'Lord Randolph Churchill and Tory Democracy 1880–85', *Historical Journal*, 22 (1979), pp. 144–5.
7 National Union (Pamphlet No. 24, 1873), p. 4.

8   Quinault, 'Randolph Churchill', pp. 152, 158–9.

9   Peter Marsh, *The Discipline of Popular Government* (1978), p. 152.

10 R. B. McDowell, *British Conservatism 1832–1914* (1959); Samuel Beer, *Modern British Politics* (1965).

11 R. J. Olney, *Lincolnshire Politics 1832–85* (1973), pp. 188–9, 217.

12 *Campaign Guide* (1892).

13 Marsh, *The Discipline of Popular Government*, p. 160.

14 J. P. D. Dunbabin, 'The Politics of the Establishment of County Councils', *Historical Journal*, 6 (1963), pp. 228–36.

15 Stedman Jones, *Outcast London* (1971), pp. 227–30.

16 Quoted in Dunbabin, 'County Councils', pp. 239–40.

CHAPTER 4: *The Social Roots of Political Change in Late Victorian Britain*

1   T. J. Nossiter, *Influence, Opinion and Political Idioms in Reformed England* (1975), pp. 177–92.

2   H. M. Pelling, *Social Geography of British Elections 1885–1910* (1967), p. 415.

3   Quoted in R. J. Olney, *Lincolnshire Politics 1832–85* (1973), p. 229.

4   See Raphael Samuel, *Village Life and Labour* (1975) on Headington Quarry in Oxfordshire.

5   Peter Marsh, *The Discipline of Popular Government* (1978), p. 207.

6   Olney, *Lincolnshire Politics*, p. 214.

7   Karl Marx 'The Chartists', *New York Daily Tribune*, 25 August 1852.

8   Pelling, *Social Geography of British Elections*, p. 419.

9   Frank Gray, *Confessions of a Candidate* (1925), pp. 9–10.

10 Countess of Warwick, *Joseph Arch: the Story of his Life Told by Himself* (1898), p. 55.

11 Ramsay MacDonald, *The Socialist Movement* (1911), p. 93.

12 NUCCA Annual Conference Minutes, 13–14 November 1892.

13 C. Green, 'Birmingham's Politics 1873–91: the Local Basis of Change', *Midland History*, 2 (1973), p. 92.

14 Quoted in A. McKenzie and A. Silver, *Angels in Marble* (1968), p. 60.

15 R. Price, *An Imperial War and the British Working Class* (1972), pp. 200–28.

16 National Union pamphlet no. 3 (1892), 'Promise Versus Performance'.

17 *Campaign Guide* (Conservative Party) (1892), 'Labour Problems'.

18 Countess of Warwick, *Joseph Arch*, p. 255.

19 *Campaign Notes* (Conservative Party) (1901), p. 516.

20 Green, 'Birmingham's Politics 1873–91', p. 91.

21 ibid.

22 Nossiter, *Influence, Opinion and Political Idioms*, pp. 163–7, 147–8.

CHAPTER 5: *The Edwardian Crises 1895–1914*

1   H. A. Tulloch, 'Changing British Attitudes towards America in the 1880s', *Historical Journal*, 20 (1977).

2   H. C. G. Matthew, R. I. McKibbin and J. A. Kay, 'The Franchise Factor in the Rise of the Labour Party', *English Historical Review*, 91 (1976), pp. 742–3.

3   Minutes of the Society of Certificated and Associated Liberal Agents, 1895–1945.

4   For a valuable discussion of the problem see A. J. Lee, *The Origins of the Popular Press 1855–1914* (1976); and S. E. Koss, *Fleet Street Radical: A. G. Gardiner and the Daily News* (1973), p. 40.

5   S. E. Koss, 'Wesleyanism and Empire', *Historical Journal*, 18 (1975).

6   Correspondence for 1897–98 in C. P. Trevelyan Papers, vol. 4, Newcastle University; M. D. Pugh, 'Yorkshire and the New Liberalism?' *Journal of Modern History*, 50 (1978), p. 1142; L. Kitchen, 'The 1892 Election in the Tyneside Area' (Newcastle M. Litt. thesis, unpublished, 1979), pp. 70–1.

7   M. Barker, *Gladstone and Radicalism* (1975), pp. 50, 89–96, 197–8.

8   C. P. Trevelyan to Herbert Samuel, 2 October 1898, Trevelyan Papers, 4.

9   T. Boyle, 'The Liberal Imperialists, 1892–1906', *Bulletin of the Institute of Historical Research*, 52 (1979), pp. 51–5.

10   R. B. Haldane to Rosebery, 24 April 1895, Rosebery Papers, 24.

11   Peter Cain, 'Political Economy in Edwardian England: the Tariff Reform Controversy', A. O'Day (ed.), *The Edwardian Age* (1979), p. 37.

12   Contemporary estimates after the 1906 election suggested that the MPs comprised 11–16 free traders, 32 Balfourites and 109 tariff reformers, though historians have thought this an exaggeration of protectionist strength.

13   R. Rempel, *Unionists Divided* (1972), pp. 94–5.

14   G. R. Searle, 'Critics of Edwardian Society: the Case of the Radical Right', in O'Day (ed.), *The Edwardian Age*.

15   He had been parliamentary secretary at the Board of Trade 1902–5 and had worked for a firm of merchant bankers and become a partner in a Glasgow iron merchant's company.

16   Lord Oxford and Asquith, *Memories and Reflections 1852–1927* (1928), vol. 1, p. 202.

17   H. H. Asquith to W. S. Churchill, 12 September 1913, Randolph S. Churchill, *Winston S. Churchill*, vol. II, Companion, part 3 (1969), p. 1399.

18   See P. F. Clarke, *Lancashire and the New Liberalism* (1971), p. 387.

19   J. Liddington and J. Norris, *One Hand Tied Behind Us: the Rise of the Women's Suffrage Movement* (1979), pp. 193, 205, 219.

20   Paul Thompson, *The Edwardians: the Remaking of British Society* (1975), pp. 240–64.

21   D. Lloyd George, *Better Times: Speeches on the Social Question* (1910).

CHAPTER 6: *Edwardian Progressivism*

1   See, for example, J. R. Vincent, 'The Electoral Sociology of Rochdale', *Economic History Review*, 16 (1963–4), p. 85.

2 Published as Charles Booth, *Life and Labour of the People of London*, 17 vols (1902–4); B. S. Rowntree, *Poverty: a Study of Town Life* (1901).

3 J. M. Robertson, *The Meaning of Liberalism* (1912), p. 64.

4 P. F. Clarke, *Lancashire and the New Liberalism* (1971), p. 223.

5 Herbert Gladstone Papers 46106, memorandum, 6 September 1903.

6 C. P. Trevelyan to W. S. Churchill, draft, undated, December 1903, Trevelyan Papers 13, Newcastle University.

7 Bruce K. Murray, *The People's Budget 1909–10* (1980), pp. 112–21.

8 Notably the British Medical Association, friendly societies and insurance companies with their armies of collectors. Part I of the Act provided health insurance and Part II unemployment insurance for three groups of workers.

9 A. E. Pease to Herbert Samuel, 19 August 1908, Samuel Papers A/155 (III) House of Lords Record Office.

10 Runciman to Asquith (copy) 27 February 1908, Crawshaw to Runciman 2 April 1912, Runciman Papers 21 and 63, Newcastle University.

11 See Lloyd George Papers C/21/1/17, House of Lords Record Office.

12 W. D. Rubinstein, 'Wealth, Elites and the Class Structure of Modern Britain', *Past and Present*, 76 (1977); and 'The Victorian Middle Classes: Wealth, Occupation and Geography', *Economic History Review*, 30 (1977).

13 See Runciman Papers 66 and 74.

14 H. V. Emy, *Liberals, Radicals and Social Politics 1892–1914* (1973), p. 219.

15 Leslie Scott to Lloyd George, 29 September 1913, Lloyd George Papers C/8/2/1.

16 P. Poirer, *The Advent of the Labour Party* (1958), p. 110.

17 Memorandum, MacDonald Papers 30/69/5/81, Public Record Office.

CHAPTER 7: *The Electoral Struggle 1906–1914*

1 Roy Gregory, *The Miners and British Politics 1906–14* (1968), p. 189.

2 Neal Blewett, 'The Franchise in the United Kingdom 1885–1918', *Past and Present*, 32 (1965), pp. 30–42.

3 Duncan Tanner, *Political Change and the Labour Party 1900–1918* (1990), pp. 111–23.

4 The *Labour Leader*, 18 July 1912.

5 CAB 37/108/148, 16 November 1911.

6 Gregory, *The Miners and British Politics*, p. 9.

7 J. Blackley to Walter Runciman, 15 September 1906, Runciman Papers 14, Newcastle University.

8 T. Catterall, 2 July 1903, C. P. Trevelyan Papers 13, Newcastle University.

9 Labour Party Archives, LP/EL/08, Manchester.

10 Alexander Murray to Lord Knollys (copy), 7 November 1906, and 'Memorandum on the Socialist and Labour Movements in Scotland', by D. A. Wood and W. Webster, Elibank Papers 8801, National Library of Scotland.

11 P. F. Clarke, 'The Electoral Position of the Liberal and Labour Parties 1910–14', *English Historical Review*, 90 (1975), pp. 829–35.

12 Alan Sykes, *Tariff Reform in British Politics 1903–13* (1979), p. 273.

13 Austen Chamberlain, 9 March 1910, Chamberlain Papers AC/8/8/15, Birmingham University.

14 Josiah Wedgwood to Ramsay MacDonald, 12 June 1913, MacDonald Papers 30/69/5/23, Public Record Office.

15 Private Memorandum, 3 March 1914, MacDonald Papers 30/69/8/1.

16 Tanner, *Political Change*, pp. 325–37.

17 George Young to C. P. Trevelyan, 28 June 1906, Trevelyan Papers 16.

18 J. Cochrane Shanks to D. Lloyd George, 9 February 1914, Lloyd George Papers C/10/3/19, House of Lords Record Office.

19 Mrs L. Bulley to Mrs Lloyd George, Lloyd George Papers C/10/1/68.

20 Catherine Marshall to Arthur Henderson, 14 October 1912, Marshall Papers, Cumbria Record Office.

21 Undated memorandum, J. A. Pease Papers 88, Nuffield College.

22 Asquith Papers 23, fol. 298, Bodleian Library.

23 Trevelyan to Walter Runciman, 25 March 1912, Runciman Papers 63.

24 Lloyd George to Christopher Addison (copy), 11 November 1913, Lloyd George Papers C/10/2/24.

25 Trevelyan to Walter Runciman, 3 November 1913, Runciman Papers 82.

CHAPTER 8: *The Impact of the Great War on British Politics*

1 Ponsonby to W. S. Churchill, 31 July 1914, Churchill Papers.

2 E. I. David (ed.), *Inside Asquith's Cabinet: from the Diaries of Sir Charles Hobhouse* (1977), pp. 179–80.

3 A. Bonar Law to H. H. Asquith, 2 August 1919, quoted in R. Blake, *The Unknown Prime Minister* (1955), p. 222.

4 The Union of Democratic Control had been founded in August 1914 by MacDonald, E. D. Morel, C. P. Trevelyan, Arthur Ponsonby and Norman Angell and was dedicated to restoring parliamentary control of foreign policy.

5 *The Times*, 18 September 1914.

6 David French, 'The Military Background to the "Shell Crisis" of May 1915', *Journal of Strategic Studies*, 2 (1979), pp. 199–200.

7 Bonar Law Papers 36/1/12, 14, 18, House of Lords Record Office, for correspondence with Lord Crewe on this point.

8 Bonar Law to Curzon (copy), 29 January 1915, and memoranda by Curzon and Long in Balfour Papers 49693, British Library.

9 Richard Denman to C. P. Trevelyan, 28 May 1915, quoted in M. Swartz, *The Union of Democratic Control in British Politics during the First World War* (1971), p. 66.

10 C. P. Scott's Diary, 3 September 1915, British Library.

11 Report of Proceedings of the National Union Special Conference, 30 November 1917.

12 M. D. Pugh, *Electoral Reform in War and Peace 1906–18* (1978), pp. 98–9, 103–35, 156–7.

13 Notes on the Report of the Speaker's Conference, 3 February 1917, Steel-Maitland Papers 202, Scottish Record Office.

14 F. E. Guest to Lloyd George, 20 July 1918, Lloyd George Papers F/21/2/28, House of Lords Record Office.

15 I. G. Hunter, 'Working Class Representatives on Elective Local Authorities on Tyneside 1883–1921' (unpublished Newcastle M. Litt. thesis 1979), pp. 115–38.

16 ibid., pp. 124–5.

17 Annual Conference Reports, Labour Party Archives, Manchester.

18 Labour Party Archives, ORG/14/1 & 2.

CHAPTER 9: *A Mass Electorate at War*

1 Quoted in P. F. Clarke, *Liberals and Social Democrats* (1978) p. 175.

2 Philip Gibbs, quoted in P. Knightley, *The First Casualty* (1978), p. 97.

3 Diary of Miss K. M. B. Alexander (aged 11), 29 February 1916; Peter Liddle's 1914–18 Personal Experience Archives, Leeds University.

4 See M. D. Pugh, *Women's Suffrage in Britain 1867–1928* (Historical Association G97, 1980).

5 M. D. Pugh, *Electoral Reform in War and Peace 1906–18* (1978), pp. 84–6, 136–54.

6 G. Slater (ed.), *My Warrior Sons: the Borton Family Diary 1914–18* (1970), p. 51; also M. Moynihan (ed.), *A Place Called Armageddon* (1975), pp. 134–59.

7 Julian Grenfell to Lady E. Desborough, 17 October 1914.

8 M. Moynihan (ed.), *People at War 1914–18* (1973), p. 48.

9 H. J. Odell to his mother, 30 August 1917; Peter Liddle, Personal Experience Archives.

10 H. J. Odell to his mother, 13 January 1918; Peter Liddle, ibid.

11 S. Sassoon, *Seigfried's Journey* (1946), p. 51.

12 D. Englander and J. Osborne, 'Jack, Tommy and Henry Dubb: the Armed Forces and the Working Class', *Historical Journal*, 21 (1978), pp. 603–5.

13 ibid., p. 620.

14 Addison Papers, vol. 80, Bodleian Library.

15 Stansgate Papers, 40/1, House of Lords Record Office.

16 R. B. MacCallum and A. Readman, *The British General Election of 1945* (1947), p. 239.

17 J. Davidson to Arthur Ponsonby, 29 December 1918, Ponsonby Papers 667, Bodleian Library.

18 MacDonald Papers 30/69/7/51, Public Record Office.

19 G. Morgan to Arthur Ponsonby, 20 December 1917, Ponsonby Papers 666.

20 A. Rowntree to Arthur Ponsonby, 3 January 1919, Ponsonby Papers 667; K. O. Morgan, *Consensus and Disunity: the Lloyd George Coalition Government 1916–22* (1979), pp. 152–3; D. Marquand, *Ramsay MacDonald* (1977), p. 235.

21 Report by S. Higgenbotham, 17 January 1919, MacDonald Papers 30/69/7/51.

22 John Turner, 'The Labour Vote and the Franchise after 1918', in P. R. Denley and D. Hopkins (eds), *History and Computing* (1987), pp. 139–40.
23 Report by S. Higgenbotham, 17 January 1919, MacDonald Papers 30/69/7/51; A. Rowntree to Arthur Ponsonby, 3 January 1919, Ponsonby Papers 667.

CHAPTER 10: *Party, Ideology and the State in the Great War*

1 See A. J. P. Taylor, *English History 1914–45* (1970), pp. 57, 64–5, 98–101, 113.
2 David French, 'Some Aspects of Social and Economic Planning for War in Great Britain 1905–15' (University of London Ph.D. thesis 1978), pp. 63–5.
3 David French, 'The Military Background to the "Shell Crisis" of May 1915', *Journal of Strategic Studies*, 2 (1979), pp. 192–7.
4 CAB 42/1/21, 25 January 1915.
5 French, 'Some Aspects of Social and Economic Planning', p. 160.
6 17 February 1915 (French, ibid., p. 176).
7 Alan Sykes, *Tariff Reform in British Politics 1903–13* (1979), p. 278.
8 J. Turner, 'The British Commonwealth Union and the General Election of 1918', *English Historical Review*, 93 (1978), pp. 530–9.
9 Rodney Lowe, 'The Erosion of State Intervention in Britain 1917–24', *Economic History Review*, 31, 2 (1978), p. 278.
10 K. O. Morgan, *Consensus and Disunity: the Lloyd George Coalition Government 1916–22* (1979), pp. 105–7.
11 H. C. Deb., 23 June 1921, c. 1600.
12 J. M. McEwen, 'The Coupon Election of 1918 and the Unionist Members of Parliament', *Journal of Modern History*, 34 (1962), pp. 298–302.
13 J. O. Stubbs, 'The Impact of the Great War on the Conservative Party', in G. Peele and C. Cook (eds), *The Politics of Reappraisal* (1975), p. 34.
14 C. P. Scott's Diary, 11–12 December 1917, British Library.
15 C. P. Trevelyan, *From Liberalism to Labour* (1921), p. 17.
16 C. V. Wedgwood, *The Last of the Radicals* (1951), p. 154.
17 Addison to Arthur Henderson (copy), 19 November 1923, Addison Papers 82, Bodleian Library.
18 Kenneth and Jane Morgan, *Portrait of a Progressive* (1980), pp. 182–7.
19 C. P. Trevelyan, *From Liberalism to Labour* (1921).
20 W. Wedgwood Benn to A. Munro (copy), 25 January 1927, Stansgate Papers 85/1, House of Lords Record Office.

CHAPTER 11: *The Elevation of Labour and the Restoration of Party Politics 1918–1924*

1 M. Kinnear, *The Fall of Lloyd George* (1973), pp. 79–85.
2 John Ramsden, *The Age of Balfour and Baldwin* (1978), pp. 134–5.
3 M. Cowling, *The Impact of Labour* (1971), pp. 72–5.

4   Kinnear, *The Fall of Lloyd George*, pp. 89–90.

5   K. Middlemas and J. Barnes, *Baldwin* (1969), p. 216.

6   Lloyd George to C. P. Scott 27 December 1923, quoted in R. Douglas, *The History of the Liberal Party 1895–1970* (1971), p. 175.

7   MacDonald's Diary 7 June 1920, quoted in D. Marquand, *Ramsay MacDonald* (1977), p. 268.

8   Sir Keith Feiling, *Life of Neville Chamberlain* (1946), p. 111.

9   Middlemas and Barnes, *Baldwin*, p. 268.

10 MacDonald's Diary 26 September 1924, Public Record Office.

11 Middlemas and Barnes, *Baldwin*, p. 273.

CHAPTER 12: *Origins of the Conservative Electoral Hegemony 1918–1931*

1   For 1922 the total poll can be recalculated by estimating the likely vote in the 42 Conservative seats uncontested and in the 14 Liberal and Labour ones on the basis of subsequent performances; this would raise the Conservative share by around 3 per cent, from 38 per cent to 41 per cent.

2   MacDonald Papers PRO 30/69/5/166.

3   M. Kinnear, *The British Voter: an Atlas and Survey 1885–1964* (1969), pp. 70–1.

4   They were: Cambridge 2; Oxford 2; London 1; Combined English Universities 1; Wales 1; Combined Scottish Universities 3: Dublin 2; National University 1; Belfast 1.

5   Memorandum dated October 1916, Steel-Maitland Papers 202, Scottish Record Office.

6   Col. R. A. Sanders Diary, 15 June 1917.

7   Memorandum on seats by Walter Long (copy), 19 January 1918, Long Papers, Wiltshire County Record Office.

8   J. P. D. Dunbabin, 'British Elections in the Nineteenth and Twentieth Century: a Regional Approach', *English Historical Review*, 95 (1980), pp. 244–5.

9   Kinnear, *The British Voter*, pp. 122–4.

10 John Ramsden, *The Age of Balfour and Baldwin 1902–40* (1978), p. 239.

11 ibid., p. 249.

12 R. I. McKibbin, *The Evolution of the Labour Party 1910–24* (1974), p. 145.

13 J. Rasmussen, 'Women in Labour: the Flapper Vote and Party System Transformation in Britain', *Electoral Studies*, 3, 1 (1984) pp. 55–8.

14 Michael Savage, *The Dynamics of Working-Class Politics* (1987), pp. 162–73.

15 Mark Abrams, 'Social Class and British Politics', in Lewis A. Coser (ed.), *Political Sociology* (1966), pp. 206–71.

16 Dunbabin, 'British Elections', p. 243.

17 D. Butler and D. Stokes, *Political Change in Britain* (1971 edn), pp. 65–89.

18 ibid., p. 77.

19 MacDonald Papers PRO 30/69/5/160.

20 S. E. Koss, *Nonconformity in Modern British Politics* (1975), p. 234.

21 Butler and Stokes, *Political Change in Britain*, p. 163.

22 ibid., pp. 166–7.
23 W. G. Runciman, *Relative Deprivation and Social Justice* (1972 edn), p. 82.

CHAPTER 13: *The Eclipse of the Extremes 1931–1939*

1   A. Oldfield, 'The Independent Labour Party and Planning 1920–26', *International Review of Social History*, 21 (1976), p. 21.
2   D. Marquand, *Ramsay MacDonald* (1977), pp. 478–9.
3   Quoted in R. Skidelsky, *Politicians and the Slump* (1967), p. 241.
4   MacDonald to V. Hartshorn (copy), 20 December 1930; MacDonald to Graham (copy), 2 October 1930, MacDonald Papers 30/69/5/174, Public Record Office.
5   See correspondence of MacDonald and Lloyd George, Snowden and Hartshorn, autumn 1930, MacDonald Papers 30/69/5/174, and for 1931 MacDonald Papers 30/69/5/175.
6   MacDonald Papers 30/69/5/166, memoranda and correspondence on electoral reform 1929–30.
7   B. C. Malament, 'British Labour and Roosevelt's New Deal: the Response of the Left and the Unions', *Journal of British Studies* (Spring, 1978), pp. 158–9.
8   MacDonald to Baldwin (copy), 5 September 1931, MacDonald Papers 30/69/5/180.
9   MacDonald to the King (copy), 14 September 1931, MacDonald Papers 30/69/5/180.
10 C. T. Stannage, 'The General Election of 1935' (Cambridge Ph.D. thesis 1973), pp. 30–1.
11 Quoted in David Dilks, *The Conservatives*, ed. Lord Butler (1977), p. 312.
12 A. Mason, 'The Government and the General Strike, 1926', *International Review of Social History*, 14 (1969), pp. 3–8.
13 M. Cowling, *The Impact of Hitler* (1975), p. 63.
14 ibid., p. 81.
15 H. C. Deb., 14 June 1934, c. 2018.
16 See K. Middlemas and J. Barnes, *Baldwin* (1969), pp. 744–7, 764, 791.
17 ibid., pp. 863–8; Dilks, *The Conservatives*, p. 366.
18 Stannage, 'The General Election of 1935', pp. 287–99.

EPILOGUE

1   The title of a book by Michael Foot, Frank Owen and Peter Howard which went through ten impressions in July 1940.
2   Paul Addison, *The Road to 1945 (1975)*.

Guide to Further Reading

CHAPTER 1: *Party and Participation 1867–1900*

Mid to late Victorian attitudes towards the franchise and representative government are perceptively revealed in F. B. Smith, *The Making of the Second Reform Act* (1967); Brian Harrison, *Separate Spheres: the Opposition to Women's Suffrage in Britain* (1978); and Walter Bagehot, *The English Constitution* (1867, reprinted 1963). Specifically on franchise changes see C. Seymour, *Electoral Reform in England and Wales 1832–85* (1915); the indispensable article by Neal Blewett, 'The Franchise in the United Kingdom 1885–1918', *Past and Present*, 32 (1965); G. A. Jones, 'Further Thoughts on the Franchise', *Past and Present*, 34 (1966); and important revisionism by Duncan Tanner in 'The Parliamentary Electoral System, the "Fourth" Reform Act and the Rise of Labour in England and Wales', *Bulletin of the Institute of Historical Research*, 56, 134 (1983).

Much the most valuable single volume on the operation of the political system in the country is H. J. Hanham's *Elections and Party Management: Politics in the Time of Disraeli and Gladstone* (1959). Excellent insights into particular aspects of elections at this time are to be found in: R. Kelley, 'Midlothian: a Study in Politics and Ideas', *Victorian Studies*, 4 (1960); Trevor Lloyd, *The General Election of 1880* (1968); D. Richter, 'The Role of Mob Riot in Victorian Elections', *Victorian Studies*, 15 (1971); C. C. O'Leary, *The Elimination of Corrupt Practices in British Elections* (1962); and W. B. Gwyn, *Democracy and the Cost of Politics in Britain* (1962). For an overview see the Historical Association pamphlet by Martin Pugh, *The Evolution of the British Electoral System 1832–1987* (1988).

A highly perceptive analysis of the gradual shift from local to national patterns in both county and borough constituencies is T. J. Nossiter's *Influence, Opinion and Political Idioms in Reformed England: Case Studies from the North-East* (1975). On largely rural developments the following are useful: R. J. Olney, *Lincolnshire Politics 1832–85* (1973); J. Howarth, 'The Liberal Revival in Northamptonshire 1885–95', *Historical Journal*, 12 (1969). On urban changes there are two important and stimulating contributions: J. A. Garrard shows the response of the parliamentarians to the new electorate in 'Parties, Members and Voters after 1867', *Historical Journal*, 20 (1977); Patrick Joyce argues for the continuing strength of non-political voting behaviour after 1867 in 'The Factory

Politics of Lancashire in the Later Nineteenth Century', *Historical Journal*, 18 (1975), and in *Work, Society and Politics* (1980). Useful on the extension of party influence are Derek Fraser, *Urban Politics in Victorian England* (1976); and Trevor Lloyd, 'Uncontested Seats in British General Elections 1852–1910', *Historical Journal*, 8 (1965).

W. L. Guttsman's *The British Political Elite* (1965) analyses the changing social composition of the parties. Valuable studies of the tightening party control at Westminster are Hugh Berrington's 'Partisanship and Dissidence in the Nineteenth Century House of Commons', *Parliamentary Affairs*, 21 (1967–8); and P. Fraser's 'The Growth of Ministerial Control in the Nineteenth Century House of Commons', *English Historical Review*, 75 (1960). For a fascinating examination of political honours and fund-raising see G. R. Searle, *Corruption in British Politics, 1895–1930* (1987); H. J. Hanham, 'The Sale of Honours in Late Victorian England', *Victorian Studies*, 3 (1960); R. Pumphrey, 'The Introduction of Industrialists into the British Peerage', *American Historical Review*, 65 (1959–60); and Trevor Lloyd, 'The Whip as Paymaster: Herbert Gladstone and Party Organisation', *English Historical Review*, 89 (1974). See also David Cannadine's *The Decline and Fall of the British Aristocracy* (1990).

CHAPTER 2: *The Evolution of the Gladstonian Liberal Party 1867–1895*

The seminal work here is J. R. Vincent, *The Formation of the British Liberal Party 1857–68* (1966). A number of works shed interesting light on the development of Liberal attitudes and policies: F. B. Smith, *The Making of the Second Reform Act* (1967); R. T. Shannon, *Gladstone and the Bulgarian Agitation 1876* (1963); C. Harvie, *The Lights of Liberalism: University Liberals and the Challenge of Democracy* (1976); Ian Bradley, *The Optimists: Themes and Personalities in Victorian Liberalism* (1980); H. Pelling, *America and the British Left* (1956); A. Briggs, *Victorian People* (1954); H. A. Tulloch, 'Changing British Attitudes towards America in the 1880's', *Historical Journal*, 20 (1977).

The local fabric of Liberalism is lucidly analysed in D. A. Hamer's *The Politics of Electoral Pressure* (1977). The centrality of religion has been expertly analysed in recent books by J. P. Parry, *Democracy and Religion: Gladstone and the Liberal Party 1867–1875* (1986); G. I. T. Machin, *Politics and the Churches in Great Britain, 1869–1921* (1987); and D. W. Bebbington, *The Nonconformist Conscience* (1982). Also valuable on the local basis of party organization are: R. Spence Watson, *The National Liberal Federation 1877–1906* (1907); B. McGill, 'Francis Schnadhorst and Liberal Party Organisation', *Journal of Modern History*, 34 (1962); C. D. H. Howard, 'Joseph Chamberlain and the Unauthorised Programme', *English Historical Review*, 65 (1950); D. A. Hamer (ed.), *Joseph Chamberlain: the Radical Programme* (1971); K. O. Morgan, *Wales in British Politics* (1970); James Hunter, 'The Politics of Highland Land Reform 1873–95', *Scottish Historical Review*, 53 (1974).

Several works examine the relationship between the parliamentary leadership and the wider party. T. A. Jenkins argues for the resilience of the Whig elements in *Gladstone, Whiggery and the Liberal Party 1874–1886* (1988). E. F. Biagini emphasizes the working-class loyalty to Gladstonianism in 'Popular Liberals, Gladstonian Finance and the Debate on Taxation, 1860-1874', in E. F. Biagini and A. S. Reid, *Currents of Radicalism* (eds), (1990), and in *Liberty, Retrenchment and Reform: Popular Liberalism in the Age of Gloadstone, 1860-1880* (1992). There is a detailed study of Gladstone's final decade in Michael Barker, *Gladstone and Radicalism 1885-94* (1975), and a wide-ranging treatment in D. A. Hamer's *Liberal Politics in the Age of Gladstone and Rosebery* (1972), though the latter book seems to me to mislead by emphasizing the negative aspects above all else. There are two important corrective articles by T. W. Heyck, 'Home Rule, Radicalism and the Liberal Party 1886-95', *Journal of British Studies*, 13 (1974); and P. C. Griffiths, 'The Caucus and the Liberal Party in 1886', *History*, 61 (1976). The most penetrating analysis of the parliamentarians' motives in 1886, and particularly the tactical calculations of Chamberlain, Gladstone and Hartington, is A. B. Cooke and J. R. Vincent, *The Governing Passion* (1974). The importance of 1886 in the evolution of the party is also analysed in W. C. Lubenow, 'Irish Home Rule and the Social Basis of the Great Separation in the Liberal Party in 1886', *Historical Journal*, 28, 1, (1985); J. G. Kellas, 'The Liberal Party in Scotland 1876-95', *Scottish Historical Review*, 44 (1965); D. C. Savage, 'Scottish Politics 1885-86', *Scottish Historical Review*, 40 (1961); Janet Howarth, 'The Liberal Revival in Northamptonshire 1880-95', *Historical Journal*, 12 (1969); D. Southgate, *The Passing of the Whigs* (1962). Useful biographies are: E. J. Feuchtwanger, *Gladstone* (1975); Richard Shannon, *Gladstone 1809-65* (1982); H. G. C. Matthew, *Gladstone 1809-74* (1986); and D. A. Hamer, *John Morley: Liberal Intellectual in Politics* (1968). There is an excellent biography of Chamberlain by Richard Jay, *Joseph Chamberlain: a Political Study* (1981). Also on the Liberal Unionists see: M. Hurst, *Joseph Chamberlain and Liberal Reunion 1887* (1967); Peter Fraser, *Joseph Chamberlain* (1966); 'The Liberal Unionist Alliance: Chamberlain, Hartington and the Conservatives 1886-1905', *English Historical Review*, 77 (1962); and Dennis Judd, *Radical Joe* (1977).

CHAPTER 3: *The Conservative Revival 1874-1900*

Several general works on the Conservative Party cover this period: Bruce Coleman, *Conservatism and the Conservative Party in Nineteenth Century Britain* (1988); Robert Blake, *The Conservative Party from Peel to Churchill* (1970); D. Southgate (ed.), *The Conservative Leadership 1832-1932* (1974); and Lord Butler (ed.), *The Conservatives* (1977).

All previous works are superseded by Peter Marsh's *The Discipline of Popular Government: Lord Salisbury's Domestic Statecraft 1881-1902* (1978) which fills a major gap; the author emphasizes the adaptive qualities of Salisbury rather than the inflexibility. See also the useful revisionary article by R. E. Quinault, 'Lord Randolph Churchill and Tory Democracy 1880-85', *Historical Journal*, 22 (1979); Viscount Chilston, *Chief Whip* (1961); Andrew Jones, *The Politics of Reform 1884* (1972); M. E. Chadwick, 'The Role of Redistribution in the Making of the Third Reform Act', *Historical Journal*, 19 (1976); A. B. Cooke and J. R. Vincent, *The Governing Passion* (1974).

There are several stimulating works on Conservative strength in the country: J. P. Cornford's seminal article, 'The Transformation of Conservatism in the Late Nineteenth Century', *Victorian Studies*, 7 (1963), and 'Parliamentary Foundations of the Hotel Cecil', in R. Robson (ed.), *Ideas and Institutions of Victorian Britain* (1967); H. J. Hanham, *Elections and Party Management: Politics in the Time of Disraeli and Gladstone* (1959); Martin Pugh, *The Tories and the People 1880–1935* (1985); J. P. D. Dunbabin, 'Parliamentary Elections in Great Britain 1868–1900: a Psephological Note', *English Historical Review*, 81 (1966); E. J. Feuchtwanger, *Disraeli, Democracy and the Tory Party* (1968); R. T. McKenzie, *British Political Parties* (1955); D. W. Urwin, 'The Development of Conservative Party Organisation in Scotland before 1912', *Scottish Historical Review*, 44 (1965).

On Disraeli, Paul Smith's *Disraelian Conservatism and Social Reform* (1967) attacks the traditional mythology; Robert Blake's *Disraeli* (1966) remains the standard biography. For some recent revisionism see the articles by Peter Ghosh, 'Disraelian Conservatism: a Financial Approach', *English Historical Review*, 99 (1984); and Paul Smith, 'Disraeli's Politics', *Transactions of the Royal Historical Society*, 37 (1987).

Salisbury's ideas are examined in Paul Smith's *Lord Salisbury on Politics* (1972); M. Pinto-Duschinsky, *The Political Thought of Lord Salisbury* (1967); and in a wider context in the following: Noel O'Sullivan, *Conservatism* (1976); Samuel Beer, *Modern British Politics* (1965); and R. B. McDowell, *British Conservatism 1832–1914* (1959). Useful on particular aspects are: J. E. B. Munson, 'The Unionist Coalition and Education 1895–1902', *Historical Journal*, 20 (1977); J. P. D. Dunbabin, 'The Politics of the Establishment of County Councils', *Historical Journal*, 6 (1963); Peter Davis, 'The Liberal Unionist Party and the Irish Policy of Lord Salisbury's Government 1886–92', *Historical Journal*, 18 (1975). See also chapter 2 for works on Chamberlain and Liberal Unionism. Among the biographies the following are useful: R. Rhodes James, *Lord Randolph Churchill* (1960); Viscount Chilston, *W. H. Smith* (1965); T. J. Spinner, *George Joachim Goschen* (1973); S. H. Zebel, *Balfour* (1973); and R. Taylor, *Salisbury* (1975).

CHAPTER 4: *The Social Roots of Political Change in Late Victorian Britain*

Henry Pelling's *Social Geography of British Elections 1885–1910* (1967) is an invaluable guide to the themes treated in this chapter. There are several other original interpretations of popular politics in this period. T. J. Nossiter, *Influence, Opinion and Political Idioms in Reformed England* (1975) is the best analysis of the breakdown of traditional, deferential patterns of politics; H. J. Hanham's *Elections and Party Management: Politics in the Time of Disraeli and Gladstone* (1959) is essential reading: J. R. Vincent's *Pollbooks: How Victorians Voted* (1967) throws fascinating light on the occupational basis of party support before 1872. See also two articles by J. P. D. Dunbabin, 'Parliamentary Elections in Great Britain 1868–1900', *English Historical Review*, 81 (1966); and 'British Elections in the Nineteenth and Twentieth Century: a Regional Approach', *English Historical Review*, 95 (1980).

A number of works help to bring out the political significance of particular issues: Brian Harrison's excellent *Drink and the Victorians* (1971); J. S. Hurt, *Elementary Schooling and the Working Classes 1860–1918* (1979); Alan Simon, 'Church Disestablishment as a Factor in the General Election of 1885', *Historical Journal*, 18 (1975); Ian Sellers, *Nineteenth Century Nonconformity* (1977); K. S. Inglis, *Churches and the Working Classes in Victorian England* (1963); S. E. Koss, 'Wesleyanism and Empire', *Historical Journal*, 18 (1975); H. Pelling and K. O. Morgan, 'Wales and the Boer War', *Welsh History Review*, 4 (1968–9); J. A. Garrard, *The English and Immigration 1880–1910* (1971); and Catherine Jones, *Immigration and Social Policy in Britain* (1977).

The social context of rural politics is admirably reconstructed in Raphael Samuel (ed.), *Village Life and Labour* (1975); and in Flora Thompson's classic account, *Lark Rise to Candleford* (1939, reprinted 1973). There are several works on the political manifestations of agricultural areas by J. P. D. Dunbabin, *Rural Discontent in Nineteenth Century Britain* (1974); and 'The Revolt of the Field: the Agricultural Labourers' Movement in the 1870's', *Past and Present*, 26 (1963). See also: F. M. L. Thompson, 'Land and Politics in England in the Nineteenth Century', *Transactions of the Royal Historical Society*, 15 (1965); Roy Douglas, *Land, People and Politics* (1976); Countess of Warwick, *Joseph Arch: the Story of his Life Told by Himself* (1898); P. Horn, 'Agricultural Trade Unionism and Emigration 1872–81', *Historical Journal*, 15 (1972); R. J. Olney, *Lincolnshire Politics 1832–85* (1973); L. Marion Springhall, *Labouring Life in Norfolk Villages 1834–1914* (1936); F. M. L. Thompson, *English Landed Society in the Nineteenth Century* (1968); G. Mingay, *The Gentry* (1978); and T. W. Fletcher, 'The Great Depression of British Agriculture 1873–1896', *Economic History Review*, 13 (1961).

On the attitudes of urban working-class people towards politics see three stimulating works: Robert Tressel, *The Ragged Trousered Philanthropists* (1955, reprinted 1967); Stephen Reynolds, *Seems So! A Working Class View of Politics* (1911); and Robert Roberts, *The Classic Slum* (1971). The hostility to authority indicated in the latter two volumes is discussed by Henry Pelling in 'The Working Class and the Origins of the Welfare State' in a valuable collection of essays, *Popular Politics and Society in Late Victorian Britain* (1968). Much incidental light is thrown upon political attitudes in: R. Moore, *Pitmen, Preachers and Politics* (1974), which examines Methodist mining villages in Durham; Paul Thompson, *The Edwardians* (1975), an excellent social history based on oral sources; G. Stedman Jones, *Outcast London* (1971); and S. Meacham, *A Life Apart* (1977). For a stimulating discussion of working-class society see Ross McKibbin's 'Why was there no Marxism in Great Britain?' *English Historical Review*, 99, (1984); and Gareth Stedman Jones, *Languages of Class* (1983). On trade unions see E. H. Hunt, *British Labour History 1815–1914* (1981); H. A. Clegg, A. Fox and A. F. Thompson, *A History of British Trade Unions Since 1889*, vol. 1 (1964); E. H. Phelps Brown, *The Growth of British Industrial Relations* (1965); A. E. P. Duffy, 'New Unionism in Britain 1889–90: a Reappraisal', *Economic History Review*, 14 (1961–2); Henry Pelling, *A History of British Trade Unionism* (1963); and E. F.

Biagini, 'British Trade Unions and Popular Political Economy 1860–1880', *Historical Journal*, 30, 4 (1987). Aspects of labour politics are explored in: Royden Harrison, *Before the Socialists: Studies in Labour and Politics 1861–81* (1965); R. Moore, *The Emergence of the Labour Party 1880–1924* (1978); David Howell, *British Workers and the Independent Labour Party 1888–1906* (1983); David Clark, *Colne Valley: Radicalism to Socialism* (1981); James Hinton, *Labour and Socialism* (1983); James D. Young, *Socialism and the English Working Class* (1989); Henry Pelling, *Origins of the Labour Party* (1954); A. Briggs and J. Saville (eds), *Essays in Labour History*, vol. 1 (1967), vol. 2 (1971). The idea of an elite within the working class has been vigorously debated by historians: E. J. Hobsbawm's 'The Labour Aristocracy in Nineteenth Century Britain', in *Labouring Men* (1968) is critically examined in Henry Pelling's 'The Concept of the Labour Aristocracy', in *Popular Politics*; detailed studies are: R. G. Gray, *The Labour Aristocracy in Victorian Edinburgh* (1976); and G. Crossick, *An Artisan Elite in Victorian Society: Kentish London* (1978). The whole question is put in a fresh light by Brian Harrison's 'Traditions of Respectability in British Labour History', in his *Peaceable Kingdom* (1982). The broad treatment from a Marxist viewpoint, Keith Burgess, *The Challenge of Labour* (1980), should be compared with the volume by Hunt above. The reality of working-class Liberalism is brought out in several local studies: D. Rubinstein, 'The ILP and the Yorkshire Miners: the Barnsley By-election 1897', *International Review of Social History*, 1 (1978); K. O. Fox, 'Labour and Merthyr's Khaki Election of 1900', *Welsh History Review*, 2 (1964–5). On the working-class and socialist press see the essays by Victoria Berridge and Deian Hopkin in G. Boyce (ed.), *Newspaper History: From the Seventeenth Century to the Present Day* (1978).

On the role of women see Patricia Hollis, *Ladies Elect* (1987); David Rubinstein, *Before the Suffragettes* (1986); and Elizabeth Roberts, *Women and Work 1840–1940* (1988).

For working-class Conservatism see Frank Parkin, 'Working Class Conservatives', *British Journal of Sociology*, 18 (1967); A. J. Lee, 'Conservatism, Traditionalism and the British Working Class', in D. E. Martin and D. Rubinstein (eds), *Ideology and the Labour Movement* (1979); Martin Pugh, *The Tories and the People 1880–1935* (1985); Patrick Joyce, *Work, Society and Politics* (1980); R. L. Greenall, 'Popular Conservatism in Salford 1868–1886', *Northern History*, 9 (1974); J. A. Garrard, 'Parties, Members and Voters after 1867: a Local Study', *Historical Journal*, 20 (1977); C. Green, 'Birmingham's Politics 1873–91', *Midland History*, 2 (1973); and R. T. McKenzie and A. Silver's, *Angels In Marble* (1968). Henry Pelling sceptically examines popular attitudes in 'British Labour and British Imperialism', *Popular Politics*; while Richard Price, *An Imperial War and the British Working Class* (1972), argues strongly, if unconvincingly, that imperialist sentiment was to be found only in higher social levels. An important contribution which argues that imperialism was a very extensive phenomenon is John MacKenzie's *Propaganda and Empire* (1984).

The lower middle class is considered, *inter alia*, in the works cited above by Nossiter, Vincent, Price and Paul Thompson. G. Crossick (ed.), *The Lower Middle Class in Britain 1870–1914* (1977) is a pioneering collection of essays. A useful study of one major group is G. L. Anderson's *Victorian Clerks* (1976). For a good analysis of the problems of local taxation see Avner Offer, *Property and Politics 1870–1914* (1981). For a general discussion see Arno Mayer's 'The Lower Middle Class as a Historical Problem', *Journal of Modern History*, 47 (1975), and for an amiable contemporary spoof, George and Weedon Grossmith, *The Diary of a Nobody* (1892, reprinted 1965).

CHAPTER 5: *The Edwardian Crises 1895–1914*

A valuable analysis of the ideas of the leading Liberal Imperialists is H. C. G. Matthew, *The Liberal Imperialists: the Ideas and Politics of a Post-Gladstonian Elite* (1973); for an attempt to estimate the strength of such sentiment in the Liberal ranks see T. Boyle, 'The Liberal Imperialists 1892–1906', *Bulletin of the Institute of Historical Research*, 52 (1979).

Michael Barker's *Gladstone and Radicalism: the Reconstruction of Liberal Policy 1885–94* (1975) attempts to find links between Gladstonianism and New Liberalism; it should be compared with the very different picture in D. A. Hamer, *John Morley: Intellectual in Politics* (1968). K. O. Morgan's *The Age of Lloyd George* (1971) provides an excellent introduction to the problems of this period; also useful on the high politics are Peter Stansky's *Ambitions and Strategies: the Struggle for the Liberal Leadership in the 1890's* (1964); and R. R. James, *Rosebery* (1963).

For a splendid, readable analysis of attitudes stimulated by the obsession with national decadence see G. R. Searle's *The Quest For National Efficiency* (1971). The themes and problems raised by Searle are considered further in several interesting volumes: Michael Balfour, *Britain and Joseph Chamberlain* (1985); I. F. Clarke, *Voices Prophesying War 1763–1984* (1966); B. Semmel, *Imperialism and Social Reform* (1960); R. Scally, *The Origins of the Lloyd George Coalition: the Politics of Social Imperialism 1900–1918* (1975); A. Gollin, *Proconsul in Politics* (1966); and a contemporary work of propaganda, Arnold White's *Efficiency and Empire* (reprinted 1973, ed. G. R. Searle).

Alan Sykes, *Tariff Reform in British Politics 1903–13* (1979) is an excellent, scholarly study that emphasizes the difficulties faced by the constructive protectionists in the party. A useful general guide to the arguments on tariffs is provided in Peter Cain, 'Political Economy in Edwardian England: the Tariff Reform Controversy', in A. O'Day (ed.), *The Edwardian Age* (1979). The internal factionalism among Conservatives after 1903 is examined in several works: R. Rempel, *Unionists Divided: Arthur Balfour, Joseph Chamberlain and the Unionist Free Traders* (1972); S. H. Zebel, 'Joseph Chamberlain and the Genesis of the Tariff Reform Campaign', *Journal of British Studies*, 7 (1967); P. Fraser, 'Unionism and Tariff Reform: the Crisis of 1906', *Historical Journal*, 5 (1962); N. Blewett, 'Free Fooders, Balfourites, Whole Hoggers: Factionalism within the Unionist Party 1906–10', *Historical Journal*, 11 (1968).

For the Edwardian crisis from the Conservative side see Matthew Fforde, *Conservatism and Collectivism, 1886–1914* (1990); Frans Coetzee, *For Party or Country: Nationalism and the Dilemmas of Popular Conservatism in Edwardian England* (1990); Robert Blake, *The Unknown Prime Minister: the Life and Times of*

Andrew Bonar Law (1955); and D. Southgate, *The Conservative Leadership* (1974). A stimulating view that puts the period in perspective is G. R. Searle's essay 'Critics of Edwardian Society: the Case of the Radical Right', in O'Day, *The Edwardian Age*. This, along with Paul Thompson's *The Edwardians: the Re-making of British Society* (1975), which uses oral evidence, and J. B. Priestley's *The Edwardians* (1970), serves as a corrective to the exaggerated and misleading impression given in George Dangerfield's *The Strange Death of Liberal England* (1935), and, to a lesser extent, in S. Hynes, *The Edwardian Turn of Mind* (1968). The suffragettes are placed in perspective in Andrew Rosen's, *Rise Up Women!* (1974), a critical study of the WSPU, and M. D. Pugh, *Women's Suffrage in Britain 1867–1928* (Historical Association pamphlet 1980). On the nature of Edwardian working-class action see Henry Pelling, 'The Labour Unrest 1911–14', in his *Popular Politics and Society in Late Victorian Britain* (1968); H. A. Clegg, *A History of Trade Unions Since 1889*, vol. II (1985); and R. Roberts, *The Classic Slum* (1971), an interesting autobiographical account of the period.

CHAPTER 6: *Edwardian Progressivism*

The key attempts to restate Liberalism around the turn of the century are: L. T. Hobhouse, *Democracy and Reaction* (1904, reprinted 1972, ed. P. F. Clarke), and *The Labour Movement* (1912, reprinted 1974, ed. P. Poirier); J. A. Hobson, *The Crisis of Liberalism* (1909, reprinted 1974, ed. P. F. Clarke); Herbert Samuel, *Liberalism* (1902); C. F. G. Masterman, *The Condition of England* (1912); J. M. Robertson, *The Meaning of Liberalism* (1912). For a popularization of the New Liberalism see Lloyd George's collection of 1909 speeches, *Better Times: Speeches on the Social Question* (1910).

Some excellent secondary works on the evolution of Liberal thinking have appeared in recent years: M. Richter, *The Politics of Conscience* (1964); M. Freeden, *The New Liberalism* (1978); P. F. Clarke, 'The Progressive Movement in England', *Transactions of the Royal Historical Society*, 24 (1974), and *Liberals and Social Democrats* (1978). For a general account that sets the New Liberalism in context see David Manning, *Liberalism* (1976); and for a useful cross-party treatment of attitudes towards the state among other aspects see Rodney Barker, *Political Ideas in Modern Britain* (1978).

There is an interesting and convincing exploration of the connections between ideas and political practice in H. V. Emy, *Liberals, Radicals and Social Politics 1892–1914* (1973), and 'The Impact of Financial Policy on English Party Politics Before 1914', *Historical Journal*, 15 (1972); also useful here is the detailed analysis in Bruce Murray's *The People's Budget 1909–10* (1980), and the short overview in J. R. Hay, *The Origins of the Liberal Welfare Reforms 1906–14* (1975). For changing views among Conservatives see Jane Ridley, 'The Unionist Social Reform Committee, 1911–14: Wets before the Deluge', *Historical Journal*, 30, 2 (1987). On the land question see Avner Offer, *Property and Politics 1870–1914* (1981); H. V. Emy, 'Lloyd George as a Social Reformer: the Land Campaign', in A. J. P. Taylor (ed.), *Lloyd George: Twelve Essays* (1971); and Roy Douglas, 'God Gave the Land to the People', in A. J. A. Morris (ed.), *Edwardian Radicalism*

1900–1914 (1974). Useful studies of three rather different adherents of the New Liberalism are: E. I. David, 'The New Liberalism of Charles Masterman', in K. D. Brown (ed.), *Essays in Anti-Labour History* (1974); S. E. Koss, *Sir John Brunner: Radical Plutocrat* (1970); and S. E. Koss, *Fleet Street Radical: A. G. Gardiner and the Daily News* (1973). See also a counter-argument by G. R. Searle, 'The Edwardian Liberal Party and Business', *English Historical Review*, 98, 386, (1983). In addition to the collections of essays on the Edwardian period edited by Morris, Brown and Taylor cited above, the following are useful and readable: K. O. Morgan, *The Age of Lloyd George* (1971), which ranges from 1890 to 1929; and Alan O'Day (ed.), *The Edwardian Age* (1979). For biographical treatment see John Grigg, *Lloyd George: the People's Champion 1902–11* (1978); Roy Jenkins, *Asquith* (1964); S. E. Koss, *Asquith* (1976); Lucy Masterman, *C. F. G. Masterman* (1939); and R. S. Churchill, *Winston S. Churchill: the Young Statesman 1901–14* (1967).

Essential on the Liberal–Labour alliance are Frank Bealey, 'The Electoral Arrangement between the Labour Representation Committee and the Liberal Party', *Journal of Modern History* (December 1956); Frank Bealey and H. Pelling, *Labour and Politics 1900–1906* (1958). The most persuasive explanation of Labour ideology in the 1900s may be found in several works by Rodney Barker: 'Socialism and Progressivism in the Political Thought of Ramsay MacDonald', in Morris, *Edwardian Radicalism*; and *Education and Politics 1900–51* (1972). For a hostile critique see Ralph Miliband's *Parliamentary Socialism* (1961); and for a valuable examination of the role of the Fabians, A. M. McBriar, *Fabian Socialism and English Politics 1884–1918* (1966). K. D. Brown's *Labour and Unemployment 1900–14* (1971) demonstrates the limitations on the parliamentary party's ability to influence government policy. There is a recent short account of the party in Roger Moore's *The Emergence of the Labour Party 1880–1924* (1978). Although there are still, unavoidably, gaps in Labour biography several excellent volumes appeared in the 1970s. David Marquand's *Ramsay MacDonald* (1977) puts its subject in the Progressive tradition and demonstrates his consistency of thought and objectives. Two admirable works on Hardie tend to emphasize his Lib–Lab traditions: K. O. Morgan, *Keir Hardie: Radical and Socialist* (1975); and I. S. McLean, *Keir Hardie* (1975). Fred Reid in *James Keir Hardie* (1978) does argue for a more distinctively socialist ideology for his subject.

For some interesting analysis of popular reactions to social reform see: Pat Thane, 'The Working Class and State Welfare in Britain, 1880–1914', *Historical Journal*, 27, 4 (1984); Sheila Blackburn, 'Working-Class Attitudes to Social Reform': Black Country Chainmakers and Anti-Sweating Legislation, 1880–1930, *International Review of Social History*, 33, (1988); and Henry Pelling, 'The Working Class and the Origins of the Welfare State', in *Popular Politics and Society in Late Victorian Britain* (1968).

CHAPTER 7: *The Electoral Struggle 1906–1914*

The most original and compelling interpretation of pre-1914 electoral politics is P. F. Clarke's *Lancashire and the New Liberalism* (1971), which argues for the adaptation of Liberalism to a working-class electorate and for the arrival of class-based politics before rather than after the First World War. Several other published studies of the regions are available though many more exist as postgraduate theses: Paul Thompson's *Socialists, Liberals and Labour: the Struggle for London 1885–1914* (1967) reaches conclusions quite inconsistent, in my view, with the evidence in the book which tends to confirm Clarke's line of argument; A. W. Purdue, 'Arthur Henderson and Liberal, Liberal–Labour and Labour Politics in North-East England 1892–1903', *Northern History*, 11 (1975); K. O. Morgan, 'The New Liberalism and the Challenge of Labour: the Welsh Experience 1885–1929', *Welsh History Review*, 6 (1973); M. D. Pugh, 'Yorkshire and the New Liberalism?' *Journal of Modern History*, 50 (1978). There are Nuffield-type studies of the general elections of 1906 in A. K. Russell's *Liberal Landslide* (1973); and of 1910 in Neal Blewett's invaluable *The Peers, the Parties and the People* (1972), whose findings tend to corroborate Clarke's case. The most important and original recent contribution to the debate is Duncan Tanner's *Political Change and the Labour Party 1900–1918* (1990); this modifies Clarke's thesis in some respects, but its overall effect is to strengthen his interpretation by means of a critical analysis of the franchise and of Labour's strength at the grass roots.

R. I. McKibbin's *The Evolution of the Labour Party 1910–24* (1974) accepts the ideological cohesion of Labour and Liberalism but argues lucidly that a politicized working class could not be contained within the alliance; Henry Pelling also argues for the long-term importance of social changes in his essay 'Labour and the Downfall of Liberalism', in *Popular Politics and Society in Late Victorian Britain* (1968); similarly Roy Gregory's *The Miners and British Politics 1906–14* (1968) argues for a collapse of the politics of the pact.

A number of writers have examined the problems encountered by the electoral pact strategy particularly after 1910: M. Petter, 'The Progressive Alliance', *History*, 58 (1973); R. I. McKibbin, 'James Ramsay MacDonald and the Problem of the Independence of the Labour Party 1910–14', *Journal of Modern History*, 42 (1970); Roy Douglas, 'Labour in Decline', in K. D. Brown (ed.), *Essays in Anti-Labour History* (1974); M. D. Pugh, *Electoral Reform in War and Peace 1906–18* (1978), and 'New Light on Edwardian Voters: the Model Elections of 1906–12', *Bulletin of the Institute of Historical Research*, 51 (1978). Finally a convincing case for Liberal vitality on the eve of war is made by P. F. Clarke from an analysis of the 1911–14 by-elections in 'The Electoral Position of the Liberal and Labour Parties 1910–14', *English Historical Review*, 90 (1975).

An important attack on the new orthodoxy has come from H. C. G. Matthew, R. I. McKibbin and J. A. Kay, 'The Franchise Factor in the Rise of the Labour Party', *English Historical Review*, 91 (1976); a similar line is pursued in C. Chamberlain, 'The Growth of Support for the Labour Party in Britain', *British Journal of Sociology*, 24 (1973). Another area of debate is opening up on the municipal elections front: C. Cook, 'Labour and the Downfall of the Liberal Party 1906–14', in A. Sked and C. Cook (eds), *Crisis and Controversy: Essays in Honour of A. J. P. Taylor* (1976). Several authors have argued that New Liberalism was not viable and was in decline but support this by making rather selective use of evidence: K. Laybourn and J. Reynolds, *Liberalism and the Rise of*

Labour 1890–1918 (1984); George Bernstein, *Liberalism and Liberal Politics in Edwardian England* (1986).

CHAPTER 8: *The Impact of the Great War on British Politics*

Zara Steiner's *Britain and the Origins of the First World War* (1977) is a superb synthesis, treating domestic political aspects as well as diplomatic and military; detailed essays on foreign policy are to be found in F. H. Hinsley (ed.), *British Foreign Policy under Sir Edward Grey* (1977); for military preparations and thinking see John Gooch's *The Plans of War* (1974), and the short, masterly study by Michael Howard, *The Continental Commitment* (1972). For comprehensive treatment of the war see Trevor Wilson, *The Myriad Faces of War* (1986); and John Bourne, *Britain and the Great War 1914–18* (1989).

Useful analysis of the weakness of radical criticism of foreign and defence policy may be found in: Howard Weinroth, 'The British Radicals and the Balance of Power 1902–14', *Historical Journal*, 13 (1970), and 'Left-wing Opposition to Naval Armaments in Britain before 1914', *Journal of Contemporary History*, 6 (1971); M. Swartz, 'A Study in Futility: the British Radicals at the Outbreak of the First World War', in A. J. A. Morris (ed.), *Edwardian Radicalism* (1974); A. J. A. Morris, *Radicalism Against War 1906–14* (1972), and 'Haldane's Army Reforms 1906–08: the Deception of the Radicals', *History*, 56, 189 (1971).

Cameron Hazelhurst's *Politicians at War* (1971) provides a readable and detailed examination of the Cabinet's decision for war and the high politics of the first nine months; also useful is John Turner, *British Politics and the Great War* (1992); E. I. David (ed.), *Inside Asquith's Cabinet: From the Diaries of Sir Charles Hobhouse* (1977). The strains and stresses on the Liberals are fully exposed in Trevor Wilson (ed.), *The Political Diaries of C. P. Scott 1911–28* (1970); B. McGill, 'Asquith's Predicament 1914–18', *Journal of Modern History*, 39 (1967); and M. Howard, *War and the Liberal Conscience* (1978). Trevor Wilson's fine, readable analysis, *The Downfall of the Liberal Party 1914–35* (1966), tends to place the blame on Lloyd George; it sees the 1915 Coalition in terms of the shells crisis and party warfare; S. E. Koss, *Lord Haldane: Scapegoat for Liberalism* (1969), finds an improbable explanation in a conspiracy; Lord Beaverbrook's *Politicians and the War* (1928) was for long an influential account because of the author's supposedly close involvement in the events; M. D. Pugh, 'Asquith, Bonar Law and the First Coalition', *Historical Journal*, 17 (1974), interprets the crisis as collusion between Law and Asquith at the expense of their parties; and David French, 'The Military Background to the Shell Crisis of May 1915', *Journal of Strategic Studies*, 2 (1979), demonstrates the vulnerability of politicians to miscalculations by the generals. Lord Hankey's *The Supreme Command 1914–18* (1961) is perceptive about the strengths and weaknesses of both Asquith and Lloyd George as wartime premiers. The nature of Liberal disintegration is analysed in Michael Hart, 'The Liberals, the War and the Franchise', *English Historical Review*, 97 (1982); E. I. David, 'The Liberal Party Divided 1916–18', *Historical Journal*, 13 (1970); J. M. McEwen, 'The Liberal Party and the Irish Question during the First World War', *Journal of British*

Studies, 12 (1972); and J. Gooch, 'The Maurice Debate', *Journal of Contemporary History*, 3 (1968); Martin Pugh, 'The Great War and the Decline of the Liberal Party', *History Sixth*, 5 (1989); and G. L. Bernstein, 'Yorkshire Liberalism during the First World War', *Historical Journal*, 32 (1989).

A. J. P. Taylor provides a lively overview in 'Politics in the First World War', and 'Lloyd George: Rise and Fall', in *Politics in Wartime* (1964). For accounts of the December 1916 crisis sympathetic to Lloyd George see Peter Lowe, 'The Rise to the Premiership', in A. J. P. Taylor (ed.), *Lloyd George: Twelve Essays* (1971); P. Rowland, *Lloyd George* (1975); and K. O. Morgan, *Lloyd George* (1974). A. J. P. Taylor's *Beaverbrook* (1972) throws light on Conservative motivation as does Austen Chamberlain, *Down the Years* (1935). Roy Jenkins, *Asquith* (1964) and S. E. Koss, *Asquith* (1976) are more hostile. An excellent analysis of the new coalition government is K. O. Morgan's 'Lloyd George's Premiership', *Historical Journal*, 13 (1970). Other aspects are examined in J. Turner, *Lloyd George's Secretariat (1980)*; P. A. Lockwood, 'Milner's Entry into the War Cabinet', *Historical Journal*, 7 (1964); J. F. Naylor, 'The Establishment of the Cabinet Secretariat', *Historical Journal*, 14 (1971); and J. Ehrman, 'Lloyd George and Churchill as War Leaders', *Transactions of the Royal Historical Society*, 11 (1961). On relations with the Conservatives, Robert Blake's *The Unknown Prime Minister* (1955) is the best volume. For an examination of how the Conservatives were led via franchise reform to the 1918 election see M. D. Pugh, *Electoral Reform in War and Peace 1906–18* (1978); D. Close, 'The Collapse of Resistance to Democracy: Conservatives, Adult Suffrage and Second Chamber Reform 1911–28', *Historical Journal*, 20 (1977); and D. Rolfe, 'Origins of Mr. Speaker's Conference during the First World War', *History*, 64 (1979).

M. Swartz, *The Union of Democratic Control in British Politics during the First World War* (1971), is good on the shifting allegiances of Liberal and Labour opponents of the war; see also D. Marquand's *Ramsay MacDonald* (1977) and C. Howard's 'MacDonald, Henderson and the Labour Party in 1914', *Historical Journal*, 20 (1977). Essential reading on Labour's wartime activity is Royden Harrison, 'The War Emergency Workers National Committee', in A. Briggs and J. Saville (eds), *Essays in Labour History 1886–1924* (1971); for the local level see Julia Bush, *Behind the Lines: East London Labour 1914–19* (1984); and A. Clinton's 'Trades Councils during the First World War', *International Review of Social History*, 15 (1970); and for a typically pragmatic trade union leader see A. Bullock, *The Life and Times of Ernest Bevin*, vol. 1 (1960). An important article on Labour's turning point is J. M. Winter, 'Arthur Henderson, the Russian Revolution and the Reconstruction of the Labour Party', *Historical Journal*, 15 (1972); the same author's *Socialism and the Challenge of War* (1974) analyses the growing role played by the Webbs and other middle-class socialists in the party at this time. The best treatment of the organizational breakthrough is R. I. McKibbin's indispensable *The Evolution of the Labour Party 1910–24* (1974).

CHAPTER 9: *A Mass Electorate at War*

There is an interesting examination of pre-war attitudes in I. F. Clarke, *Voices Prophesying War 1763–1984* (1966); and a credible explanation for contradictory attitudes towards the army in Anne Summers, 'Militarism in Britain Before the Great War', *History Workshop Journal*, 2 (1976). C. Haste's, *Keep the Home Fires Burning* (1977) is a general survey of domestic propaganda in wartime. Specialist studies are: M. L. Sanders, 'Wellington House and British Propaganda during the First World War', *Historical Journal*, 18 (1975); D. G. Wright, 'The Great War, Government Propaganda and English Men of Letters', *Literature and History*, 7 (1978); D. Hopkin, 'Domestic Censorship in the First World War', *Journal of Contemporary History*, 5 (1970); C. Lovelace, 'British Press Censorship during the First World War', in G. Boyce (ed.), *Newspaper History* (1978); and P. Knightley, *The First Casualty* (1978).

K. G. Robbins analyses the whole range of anti-war activity in *The Abolition of War* (1976); see also M. Swartz, *The Union of Democratic Control in British Politics during the First World War* (1971), and H. Hanak, 'The Union of Democratic Control', *Bulletin of the Institute of Historical Research*, 36 (1963). An excellent, dispassionate analysis of conscientious objection is John Rae, *Conscience and Politics* (1971). Also helpful on the anti-war forces are: A. Marwick, *Clifford Allen: the Open Conspirator* (1964); S. E. Koss, *Nonconformity in Modern British Politics* (1975); A. J. A. Morris, *Charles Trevelyan* (1977); and A. J. P. Taylor, *The Trouble Makers* (1957).

J. M. Winter argues convincingly for improving wartime living standards in *The Great War and the British People* (1985); see also A. Marwick, *The Deluge* (1965); R. Mitchison, *British Population Growth since 1860* (1977); and Robert Roberts, *The Classic Slum* (1971). On radical tendencies among trade unions see James Hinton, *The First Shop Stewards Movement* (1973), and S. R. White, 'The Leeds Soviet', *International Review of Social History*, 19 (1974); the narrow base of radicalism is well brought out by I. S. McLean, 'Red Clydeside 1915–19', in J. Stevenson and R. Quinault (eds), *Popular Protest and Public Order* (1974), and for a union leader hostile to the shop stewards movement see A. Bullock, *The Life and Times of Ernest Bevin*, vol. 1 (1960). C. Wrigley, *Lloyd George and the British Labour Movement* (1976) provides a detailed account of union–government relations.

On the response of men to the call for volunteers see R. Douglas, 'Voluntary Enlistment in the First World War', *Journal of Modern History*, 42 (1970); and the superb account by Martin Middlebrook, *The First Day on the Somme* (1971). In addition to the latter there are some stimulating recent examinations of battle experience and the attitudes of the men: John Keegan, *The Face of Battle* (1976); and Denis Winter, *Death's Men: Soldiers of the Great War* (1978). Evidence of discontent in the army and its political significance is analysed in a valuable article by D. Englander and J. Osborne, 'Jack, Tommy and Henry Dubb: the Armed Forces and the Working Class', *Historical Journal*, 21 (1978); see also G. Dallas and D. Gil, 'The Mutiny at Etaples Base in 1917', *Past and Present*, 69 (1975); and a general account of trench life in John Ellis, *Eye Deep in Hell* (1976).

On the Coupon Election there are some useful publications on the circumstances in which it was fought: R. Douglas, 'The Background to the Coupon Election Arrangements', *English Historical Review*, 86 (1971); T. Wilson, *The Downfall of the Liberal Party 1914–35* (1966), and 'The Coupon and the British

General Election of 1918', *Journal of Modern History*, 36 (1964); B. McGill, 'Lloyd George's Timing of the 1918 Election', *Journal of British Studies*, 14 (1974); M. D. Pugh, *Electoral Reform in War and Peace 1906–18* (1978). For analysis of the outcome of the election see: Duncan Tanner, *Political Change and the Labour Party* (1990); John Turner, 'The Labour Vote and the Franchise after 1918' in P. R. Denley and D. Hopkin (eds), *History and Computing* (1987); Michael Hart, 'The Liberals, the War and the Franchise', *English Historical Review*, 97 (1982); and R. I. McKibbin, *The Evolution of the Labour Party 1910–1924* (1974). See also guide to further reading for chapter 8.

CHAPTER 10: *Party, Ideology and the State in the Great War*

There are useful general accounts of the questions raised in this chapter in James Cronin, *The Politics of State Expansion: War, State and Society in the Twentieth Century* (1991); S. Pollard, *The Development of the British Economy 1914–67* (1962); and C. L. Mowat, *Britain between the Wars 1918–40* (1955). E. M. H. Lloyd's *Experiments in State Control at the War Office and the Ministry of Food* (1924) expresses a contemporary civil servant's enthusiasm for controls and sees political ideology as the obstacle; more recent secondary works in a similar vein are A. Marwick, *The Deluge* (1965), and A. J. P. Taylor, *English History 1914–45* (1965). An essential corrective to all this for the early phase of the war is David French's *British Economic and Strategic Planning 1905–15* (1982). For the later stages the fragility of Lloyd George's system is well analysed in Rodney Lowe, 'The Erosion of State Intervention in Britain 1917–24', *Economic History Review*, 31 (1978); see also R. H. Tawney, 'The Abolition of Economic Controls 1918–21', *Economic History Review*, 13 (1943); Keith Grieves, *Sir Eric Geddes* (1989); K. Burke (ed.), *War and the State: the Transformation of British Government 1914–19* (1982); and P. K. Cline, 'Eric Geddes and the Experiment with Businessmen in Government 1915–22', in K. D. Brown (ed.), *Essays in Anti-Labour History* (1974).

The optimistic view of the impact of war on social policy is lucidly stated by Richard Titmuss in *Essays on the Welfare State* (1958) and in the controversial study by S. Andreski, *Military Organisation and Society* (1954). This view has never recovered from the criticism offered in P. Abrams, 'The Failure of Social Reform 1918–20', *Past and Present*, 24 (1963). A useful summary is A. Marwick, 'The Impact of the First World War on British Society', *Journal of Contemporary History*, 3 (1968). P. B. Johnston's *Land Fit for Heroes* (1968) is a detailed examination of the reconstruction ideology, and P. F. Clarke's *Liberals and Social Democrats* (1979) throws valuable light on the alienation of Progressives from Lloyd George. Against a strong tide K. O. Morgan, *Consensus and Disunity: the Lloyd George Coalition 1918–22* (1979) attempts to defend the liberal, reforming credentials of its subject.

The general volumes on the Conservative Party by Blake, Beer, Butler, Southgate and Ramsden tend to overlook either the war or ideas. One has to turn to more specialist studies. One essay that tends to ascribe to the war much that existed already is J. O. Stubbs, 'The Impact of the Great War on the

Conservative Party', in G. Peele and C. Cook (eds), *The Politics of Reappraisal* (1975). The role of business pressure is examined in J. Turner, 'The British Commonwealth Union and the General Election of 1918', *English Historical Review*, 93 (1978); and for changes in party personnel see the useful article by J. M. McEwen, 'The Coupon Election of 1918 and Unionist Members of Parliament', *Journal of Modern History*, 34 (1962). R. Scally, *Origins of the Lloyd George Coalition: the Politics of Social Imperialism* (1975), probably exaggerates the coherence of the phenomenon but is a valuable treatment of right-wing interventionist elements within the party and on its peripheries. The ideas of one right-wing breakaway from the Conservatives are considered in D. Rubinstein, 'Henry Page-Croft and the National Party 1917–22', *Journal of Contemporary History*, 9 (1974).

An excellent analysis of wartime socialism especially Webbian is J. M. Winter's *Socialism and the Challenge of War* (1974); on the decline of the ILP see A. Marwick, 'The ILP in the Nineteen Twenties', *Bulletin of the Institute of Historical Research*, 35 (1962), and R. E. Dowse, *Left in the Centre* (1966). The most cogent and forceful statement of the view that Clause IV was without significance is in R. I. McKibbin's *The Evolution of the Labour Party 1910–24* (1974). A persuasive and credible explanation of the positive value of the socialist commitment is Rodney Barker's 'Political Myth: Ramsay MacDonald and the Labour Party', *History*, 61 (1976). The elements of continuity between pre- and post-war Labour politics are well brought out in R. I. McKibbin, 'Arthur Henderson as Labour Leader', *International Review of Social History*, 23 (1978). For the motives behind Liberal changes of allegiance see the invaluable book by C. A. Cline, *Recruits to Labour* (1963); also on this theme are: C. P. Trevelyan, *From Liberalism to Labour* (1921); A. J. A. Morris, *Charles Trevelyan* (1977); and Jane and Kenneth Morgan, *Portrait of a Progressive: the Political Career of Viscount Addison* (1980).

CHAPTER 11: *The Elevation of Labour and the Restoration of Party Politics 1918–1924*

Maurice Cowling's *The Impact of Labour 1920–24* (1971) analyses in detail politicians' motivations and strategies after the war. The Conservatives' detachment from Lloyd George is well brought out in R. Blake, *The Unknown Prime Minister* (1955) and M. Kinnear, *The Fall of Lloyd George* (1973). Also useful on the Conservatives are R. Blake, *The Conservative Party from Peel to Churchill* (1970); Lord Butler (ed.), *The Conservatives* (1977); D. Southgate (ed.), *The Conservative Leadership 1832–1932* (1974); J. Ramsden, *The Age of Balfour and Baldwin 1902–40* (1978); K. Middlemas and J. Barnes, *Baldwin* (1969).

The collapse of the Coalition is examined sympathetically from the Liberal side in K. O. Morgan, *Consensus and Disunity: the Lloyd George Coalition Government 1918–22* (1979). Also valuable is the same author's essay 'Lloyd George's Stage Army: the Coalition Liberals', in A. J. P. Taylor (ed.), *Lloyd George: Twelve Essays* (1974). For the seamier side see G. R. Searle, *Corruption in British Politics 1895–1930* (1987). John Campbell's *Lloyd George: The Goat in the*

Wilderness (1977) is a very readable account of his post-war career, sympathetic to its subject. More 'Asquithian' versions are Trevor Wilson, *The Downfall of the Liberal Party 1914–35* (1966); R. Douglas, *The History of the Liberal Party 1895–1970* (1971); Roy Jenkins, *Asquith* (1964); and S. E. Koss, *Asquith* (1976). On Labour strategy see the valuable biographies by David Marquand, *Ramsay MacDonald* (1977); and Chris Wrigley, *Arthur Henderson* (1990); a hostile view of Labour's search for respectability within the system is Ralph Miliband's *Parliamentary Socialism* (1961); for an interesting study of direct action in the Labour movement see L. J. MacFarlane's 'Hands Off Russia: British Labour and the Russo-Polish War 1920', *Past and Present*, 38 (1967). Also useful are C. L. Mowat, 'Ramsay MacDonald and the Labour Party' in A. Briggs and John Saville, *Essays in Labour History 1886–1923* (1971); G. D. H. Cole's *A History of the Labour Party from 1914* (1948); R. Lyman, *The First Labour Government* (1957); C. Cook and J. Ramsden (eds), *By-Elections in British Politics* (1975).

CHAPTER 12: *Origins of the Conservative Electoral Hegemony 1918–1931*

David Butler's *The Electoral System in Britain 1918–51* (1953) provides a good introduction to the subject. There is a valuable discussion of the effects of different voting systems in Enid Lakeman, *Voting in Democracies* (1955), reprinted as *How Democracies Vote* (1959). A sign of the growing academic interest in and concern about the British system is S. E. Finer (ed.), *Adversary Politics and Electoral Reform* (1975). On the emergence of the post-1918 constituency pattern and attempted modifications of the electoral system see M. D. Pugh, *Electoral Reform in War and Peace 1906–18* (1978), and 'Political Parties and the Campaign for Proportional Representation 1905–14', *Parliamentary Affairs*, 33 (1980).

Students will find general elections brought to life in Michael Kinnear's *The British Voter: an Atlas and Survey since 1885* (1969). For evidence on Conservative organization centrally and locally John Ramsden, *The Age of Balfour and Baldwin 1902–40* (1978) is essential reading. For Labour there is a more interpretative treatment which also provides important evidence in R. I. McKibbin, *The Evolution of the Labour Party 1910–24* (1974); the evidence on party organization should be considered in conjunction with the different assumptions in the important article by H. C. G. Matthew, R. I. McKibbin and J. A. Kay, 'The Franchise Factor in the Rise of the Labour Party', *English Historical Review*, 91 (1976). A useful corrective on Labour Party membership and related themes is I. S. McLean, 'Party Organisation', in C. Cook and I. Taylor (eds), *The Labour Party* (1980). Also interesting because of its subject's role as an organizer is B. Donoughue and G. W. Jones, *Herbert Morrison: Portrait of a Politician* (1973).

A cogent and original analysis of politics in Preston which, unusually, includes women is Michael Savage, *The Dynamics of Working-Class Politics* (1987). Various aspects of women's role are discussed in Martin Pugh, *Women and the Women's Movement in Britain 1914–1959* (1992), and 'Women, Food and Politics 1880–1930', *History Today*, 41, (March 1991); Brian Harrison, *Prudent Revolutionaries: Portraits of British Feminists between the Wars* (1987), and 'Women in a Men's House: the Women MP's 1919–45', *Historical Journal*, 29, 3 (1986);

and J. Rasmussen, 'Women in Labour: the Flapper Vote and Party System Transformation in Britain', *Electoral Studies*, 3, 1 (1984).

On the realignment of voters during the twentieth century David Butler and Donald Stokes, *Political Change in Britain* (1969) is fascinating and essential, though flawed by the assumption that class-based politics must have arisen *after* the First World War. C. Cook's *The Age of Alignment* (1975) charts party fortunes in the general elections of the 1920s, and the same author examines the municipal pattern in 'Liberals, Labour and Local Elections', in C. Cook and G. Peele (eds), *The Politics of Reappraisal* (1975). Robert Moore's *Pitmen, Preachers and Politics* (1974) is an illuminating study of shifting allegiance among Methodist working men in Durham; the declining role of the free churches in national politics is examined in S. E. Koss, *Nonconformity in Modern British Politics* (1975). W. G. Runciman's *Relative Deprivation and Social Justice* (1966) offers, *inter alia*, an original interpretation of the defensive nature of working-class politics in the inter-war years. On 1931 see Andrew Thorpe, *The British General Election of 1931* (1991); and D. H. Close, 'The Realignment of the British Electorate in 1931', *History*, 67, 221 (1982). Also useful on changing party fortunes are C. Cook and J. Ramsden (eds), *By-Elections in British Politics* (1973); Philip Williamson, 'Safety First; Baldwin, the Conservative Party and the 1929 General Election', *Historical Journal*, 25, 2 (1982); and Trevor Wilson, *The Downfall of the Liberal Party 1914–35* (1966).

CHAPTER 13: *The Eclipse of the Extremes 1931–1939*

Among the many publications on inter-war economic problems and policies the following are particularly useful: P. Fearon, *The Origins and Nature of the Great Slump 1929–32* (1979); D. Winch, *Economics and Policy: an Historical Study* (1969); Peter Clarke, *The Keynesian Revolution in the Making, 1924–1936* (1988); Rodney Lowe, *Adjusting to Democracy: the Role of the Ministry of Labour in British Politics 1916–1939* (1986); James Cronin, *The Politics of State Expansion: War, State and Society in the Twentieth Century* (1991); K. J. Hancock, 'The Reduction of Unemployment as a Problem of Public Policy 1920–29', *Economic History Review*, 15 (1962–3); and C. L. Mowat, *Britain between the Wars 1918–40* (1955).

A credible account of the evolution of Labour's policy and programme during the twentieth century is David Howell's *British Social Democracy* (1976). Two valuable studies of attitudes to economic questions by Adrian Oldfield are 'The Independent Labour Party and Planning 1920–26', *International Review of Social History*, 21 (1976), and 'The Labour Party and Planning – 1934 or 1918?' *Bulletin of the Society for the Study of Labour History*, 25 (1972). The reluctant acceptance of Keynesianism is analysed in Barbara Malament's important article, 'British Labour and Roosevelt's New Deal: the Response of the Left and the Unions', *Journal of British Studies*, (Spring 1978); and in Henry Pelling, *America and the British Left* (1956). An excellent recent interpretation of the 1931 crisis which argues that there were economic and political alternatives available to the MacDonald government during 1929–31 is Robert Skidelsky's *Politicians and the Slump* (1967); there is a rebuttal, on the grounds that Keynesianism did not succeed in countries where it was tried, in R. I. McKibbin, 'The Economic Policy of the Second Labour Government', *Past and Present*, 36 (1975). Also useful are: B. Donoughue and G. W. Jones, *Herbert Morrison: Portrait of a Politician* (1973); David Marquand, *Ramsay MacDonald* (1977); A. Bullock, *The Life and Times of Ernest Bevin* (1960); R. Bassett, *1931: Political Crisis* (1958); and S. Beer, *Modern British Politics* (1965).

On the background to 1931 from the Tory side see Stuart Ball, *Baldwin and the Conservative Party: the Crisis of 1929–31* (1988); and Philip Williamson, 'A "Bankers' Ramp"? Financiers and the British Political Crisis of August 1931', *English Historical Review*, 99 (1984). A comprehensive account of the emergence of the National Government from a high politics perspective is Philip Williamson's *National Crisis and National Government* (1992). A perceptive treatment of the Conservative leaders in the National Government is to be found in David Dilks' section in Lord Butler (ed.), *The Conservatives* (1977); see also David Butler (ed.), *Coalitions in British Politics* (1978). Baldwin receives sympathetic handling in John Ramsden, *The Age of Balfour and Baldwin 1902–40* (1979), and in the monumentally tedious and pedestrian biography by K. Middlemas and J. Barnes, *Baldwin: a Biography* (1969). J. A. Cross, *Sir Samuel Hoare* (1977) throws useful light on an important liberal Conservative. The boundaries between liberal and right-wing Toryism are also drawn in Gillian Peele's essay on India in G. Peele and C. Cook (eds), *The Politics of Reappraisal* (1975); A. Marwick, 'Middle Opinion in the Thirties: Planning, Progress and Political Agreement', *English Historical Review*, 79 (1965); and R. R. James, *Churchill: a Study in Failure 1900–39* (1970). On the fascist challenge Robert Skidelsky's sympathetic biography *Oswald Mosley* (1975) interprets its subject as an authoritarian modernizer. Also useful on this aspect are: R. Benewick, *The Fascist Movement in Britain* (1972); K. Lunn and R. C. Thurlow's collection of essays, *British Fascism* (1980); Richard Thurlow, *Fascism in Britain* (1987); Tony Kushner and K. Lunn (eds), *The Politics of Marginality* (1990); and C. Cook and J. Stevenson, *The Slump: Society and Politics in the Depression* (1977).

A number of recent publications explore the reasons for the weakness of the left in the 1930s: Ben Pimlott, *Labour and the Left in the 1930s* (1977); and James Jupp, *The British Radical Left 1931–41* (1978); John Stevenson emphasizes the absence of radical inclinations among the unemployed in two essays, 'Myth and Reality: Britain in the 1930's', in A. Sked and C. Cook (eds), *Crisis and Controversy* (1976), and 'The Politics of Violence', in G. Peele and C. Cook (eds), *The Politics of Reappraisal* (1975); the erosion of the pacifist left's influence on Labour foreign policy is explained in John Naylor's *Labour's International Policy* (1969), and in H. R. Winkler, 'The Emergence of a Labour Foreign Policy in Great Britain 1918–29', *Journal of Modern History*, 28 (1956).

The traditional, Baldwinian view of public opinion and rearmament is exploded in C. T. Stannage's, 'The East Fulham By-Election', *Historical Journal*, 14 (1971). A balanced and critical study of one manifestation of opinion is Martin Ceadel's, 'The First British Referendum: the Peace Ballot 1934–35', *English Historical Review*, 95 (1980): for a more wide-ranging study see the same author's *Pacifism in Britain 1914–45* (1980). Other works which examine the political calculations behind rearmament are: M. Cowling, *The Impact of Hitler*

(1975); F. Coughlan, 'Armaments, Economic Policy and Appeasement: the Background to British Foreign Policy 1931–37', *History*, 57 (1972); J. P. D. Dunbabin, 'British Rearmament in the 1930's: a Chronology and Review', *Historical Journal*, 17 (1975). The essential work on changing political allegiance in the mid-1930s is C. T. Stannage, 'The General Election of 1935' (Cambridge Ph.D. thesis, 1973), now published as *Baldwin Thwarts the Opposition* (1980). Other useful studies of opinion in the last years of peace are: Nicholas Pronay's two articles on 'British Newsreels in the 1930's', *History*, 56 (1971) and 57 (1972); T. J. Hollins, 'The Conservative Party and Film Propaganda between the Wars', *English Historical Review*, 96 (1981); I. S. McLean, 'Oxford and Bridgewater', in C. Cook and J. Ramsden (eds), *By-Elections in British Politics* (1975); R. Eatwell, 'Munich, Public Opinion and the Popular Front', *Journal of Contemporary History*, 6 (1971).

Index

Abraham, William, 29
Addison, Dr Christopher, 119, 150, 171, 172, 175, 178, 194, 208–9, 220; joins Labour, 214, 215–16
Afghanistan, 33, 35
agents, 16, 99, 244, 247
Agricultural Labourers' Union, 11, 75
Aitken, Sir Max, 170, 184, 208
Akers-Douglas, Aretas, 59
Alden, Percy, 118–19, 215
alien immigration, 51, 67, 86–8
Allendale, Lord, 21
allotments acts (1887, 1890), 64
American Civil War, 28
Amery, L. S., 108, 222
Anderson, W. C., 154, 177
Anglicans, 70–1, 97, 258
appeasement, 280–1, 287–8
Arch, Joseph, 11, 29, 75, 86
Argyll, Duke of, 33, 38
Armstrong, Lord, 21
Arnold, Sydney, 213, 214
Artisans Dwellings Act, 54, 74, 88
Askwith, Sir George, 111
Asquith, H. H., 24, 97, 102, 115, 176, 197, 231–4, 255; as Liberal Imperialist, 104–5, and New Liberalism, 115, 120, 135; as prime minister, 110, 156–7, 161–71, 201–3
Astor, Lady Nancy, 249
Atholl, Duchess of, 287
Attlee, Clement, 278, 279, 281, 286, 289, 290–1

Baldwin, Oliver, 208, 270
Baldwin, Stanley, 208, 210, 223, 225–6, 248; as prime minister, 225–7, 248, 255–6, 271, 291; attitude to Labour, 233, 235, 248, 255–6, 271; and National Governments, 270–5, 287
Balfour, A. J., 20, 49, 55, 57, 58, 63, 65, 86, 105, 106, 108, 154, 166, 175, 225
ballot, 11–12, 31, 73

Barnes, George, 154, 179, 208
Beaverbrook, see Aitken, Sir Max
Bedford, Duke of, 38
Bell, Richard, 134
Bennett, Arnold, 165
Bevan, Aneurin, 277, 280
Beveridge, William, 115, 264, 289, 291
Bevin, Ernest, 255, 278, 281, 283, 285, 289
Birkenhead, see Smith, F. E.
Birrell, Augustine, 22
Blatchford, Robert, 79
Boer War, see South African War
Bondfield, Margaret, 83, 255
Booth, Charles, 103, 114
Bottomley, Horatio, 192, 222
Bowerman, C. W., 177
Bradlaugh, Charles, 25, 29, 35
Bramley, Fred, 177
Bridgeman, W. C., 222
Bright, John, 24, 28, 29
Broadhurst, Henry, 81
British Broadcasting Company, 272, 286
British Commonwealth Union, 206
British Expeditionary Force, 161–2, 164, 201
British Socialist Party, 147, 212
British Union of Fascists, 275–8
British Workers League, 173
Brittain, Vera, 281
Brunner, Sir John, 13, 14, 100, 119, 150
Bryce, James, 28, 98, 102, 165, 187
Bulgarian atrocities, 3–5, 26, 33, 34
Burnham, Lord, 21
Burns, John, 134, 135, 163
Burt, Thomas, 29, 78, 134
Butler, R. A., 272, 291
Buxton, Noel, 214, 231
Buxton, Sydney, 119, 150

Cadbury, George, 100, 119
Campbell, J. R., 233–4
Campbell-Bannerman, Sir Henry, 102, 104–5, 120, 122

Carson, Sir Edward, 170–1, 172, 205, 208
Cavendish, Richard, 124
Chamberlain, Austen, 110, 129–30, 154, 166, 209, 210, 223–4, 225, 271
Chamberlain, Joseph: and the Liberal Party, 9, 18, 24, 26, 33–6, 38, 39–40, 74; the Unauthorised Programme, 35, 70; and the Conservative Party, 61, 65, 66–7, 102, 107–8; see also tariff reform
Chamberlain, Neville, 233, 271, 283, 284, 285
Champion, H. H., 79
Chanak crisis, 221
Channing, Francis, 119
Chelmsford, Lord, 231
'Chinese Slavery', 120
Church Burials Act (1880), 71
Churchill, Lord Randolph, 18, 49, 51–2, 58, 61
Churchill, Winston, 84, 120, 124, 133, 150, 152, 273–5, 285, 289; in First World War, 164, 167, 169, 182, 187; rejoins Conservatives, 220, 228, 271
Clarion, 79
Clyde Workers Committee, 183
Clynes, J. R., 198, 220, 230, 278
Cockerton Judgement, 65
Cole, G. D. H., 177, 211, 279
Coleman, J. J., 13
Committee of Imperial Defence, 107
Communist Party, 79, 280, 286
Conservative Central Office, 50, 174
Conservative Party, 19–20, 44–50, 53–4, 107–10, 152–3; working-class Conservatives, 17, 50, 83–90, 142; and the 1909 budget, 124–6; and the First World War, 165–7, 169–71, 173–5, 194–9, 204–10; inter-war organization, 236–44; and women, 249–50; and the National Governments, 269–70, 274–5; and the British Union of Fascists, 276–7; see also National Union of Conservative and Constitutional Associations, Primrose League, tariff reform
Contagious Diseases Acts, 27
Cooper, Duff, 274
Corrupt and Illegal Practices (Prevention) Act (1883), 12, 51
county councils, 64–5
'Coupon Election', 175–6, 193–9, 254
Courtney, Leonard, 47
Craig, Captain James, 110
Cranbrook, see Gathorne-Hardy, G.
Cremer, Randall, 29
Cripps, C. A., 231
Cripps, Sir Stafford, 208, 280, 283, 285, 286
crofters, 12, 40
Crooks, Will, 80, 122, 134
Cross, Richard, 49
Crowe, Sir Eyre, 166
Curragh Mutiny, 109
Curzon, Lord, 126, 167, 172, 220, 223, 271

Daily Chronicle, 119, 286
Daily Herald, 286
Daily Mail, 91, 100, 185
Daily Mirror, 286
Daily News, 29, 71, 91, 119
Daily Telegraph, 21, 184
Dalton, Hugh, 278, 281, 285
Davis, W. J., 177
death duties, 42, 101, 117, 127
Derby, 14th Earl, 45
Derby, 17th Earl, 154, 190, 223
Development Commission, 121
Devonport, Lord, 204
Dicey, A. V., 33
Dickinson, Willoughby, 103, 150, 217
Dilke, Sir Charles, 24, 35, 36, 102, 119
disestablishment, 25, 31–2, 40, 41, 42–3, 70–1, 128
Disraeli, Benjamin, 3, 7, 33, 44–5, 49, 50–2, 53–4, 57, 64, 84
Dreadnought, 120, 161
Dubery, H., 177
Dunraven, Lord, 66

East Fulham by-election, 282–3
Eden, Sir Anthony, 273, 291
Education Act (1870), 26, 32
Education Act (1902), 65, 105, 107, 133, 135
Education Bill (1896), 62, 65
educational reform, 78; see also Forster, W. E.
elections, general: (1865) 15, 46, 69; (1868) 12, 15, 31, 46, 69–70; (1874) 12, 15, 32–3, 45–6, 69–70; (1880) 3–4, 12, 15, 34, 69–70; (1885) 12, 15, 35, 46–7, 68–9, 70; (1886) 15, 38–9, 47, 69, 71; (1892) 15, 41, 69, 72, 139; (1895) 15, 69, 70, 73, 139; (1900) 15, 46, 69, 73, 139, 248; (1906) 15, 121–3, 138–40; (January 1910) 15, 112, 126, 138–40; (December 1910) 15, 112, 126, 138–40; (1918) 175–6, 179–81, 193–9, 246; (1922) 224–5, 237–9, 246; (1923) 225–6, 237–8, 246; (1924) 233–5, 237–8, 242–3, 246; (1929) 237–8, 246–7, 256; (1931) 246, 259–60, 269–70; (1935) 253, 275, 284–8; (1945) 253, 289, 292
Elibank, Master of, 98, 152
Elliott, Arthur, 124
Ellis, Tom, 38
Employers Liability Act (1880), 33
Estimates Committee, 19

Fabian Essays, 30
Fabian Society, 63, 82, 115, 133; see also Webb, Sidney
fascists, see British Union of Fascists
Fawcett, Henry, 28, 29, 78
Fawcett, Millicent Garrett, 157; see also National Union of Women's Suffrage Societies
Fenwick, Charles, 29, 134, 180

Fisher, H. A. L., 175, 207
Fisher, Hayes, 207
Fisher, Admiral Sir John, 167, 187
Forster, W. E., 24, 31, 70
Fourth Party, 52, 58
Fowler, Sir Henry, 104
franchise, see parliamentary franchise;
   municipal franchise
free trade, 25, 30, 32, 63, 73, 75, 77, 120,
   122, 124, 131, 134, 154, 260
French, Field Marshall Sir John, 166
Frere, Sir Bartle, 33
friendly societies, 77
Furness, Sir Christopher, 151

Galsworthy, John, 165
Gardiner, A. G., 119
Gathorne-Hardy, G., 49
Geddes, Sir Eric, 206–7, 209–10
general strike, 255–6, 263–4, 271
George, David Lloyd, see Lloyd George,
   David
George, Henry, 29, 130, 131
Gilbert, W. S., 49
Gladstone, Herbert, 36, 98, 100, 102, 119,
   227; pact with Labour, 121–3, 152
Gladstone, W. E., 3–5, 7, 11, 12, 21, 23–6,
   28–9, 30–5, 42–3, 70, 74, 85, 88, 101–2;
   and Home Rule, 36–43, 103–4
Glenesk, Lord, 21
Gordon, General Charles, 56, 70, 85
Gorst, John, 50–3, 58
Goschen, George, 36, 49, 61
Graves, Robert, 191, 281
Grayson, Victor, 135, 150
Green, T. H., 114–15
Greene, Ben, 280
Greenwood, Sir Hamar, 220
Gregory, Maundy, 221
Grenfell, Julian, 189
Grey, Sir Edward, 102, 104, 156, 161–4
Griffith-Boscawen, Sir Arthur, 223
Guest, F. E., 175

Haig, Sir Douglas, 187, 188, 190–1
Haldane, R. B., 102, 104, 161, 164, 166, 187,
   214–15, 231
Hankey, Sir Maurice, 202
Hannington, Wal, 279
Harcourt, Lewis, 101, 157, 162, 164
Harcourt, Sir William, 18, 24, 37, 42, 72,
   98, 102, 117
Hardie, James Keir, 77, 79, 80, 129, 130–3,
   135, 139, 148, 154, 186
Hardy, Thomas, 165
Harmsworth, Alfred, see Northcliffe, Lord
Hartington, Lord, 36–8, 39, 61
Hartshorn, Vernon, 198, 266
Hastings, Sir Patrick, 214
Heath, Edward, 291
Hemmerde, Edward, 129, 151, 213, 215

Henderson, Arthur, 100, 122, 134, 136, 148,
   171, 174, 177, 178–9, 192, 212, 215, 245,
   247, 259, 267, 273, 278, 286
Henderson, Hubert, 264
Hicks-Beach, Sir Michael (Earl St
   Aldwyn), 46, 166
Hoare, Sir Samuel, 273–4; Hoare–Laval
   Pact, 282
Hobhouse, Sir Charles, 164, 197
Hobhouse, L. T., 114, 115
Hobson, J. A., 114, 117–19, 214, 264
Hodge, John, 177
Holt, Richard, 14, 119
Horne, Sir Robert, 206, 225
House of Lords, 59, 98, 104; and the
   'People's Budget', 108; in the First
   World War, 174, 175, 221
housing, 129, 178, 209; royal commission
   on (1885), 65
Howell, George, 29
Hyndman, H. H., 79, 177

income tax, 30, 33, 43, 64, 101, 117–18,
   120–1, 127, 130, 209
Independent Labour Party, 79–80, 82, 83,
   122, 144–7, 231, 262–4, 279;
   membership, 79–80, 82; and the First
   World War, 165, 192–3, 198, 211–12
India, 74, 220, 274–5
Inverclyde, Lord, 21
Ireland: Home Rule, 20, 36–9, 42–3, 71–2,
   88–9, 102, 104, 109–10, 133, 134; Home
   Rule Party, 12, 19, 35, 36, 109–10, 242,
   257; Irish Church, 25, 31; Irish Land
   Act (1881), 31, 33; Conservative reforms,
   62, 65–6; Irish Universities Bill (1873),
   25, 32
Irwin, Lord (Edward Wood), 222, 274

Jackson, W. L., 49
James, Sir Henry, 39
Jellicoe, Admiral Sir John, 187
John, E. T., 213
Joicey, Lord, 21, 119, 151
Jowett, Fred, 177, 214, 231

Keynes, J. M., 209, 263, 264, 291
Keynesianism, 118, 261, 265, 267–8, 291
Kimberley, Lord, 24, 102
King, Joseph, 213
Kitchener, Lord, 56, 105, 132, 164, 166,
   169, 185–8, 189, 202

Labouchere, Henry, 41
labour exchanges, 67, 111, 120, 136
Labour Leader, 79
Labour Party, 18, 81–2, 111–12, 145–53,
   156, 223, 238–40, 244–9; relations with
   Liberals, 121–3, 130–6, 156–8;
   'Labourism', 130–6; and the franchise,
   141–5; and women voters, 249–52; and

the First World War, 176–81, 193, 195, 197–9, 210–16; and direct action, 229; the 1924 government, 228–35; and the general strike, 252–9; the 1929–31 government, 261–9; in the 1930s, 260, 278–81, 283–4; the Constituency Parties Movement, 280; and the 1935 election, 284–7; and the 1945 election, 289–90; see also Labour Representation Committee

Labour Representation Committee, 81–2, 122–3, 133–5

laissez-faire, 30, 33, 62–4, 66–7, 113, 115–17, 131, 200–4

Lambert, Richard, 213

land reform, 33, 35, 64, 65–6, 74–6, 92, 117, 125, 131, 134; and the Land Campaign, 128–30, 136, 153

Lansbury, George, 80, 278, 283, 286

Lansdowne, Marquess of, 38, 164, 173, 186

Larkin, Jim, 111, 158

Laski, Harold, 280–1

Law, Andrew Bonar, 108, 109–10, 112, 127, 154, 164, 166–7, 170–1, 172–3, 174–5, 205, 223–4; becomes prime minister, 221–5

Layton, Walter, 264

League of Nations, 175, 273, 281–2, 285

Leeds Mercury, 28

Lees-Smith, H. B., 213, 214

Lever, Sir William, 100, 119, 128, 150

Liberal Imperialism, 103–6, 156

Liberal Party, 11–12, 15, 19–21, 23–31, 97–102, 121–30, 137–41, 156–8, 226–8, 231, 233, 234, 235, 253–8, 260, 292; relations with Conservatives, 124, 148, 255; and the First World War, 161–2, 167–9, 171–2, 193–4, 197, 199, 200–4, 213–16; Coalition Liberals, 220, 222, 227; the Liberal Yellow Book, 264–5; see also National Liberal Federation, Liberal Imperialism, Liberal Unionists, 'Lib–Labs', Progressivism, New Liberalism

Liberal Unionists, 36, 38–9, 40–1, 53, 59–62, 66–7, 72–3, 100

Liberation Society, 27, 40; see also Nonconformists

Liberty and Property Defence League, 33

'Lib–Labs', 29, 81, 101, 130, 133–4, 139, 151

Lincoln, Abraham, 28, 29

Lloyd George, David, 99, 110, 111, 112, 113, 154, 158, 225–7, 227–8, 239, 255–6, 264–5, 270; as chancellor of the exchequer, 117, 118, 120–1, 125, 126–30, 133, 138; in the First World War, 162–3, 167, 169–76, 187, 193, 203–4, 207–8, 209; loses office, 221–5; see also Liberal Party, Coalition Liberals; Liberal Party, Liberal Yellow Book

Lloyd-Greame, Sir P., 222

Lloyds Weekly News, 29

London County Council, 65, 80, 103, 119, 134, 150, 284

Long, Walter, 66, 110, 166, 174, 205, 207

Lowell, A. L., 18

Lubbock, Sir John, 47

Lyons v. Wilkins, 81

Lytton, Lord, 33

MacDonald, Alexander, 29

MacDonald, James Ramsay, 79, 82, 93, 115, 129, 130–3, 135–6, 157; pact with Liberals, 121–3, 130–9, 144, 147–8, 154–5; in the First World War, 165, 177, 179, 198, 213, 215; as prime minister, 228–35, 239–40, 248, 262, 264–7; and the National Government, 269–70

McKenna, Reginald, 159, 168, 187, 197, 202, 203, 204, 225, 227

Maclay, Sir Joseph, 208

Macmillan, Harold, 272, 291

Macnamara, T. J., 150

Majuba Hill, 85

Manchester Guardian, 28, 119

Mann, Tom, 158

Manners, Lord John, 63

Markham, Sir Arthur, 13, 151

Married Women's Property Acts, 6

Martin, Joseph, 213

Marx, Karl, 76, 130

Masefield, John, 165

Massingham, W. H., 119

Masterman, Charles, 119, 150, 165, 264

Matthews, Henry, 26

Maudling, Reginald, 291

Maurice Debate, 173

Mawdsley, James, 84

Maxton, James, 277

Middleton, Jim, 177

Middleton, R. W. E., 53

Midlothian campaigns, 3–5, 33, 34, 70

Mill, John Stuart, 28, 29, 78, 130

Milner, Sir Alfred, 104, 106, 172, 173, 208, 219

miners federation, 29, 134, 139, 247; minimum wages, 111

Mond, Sir Alfred, 14, 220

Money, L. C., 151, 215

Montagu, Edwin, 172, 208, 220, 274

Morley, Arnold, 38

Morley, John, 23–4, 35, 36, 41, 98, 100, 102, 103, 132

Morning Post, 21

Morrell, Philip, 154

Morris, William, 79

Morrison, Herbert, 93, 193, 216, 248, 268, 272, 278, 289

Mosley, Lady Cynthia, 208

Mosley, Sir Oswald, 208, 230, 263, 264, 266, 267; as a fascist, 275–7

Muir, Ramsay, 264
Municipal Corporations Act (1835), 15, 90
municipal franchise, 65, 149, 199
municipalization, 35, 80, 113
Munitions, Ministry of, 169, 183, 203
Munro-Ferguson, R., 104
Murray, Alexander, see Elibank, Master of
Murray, Gilbert, 165

National Democratic Party, 173, 175
National Education League, 27, 32, 40
'National Efficiency', 106–7, 133, 208
National Governments, 259–60, 269–75,
    284–8
National Insurance Act (1911), 111, 120,
    126, 135, 141, 154
National Liberal Federation, 17, 19–20,
    33–4, 39–42, 100, 102
National Service League, 189
National Unemployed Workers Movement,
    279
National Union of Conservative and
    Constitutional Associations, 17–18,
    50–3, 84
National Union of Women's Suffrage
    Societies, 97, 157
nationalization, 134, 206–7, 212, 221,
    268–9, 272
'New Deal', 268
New Liberalism, 113–21
Newcastle Chronicle, 28
'Newcastle Programme', 41–2, 102, 119
News of the World, 29
1922 Committee, 205, 224
No Conscription Fellowship, 186
Nonconformists, 25–6, 27–8, 36, 70, 71, 74,
    91, 100, 257–9
Northcliffe, Lord, 21, 208, 222
Northcote, Sir Stafford, 52, 57–8

O'Connor, T. P., 257
O'Grady, James, 177
old age pensions, 67, 74, 101, 119, 120, 125,
    135, 136, 271
opinion polls, 287, 289
Osborne Judgement, 135, 157, 179
Ostrogorski, M., 18
Outhwaite, R. L., 129, 151, 213, 215

Palmer, Charles Mark, 13, 14, 151
Palmerston, Lord, 23–4, 32, 44–5
Pankhurst, Emmeline and Christabel,
    10–11
parish councils, 11, 64
Parliament Act (1911), 153, 291
parliamentary constituencies, 8–9, 46,
    240–2
parliamentary franchise: (pre-1918) 5–9,
    16, 31, 35, 45, 46, 76, 90, 142–5, 153; (in
    1917–18) 174, 180, 198–9; (1918–29) 249
Parliamentary Recruiting Committee, 184

Parmoor, Lord, see Cripps, C. A.
Parnell, C. S., 41, 70
Peace Ballot, 282
Peace Society, 27
Pease, Alfred, 127
Pease, J. A., 98, 164
Pease, Sir Joseph, 13, 122
Peel, Sir Robert, 23–4, 41; Peelites, 44
peerage, 21
Perks, Robert, 104
Pickard, Ben, 29, 134
Plunkett, Horace, 66
Ponsonby, Arthur, 161–2, 172, 195, 198,
    214, 283, 286
poor law, 63, 120, 134, 271; poor law
    guardians, 5, 77, 83; Royal Commission
    on the, 66, 107, 133
press, 28, 99–100; in the First World War,
    184–5, 193–4; in the 1930s, 286
Primrose League, 17, 54–7, 76, 83, 84
Pritt, D. N., 280–1
Progress and Poverty, 29, 130, 131
Progressivism, 118–19, 133, 137–8, 150–3,
    216
proportional representation, 238–40
Public Accounts Committee, 19

Rainbow Circle, 118, 132
Rathbone, Eleanor, 249
rearmament, 280–4, 285
Redmond, John, 165, 168
Reform League, 27
Reform Union, 27
Reynolds Newspaper, 29
Rhondda, Lord, 204
Richie, C. T., 49, 63, 65
Ripon, Lord, 24, 26
Roberts of Khandahar, Lord, 56, 189
Robertson, J. M., 115, 118–19
Robertson, Sir William, 189
Roosevelt, F. D., 268
Rosebery, Earl of, 70, 71, 72, 94, 103,
    104–6; Chesterfield speech, 97, 105
Rothermere, Lord, 222, 274–5
Rowlands, James, 29
Rowntree, Joseph, 100, 119, 128
Rowntree, Seebohm, 103, 114
Runciman, Walter, 14, 103, 119, 128, 129,
    152, 227; in the First World War, 162,
    164, 183, 197, 202, 203, 204
Russell, Lord John, 31

Safeguarding of Industries Act (1921), 206,
    220
St Aldwyn, Earl, see Hicks-Beach, Sir
    Michael
Salisbury, 3rd Marquess of, 5, 19, 21, 36,
    46, 49, 50, 52, 55, 82; political
    philosophy, 57–9; and domestic policy,
    62–7; as party leader, 57–9; and Liberal
    Unionists, 57–62

Salisbury, 4th Marquess of, 208, 223
Salvidge, Archibald, 88
Samuel, Sir Herbert, 103, 115, 118, 119, 152, 197, 269, 270
Sankey, Lord, 207, 208, 221, 254
Sassoon, Siegfried, 191, 192, 196
Schlieffen Plan, 164
Schnadhorst, Francis, 39, 99
school boards, 31, 32, 40, 65, 83
Scott, C. P., 119, 120, 150, 154, 161
Scott, Leslie, 130, 154
Scott, Ted, 264
Seager, J. Renwick, 99
Seddon, J. A., 177
Seeley, J. E. B., 124
Selbourne, Earl of, 208, 223
Shackleton, David, 122, 134
Simon, E. D., 264
Simon, Sir John, 164, 227, 255, 273, 285, 286
Sinn Fein, 220, 242, 252
Smallholdings Act (1892), 64
Smillie, Robert, 122, 177
Smith, F. E., 126, 154, 175, 219, 225
Smith, Hubert Llewellyn, 202
Smith, W. H., 49
Snowden, Philip, 77, 135, 154, 157, 196, 198; as chancellor of the exchequer, 214, 232, 263, 266-7
Social Democratic Federation, 79-82, 134
socialism, 78-80, 103, 115, 130-5, 201, 210-13, 261-3, 265-9
Socialist League, 279
South African War (1899-1902), 67, 73, 91, 105-7
Spencer, Lord, 24
Stanton, C. B., 186
Steel-Maitland, Sir Arthur, 130, 222
Sutherland, Sir William, 221
syndicalism, 109, 111

Taff Vale judgement, 63, 111, 123, 134
Talbot, Lord Edmund, 130
tariff reform, 51, 88, 89, 106-8, 124, 125, 154, 205-6, 220, 225-6, 277; and the United Empire Campaign, 273, 274-5
Tawney, R. H., 115, 210-11, 280
temperance, 27, 32-3, 72-3, 75, 135
Thomas, J. H., 139, 171, 198, 220, 266
Thorne, Will, 81, 177
Tillett, Ben, 81, 135, 177
Times, The, 184, 185
Trade Boards Act (1909), 111, 128, 136
trade union membership, 76, 81, 83, 123, 157-8, 229, 247, 254
Trades Disputes Act (1906), 111, 124
Trades Union Congress, 28, 77-8, 81, 263, 267, 283
Trevelyan, Charles, 103, 118, 119, 124, 152, 162, 172, 195, 198; joins the Labour Party, 214-16, 231, 280, 283

Trevelyan, Sir G. O., 36
Triple Alliance (industrial), 111, 221, 229
Truck Act (1897), 88

Ulster Unionists, 89, 109-10, 197, 221
Unemployed Workmen's Act (1905), 66, 132
Union of Democratic Control, 165, 173, 179, 186, 197
Unionist Business Committee, 166, 170, 205
Unionist Social Reform Committee, 126
United Kingdom Alliance, 27
University Tests Act (1871), 71

Victoria, Queen, 44, 56, 57

Wake, Egerton, 245
Wallas, Graham, 18, 115
War Emergency Workers National Committee, 177-8, 210, 215
Webb, Beatrice, 106, 115, 133, 231
Webb, Sidney, 106, 115, 133, 177, 179, 210-11, 286
Wedgwood, Josiah, 151, 154, 214-16, 231
Wedgwood Benn, William, 194, 200, 214-17
Wells, H. G., 165
Wesleyan Methodists, 71, 100, 258
Westminster Gazette, 119
Wheatley, John, 231, 233
White, J. D., 213, 215
Whitley Councils, 210, 255
Widows Pensions Act (1925), 250, 271
Wilkinson, Ellen, 280, 287
Williams, Powell, 39
Wilson, Havelock, 177, 211
Wilson, John, 29, 151
Wilson, Thomas Woodrow, 186
Wolff, Sir Henry Drummond, 58
women in politics, 56-7, 82-3, 174, 196-7, 249-52, 272
Women's Co-operative Guild, 83
Women's Liberal Federation, 83, 98, 157
Women's Social and Political Union, 110-11, 157, 249
women's suffrage, 6, 51, 57, 97, 110-11, 135, 156-7, 174, 188, 249, 272; see also National Union of Women's Suffrage Societies
Women's Trade Union League, 83
Wood, Edward, see Irwin, Lord
Wood, T. McKinnon, 197
Woods, Sam, 122
Workmen's Compensation Bill: (1897), 62; (1906), 135
Worthington-Evans, Sir L., 220, 225
Wyndham, George, 66

Younger, Sir George, 175, 223-4

Zinoviev Letter, 234